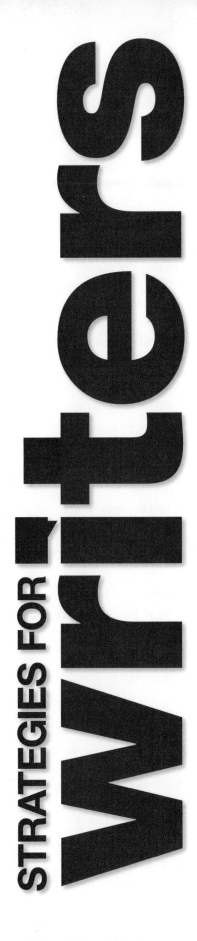

STRATEGIES FOR writers

6

Senior Author
Rebecca Bowers Sipe, Ed.D.
Eastern Michigan University

Consulting Authors
Julie Coiro, Ph.D.
University of Rhode Island

Amy Humphreys, Ed.M., NBCT
Educational Consultant

Sara B. Kajder, Ph.D.
University of Pittsburgh

Mark Overmeyer, M.A.
Cherry Creek School District, Colorado

Senior Consultant
James Scott Miller, M.Ed.
National Writing Consultant

ZB **Zaner-Bloser**

Program Reviewers

Zaner-Bloser wishes to thank these educators who reviewed portions of this program and provided comments prior to publication.

Joe Anspaugh
Shelbyville Middle School
Shelbyville, IN

Michele Barto, Ed.D.
Fairleigh Dickinson University
Madison, NJ

Jackie Blosser
Lima City Schools
Lima, OH

Kim Bondy
South Arbor Academy
Ypsilanti, MI

Kelly Caravelli
Meadowbrook Middle School
Poway, CA

Cathy Cassy
St. Louis Public Schools
St. Louis, MO

Penny Clare
Educational Consultant
Lee, NH

Mary Dunton
Literacy Consultant
Sparks, NV

Emily Gleason
Beaverton School District
Beaverton, OR

Denise Gray, Ed.D.
Whiteriver Elementary School
Whiteriver, AZ

Laura Hall
Walton Charter Academy
Pontiac, MI

Donna Jett
Rockwood South Middle School
Fenton, MO

Christine Johnson, Ed.D.
Boonton Public Schools
Boonton, NJ

Dr. Roma Morris
Columbia School District
Columbia, MS

Rosanne Richards
Southern Nevada Regional
Professional Development
Program
North Las Vegas, NV

Sharlene E. Ricks
Alpine School District
American Fork, UT

Debbie Rutherford
Independent National Consultant
Omaha, NE

Melinda Springli
Lawton Public Schools
Lawton, OK

Kerry Stephenson
Pendleton County School District
Butler, KY

Photography: Cover © Purestock/age fotostock; Interior models, Tom Dubanowich; Stopwatch image © Royalty-Free/Corbis; p. 3 © Strauss/Curtis/Corbis; p. 33 © Marvin E. Newman/Getty Images; p. 81 © Bettmann/Corbis; pp. 99–101 © iStockphoto.com/sonia_ai; p. 101 © iStockphoto.com/Graffizone and © Corbis; p. 125 © George Ostertag/Superstock Inc/Photolibrary; p. 138 © Burstein Collection/Corbis; p. 139 Quarter-dollar coin images from United States Mint; p. 227 © iStockphoto.com/Mark Stay; p. 227 © iStockphotocom/essxboy; p. 251 © iStockphoto.com/David Liu; p. 367 © Comstock/Photolibrary; p. 371 © Mike Dobel/Masterfile; pp. 378, 379, 381, 391 © Dave Robertson/Masterfile

Art Credits: pp. 4, 28, 54, 126, 152, 176, 227, 252, 278, 300, 368, 392, 416 Illustrated by Alaskan Moose Studio; pp. 395, 399, 414 Sandy Joncas; p. 233 Tammie Lyon; pp. 76, 204, 322, 438, 441 Chris Vallo

Literature Credits: pp. 129–131 *A Touch of Genius* by Patricia Millman © 2000 by Highlights for Children, Inc., Columbus, Ohio; pp. 138–139 *The Tree That Saved History* by Jane Sutliffe © 2000 by Highlights for Children, Inc. Columbus, Ohio

ISBN 978-0-7367-7281-5

Zaner-Bloser, Inc.
1-800-421-3018
www.zaner-bloser.com
Printed in the United States of America   12   13   14   15   19840   5   4   3   2

SUSTAINABLE FORESTRY INITIATIVE
Certified Chain of Custody
Promoting Sustainable Forestry
www.sfiprogram.org
SFI-00993

Hi, there!

We're your *Strategies for Writers Writing Partners!*

We're here to guide you step-by-step through the stages of the writing process: Prewrite, Draft, Revise, Edit, and Publish.

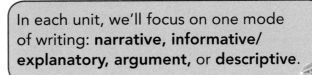

In each unit, we'll focus on one mode of writing: **narrative, informative/ explanatory, argument,** or **descriptive**.

Have you ever wondered what makes a good historical episode? Or what the elements of a cause-and-effect report are? How about some reasons for writing a business letter or a descriptive article? We'll answer those questions and more.

We'll focus on these six traits of effective writing: **Ideas, Organization, Voice, Word Choice, Sentence Fluency,** and **Conventions**. We'll explain how to apply the traits to each genre of writing, and we'll show you how the traits work together.

In each chapter, we'll first review a model writing sample. Then we'll use a rubric to score the model. Rubrics are a great way to know exactly what is expected as you plan and evaluate your writing. After that, it's your turn to write!

Narrative writing

Table of Contents

Informative/Explanatory writing

Table of Contents

Argument writing

Table of Contents

Descriptive writing

Table of Contents

Appendices

Appendix A: Grammar Practice

Table of Contents

Narrative writing tells a story to the audience.

Hi, there! I'm Marco. I'm learning about narrative writing in school, and I really think I'm going to like this stuff. I share stories with my friends all the time. They always tell me I should write them down, and now I'll get the chance to do it!

IN THIS UNIT

- ☐ **Eyewitness Account**
- ☐ **Historical Episode**
- ☐ **Short Story**
- SOCIAL STUDIES CONNECTION ▷ **Biography**
- ☐ **Writing for a Test**

Name: Marco
Home: Arizona
Hobbies: rodeos, raising calves, reading about history
Favorite Book: *Walker's Crossing,* by Phyllis Reynolds Naylor
Favorite Food: macaroni and cheese

What's an Eyewitness Account?

It's a true report of something that happened in real life. I think this kind of writing is fun because I can pretend I'm a newspaper reporter!

What's in an Eyewitness Account?

Narrator
That's me! The narrator is the person who tells about something he or she saw. I've seen a lot of things that I'd like to report on, so now I'll tell my audience about one of them!

Order
This is the order in which I saw things happen. I'll describe the events as they really happened because I want my reader to understand the big picture.

Tone
This is how I want my story to sound and how I want my readers to feel. I can change the tone depending on what I'm writing. I can use short sentences to build suspense, powerful verbs to create drama, or descriptive words to create a serious, sad, or funny mood.

The 5 W's
These are the details of *who, what, when, where,* and *why* in my account. I'll use all of these, but I'll have to remember to keep each detail accurate and true!

Why write an Eyewitness Account?

There are many reasons to write an eyewitness account. I listed some here, since I'm still thinking about why I want to write.

Entertainment
Entertaining the reader is one good reason to write an eyewitness account. When I see something that is funny, exciting, or sad, I just want to share it with someone else.

Personal Reflection
Reflecting can help me understand how I've been affected by something I've seen. Writing helps me reflect, or make sense out of the things I see.

Information
I can write my account to educate, instruct, or inform my reader. He or she might find useful or interesting new information in my account.

Summarize
Sometimes the events I see are long and complicated. Often, there are smaller details that lead up to one main event, so it's important for me to summarize only the details my reader really needs to know. It's also good practice to use my summarization skills, especially since I'll use them a lot in school.

Linking Narrative Writing Traits to an Eyewitness Account

In this chapter, you will write about something that happened in real life. This type of narrative writing is called an eyewitness account. Marco will guide you through the stages of the writing process: Prewrite, Draft, Revise, Edit, and Publish. In each stage, Marco will show you important writing strategies that are linked to the Narrative Writing Traits below.

Narrative Writing Traits

Ideas	• a focused topic, experience, or series of events • engaging, accurate details that develop and describe the topic, experience, or series of events
Organization	• logically sequenced events, often in chronological order • an interesting beginning and a satisfying ending • transitions that signal the sequence of events as well as shifts in time or setting
Voice	• a voice and tone that are appropriate for the purpose and audience • dialogue that, if used, fits the characters
Word Choice	• precise, descriptive words and phrases
Sentence Fluency	• a variety of sentences that flow and are a pleasure to read aloud
Conventions	• no or few errors in grammar, usage, mechanics, and spelling

Before you write, read Joe Torelli's eyewitness account on the next page. Then use the eyewitness account rubric on pages 8–9 to decide how well he did. (You might want to look back at What's in an Eyewitness Account? on page 4, too!)

THE GREAT CIRCUS PARADE

by Joe (Bongo the Clown) Torelli

Narrator

Last week I was amazed, astounded, flabbergasted, and stupefied! I saw wild animals, dozens of circus wagons and bands, hundreds of horses, and thousands of people in costumes. I, Bongo the Clown, fell under the spell of the Great Circus Parade.

Why | Who | What | When

As a professional clown, I had to see the parade. Every July, it winds three miles through downtown Milwaukee, Wisconsin. From near and far, people come to see the spectacle.

5 W's

Where

Order

The day I attended was cloudless and bright; a faint breeze floated in from Lake Michigan. A drum troop at the start of the parade stirred up the crowd. Following close behind, young men in knickers pedaled high-wheeled bicycles, and mounted police waved from their saddles. By the time the clown snake charmers arrived, the parade was in full swing.

The clowns were funny, but I was more impressed by the historic circus wagons. Each one showed off a dazzling color scheme. As the wheels turned, yellow and orange webbing between the spokes swirled like sunbursts. Huge draft horses with fancy brass harnesses hauled most of the wagons, some weighing more than a ton.

Magnificent bandwagons carried musicians playing grand old tunes. One bandwagon stood out. Sparkling with gold mermaids and swans, it was like something from a fairy tale.

Tone

The cage wagons displayed exotic animals, including a pygmy hippo, a buffalo, and a giraffe. I even saw a liger (a cross between a lion and a tiger).

Most splendid were the tableau wagons. Filled with carved and painted wooden figures, they are historical scenes on wheels. A woman dressed as Cleopatra rode a tableau pulled by camels. A two-headed green dragon roared from the top of a tableau that celebrated the age of knights and castles.

At the end of the parade were lumbering elephants and a steam calliope. Belching out plumes of smoke and hooting old-time melodies, the calliope bid farewell to the satisfied crowd. I smiled all the way home, thinking about those sunburst wheels. I'm still smiling. Maybe I should run off to join the circus parade.

CIRCUS

Rubric

Use this 6-point rubric to plan and score an eyewitness account.

	6	5	4
Ideas	The narrator uses the 5 W's to establish a context for the event. Strong details engage the reader and develop the event.	The narrator answers the 5 W's. Details engage the reader and develop the event.	The writer answers most of the 5 W's. Details are mostly engaging and develop the event.
Organization	An engaging lead introduces the event; the ending follows from the narrated event.	The lead introduces the event, and the ending follows from the narrated event.	The lead introduces the event, but the ending could be stronger.
Voice	The voice is expressive and engages the reader throughout.	The voice is expressive most of the time. The writing connects with the reader.	The voice is sometimes inconsistent. The writer sometimes seems unaware of the audience.
Word Choice	Descriptive and sensory language helps the reader create a precise picture of the event.	Descriptive and sensory words strengthen the writing.	Words are usually clear and sensory but not always the best choice.
Sentence Fluency	Variety in sentence beginnings makes the writing interesting to the reader.	Most sentences begin in different ways. The writing is easy to read.	There is some variety in sentence beginnings. The report isn't always smooth to read.
Conventions	All the sentences are correct and complete.	A few minor errors with sentences are difficult to spot.	Some sentences are incorrect or incomplete and distract the reader.
✛ Presentation	The eyewitness account is legible and neat.		

3	2	1	
Several of the 5 W's are missing. Several details are weak, irrelevant, or missing.	It is not clear what event the writer is describing. Details are sketchy and not engaging.	The writing does not attempt to describe an event. Details seem to have been included for no reason.	**Ideas**
The lead is present but does not pull the reader in. The ending does not follow from the event or is missing.	The organization is hard to follow. The lead and ending need work.	The writing is not organized. The lead and ending are missing.	**Organization**
The voice is sometimes dull and unengaging.	The voice is wrong for this piece of writing. It does not draw the reader in.	The writing is dull and has no voice.	**Voice**
Some of the words are unclear and misused. They don't help the reader get a clear picture.	The writer's words are ordinary and repetitive.	The writing doesn't make sense. The words are confusing.	**Word Choice**
Sentence beginnings are repeated in places, creating patches that are dull or hard to read.	Many sentences begin the same way, making the report hard to read.	Sentences are incomplete or run-on. The report is very hard to read.	**Sentence Fluency**
Several noticeable errors with sentences slow down the reader.	Errors with sentences are frequent and get in the way of reading the writing.	Many errors with sentences make the writing very difficult to read.	**Conventions**

See Appendix B for 4-, 5-, and 6-point narrative rubrics.

Using the Rubric to Study the Model

Eyewitness Account

Did you notice that the model on page 7 points out some key elements of an eyewitness account? As he wrote "The Great Circus Parade," Joe Torelli used these elements to help him tell about a real-life event. He also used the 6-point rubric on pages 8–9 to plan, draft, revise, and edit the writing. A rubric is a great tool to evaluate writing during the writing process.

Now let's use the same rubric to score the model. To do this, we'll focus on each trait separately, starting with Ideas. We'll use the top descriptor for each trait (column 6), along with examples from the model, to help us understand how the traits work together. How would you score Joe on each trait?

Ideas

- The narrator uses the 5 W's to establish a context for the event.
- Strong details engage the reader and develop the event.

Joe answers the 5 W's early on to set the scene of his event. Strong, vivid details like *faint breeze* and *high-wheeled bicycles* keep me interested and wanting to know more.

[from the writing model]

The day I attended was cloudless and bright; a faint breeze floated in from Lake Michigan. A drum troop at the start of the parade stirred up the crowd. Following close behind, young men in knickers pedaled high-wheeled bicycles, and mounted police waved from their saddles.

Organization

• An engaging lead introduces the event; the ending follows from the narrated event.

Joe's lead paragraph pulls me in immediately. I need to know more about this amazing event! I also like the way Joe's ending ties into the astounded feelings he describes in the lead. This helps the account feel well-rounded and complete.

[from the writing model]

Last week I was amazed, astounded, flabbergasted, and stupefied! I saw wild animals, dozens of circus wagons and bands, hundreds of horses, and thousands of people in costumes.

[from the writing model]

I smiled all the way home, thinking about those sunburst wheels. I'm still smiling. Maybe I should run off to join the circus parade.

Voice

• The voice is expressive and engages the reader throughout.

Joe uses an enchanting tone to describe the parade. His use of the words *magnificent, grand,* and *sparkling* remind me of the way a ringmaster describes a circus.

[from the writing model]

Magnificent bandwagons carried musicians playing grand old tunes. One bandwagon stood out. Sparkling with gold mermaids and swans, it was like something from a fairy tale.

Word Choice

- Descriptive and sensory language helps the reader create a precise picture of the event.

Interesting and colorful sensory language helps me picture what's happening. For example, the elephants don't just walk, they *lumber*. And the smoke doesn't just come out of the calliope, it *belches* out in *plumes*. Joe's excellent use of description is truly inspiring!

[from the writing model]

At the end of the parade were lumbering elephants and a steam calliope. Belching out plumes of smoke and hooting old-time melodies, the calliope bid farewell to the satisfied crowd.

Sentence Fluency

- Variety in sentence beginnings makes the writing interesting to the reader.

Joe uses many different sentence beginnings and patterns to help his writing flow. This variety not only makes the reading easier for me, but it also helps keep me interested the whole way through.

[from the writing model]

Most splendid were the tableau wagons. Filled with carved and painted wooden figures, they are historical scenes on wheels. A woman dressed as Cleopatra rode a tableau pulled by camels. A two-headed green dragon roared from the top of a tableau that celebrated the age of knights and castles.

Conventions

- **All the sentences are correct and complete.**

I went back and checked Joe's account to see if there were any mistakes. There aren't any sentence fragments or run-ons because every sentence has a subject and a verb. Joe also uses coordinating conjunctions such as *but* to join shorter sentences. None of the words are misspelled, and all sentences are capitalized and punctuated correctly.

[from the writing model]

The clowns were funny, but I was more impressed by the historic circus wagons. Each one showed off a dazzling color scheme. As the wheels turned, yellow and orange webbing between the spokes swirled like sunbursts.

✚ Presentation   The eyewitness account is legible and neat.

My Turn!

I'm going to write an eyewitness account of something that I have seen. I'll follow the rubric and use good writing strategies. Read on to see how I do it!

Prewrite

Focus on **Ideas**

The Rubric Says   The narrator uses the 5 W's to establish a context for the event.

Writing Strategy   Choose an incident and record details to help answer the 5 W's.

I knew what I wanted to write about as soon as my teacher announced the assignment: the rodeo I saw last summer in Cody, Wyoming. There are so many details I remember. I think I'll jot down what I remember while keeping the 5 W's in mind. Using details to answer *who, what, where, when*, and *why* will help my reader better experience the event. It's amazing how vivid the sights, sounds, and smells of the rodeo still are in my mind.

My Notes on the Cody Stampede Rodeo

✔ every year during July 1–4, in Cody, Wyoming (when/where)

✔ smells like animal sweat and dust

✔ noisy: announcer, crowd cheering, buzzers, animals banging against fences

✔ Grand Entry parade: flag colors, 4th of July

✔ timed events: calf roping, barrel racing—fast cowgirl event

✔ bulldogging (steer wrestling): invented in early 1900s by Will Pickett, an African American cowboy (what)

✔ rough stock events: bareback, saddle bronc, bull riding—8 seconds and one hand (what)

✔ rodeo clowns: protect bull riders from bulls (who)

✔ pickup men: protect bronc riders from broncs (who)

✔ winners get prize money and rodeo buckle (why)

Apply

Choose an event you've witnessed. Then record what you remember, keeping in mind the 5 W's.

The Rubric Says   An engaging lead introduces the event; the ending follows from the narrated event.

Writing Strategy   Make a 5 W's Chart to organize the notes.

Writer's Term

5 W's Chart
A **5 W's Chart** organizes information according to what happened, who was there, why it happened, when it happened, and where it happened.

Now I need to organize my notes into a 5 W's chart. The chart will help me as I write my draft. With all my details organized, it'll be easier to write a strong, interesting lead and solid ending.

5 W's Chart

What **happened?** Buffalo Bill Cody Stampede Rodeo, bronc rider bucked high, bull rider thrown over horns, sharpshooter act

Who **was there?** my dad and I, cowboys and cowgirls, crowd, rodeo announcers and judges, clowns, animals, sharpshooter

Why **did it happen?** so cowboys and cowgirls can show off their skills and entertain people

When **did it happen?** July 1–4 last summer (and annually)

Where **did it happen?** Cody, Wyoming

Reflect
How will Marco's 5 W's chart help him write his draft?

Apply
Organize your ideas by using your notes to make a 5 W's Chart.

Draft

Focus on **Ideas**

The Rubric Says	Strong details engage the reader and develop the event.
Writing Strategy	Use the best details to describe the event and keep readers interested.

Now I'll use my 5 W's Chart to write my draft. According to the rubric, I need to use strong details to engage my reader and develop the event. I've included lots of details in my 5 W's chart, but I'll be sure to use only the most vivid and descriptive details in my writing. Vague or incomplete details will only weaken my account and bore or confuse my readers. The rodeo was so exciting—I want my audience to feel that excitement, too!

I think I'll open with the announcer welcoming folks to the rodeo. That will be a really engaging lead! I'll begin writing and see how it goes. I'll do my best with spelling and grammar, but I won't worry too much about mistakes right now. I can always fix those later!

Proofreading Marks

⅂ Indent	ℓ Take out something
≡ Make uppercase	⊙ Add a period
/ Make lowercase	⌗ New paragraph
∧ Add something	ⓈⓅ Spelling error

[DRAFT]

Ride 'em, Cowboy!

[engaging lead]

 "Welcome, folks! Welcome to the annual Buffalo Bill Cody Stampede Rodeo in Cody, Wyoming!" the announcer's voice blared from the loudspeakers. "Let the Grand Entry begin!"

 My dad and I yelled as the cowboys and cowgirls came by [detail] wearing colorful western clothes. Some of them wore patriotic colors because the rodeo took place over the Fourth of July.

 We had been to the stampede three times before. Last year we sat in the Buzzard's Roost, the best seats in the arena. [detail] I could take in everything from up there. It was dusty, and I could smell animal sweat and hear the gates banging and see the cowboys hanging out. It was like a big stable.

 Timed events were first on the program. Mainly ropeing and racing against the clock. Calf ropeing shows off ranching skills. I was watching to learn more about ropeing, I had to feel for the calves. A calf would take off from the shoot. Then suddenly it would be on the ground with a rope tied in a half hitch around three legs.

Reflect

What do you think of Marco's lead? Is it engaging? Has he included interesting details to hold his readers' attention?

Apply

Use your 5 W's chart to help you write a draft of your account. Include engaging details to hold your readers' interest.

Revise

Focus on Organization

The Rubric Says   An engaging lead introduces the event; the ending follows from the narrated event.

Writing Strategy   Write a strong beginning and ending.

After I wrote my draft, I checked the beginning again and decided that it is strong. It's interesting and engages the reader. But my ending needs work. I want my reader to take away the idea that the rodeo experience was fun and memorable. I think I'll add details to the last sentence.

[DRAFT]

On the last night, the winners got to take home prize money and a rodeo trophy: a belt buckle. ~~It was late and I went home tired.~~

I took home a new rodeo poster and a saddlebag of memories.

Apply

Try adding details to your account that make the beginning and ending strong and engaging.

Revise

The Rubric Says	The voice is expressive and engages the reader throughout.
Writing Strategy	Share your feelings about the topic.

One way I can be expressive is by using words and phrases that let my reader know how I feel, such as *Let the grand entry begin!* and *the best seats in the arena.* If I reveal a variety of feelings, I'll help the reader share my experience. Take a look at how I changed the sentences below to convey how scary it was to see a cowboy almost get hurt.

[DRAFT]

At the stampede, I saw a Brahma Bull ~~come out of~~ the shoot
explode from
, twisting like a tornado   flipped over the bull's horns and flopped
~~and twist around a lot~~. The rider ~~fell off the bull and landed~~ at

its feet.

Reflect

How do Marco's changes help you as a reader share his feelings?

Apply

Add expressive words and phrases that show your feelings about what is happening.

Revise

Focus on Word Choice

The Rubric Says   Descriptive and sensory language helps the reader create a precise picture of the event.

Writing Strategy   Choose words and phrases to convey ideas precisely.

The rubric encourages me to use descriptive sensory language. I know that I enjoy reading descriptions that help me create images in my mind. I'll be sure to choose my words carefully so that I can help readers "see" and "hear" the rodeo in their own minds.

Writer's Term

Common Words

Common words are plain and boring. Their meanings are so general that they do not create a clear picture in the reader's mind. Words such as **nice, good, big,** and **beautiful** are examples of common words.

[DRAFT]

My dad and I ~~yelled~~ whooped as the cowboys and cowgirls ~~came by~~ paraded past, decked out in ~~wearing~~ colorful western ~~clothes~~ shirts, hats, belts, boots, and chaps.

[replaced common words]

Apply

Replace common words with descriptive sensory language to help your readers clearly picture your event.

Edit

The Rubric Says   All the sentences are correct and complete.

Writing Strategy   Fix sentence fragments, run-on sentences, and comma splices.

Writer's Term

Sentence Fragments/Run-Ons

A **sentence fragment** is a group of words that begins with a capital letter and ends with a period or other end punctuation but does not state a complete thought. A **run-on sentence** and a comma splice are made up of two simple sentences that are run together and are not joined properly by a conjunction or a semicolon.

I need to check my spelling, punctuation, and capitalization. The rubric also says that all sentences should be correct and complete. That means there should be no sentence fragments, run-on sentences, or comma splices. A sentence fragment is missing a subject or a predicate. A run-on sentence and a comma splice string thoughts together without a conjunction or a semicolon.

[DRAFT]

[fixed capitalization and spelling]

Cowboys called "pickup men" protect the bronc riders from the
, and
broncs rodeo clowns protect the bull riders from the bulls.

At the stampede, I saw a Brahma Bull explode from the
chute
shoot, twisting like a tornado.

[joined compound sentence correctly]

Reflect

Is Marco's account free of sentence fragments, run-on sentences, and comma splices? Are the sentences correct and easy to follow?

Apply

Edit your draft for spelling, punctuation, and capitalization. Be sure to fix sentence fragments, run-ons, and comma splices.

For more practice fixing fragments, run-ons, and comma splices, use the exercises on the next two pages.

Sentence Fragments, Run-ons, and Comma Splices

Know the Rule

A sentence that is missing a subject or a predicate is called a **fragment**.
    Fragment: Looked forward to the rodeo. (subject missing)
    Fragment: A clown on the fence. (predicate missing)
When you join two sentences as a **compound sentence,** put a comma followed by a conjunction between them. You can also join them with a semicolon. Sentences that are not joined correctly are called **run-ons** or **comma splices**.
    Run-on: Rodeo clowns look funny they take their work seriously.
    Comma splice: Rodeo clowns look funny, they take their work seriously.
    Correct: Rodeo clowns look funny, but they take their work seriously.
    Correct: Rodeo clowns look funny; they take their work seriously.

Practice the Rule

Number a sheet of paper 1–10. Identify the problem with each item below. Write the problem on your paper. Then rewrite sentences 8–10 correctly.

1. Gripping the reins tightly.
2. Bulls with names like Turbo and Jackhammer.
3. Streaked from the chute like a shot from a cannon.
4. The announcer named the winners, the crowd cheered for each one.
5. Some people protest the use of animals in rodeos rodeo animals are treated well.
6. Compete for money and prizes.
7. Rodeo performers work hard, they enjoy their work.
8. The cowboy hit the ground hard the crowd gasped.
9. Was handed the grand prize as the crowd clapped and cheered.
10. Fearless Frank, last year's champion.

Coordinating Conjunctions

Know the Rule

Coordinating conjunctions (*and, but, or*) connect words or groups of words (including independent clauses) that are similar. They can be used to fix run-on sentences, sentence fragments, and comma splices.

Examples: Elephants decorated with jewels paraded down Main Street, and two camels pulled a fancy circus wagon.

The clowns are funny, but some people like the trapeze artists better.

You can see the main act in the Big Top, or you can go to the smaller carnival acts.

Practice the Rule

Number a sheet of paper 1–10. Use coordinating conjunctions to correct the sentence fragments, run-on sentences, and comma splices. Then write the complete sentences on a separate piece of paper.

1. At the rodeo you can sit in the stands, you can walk around and buy food at the stalls.
2. Steer wrestling is one of the fastest rodeo events, it often takes only three or four seconds.
3. Two cowboys try to rope the head of a cow in team roping they can rope the legs.
4. In barrel racing, a horse and rider race around barrels set in a pattern, this event is about speed.
5. You can see calf roping you can also see bull riders.
6. A rodeo cowboy competes in rodeo events he earns more money when he wins.
7. The saddles used in saddle bronc riding are lightweight, they have no saddle horn.
8. The pickup men at a rodeo rescue riders from their horses they manage horses and bulls.
9. This year I'm taking Grandpa Jack, we'll celebrate his birthday at the rodeo.
10. He's always wanted to go he's always been too busy to attend.

Publish

✚ Presentation

Publishing Strategy	Add your account to a class journal.
Presentation Strategy	Use neat handwriting or word processing.

Now it's time to publish my eyewitness account. There are a lot of ways to publish my work, but I've decided to put my account into my class journal. I want my account to be easy to read, so I need to make sure I use neat handwriting and watch the letter and word spacing. Or I could choose a couple of clear readable fonts on the computer. Before publishing my work, I want to read through it one last time to make sure it includes all the items on my final checklist.

My Final Checklist

Did I—

✔ check for sentence fragments, run-on sentences, and comma splices?

✔ use neat handwriting or a couple of clear fonts on the computer?

✔ check spelling, capitalization, and punctuation?

Apply

Check your eyewitness account against your own checklist. Then make a final copy to publish.

RIDE 'EM, COWBOY!

by Marco

"Welcome, folks! Welcome to the annual Buffalo Bill Cody Stampede Rodeo in Cody, Wyoming!" the announcer's voice blared from the loudspeakers. "Let the Grand Entry begin!"

My dad and I whooped as the cowboys and cowgirls paraded past, decked out in colorful western shirts, hats, belts, boots, and chaps. Some wore red, white, and blue because the rodeo took place over the Fourth of July.

We had been to the Stampede three times before, but this time we sat in the Buzzard's Roost, the best seats in the arena. From up there, I could take in the entire scene. I could smell animal sweat, hear the gates banging, and see the cowboys hanging out. It was like a big, dusty stable.

Timed events were first on the program. I was jumping out of my seat, waiting for the roping and racing against the clock. Calf roping shows off ranching skills. I was eagerly watching to learn more about roping, but I had to feel sorry for the calves. One second a calf was running from the chute, and less than 30 seconds later it was on the ground bawling, with a rope tied in a half hitch around three legs.

Barrel racing is another timed event. If I remember correctly, it's the only event for women in this rodeo. Racing around three barrels, the cowgirls spurred their horses in a cloverleaf pattern. Skillfully, they avoided knocking down any barrels.

Almost 100 years ago, an African American cowboy named Will Pickett invented steer wrestling—my favorite timed event. Leaning off the side of his horse, he seized a steer by its horns and slid to the ground. Then he dug in his boot heels and twisted the steer over onto its side. Pickett called it "bulldogging." At the Stampede, the steers were dropping like flies.

Rough stock is the tough stuff: bareback riding, saddle bronc riding, and bull riding. To qualify for the next round in rough stock events, a cowboy has to hang on to a bucking beast with one hand and hold out for at least eight seconds. The first bareback rider flew so high you could see daylight between him and the horse. Yee haw! If the rider's free hand touches anything, the judges disqualify him. Then the announcer always remarks, "Let's give him a hand, folks. It may be all he's taking home tonight."

Rodeo is downright dangerous. Broken bones, cuts and bruises, pulled muscles, and concussions are common. Riders are sometimes trampled. Cowboys called "pickup men" protect the bronc riders from the broncs, and rodeo clowns protect the bull riders from the bulls. At the Stampede, I saw a Brahma bull explode from the chute, twisting like a tornado. The rider flipped over the bull's horns and flopped at its feet. In a flash, a red-nosed rodeo clown distracted the bull, and the cowboy sprang up and scrambled over the fence to safety.

The Stampede always has a famous specialty act. One year, it was a trained buffalo. Last summer, it was a sharpshooter who also did tricks with a bullwhip and a lasso. He snapped a target from his own mouth with the whip! Crrrrack!

On the last night, the winners got to take home prize money and a rodeo trophy: a belt buckle. I took home a new rodeo poster and a saddlebag of memories.

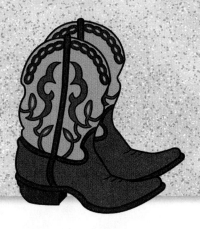

Reflect

What do you think? Did Marco use all the traits of a good eyewitness account in his writing? Does your writing have all the traits of a good eyewitness account? Be sure to check it against the rubric.

What's a Historical Episode?

It's a story that's based on an actual time, place, event, or person in history. Both fact and fiction can be woven together. I like this kind of writing because I can be creative while making history come alive.

What's in a Historical Episode?

Setting
This is the time and place of my story. I want to make sure my readers understand the historical period I'm writing about.

Characters
I can write about real people from history or make up fictional characters. I just need to be sure my characters act like real people from the past.

Accuracy
This is important for the true parts of my story. I don't want to give my readers incorrect information, so I'll research my facts very carefully.

Interest
My story won't bring history to life if it's just a list of facts. I need to focus on an exciting problem or a fascinating event. I'll use an interesting beginning and clear details to keep my readers involved.

Why write a Historical Episode?

Since I'm interested in history, I enjoy this kind of writing. There are many other reasons for writing a historical episode. I've listed some here.

Information
My readers can learn more about familiar topics or find out something completely new about history. I can share real information about historical people and events.

Entertainment
History is really interesting! It's fun to read about how people in the past lived, what they thought, and how they coped with life. I want to share that with my readers.

Research Skills
Even though a historical episode is partly fiction, I have to do a lot of research before writing. Practicing my research skills is important since I'll use them throughout my education.

Linking Narrative Writing Traits to a Historical Episode

In this chapter, you will write a story that takes place in a specific time period. This type of narrative writing is called a historical episode. Marco will guide you through the stages of the writing process: Prewrite, Draft, Revise, Edit, and Publish. In each stage, Marco will show you writing strategies that are linked to the Narrative Writing Traits below.

Narrative Writing Traits

- a focused topic, experience, or series of events
- engaging, accurate details that develop and describe the topic, experience, or series of events

- logically sequenced events, often in chronological order
- an interesting beginning and a satisfying ending
- transitions that signal the sequence of events as well as shifts in time or setting

- a voice and tone that are appropriate for the purpose and audience
- dialogue that, if used, fits the characters

- precise, descriptive words and phrases

- a variety of sentences that flow and are a pleasure to read

- no or few errors in grammar, usage, mechanics, and spelling

Before you write, read Kim Lee's historical episode on the next three pages. Then use the rubric on pages 34–35 to decide how well she did. (Look back at What's in a Historical Episode? on page 28, too!)

Conquest of the Stratosphere

by Kim Lee

Setting

Characters

Two men sat across from each other on a train chugging through the Swiss Alps. They had met only an hour earlier, but they were enjoying each other's company. Auguste Piccard, the elder one, was a long-limbed professor. A wreath of wild hair encircled his balding crown. Small round glasses perched on his long slender nose. His mustache wiggled as he talked. Paul Kipfer, the younger man, had sandy hair and soft blue eyes. He didn't talk much. Instead, he listened intently as Auguste described his research on cosmic rays in the atmosphere.

After a pause in the conversation, Auguste asked Paul, "Are you married?"

"No," Paul replied.

Interesting beginning →

"Good," Auguste said eagerly. "Are you engaged?"

"No," said Paul, puzzled by Auguste's questions.

"Ah, wonderful!" Auguste exclaimed. "Would you like to go up into the stratosphere in a balloon with me? We could study the cosmic rays!"

In 1930, this was a dangerous proposal. The stratosphere begins six to eight miles above Earth's surface. It is deadly cold and lacks enough oxygen for survival. Paul knew that no one had ever been up there and returned alive. Balloons had only open-air baskets. Even airplanes did not yet have pressurized cabins to hold in oxygen. Accurate historical details

Auguste knew it was risky, too. That was why he wanted an assistant without a wife and family. Auguste's family accepted his determination to make the hazardous trip. Paul also felt the force of that determination. He listened to Auguste's plan. By the time the train arrived in Brussels, Belgium, where Auguste lived, Paul had agreed to be his assistant. Setting

Auguste took care of every detail. The giant balloon was made of rubberized cotton. Attached to it was a pressurized cabin. It consisted of an airtight aluminum sphere with portholes as windows. It included a system that recycled oxygen so it would last longer. No lightweight crash helmets were available in those days, so Auguste created some out of upside-down sewing baskets. He added seat cushions for padding.   **Accurate historical details**

Accurate historical facts

On the morning of May 27, 1931, Paul and Auguste prepared for take-off in Augsburg, Germany. As the balloon was being inflated, Auguste imagined all he would learn on this scientific adventure. Suddenly, a gust of wind rolled the cabin off its platform, and it crashed to the ground. It had only slight damage, so the launch continued as scheduled.

A few minutes later, however, the men heard a hissing sound. The cabin was leaking air. Auguste patched the leak with petroleum jelly and waited with his fingers crossed.

Communication with the ground crew would be impossible. Radio was only in its infancy, and satellite technology was decades in the future. Like the early explorers, the scientists sailed alone into an uncharted world.

By afternoon, the balloon had safely risen nearly ten miles, well into the stratosphere. Auguste and Paul made some observations and measurements. Then they prepared for their descent, but something went wrong. The ropes that release the gas from the balloon had become tangled. The two men were stuck in the stratosphere!

Hours passed. The sun's heat raised the temperature inside the cabin to over 90 degrees. Sweating, the men eyed the gauges on the oxygen tanks in their silver bubble.

Accurate historical facts

Auguste was certain that at nightfall the air in the balloon would cool, and they would start to descend. Yet even after the sun went down, the balloon did not. Around 6:00 A.M., Auguste wrote in his log, "We have oxygen left for only four hours."

In the meantime, people around the world waited for each day's newspaper to learn about the fate of the scientists. Readers were troubled by headlines that the balloon was out of control. In the midst of a worldwide economic depression, people craved hope and heroes.

Finally, the balloon started to float slowly down. Auguste and Paul landed the next night on top of a glacier—but where? They crawled from the cramped cabin. Unprepared for a freezing climate, they wrapped themselves in the balloon fabric to stay warm. At dawn, they picked their way down the ice slope. A rescue party soon caught up with them.

Shivering, Auguste asked a round man with a pointed wool hat, "Wh—wh—what country are we in?"

"Austria," the man answered. "We're near a village called Obergurgl."

Auguste Piccard and Paul Kipfer had spent 16 hours inside the sphere. They had ascended 51,775 feet, a height no one had reached before. Not only did they gather valuable scientific data, but they also proved that people could survive in pressurized cabins high above Earth. Their conquest of the stratosphere paved the way for future air and space travel.

Rubric

Use this 6-point rubric to plan and score a historical episode.

	6	5	4
Ideas	The episode focuses on one historical event. Details and quotes are credible, accurate, and interesting.	The writing focuses mainly on one event. Details and quotes are accurate and credible.	The writing sometimes strays from the historical event. Some details are vague or inaccurate.
Organization	The sequence of events in the episode unfolds naturally. Transitions guide the reader smoothly from the beginning to the end. There is a clear beginning, middle, and end.	The sequence of events is logical. Transitions guide the reader. There is a clear beginning, middle, and end.	The events are mostly easy to follow. Several transitions are used. There is a beginning, middle, and end.
Voice	The writer's voice is knowledgeable and connects with the audience throughout the episode.	The writer's voice is knowledgeable and engaging throughout most of the episode.	The writer's voice starts out strong and engaging but fades as the episode goes on.
Word Choice	Unfamiliar words are clearly defined for the reader.	Unfamiliar words are defined for the reader.	Some unfamiliar words are poorly defined, forcing the reader to stop and reread.
Sentence Fluency	There is great variety in length and structure of sentences. The writing is enjoyable to read.	Variety in sentence length and structure makes the writing easy to read.	There is some variety in sentence length and structure. The writing is easy to read.
Conventions	Quotation marks and commas are used correctly. The episode is easy to read and understand.	A few errors with quotation marks and commas do not distract the reader.	Some noticeable errors in quotation marks don't confuse the reader.

✚ **Presentation** All the pages are labeled and numbered.

3	2	1	
It is not always clear which event is being described. Details may be lacking, and some are vague.	The episode does not focus on one event. The details are weak or incorrect.	The episode does not attempt to tell about an event. Details are missing or unrelated.	**Ideas**
Some of the events are out of order. More transitions would help the reader follow the story. The beginning or the end is weak and needs work.	The events are difficult to follow. Very few transitions are used. Both the beginning and the end need work.	The reader feels lost with the writer's list of random details. The beginning and the end are missing.	**Organization**
Sometimes the voice is present; sometimes it disappears. There is little connection to the reader.	The writer's voice is weak and does not engage with the reader.	The writer's voice is absent from the writing.	**Voice**
Several unfamiliar words are not defined or are poorly defined, making it hard for the reader to understand the episode.	The writer does not bother defining unfamiliar words, leaving the reader in the dark.	Words are incorrectly used, and definitions are missing.	**Word Choice**
Sentences are repetitive in beginnings and similar in length. The writing is choppy in places.	There are many choppy or incomplete sentences and very little variety in length or beginnings.	Many sentence problems make the writing a challenge to read.	**Sentence Fluency**
Many errors in the use of quotation marks and commas interfere with meaning.	The writing has many errors with quotation marks, commas, and other conventions that get in the way of the message.	The writing has not been edited and is very difficult to read.	**Conventions**

See Appendix B for 4-, 5-, and 6-point narrative rubrics.

Historical Episode

Using the ^ Rubric to Study the Model

Did you notice that the model on pages 31–33 points out some key elements of a historical episode? As she wrote "Conquest of the Stratosphere," Kim Lee used these elements to help her describe an event in history. She also used the 6-point rubric on pages 34–35 to plan, draft, revise, and edit the writing. A rubric is a great tool to evaluate writing during the writing process. Now let's use the same rubric to score the model.

To do this, we'll focus on each trait separately, starting with Ideas. We'll use the top descriptor for each trait (column 6), along with examples from the model, to help us understand how the traits work together. How would you score Kim on each trait?

- **The episode focuses on one historical event.**
- **Details and quotes are credible, accurate, and interesting.**

Kim focuses on one historical event throughout the episode. She includes details about the people and the event that are interesting and accurate. Her quotes sound like real conversation.

[from the writing model]

Auguste Piccard, the elder one, was a long-limbed professor. A wreath of wild hair encircled his balding crown. . . .

"Ah, wonderful!" Auguste exclaimed. "Would you like to go up into the stratosphere in a balloon with me?"

Organization

- The sequence of events in the episode unfolds naturally.
- Transitions guide the reader smoothly from the beginning to the end.
- There is a clear beginning, middle, and end.

Kim sequences the episode's events in chronological order, which makes sense. She uses transitions, such as *In the meantime* and *Suddenly*, to help the reader follow along. It's easy to tell which parts of the story are the beginning, middle, and end.

[from the writing model]

As the balloon was being inflated, Auguste imagined all he would learn on this scientific adventure. Suddenly, a gust of wind rolled the cabin off its platform, and it crashed to the ground.

Voice

- The writer's voice is knowledgeable and connects with the audience throughout the episode.

Kim's voice makes it easy for the reader to stay connected to the events of the balloon ride. In this paragraph, Kim describes the beginning of the men's descent. Notice how she draws the audience in with an exclamation about the danger the men are in.

[from the writing model]

Then they prepared for their descent, but something went wrong. The ropes that release the gas from the balloon had become tangled. The two men were stuck in the stratosphere!

• Unfamiliar words are clearly defined for the reader.

Kim makes sure her readers know the meanings of unfamiliar words, such as *stratosphere* and *pressurized cabin*, so they can fully understand the story.

[from the writing model]

The stratosphere begins six to eight miles above Earth's surface. It is deadly cold and lacks enough oxygen for survival.

[from the writing model]

The giant balloon was made of rubberized cotton. Attached to it was a pressurized cabin. It consisted of an airtight aluminum sphere with portholes as windows. It included a system that recycled oxygen so it would last longer.

• There is great variety in length and structure of sentences. The writing is enjoyable to read.

Kim varies her sentences to make her writing flow and to keep it lively. Read the following paragraph. Do you see how Kim uses sentences of different lengths? Some of her sentences start with a subject, and others start with a phrase. She even ends one sentence with a question!

[from the writing model]

Finally, the balloon started to float slowly down. Auguste and Paul landed the next night on top of a glacier—but where? They crawled from the cramped cabin. Unprepared for a freezing climate, they wrapped themselves in the balloon fabric to stay warm. At dawn, they picked their way down the ice slope. A rescue party soon caught up with them.

Conventions

- Quotation marks and commas are used correctly. The episode is easy to read and understand.

Kim really knows how to use quotes. Every time a character speaks in this story, his exact words have quotation marks around them. She even uses dashes to help the reader understand how the character is speaking. It's a little unusual, but it's very effective!

[from the writing model]

Shivering, Auguste asked a round man with a pointed wool hat, "Wh—wh—what country are we in?"

"Austria," the man answered. "We're near a village called Obergurgl."

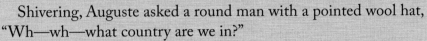

✛**Presentation** All the pages are labeled and numbered.

My Turn!

Now I'm going to use the rubric to help me write a historical episode. Read along and see how I do it.

Prewrite

Focus on (**Ideas**)

The Rubric Says   The episode focuses on one historical event.

Writing Strategy   Use several credible sources to take notes on a historical event.

I found out about the Cardiff Giant hoax online. I was fascinated! When my teacher asked us to write a historical episode, I decided to write about the Giant.

First, I read an overview of the event in an encyclopedia. Then I looked at a library book and some reliable websites on the topic. Here are some of the notes I took.

My Notes on the Cardiff Giant

- ☒ 1866: George Hull heard some people talk about giants on Earth—he got an idea
- ☒ 1868: Hull sent a chunk of gypsum from Ft. Dodge to Chicago
- ☒ stonecutters made 10-foot man, twisted body, calm face—acid to make it look old
- ☒ Hull buried statue near Cardiff, NY, on farm of William Newell, his relative who was in on hoax
- ☒ Oct. 16, 1869: well diggers found giant, Newell put up tent, charged 300–500 people daily to see statue
- ☒ people say they saw Hull and wagon with box the year before—Hull admits hoax on Dec. 10
- ☒ "We'll make a fortune off the fools."—Hull's partner
- ☒ giant stored, exhibited at fairs, bought by Farmers' Museum in Cooperstown, NY, in 1947
- ☒ period: after Civil War, mid-Victorian Age—growth in business, science, and technology (no cars or phones)

Apply

Choose an interesting historical event. Gather information from credible sources, and take notes.

Prewrite

The Rubric Says	The sequence of events in the episode unfolds naturally.
Writing Strategy	Make a Story Map to organize the notes.

Writer's Term

Story Map
A **Story Map** organizes the setting, characters, problem, plot, and ending of a story.

The rubric reminds me to order events naturally. A historical episode is a story, so the events should unfold logically. A Story Map will help me organize the events into a natural sequence so my audience can easily follow along.

Story Map

Setting Time 1866–1869 **Place** farm near Cardiff, NY

Characters George Hull, William Newell, well diggers, scientist

Problem Hull has to convince people that a stone sculpture is a giant fossilized prehistoric man and get them to pay to see it.

Plot/Events Hull learns about the giant story, comes up with a hoax, has a stone sculpture made, and has it buried on a relative's farm. It's discovered, people pay to see it, and Hull sells part ownership of it. People start to doubt Hull's claims and check into them.

Ending (Resolution) Hull admits the hoax. The giant is moved around for years. It finally ends up in a NY museum.

Reflect

Think about Marco's Story Map. Are the events organized in a clear and natural way?

Apply

Organize your ideas by using your notes to make a Story Map.

Draft

The Rubric Says   Transitions guide the reader smoothly from the beginning to the end. There is a clear beginning, middle, and end.

Writing Strategy   Make sure your writing has a clear organization.

Now I'll use my Story Map to write my draft. According to the rubric, I need a clear and interesting beginning, middle, and end for my historical episode, and I should use transitions to guide my reader along. As I said before, I'll present the plot in the order it happened. That will help me keep the story clear and focused on the event. Using transitions such as *First, Two years later,* and *After several months* will help my readers understand how the story is moving along.

Right from the start, I'll include important facts so my audience will understand when and where this event took place. To grab my readers' interest, I'll hint at what's to come but leave them wondering for a while. This is my draft, so I'll just write now and worry about spelling and grammar later.

[DRAFT]

[places readers into the historical period]

[clear beginning introduces historical event]

The Cardiff Giant

In 1866, the Civil War had just ended, and the nation was looking towards a bright future. George Hull of Binghamton, New York, was visiting his sister in Iowa. During his visit, he learned that some people believed there were giants on Earth long ago. That gave Hull an idea. Hull began to make plans to put his own giant on Earth.

[hint of what's to come]

Two years later, Hull returned to Iowa. He sent a block of gypsum from a quarry near Fort Dodge to Chicago. Then he hired stonecutters to carve it into a man. Hull wanted it to look like a prehistoric man, so he "aged" it with acid. To create the look of skin pores, he poked the stone with darning needles.

When the sculpture was completed, Hull shipped it to the farm of William Newell, a relative who was in on the skeem. Newell lived near Cardiff, New York, south of Syracuse Together they buried the giant behind Newell's barn.

[grabs audience interest and makes readers wonder what will happen next]

Reflect

Does the beginning of the story make the historical period clear? Is it interesting enough to get the audience's attention?

Apply

Write a draft using your Story Map as a guide. Make your beginning clear so your readers are placed right into the historical period.

Revise

Focus on Voice

The Rubric Says	The writer's voice is knowledgeable and connects with the audience throughout the episode.
Writing Strategy	Sound like I know and care a lot about the topic.

I know that a historical episode can both inform and entertain. If I want my reader to believe me, I have to sound knowledgeable about my topic. To connect with and entertain my audience, I'll write as if I'm speaking directly to my readers. See where I added information to sound more knowledgeable.

[DRAFT]

Geology was a new science in the mid-1800s, but paleontologists knew that flesh could not be turned to stone.

Most scientists were certain it was a fake. This judgment led

to another theory . . .

Apply

Make sure your voice connects with the audience. Does it sound like you know your topic and care about it?

Revise

The Rubric Says   Unfamiliar words are clearly defined for the reader.

Writing Strategy   Explain the meanings of any unfamiliar words.

After I wrote my draft, I looked at the rubric again. It says that I should explain any domain-specific vocabulary that is specific to my topic. I see some words like that in my draft. I think I'll add some phrases to make their meaning more clear.

[DRAFT]

Two years later, Hull returned to Iowa. He sent a block of **, a soft, light-colored mineral,** ← **[explains meaning of gypsum]** gypsum from a quarry near Fort Dodge to Chicago. Then he hired

stonecutters to carve it into a man. Hull wanted it to look like a

prehistoric man, so he "aged" it with acid. To create the look of

skin pores, he poked the stone with darning needles.

[explains meaning of darning needles] → **These long needles were usually used for mending holes in knitted clothing, not for creating fake fossils!**

Reflect

What do you think? Does Marco sound knowledgeable about his subject? How do his explanations strengthen his writing?

Apply

Add words or phrases that will explain any difficult vocabulary in your episode.

Revise

Focus on Sentence Fluency

The Rubric Says	There is great variety in length and structure of sentences. The writing is enjoyable to read.
Writing Strategy	Vary sentence patterns for meaning, reader interest, and style.

Time to check sentence fluency. The rubric says I should use different sentence lengths and structures to make my writing enjoyable to read. Let's look at another section of my draft. All the sentences here began with the subject, and most were about the same length. But look how I changed some of the sentences to vary my writing. Now this section reads much more smoothly.

[DRAFT]

After clearing away the rest of the dirt,
the workman
~~He cleared away the rest of the dirt and~~ ran to fetch Newell.
Rubbing his beard,
Newell peered down into the pit ~~and rubbed his beard~~. A silent

stone giant stared back. It's body was twisted as if in pain, but

it's face had a peaceful expression. Newell said ride into town

boys and tell them what we've got here. [added introductory phrases]

Apply

Do your sentences all sound the same? If so, add some descriptive phrases or rewrite some sentences into different patterns.

The Rubric Says	Quotation marks and commas are used correctly. The episode is easy to read and understand.
Writing Strategy	Check the use of quotation marks and commas.

Writer's Term

Quotation

A **quotation** restates the exact words of a speaker or writer. A quotation is placed within quotation marks and is credited to the speaker or writer.

Now I need to check my draft for errors. I will check my spelling, grammar, and capitalization. I will pay special attention to punctuation. If quotations are not punctuated correctly or if commas are out of place, the reader will be confused.

[DRAFT]   [punctuated quotes correctly]

When the sculpture was completed, Hull shipped it to the farm of

William Newell, a relative who was in on the ~~skeem~~ scheme. Newell lived near

Cardiff, New York, south of Syracuse. Together they buried the

giant behind Newell's barn. Wiping the dirt from his hands, Hull said,

"We'll make a fortune off the fools, but we must wait until the time is

right."

Reflect

How did Marco's sentence structure revisions improve the flow of his writing? How do his edits help you better understand his historical episode?

Apply — Conventions

Edit your draft for spelling, punctuation, and capitalization. Be sure quotations are punctuated correctly and commas are correct.

For more practice correcting quotation and comma errors, use the exercises on the next two pages.

Quotations

Know the Rule

A **quotation** is the exact words of a speaker or a writer. Quotations can add interest to nearly every piece of writing. Quotations must be punctuated correctly.

Use **quotation marks** at the beginning and end of a quote. Use a comma to separate the speaker's words from the rest of the sentence. If a quotation is a complete sentence, begin it with a capital letter. Add the correct end punctuation before the last quotation mark.

> **Examples:** "Will people believe us?" asked Newell.
> Hull said, "Of course they will!"

Practice the Rule

Correct the punctuation of each quotation below. Then write the correct sentences on a separate piece of paper.

1. To the people at the quarry, Hull said The stone is for a patriotic statue.
2. One article said, Hull was the model for the giant's face.
3. Newell asked "Should I dig up the giant myself or have it dug up by others."
4. What is it? Who carved it? How old is it? Why was it buried? everyone asked.
5. People began telling each other, The giant is a Goliath!"
6. At least one scientist exclaimed "This has to be a fake.
7. One of Newell's neighbors asked, Didn't we see Hull bring a large crate last year"
8. "I sold shares of the giant just in time", Hull admitted.
9. "Whatever happened to the Cardiff Giant"? people wondered years later.
10. "Grandpa said I think it's in a museum in New York."

Commas

Know the Rule

A **comma** tells a reader where to pause, such as the point where a **compound sentence** is connected with a coordinating conjunction.

> **Example:** People found out that the Cardiff Giant was a hoax, **but** they still go to see it at the Farmers' Museum.

A comma is used to separate an **introductory word or phrase** from the rest of the sentence.

> **Example: When they first saw the sculpture,** many people believed it was really a petrified man.

A comma is also used to separate a **noun of direct address** from the rest of a sentence. A noun of direct address names a person who is being spoken to.

> **Example:** "**William,** we can make a lot of money from this sculpture if we wait until the time is right."

Practice the Rule

Number a sheet of paper 1–8. Rewrite the following sentences with the correct punctuation.

1. There have been dozens of world fairs but the Chicago World's Fair in 1893 was one of the best of its day.

2. For the arts and architecture this fair had a strong influence.

3. Frederic Law Olmsted was a famous architect and he designed the fairgrounds.

4. In the Court of Honor buildings were constructed out of white stucco.

5. This area was called the White City and it was lighted at night with street lights.

6. In Katharine Lee Bates's poem "America the Beautiful" the phrase "alabaster cities" came from the White City.

7. Next door to the fair Buffalo Bill put on his Wild West show to entertain people.

8. Someone might have said to the mayor of Chicago "Mr. Harrison this exhibition is truly an inspiration!"

Publish

+Presentation

Publishing Strategy	Put your historical episode in a library display.
Presentation Strategy	Include a title, your name, and page numbers.

My historical episode is finished! Now it's time to publish it. I want my reader to know the title and my name, so I'll label my writing with this information. If my writing is longer than one page, I'll include a page number and my name on each page. I can use the header/footer function on my computer to do this easily. Before putting my work on display, I'll read it through one last time to make sure it includes all of the items on my final checklist.

My Final Checklist

Did I—

✔ check to make sure I punctuated quotations correctly?

✔ make sure I used commas correctly throughout the historical episode?

✔ label and number all the pages?

✔ check spelling, capitalization, and punctuation?

Apply

Check your historical episode against your checklist. Then make a final copy to publish.

The Cardiff Giant

by Marco

It was 1866. The Civil War had just ended, and the nation was looking toward a brighter future. George Hull of Binghamton, New York, was visiting his sister in Iowa. During his visit, he learned that some people believed there were giants on Earth long ago. That gave Hull an idea for a new business venture. On the long trip home by steamboat and train, Hull began to hatch a plan to put a giant on Earth.

Two years later, Hull returned to Iowa. He shipped a 3,000-pound block of gypsum, a soft, light-colored mineral, from a quarry near Fort Dodge to Chicago. Then he hired stonecutters to secretly carve the hunk of rock into the shape of a man more than ten feet tall.

Hull wanted the statue to look like a petrified prehistoric man, so he "aged" it with acid. To create the appearance of skin pores, he pounded the stone with darning needles. These long needles were usually used for mending holes in knitted clothing, not for creating fake fossils!

When the sculpture was completed, Hull shipped it to the farm of William Newell, a relative who was in on the scheme. Newell lived near Cardiff, New York, south of Syracuse. Together they buried the giant behind Newell's barn. Wiping the dirt from his hands, Hull said, "We'll make a fortune off the fools, but we must wait until the time is right."

A year later, a large bed of fossils was discovered nearby. Hull sent a mysterious telegram to Newell. It read, "Strike while the iron is hot."

On October 16, 1869, Newell hired two men to dig a well at a certain spot near the barn. A few feet down, their shovels clanked against something. "I declare, someone has been buried here!" said one of the workmen as he uncovered a stone foot.

After clearing away the rest of the dirt, the workman ran to fetch Newell. Rubbing his beard, Newell peered down into the pit. A silent stone giant stared back. Its body was twisted as if in pain, but its face had a peaceful expression. Newell said, "Ride into town, boys, and tell them what we've got here."

The Cardiff Giant was an instant celebrity. As word spread, hundreds of people came each day to gaze at the strange marvel. Four stagecoaches a day ran between the Syracuse train station and Cardiff. Newell put a tent over the site and charged 25 cents admission. As the number of visitors increased, so did the fee.

At first, many thought the sculpture really was a petrified man from an earlier time. After all, the region was known for its fossils. Recent advances in science and technology made the public believe that almost anything was possible.

Marco Page 2

Most scientists were certain it was a fake. Geology was a new science in the mid-1800s, but paleontologists knew that flesh could not be turned to stone. This judgment led to another theory: Maybe the gypsum giant was an ancient statue carved by Native Americans or by early white settlers.

Hull suspected his hoax would soon be revealed. He sold part ownership of the giant to a group of local businesspeople. It was moved to Syracuse and then toured other cities in New York.

In the meantime, an investigation was started. Local people remembered they had seen Hull traveling with a large wooden crate on a wagon the year before. On December 10, Hull admitted the hoax. One of Hull's partners commented, "What a bunch of fools!"

The Cardiff Giant toured for a while and then went into storage. Later it appeared at fairs in Iowa and New York. It was even stored in a child's playroom for a while. In 1947, the Farmers' Museum in Cooperstown, New York, bought the giant.

Today, visitors to the museum stand under a tent just like the first visitors did in 1869. There, they ponder the Cardiff Giant, America's greatest hoax.

Reflect

Did Marco use all the traits of a good historical episode? Check his writing against the rubric. Be sure to check your own story against the rubric too.

Marco Page 3

What's a Short Story?

A short story is a story that may or may not be true. It has only a few characters, and it focuses on one problem or conflict. I like using my imagination to do this kind of writing!

What's in a Short Story?

Protagonist
This is the main character in the story, the person who has the problem. I want my readers to relate to my protagonist, so I need to make his or her personality come alive.

Point of View
A short story can be written in either first person or third person. Third person works well for most stories, but sometimes nothing beats being right inside the protagonist's head!

Plot
To make my story exciting, I'll think of an interesting problem for my protagonist. Then I'll tell the events of the story in a logical order while building tension. My readers will love the climax, or high point, of my story!

Realism
Even if my story is made up, it has to seem real. My readers want to feel as if they are living the story! I need to use strong writing to capture the interest of my audience and keep them involved all the way through the story.

Why write a Short Story?

I can think of a lot of reasons to write a short story! Here are some of my ideas.

Personal Enjoyment

It's a lot of fun to write something as creative as a short story. I like making up my own characters and imagining what happens to them.

Writing Skills

Writing a short story uses a lot of important skills that I need to practice. I can get better at organizing my thoughts, writing sentences, and spelling and punctuating correctly while I do something interesting and fun!

Entertainment

Everybody enjoys a good story! I can share my short story with my family and friends and other people, too. For just a while, my readers can take a break from their real lives and experience my imagination!

Understanding

Writing my own stories can help me understand the stories I read. I can see how authors construct their stories when I've been through the process myself. And I can really appreciate the way good writers bring life into their writing!

Linking Narrative Writing Traits to a Short Story

In this chapter, you will write a story that has only one problem or conflict. This type of narrative writing is called a short story. Marco will guide you through the stages of the writing process: Prewrite, Draft, Revise, Edit, and Publish. In each stage, Marco will show you important writing strategies that are linked to the Narrative Writing Traits below.

Narrative Writing Traits

Ideas	• a focused topic, experience, or series of events • engaging, accurate details that develop and describe the topic, experience, or series of events
Organization	• logically sequenced events, often in chronological order • an interesting beginning and a satisfying ending • transitions that signal the sequence of events as well as shifts in time or setting
Voice	• a voice and tone that are appropriate for the purpose and audience • dialogue that, if used, fits the characters
Word Choice	• precise, descriptive words and phrases
Sentence Fluency	• a variety of sentences that flow and are a pleasure to read aloud
Conventions	• no or few errors in grammar, usage, mechanics, and spelling

Before you write, read Ivan Phillips's short story on the next page. Then use the short story rubric on pages 58–59 to decide how well he did. (You might want to look back at What's in a Short Story? on page 54, too!)

Loser!

by Ivan Phillips

Protagonist

Third-person point of view

"What are you doing here?" demanded David.

Stephanie hopped off her bike and looked at the other club members. Everyone stood beside a sleek, high-tech bicycle that made her rusty clunker look prehistoric. "I . . . I came for the marathon," she replied.

"But you just joined the club two days ago!" cried Jenna.
"Everybody else has trained for months," added Miller.

← Realism

They were saying she couldn't handle such a long ride. But Stephanie liked challenges. "I really want to try this," she said quietly.

David snorted. "Well, we really want to win. So don't expect us to hold back for you."

Plot—protagonist's problem

As the marathon began, Stephanie kept up with the others in her club. But soon everybody else shot ahead. "See you later, loser!" someone called back.

She tried to catch up, pumping hard until her legs ached, but the others quickly became colorful blobs in the heat waves far down the road. Then they disappeared.

Plot—building tension →

Realism

After that, Stephanie slowed to a steady pace. For a while, other bikers zoomed by, their wheels whizzing smoothly on the pavement. Then she biked on alone with just the rumbling of the support van's engine behind her. She must be the very last biker!

When the enormous hill appeared ahead, Stephanie was already exhausted from riding so long. Her lungs burned with every breath, and her rubbery legs quivered. She wouldn't give up now. She couldn't!

Plot—building tension

The bike crept upwards, rocking side-to-side as Stephanie strained against the pedals. The higher she rose, the harder she struggled. Grunting out the last of her breath, she finally felt the pedals ease beneath her. She had reached the top!

Realism

Below her stretched a golden valley of corn waving in the breeze. The flags of the finish line flapped beside a barn less than a mile away!

Plot—climax

Stephanie coasted downhill and then pedaled with new energy. Only a few people waited at the finish line, so she knew she was terribly late. Still, she lifted her arms in victory as she sailed under the flags. So what if she came in last? Completing the marathon made her feel like a real winner.

Rubric

Use this 6-point rubric to plan and score a short story.

	6	5	4
Ideas	Vivid details describe and develop the events and characters. Suspense moves the plot along.	Strong details develop the events and characters. Suspense is present in the story.	Some interesting details are used to develop events and characters. There are moments of suspense.
Organization	Events are paced so that tension builds to the climax and resolves at the end in a satisfying way.	Most of the events build tension to the climax. The story ends in a satisfying way.	The story has a climax and resolution. The reader feels tension only at times. The resolution may not be satisfying.
Voice	The writer's voice connects with the reader and brings the topic to life.	The writer is speaking to the reader, and the reader feels engaged in the story.	Sometimes the writer's voice fades, but some moments grab the reader.
Word Choice	Precise words and memorable phrases create strong images for the reader.	Precise words and phrases create pictures for the reader.	Some precise words and phrases are used well. Some moments create images for the reader.
Sentence Fluency	The story contains strong sentences written in active voice.	Most of the sentences are clear and written in active voice.	Some sentences are written in passive voice, making the writing weak in places.
Conventions	Personal, possessive, and indefinite pronouns are used correctly. The writing is easy to read.	A few errors with personal, possessive, and indefinite pronouns require careful review to spot.	Noticeable errors with personal, possessive, and indefinite pronouns don't interfere with the meaning.
✛ Presentation	All paragraphs are indented.		

3	2	1	
Plot and character details are general and not developed. The reader rarely feels suspense.	Characters are not developed, and the plot is vague. There is no feeling of suspense.	The characters and plot are hard to discern. There is no suspense because the plot is impossible to follow.	**Ideas**
The climax is hard to discern. The story has a resolution, but it is not satisfying.	The climax or resolution is missing entirely. The reader has trouble staying interested in the story.	There is no plot structure to hold the writing together, and the writing doesn't make sense.	**Organization**
The writer's voice comes and goes. The writer lacks confidence in the story.	The writer's voice is weak. The writing lacks details.	The writer's voice is absent. The reader is not sure who is telling the story.	**Voice**
Some vague or general words (*nice, fun, good*) are used. The reader has to work to form images.	Many words are vague or unclear. Verbs are weak.	Words are vague. There are no strong verbs. The writer struggled to find words.	**Word Choice**
Several sentences in a row are in passive voice, making reading dull in places.	Many sentences are weak, passive, or incorrect. The story is dull for the reader.	Sentences are incomplete or run-on. The story is almost impossible to read out loud.	**Sentence Fluency**
Noticeable errors with personal, possessive, and indefinite pronouns interfere with meaning.	Many errors with personal, possessive, and indefinite pronouns make reading a challenge.	The writing is filled with errors with personal, possessive, and indefinite pronouns that make reading difficult.	**Conventions**

See Appendix B for 4-, 5-, and 6-point narrative rubrics.

Using the Rubric to Study the Model
Short Story

Did you notice that the model on page 57 points out some key elements of a short story? As he wrote "Loser!" Ivan Phillips used these elements to help him tell a story. He also used the 6-point rubric on pages 58–59 to plan, draft, revise, and edit the writing. A rubric is a great tool to evaluate writing during the writing process. Now let's use the same rubric to score the model.

To do this, we'll focus on each trait separately, starting with Ideas. We'll use the top descriptor for each trait (column 6), along with examples from the model, to help us understand how the traits work together. How would you score Ivan on each trait?

- **Vivid details describe and develop the events and characters.**
- **Suspense moves the plot along.**

Ivan's vivid details give depth to the characters and the plot. The story has lots of suspense, and the dialogue also helps to move the plot along. Look at how the details and the dialogue make you wonder what will happen next.

[from the writing model]

They were saying she couldn't handle such a long ride. But Stephanie liked challenges. "I really want to try this," she said quietly.

David snorted. "Well, we really want to win. So don't expect us to hold back for you."

Organization

- Events are paced so that tension builds to the climax and resolves at the end in a satisfying way.

Things seem to get worse and worse for Stephanie! First, the club members leave her behind. Then the other bikers pass her by. She bikes until she's exhausted. You really wonder if she's going to make it! Finally she crosses the finish line in the exciting climax below.

[from the writing model]

Stephanie coasted downhill and then pedaled with new energy. Only a few people waited at the finish line, so she knew she was terribly late. Still, she lifted her arms in victory as she sailed under the flags.

Voice

- The writer's voice connects with the reader and brings the topic to life.

The reader is drawn into Ivan's narrative voice. I found the action and characters in the story realistic—they really came to life for me! Look at how Ivan describes the beginning of the marathon.

[from the writing model]

As the marathon began, Stephanie kept up with the others in her club. But soon everyone else shot ahead. "See you later, loser!" someone called back.

She tried to catch up, pumping hard until her legs ached, but the others quickly became colorful blobs in the heat waves far down the road. Then they disappeared.

Word Choice

- **Precise words and memorable phrases create strong images for the reader.**

Ivan chooses his words carefully. Instead of writing with overused words, he uses precise words that make the story come alive. He could have written something like this: "The bike *went* upwards, *moving* side-to-side as Stephanie *pushed* against the pedals. The higher she *went,* the harder she *worked.*" Just look at the precise, vivid words he uses instead.

[from the writing model]

The bike *crept* upwards, *rocking* side-to-side as Stephanie *strained* against the pedals. The higher she *rose,* the harder she *struggled.*

Sentence Fluency

- **The story contains strong sentences written in active voice.**

A verb is in active voice if the subject of the sentence is doing the action. A verb is in passive voice if the subject of the sentence is not doing the action. Sometimes passive voice works well, but usually sentences are stronger if they're written in active voice.

Obviously, Ivan knew that! He could have written sentences such as "Stephanie had been exhausted by the long ride" or "Her lungs were burned by every breath." But look how he used active voice to make the following paragraph strong.

[from the writing model]

When the enormous hill appeared ahead, Stephanie was already exhausted from riding so long. Her lungs burned with every breath, and her rubbery legs quivered. She wouldn't give up now. She couldn't!

Conventions

- **Personal, possessive, and indefinite pronouns are used correctly. The writing is easy to read.**

I checked Ivan's story for mistakes, but I don't see any, do you? He has spelled, capitalized, and punctuated everything correctly. And he knows how to use personal, possessive, and indefinite pronouns correctly, too. You can tell that from the paragraph below.

[from the writing model]

As the marathon began, Stephanie kept up with the others in her club. But soon everybody else shot ahead. "See you later, loser!" someone called back.

✚ **Presentation** All paragraphs are indented.

My Turn!

I'm going to write my own short story! I'll follow the rubric and use good writing strategies. You can read along and see how I do it.

Prewrite

Focus on **Ideas**

The Rubric Says   Vivid details describe and develop the events and characters.

Writing Strategy   Brainstorm characters and events to use in the story.

Ever since our teacher asked us to write a short story, I've been kicking around some ideas. To develop the plot and characters, I need to decide who the main character is and what his or her problem will be. Here are the notes I jotted down about possible characters and events for my story.

Notes

Characters:

- brave firefighter
- boy my age who's afraid of something
- cowboy
- girl my age who likes sports

Events:

- mountain-climbing expedition
- school play
- skydiving lesson
- sleepover
- camping trip

I decided I'd like to write a story about a boy my age, so I chose the boy who's afraid of something as my protagonist. I don't want him to be afraid of something obvious such as skydiving or seeing an alien, so I think I'll make him afraid of something at a sleepover. Maybe the sleepover can be held at a scary, creepy, old house. He will have to pretend he's not scared in front of his friends. Hey, I think I have a good idea for my story!

Apply

Brainstorm some ideas for characters and events for your story. Jot down your ideas and put your imagination to work!

Prewrite

Focus on **Organization**

The Rubric Says Events are paced so that tension builds to the climax and resolves at the end in a satisfying way.

Writing Strategy Make a Storyboard to organize the ideas.

Writer's Term

Storyboard

A **Storyboard** can help you plot the main parts of a story in chronological order. Each frame in the Storyboard represents a part of the story. Words and/or pictures can be used in a Storyboard.

Now that I've decided on my protagonist and his problem, I have to plan my story. I will organize the events to build tension toward the climax. I can use a Storyboard to help me. See what I did below.

STORYBOARD

EVENT 1
Chris and his best friend arrive at a creepy house for a sleepover. Chris is scared and has to hide his fear.

EVENT 2
Chris and his friend go in and find that the party is normal. Chris has a good time.

EVENT 3
At bedtime, Chris gets scared again and can't go to sleep.

EVENT 4
Chris hears footsteps and thinks someone is hurting his best friend!

EVENT 5—CLIMAX
Even though he's scared, Chris tries to save his friend. He jumps on the figure and knocks him down!

EVENT 6
It was just the host of the party sleepwalking, but Chris feels good that he handled his fear.

Reflect
How will Marco's Storyboard help him build tension in the story?

Apply
Use a Storyboard to organize the events of your short story.

Draft

Focus on Voice

The Rubric Says	The writer's voice connects with the reader and brings the topic to life.
Writing Strategy	Use first-person point of view and dialogue.

Writer's Term

Point of View

Point of view helps the reader know who is telling the story. In **first person,** the story is told from the protagonist's point of view using words such as **I** and **me** throughout. In **third person,** the writer or narrator tells the story. The writer uses words such as **he, she,** and **they** when writing in third person.

Now I'll use my Storyboard to write my draft. I know that a good way to draw the reader into the action is for the narrator to speak in first-person point of view. Then, to move the plot along and build some tension about how scared Chris is of the creepy house, I can include dialogue. I know that what my characters say may be in a different point of view so the reader will know who is talking to whom. That way the dialogue will also sound realistic.

I can't wait to start writing! I'm going to be very careful to use only complete sentences in my story—no fragments or run-ons! For now, I'll just do my best with spelling, punctuation, capitalization, and grammar while I'm getting my story down on paper. I'll fix any mistakes later!

Creepover!

by Marco

[DRAFT]

"Isn't this great, Chris?" asked my best friend, Og.

"Sure," I lied.

We stood outside the castle-sized door of the old Evans manshun. When this house was empty, everyone talked about its eerie glowing windows and strange moaning sounds. Now Roger, the new kid, lived here—and he'd invited the guys to a sleepover! I was afraid of that creepy place, but somehow I had to hide my fear from my friends.

After Og banged the iron nocker a few times, Roger opened the door with a creek and let us in. He took us to the huge, paneled room where somebody was hanging out. Any of the guys roasted marchmallows in the stone fireplace? He played cards or video games. It looked like a normal sleepover!   [first-person point of view] ◄

For a while, I actually enjoyed myself. But when we spread our sleeping bags on the floor and Roger turn off the lights, I got nervous again. I just couldn't relax.

Reflect

How does Marco build tension in the story? How does first-person point of view help you connect with the protagonist?

Apply

Write a draft using your Storyboard as a guide. Be sure to build tension throughout the story, leading up to an exciting climax.

Revise

Focus on **Ideas**

The Rubric Says   Suspense moves the plot along.

Writing Strategy   Add sensory details to build suspense.

After I wrote my draft, I read it through and noticed that I needed to build more suspense in the story. I want my reader to feel Chris's tension about the house where the sleepover is. Adding sensory details will help my readers feel what the narrator feels.

[DRAFT]

For a while, I actually enjoyed myself. But when we spread our sleeping bags on the floor and Roger turn off the lights, I got nervous again. ~~I just couldn't relax.~~

[added sensory details]

The dying fire cast strange shadows, and a dreary moan blew around the house. I burrowed into my downy sleeping bag, but I couldn't relax.

Apply

Try adding some sensory details to make your story come alive.

The Rubric Says	Precise words and memorable phrases create strong images for the reader.
Writing Strategy	Replace overused words with more exact words.

Writer's Term

Overused Words

Overused words have been used so often by writers and speakers that they have become bland and boring. Overused words carry meaning but are not precise.

Now it's time to look at my word choices. I looked at my draft again, and I have to say there are some parts that are full of overused words. The rubric tells me to use precise words and memorable phrases. Check out how I changed the paragraph below by taking out some overused words and replacing them with clearer, more precise words.

[DRAFT]

[replaced overused words]

scrambled   jumped onto   threatening   towered

I got to my feet and ran at the dark figure that stood over Og.
                    wrestled   realized
I pulled it to the floor before I saw the figure was Roger!

"Was I sleepwalking again?" he mumbled.

Reflect

How do the new word choices make Marco's writing more lively and interesting?

Apply

Replace any overused words in your draft with precise words and memorable phrases.

Revise

The Rubric Says   The story contains strong sentences written in active voice.

Writing Strategy   Use active voice to strengthen sentences.

✏ Writer's Term

Active Voice and Passive Voice
A verb is in **active voice** if the subject of the sentence is doing the action. A verb is in **passive voice** if the subject of the sentence is receiving or being affected by the action.

My short story is really coming along! The rubric says to write my sentences in active voice. That's because active voice almost always sounds stronger than passive voice.

I see one paragraph in my draft that has a lot of passive voice. I'm going to change the passive voice to active voice and make those sentences stronger!

[DRAFT]

[changed to active voice]

I still tried to save my friend
~~Even though I was frightened, my friend had to be saved!~~ So what
~~he didn't actually need my help?~~
if my help wasn't really needed? I ~~still hadn't been controlled by my~~
had controlled my fear,
~~fears~~ and that was what mattered!

Apply

Are any of your sentences written in passive voice? If they are, change them to active voice to make them stronger.

Edit

The Rubric Says   Personal, possessive, and indefinite pronouns are used correctly. The writing is easy to read.

Writing Strategy   Recognize and correct inappropriate shifts in pronoun number and person.

Writer's Term____

Indefinite Pronouns
Indefinite pronouns refer to persons or things that are not identified as individuals.

Now I need to check my spelling, punctuation, and capitalization. The rubric also says I need to use different kinds of pronouns correctly. Sometimes indefinite pronouns are confusing, and it looks like that happened in the paragraph below!

[DRAFT]

[corrected indefinite pronouns]

After Og banged the iron ^k^nocker a few times, Roger opened the
door with a creak̶e̶e̶k̶ and let us in. He took us to the huge, paneled
room where ~~somebody~~ everybody was hanging out. Any^Some^ of the guys roasted
~~marchmallows~~ marshmallows in the stone fireplace. He^Others^ played cards or video games.

It looked like a normal sleepover!

Reflect

Look at all the pronouns in the draft. Does Marco need to make any more corrections?

Apply

Edit your draft for spelling, punctuation, and capitalization. Be sure to fix any problems with pronouns.

For more practice using pronouns correctly, use the exercises on the next two pages.

Personal and Possessive Pronouns

Know the Rule

A **pronoun** can take the place of a noun.
Use the **personal pronouns** *I*, *me*, *we*, and *us* to speak or write about yourself. Use the personal pronouns *she*, *her*, *it*, *he*, *him*, *you*, *they*, and *them* to refer to other people and things.
The **possessive pronouns** *her*, *his*, *its*, *our*, *their*, *my*, and *your* show possession.

Practice the Rule

Number a sheet of paper 1–10. Rewrite each sentence with the correct pronoun(s).

1. Last year (me/my) friends gave me a surprise birthday party.
2. They blindfolded (I/me) and took me to my favorite restaurant.
3. Cara brought (she/her) camera and took pictures of all of (we/us) eating dinner.
4. Then (we/us) went to see a scary movie at the neighborhood movie theater.
5. Would (you/your) believe I was so tired that I fell asleep during the scariest part?
6. I woke up when all (me/my) friends screamed in fear.
7. My friends said (they/their) were glad I missed that part of the movie.
8. (They/Them) know I sometimes get really scared at the movies.
9. After the movie, all of (we/us) went out for ice cream.
10. That night, back in (me/my) own bedroom, I slept like a baby.

Indefinite Pronouns

Know the Rule

An **indefinite pronoun** refers to persons or things that are not identified as individuals. Indefinite pronouns include *all, any, anybody, anything, both, each, either, everybody, everyone, everything, few, many, most, nobody, no one, nothing, one, several, some,* and *someone*.

Practice the Rule

Number a sheet of paper 1–10. Rewrite each sentence by writing an indefinite pronoun from the Word Bank. Remember to capitalize any words that begin a sentence. Some sentences could have more than one correct answer. Some words may be used more than once.

Word Bank

one	many	everyone	some
no one	somebody	most	any
someone	anybody	something	several

1. _____ has lived in the Evans mansion for years.
2. Maybe that's why so _____ of us find the old house mysterious.
3. I don't believe _____ of the stories about the Evans mansion.
4. Still, _____ about that old house creeps me out.
5. _____ say they have seen strange lights glowing in its windows.
6. _____ of my friends claim to have heard eerie noises around there.
7. I think _____ of the weirdest things about the house is its enormous front door.
8. _____ of the houses today don't have doors that look like they belong on a castle!
9. People say that _____ once robbed a bank and hid the loot in the house.
10. _____ around here has heard the story.

Publish

✚Presentation

Publishing Strategy   Publish your short story in a class magazine.

Presentation Strategy   Indent every paragraph.

Now it's time to publish my short story! I could submit my story to a creative writing contest for kids, read it to my friends, or make it into a picture book using my own illustrations. I think I'll publish my story in our class magazine. To make my story easy to follow, I need to indent every paragraph and start a new, indented line for each new speaker in dialogue. Before I submit the story, I want to read it through one last time to make sure it includes all of the items on my final checklist.

My Final Checklist

Did I—

✔ check for correct use of personal, possessive, and indefinite pronouns?

✔ indent every paragraph?

✔ start a new, indented line for each speaker in dialogue?

✔ check spelling, capitalization, and punctuation?

Apply

Check your short story against your own checklist. Then make a final copy to publish.

Creepover!

by Marco

"This is going to be so great, Chris," said my best friend, Og. "Don't you think?"

"Sure," I lied.

We stood outside the castle-sized front door of the old Evans mansion. When the house stood empty, everyone talked about its eerie glowing windows and the strange moaning that couldn't be just the wind. Now Roger, the new kid, lived here—and Og and I were invited to a sleepover in the creepiest house around. I was afraid of that place, but somehow I had to hide my fear for the whole night!

After Og banged the heavy iron knocker a few times, Roger opened the door with a creak and let us in. He took us to the huge, paneled room where everybody was hanging out. Some of the guys roasted marshmallows in the stone fireplace. Others played cards or video games. It looked like a normal sleepover!

For a while, I forgot where I was and just enjoyed myself. But when we spread our sleeping bags on the floor and Roger turned off the lights, I got nervous again. The dying fire cast strange shadows, and a dreary moan blew around the house. I burrowed into my downy sleeping bag, but I couldn't relax.

Then I heard the footsteps. They creaked slowly across the floor, heading my way! Closer and closer they came. Closer . . . Closer . . .

Someone groaned in pain. Then a muffled voice choked out, "Get away from me!"

It was Og! And he needed help!

I scrambled to my feet and jumped onto the threatening figure that towered over Og. I wrestled it to the floor before I realized the figure was Roger!

"Was I sleepwalking again?" he mumbled.

"Yeah," said Og. "You stepped right on me!"

"Sorry." Roger crawled back to his spot, closed his eyes, and started snoring.

"He scared me to death," said Og, settling back down.

"Yeah, me too." As I slid into my sleeping bag, I realized something. Even though I was frightened, I still tried to save my friend. So what if he didn't actually need my help? I had controlled my fear, and that was what mattered!

Finally, I nestled into my bag and took a deep breath. Something was scratching against the windowpane, but I closed my eyes anyway.

"It's just a branch," I told myself right before I fell asleep.

Reflect

Look at the story. Does it have all the traits of a good short story? Check it against the rubric. Then use the rubric to check your own story.

What's a **Biography?**

A biography is a factual account of a person's life. However, it should be more than just a string of facts. A good biography tells a clear, engaging story about a person's life or some part of that life. A biography should not include made-up information.

What's in a **Biography?**

Subject
This is the person I am writing about. I want to be consistent and clear in identifying my subject. I should communicate the important facts about the person's life or about the part of his or her life that I'm focusing on.

Third-Person Point of View
I will use *he* or *she* because in a biography I am telling about the life of someone else. Third-person point of view is part of writing a biography.

Accuracy
I am responsible for providing accurate information about my subject from beginning to end. This means I should check figures in any dates I give. I should check spelling and facts about any names or places I mention.

Why write a Biography?

When I wrote a biography last year, I remember it was challenging but also satisfying. I have listed some reasons why I would like to write biographies.

Information
I like to discover new information about people in history, and I enjoy sharing what I learned. I want others to know about these amazing lives.

Inspiration
When I read about someone who did something that inspires me, I want to pass that on to others, too. Sometimes I'm surprised about what inspires me. I might not know until I have read a lot about the person.

Personal Enjoyment
When I choose the subject for a biography, it's like choosing a friend I want to get to know better. I personally enjoy the time I spend reading and learning about someone I am curious about.

Linking Narrative Writing Traits to a **Biography**

In this chapter, you will write about a real person's life. This type of narrative writing is called a biography. Marco will guide you through the stages of the writing process: Prewrite, Draft, Revise, Edit, and Publish. In each stage, Marco will show you important writing strategies that are linked to the Narrative Writing Traits below.

Narrative Writing Traits

Ideas
- a focused topic, experience, or series of events
- engaging, accurate details that develop and describe the topic, experience, or series of events

Organization
- logically sequenced events, often in chronological order
- an interesting beginning and a satisfying ending
- transitions that signal the sequence of events as well as shifts in time or setting

Voice
- a voice and tone that are appropriate for the purpose and audience
- dialogue that, if used, fits the characters

Word Choice
- precise, descriptive words and phrases

Sentence Fluency
- a variety of sentences that flow and are a pleasure to read aloud

Conventions
- no or few errors in grammar, usage, mechanics, and spelling

Before you write, read Cindy Lyman's biography on the next three pages. Then use the biography rubric on pages 82–83 to decide how well she did. (You might want to look back at What's in a Biography? on page 76, too!)

Mary McLeod Bethune

by Cindy Lyman

Subject of biography

Mary McLeod Bethune, a great African American educator and leader, was born in 1875 on a farm in South Carolina, where she soon learned how to plant seeds and make them grow to their full value. All through her life, Mary McLeod Bethune planted other kinds of seeds—of learning, equal rights, hope, and change. With constant dedication and wisdom, she did everything in her power to make these grow to their full value for African Americans.

In her time, African Americans in the South were free from slavery, but they were not free in some other important ways. Because of segregation, which separated people by race, African Americans could not attend public schools for white students or go to hospitals for white people. Unfortunately, in many places there were no schools for black students or hospitals for black people. One of those places was Daytona, Florida. There, Mary McLeod Bethune started a school with five black students and developed it into a highly respected college for more than a thousand young men and women. Also in Daytona she opened a very small hospital and helped it grow into a large, important one. These were just two of her numerous accomplishments that improved education, health, and opportunity for African Americans.

What seeds were planted in Mary's early life that led to such accomplishments? Her parents, Samuel and Patsy McLeod, were born in slavery, and together they had fourteen children who were born before slavery was outlawed during the Civil War. Once they were free from slavery, the McLeods bought their own land, built their own home, and ran their own farm. Mary was their first child born in freedom. In that way she was special to her parents, although they trained her to pick cotton and do other hard work that all farm children were expected to do.

Accurate facts

Sometimes in a break from the hardest work, Mary's mother told amazing stories. Mary's grandmother also shared stories about her family's heritage in Africa. Mary loved to listen to these stories and was fascinated by the spoken words. In her whole family, nobody could read or write because they were never given an opportunity to learn. Mary had looked at books in white people's homes, and she desperately wanted to understand the printed words inside. But there were no schools for black children anywhere near her home, so Mary could only hope something would change.

Third-person point of view →

Finally, one day, a young black woman in city clothes came to visit. Her name was Emma Wilson, and she was starting a mission school for black children. The McLeods could send only one child, and all agreed it would be Mary, who was then seven years old. Each day, Mary proudly walked five miles to Miss Wilson's school and then strode back eager to share the reading, writing, and math she had learned there. Later she wrote, "The whole world opened to me when I learned to read."

Mary was a serious student and a strong leader in Miss Wilson's school. When she graduated at age eleven, she hoped for further education, but in her region there were no higher schools for black students. Eventually, Miss Wilson was able to find a sponsor who paid for Mary to study at an academy in North Carolina and then at a missionary training institute in Chicago, where Mary was the only black student.

When she finished her studies, Mary dedicated herself to improving the lives of African Americans, especially in the South. Besides founding schools and hospitals, Mary McLeod Bethune formed and led organizations of black women, and she held important posts in national government as well. She advised presidents and oversaw programs for young people around the country. From age twenty until nearly seventy, she was always actively and effectively managing some major challenge to her community or her country.

Accurate facts ⌐

Certainly, one seed that grew to a towering tree in Mary's life was her love of words, in the songs and stories she learned from her family and then in the books she learned to read at Miss Wilson's school. The way she expressed herself in words became a key to her leadership and teaching. In formal speeches or friendly conversations, her confident, compelling voice convinced black people and white people to support the projects and causes she believed in. Her written words clearly conveyed her visions and convictions. Though Mary McLeod Bethune died in 1955, her words and her life story have continued to inspire others to carry on her work.

Subject of biography, summarized

Rubric

Use this 6-point rubric to plan and score a biography.

	6	5	4
Ideas	The biography is focused and developed. All details develop the subject and bring it to life.	The biography is focused. A few more details would help develop the subject.	The biography is focused. It lacks enough details to be well developed.
Organization	The events are organized in a way that unfolds naturally and logically. Smooth and effective transition words and phrases connect ideas and paragraphs.	The writing is organized. A few more transitions between paragraphs are needed.	The writing is organized. Not enough transitions are used to link ideas.
Voice	The writer uses an appropriate point of view consistently. Quotations add authenticity.	The writer uses an appropriate point of view. A few more quotations are needed.	The writer's point of view is somewhat inconsistent. Quotations don't work well with the surrounding text.
Word Choice	Precise language conveys the events and enlivens the writing.	Language is precise most of the time. A few words are weak or overused.	Some of the language is precise. Several words used are weak or overused.
Sentence Fluency	A variety of sentence structures links the ideas and moves the story along at a good pace.	Several sentences in a row share the same structure. The pace is good.	Many sentences begin the same way but vary in length. Parts of the story move along well.
Conventions	The writing has been carefully edited. Verbs are used correctly.	Minor errors are present but do not interfere with meaning. Verbs are used correctly.	A few errors cause confusion. One or two verbs or shifts in tense are problematic.
✛ Presentation	Visuals are thoughtfully integrated into the biography.		

3	2	1	
The biography is focused. Details seem undeveloped or unimportant.	The biography is not focused. Details may be unrelated.	The biography is not focused. Details are sketchy or merely listed.	**Ideas**
The writing is somewhat organized. Transitions are weak or ineffective.	Organization is unclear or inconsistent. Transitions are confusing or missing.	The writing is not organized. Transitions are not used.	**Organization**
The writer's point of view is inconsistent and confusing. Quotations may be inaccurate.	The writer's voice sounds far away or inconsistent. Quotations are not used.	The voice is weak or absent. Quotations are not used.	**Voice**
Most of the language is vague and imprecise. Overused words weaken the writing.	Ordinary and overused words make it hard for the reader to engage with the writing.	Many words are overused or used incorrectly. The writing is dull.	**Word Choice**
Most sentences share the same structure. The pace of the story is affected.	Sentences are too short. The pace is choppy.	Sentences are very basic in structure. Many are incomplete.	**Sentence Fluency**
Many errors are repeated and cause confusion. Some verbs are used incorrectly.	Serious errors interfere with meaning. Many verbs are used incorrectly.	The writing has not been edited.	**Conventions**

See Appendix B for 4-, 5-, and 6-point narrative rubrics.

Biography
Using the ︿Rubric
to Study the Model

Did you notice that the model on pages 79–81 points out some key elements of a biography? As she wrote "Mary McLeod Bethune," Cindy Lyman used these elements to help tell her subject's life story. She also used the 6-point rubric on pages 82–83 to plan, draft, revise, and edit the writing. A rubric is a great tool for evaluating writing during the writing process.

Now let's use the same rubric to score the model. To do this, we'll focus on each trait separately, starting with Ideas. We'll use the top descriptor for each trait (column 6), along with examples from the model, to help us understand how the traits work together. How would you score Cindy on each trait?

- **The biography is focused and developed.**
- **All details develop the subject and bring it to life.**

Cindy connects Mary McLeod Bethune's early life with her later accomplishments through the idea of planting seeds and making sure they grow to their full value. Then she uses details from Mary's childhood to help the reader understand the subject. Mary really came alive for me as I read!

[from the writing model]

Mary McLeod Bethune, a great African American educator and leader, was born in 1875 on a farm in South Carolina, where she soon learned how to plant seeds and make them grow to their full value. All through her life, Mary McLeod Bethune planted other kinds of seeds—of learning, equal rights, hope, and change.

Organization

- The events are organized in a way that unfolds naturally and logically.
- Smooth and effective transition words and phrases connect ideas and paragraphs.

Cindy presents the events in Mary's life in a natural and logical way. It was interesting to read about some of Mary's accomplishments, and then look back at her early experiences to see how they influenced her life. Cindy uses a question to transition to Mary's early life. I had no problem following along.

[from the writing model]

What seeds were planted in her early life that led to such accomplishments? Her parents, Samuel and Patsy McLeod, were born in slavery, and together they had fourteen children who had been born before slavery was outlawed during the Civil War. Once they were free from slavery, the McLeods bought their own land, built their own home, and ran their own farm. Mary was their first child born in freedom.

Voice

- The writer uses an appropriate point of view consistently.
- Quotations add authenticity.

Because Cindy has written a biography, she uses *she, her,* and the subject's name throughout. Her third-person perspective is consistent and leaves no confusion about who her subject is. Cindy uses a quotation that shows Mary's voice, but it fits in with her own writing.

[from the writing model]

Each day, Mary proudly walked five miles to Miss Wilson's school and then strode back eager to share the reading, writing, and math she had learned there. Later she wrote, "The whole world opened to me when I learned to read."

Word Choice

• Precise language conveys the events and enlivens the writing.

Cindy uses precise, vivid language to describe Mary's response to her first school experience. Strong action verbs help express Mary's feelings and bring a sense of reality to the entire biography. Cindy really gave me a clear picture of what life was like for Mary.

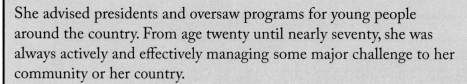

[from the writing model]

She advised presidents and oversaw programs for young people around the country. From age twenty until nearly seventy, she was always actively and effectively managing some major challenge to her community or her country.

Sentence Fluency

• A variety of sentence structures links the ideas and moves the story along at a good pace.

In her paragraphs, Cindy varies the length of sentences, so the rhythm for the reader is more lively. Find the longest and shortest sentences and compare their lengths. You'll see how much variety Cindy created!

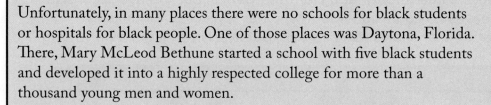

[from the writing model]

Unfortunately, in many places there were no schools for black students or hospitals for black people. One of those places was Daytona, Florida. There, Mary McLeod Bethune started a school with five black students and developed it into a highly respected college for more than a thousand young men and women.

Conventions
- **The writing has been carefully edited.**
- **Verbs are used correctly.**

Of course, this biography is about someone who is no longer alive, so it is about the past. Still, it can sometimes be tricky to decide when to use past or present tense. Cindy was careful to use verb tenses correctly throughout her writing. She also did a great job with spelling, grammar, and punctuation. I couldn't find a single error!

[from the writing model]

In formal speeches or friendly conversations, her confident, compelling voice convinced black people and white people to support the projects and causes she believed in. Her written words clearly conveyed her visions and convictions. Though Mary McLoed Bethune died in 1955, her words and her life story have continued to inspire others to carry on her work.

✛Presentation
Visuals are thoughtfully integrated into the biography.

My Turn!
Now I'm going to use the rubric to help me write a biography. Follow along to see how I do it!

Prewrite

Focus on **Ideas**

The Rubric Says   The biography is focused and developed.

Writing Strategy   Choose an interesting subject and decide on what part of the subject's life to focus.

Our teacher asked us to write a biography about someone in United States history. She posted a long list to choose from. I chose Will Rogers because I like rodeos and I knew he was a cowboy, but I didn't know much more until I read some Web biographies and lots of funny quotes. He was also featured in a book of famous Native Americans. My notes show some things I learned about Will Rogers. Looking them over, I think I'll focus on his life as a performer.

My Notes on Will Rogers

- ✔ 1879–1935, born in Indian Territory that became Oklahoma, died in plane crash in Alaska
- ✔ mother and father were part Cherokee (father, Clem Rogers, fought in Civil War, became judge)
- ✔ loved horses, learned riding and roping skills from African American ranch hand
- ✔ 1901, traveled to England, Argentina, South Africa, and Australia, did cowboy and Indian acts in Wild West show and circus
- ✔ 1905, did rope tricks on stage in New York City and got steady work in show business
- ✔ 1908 married Betty Blake and settled in New York, started popular comedy act about whatever was in the daily newspaper
- ✔ 1918 starred in silent film, then in sound films after 1929; voted most popular actor in Hollywood, 1934
- ✔ wrote newspaper column and did regular radio show with funny comments on politics and other events of the times

Apply

Choose a subject and then do some research to decide what part of the subject's life you want to focus on.

Focus on Organization

The Rubric Says	The events are organized in a way that unfolds naturally and logically.
Writing Strategy	Make a Biography Map to organize the notes.

Writer's Term___

Biography Map
A **Biography Map** organizes the important events, actions, and accomplishments of a person's life, including a summary at the end.

The rubric reminds me to organize the events in the biography naturally and logically. I will use a Biography Map because it's a good way to show the logical sequence of important events and accomplishments in my subject's life.

Biography Map

Subject: William Penn Adair Rogers
Birth facts: born November 4, 1879 in Indian Territory, later became Oklahoma.

Actions, Accomplishments:
Riding and roping on family ranch, then in Wild West shows in Africa, Australia, and back in different parts of the U.S., with success in New York.

Actions, Accomplishments:
Writing newspaper columns and speaking on radio programs with funny, thoughtful comments about politics and current events.

Actions, Accomplishments:
Acting in silent films (1918) and then star roles in talking films (1929). Flying in planes allowed him to travel widely and write about his experiences.

Summary of Life: After sudden death in plane crash, August 15, 1935, reactions around the country showed how popular and important he was as a performer.

Reflect

How will the Biography Map help Marco write his biography?

Apply

Organize your ideas by using your notes to make a Biography Map.

Draft

Focus on Word Choice

The Rubric Says	Precise language conveys the events and enlivens the writing.
Writing Strategy	Replace ordinary words and weak verbs.

I think the Biography Map has helped me see Will Rogers's life as a story or a series of connected stories. Now that the events of his life are organized into a natural and logical order, I can start writing.

The purpose of a biography is to tell the subject's story and also to give the reader as clear a picture as possible of what the person was like. To do that, I'll need to use precise, descriptive language that will add energy to my writing and bring the subject to life. Too-general or ordinary words won't help me convey Will Rogers's energy and humor. If I can't think of precise or strong words while writing my first draft, I will circle the places I want to revise. Then when I have time to reread my writing and look in a thesaurus, I can come up with better words to use.

As I write my draft, I won't worry too much about perfect grammar and spelling. I'll check for those things when I proofread my writing later.

Proofreading Marks

⌐ Indent
≡ Make uppercase
/ Make lowercase
∧ Add something

ℓ Take out something
⊙ Add a period
⌗ New paragraph
🆂🅿 Spelling error

[DRAFT]

Will Rogers

[Precise language]

Will Rogers, famous film star, humorist, writer, and stage performer, was born in 1879 on a ranch in a part of Indian Territory that would later become the state of Oklahoma. His parents, both proud of their Native American heritage, named him after a Cherokee leader, William Penn Adair. Will's father Clement Rogers, was a military and government leader who tried to keep Cherokee rights within the laws of the United States.

Growing up on the family ranch, Will loved to ride horses and rope cattle. He learned and practiced many tricks with the lariat, or rope, and hoped for success. In contrast, he did not perform well in most school subjects, and he wasn't a serious student. Yet Will Rogers became nationally known for his writing and philosophy, as well as his acting and humor. His many talents grew at different times in his life.

[Find better word]

One exciting time in his life began in 1901 when he set out from home for Argentina to find work on a cattle ranch. Though he did not find ranch work in Argentina, he got a job tending cattle and other animals on a big ship bound for South Africa.

Reflect

What do you think? How does Marco's precise language bring the subject to life? Can you find other weak words that could use replacing?

Apply

Write a draft using your Biography Map as a guide. Remember to use precise language to enliven your writing. Circle words or phrases that could use strengthening in your next draft.

Revise

Focus on **Ideas**

The Rubric Says   All details develop the subject and bring it to life.

Writing Strategy   Find details that are new to readers.

The rubric reminds me that all the details in my biography should help the reader see my subject as a living, breathing person. One way to interest my readers and bring my subject to life is to include information they don't know. I just added a detail about the Great Depression because our class hasn't studied this period in history yet. I want my readers to understand why it was so hard and why people valued what Will Rogers said.

[DRAFT]

[added detail to bring subject to life]

when large numbers of people were out of work and very poor,
Especially during the Great Depression, his words helped many

laugh and somehow feel hopeful. He was critical of Republican

presidents Calvin Coolidge and Herbert Hoover and much more

upbeat about Democrat Franklin D. Roosevelt. All three presidents

paid close attention to what he said.

Apply

Find places where you can add details that bring your subject to life.

Revise

Focus on Organization

The Rubric Says Smooth and effective transition words and phrases connect ideas and paragraphs.

Writing Strategy Use transition words and phrases.

I need to look at the way I use words to connect ideas and make the transition from one idea to another. One way to create a smooth and effective transition between paragraphs is to repeat a word, a phrase, or an idea. I found a place where I could use repetition to make one paragraph flow better into the next. What do you think of my revision?

[DRAFT]

Later on, he used a similar approach to news of the day and conditions of the times when he spoke on the <u>radio</u> or wrote a regular newspaper column. In his <u>writing</u>, he could sum up the problems and progress of the nation in a few simple words. Over the years, he compiled his thoughts in books that sold very well.

In writing and on the radio,
∧Will Rogers made fun of politics and government, but he also expressed his belief in American democracy and in ordinary human beings.

[used repeated words/ideas for transition]

[words leading to transition]

Reflect

How does the added phrase help the reader connect the ideas and make the transition between paragraphs?

Apply

Find places in your biography where you need to add transition words that connect ideas from paragraph to paragraph.

Revise

Focus on Sentence Fluency

The Rubric Says   A variety of sentence structures links the ideas and moves the story along at a good pace.

Writing Strategy   Vary the length of the sentences.

The rubric says that varying my sentence structure will link my ideas and help my writing flow well. I looked at my paragraphs to see whether each one had a good mix of sentence lengths, and I found one paragraph that was made up entirely of long sentences. It was simple to break one of the sentences into two shorter ones and give the paragraph a little more variety.

[DRAFT]

Will Rogers, sometimes called the Cherokee Kid, returned to Oklahoma in 1904, with skills that gave him opportunities to perform in other parts of the United States. In New York City, Will's quick action in one cowboy show made big news when he expertly roped a steer that had accidentally gotten loose into the audience. As his career in show business became more solid, he married a woman he had met in Oklahoma, and they settled in New York to raise a family. **[broke long sentence into two short ones]**

Apply

Check each of your paragraphs for variety in sentence lengths. Break up long sentences or combine short ones to create a good mix.

The Rubric Says	The writing has been carefully edited. Verbs are used correctly.
Writing Strategy	Recognize and correct inappropriate shifts in verb tense.

Writer's Term

Verb Tense

The **verb tense** tells the time of an action. Verbs show action that happened in the past, happens in the present, or will happen in the future. Verbs can also show that an action is ongoing.

Now I will check my draft and correct errors in spelling, capitalization, and punctuation. I'll also check the tenses of the verbs I used and correct any mistakes I made.

[DRAFT]

[corrected from present tense to past tense]

Besides newspaper and radio, film ~~is~~ was another medium that suited ~~suits~~ Will Rogers. He began as a cowboy star in silent films that were made in the New York area. When the film industry shifted location to California, Will eventually ~~moves~~ moved there with his wife and children.

Reflect

What are some reasons that using the correct tense can be challenging in writing a biography? How will Marco's edits help his readers better understand his writing?

Apply — Conventions

Edit your draft for spelling, punctuation, and capitalization. Be sure verb tenses are used correctly.

For more practice with verbs and verb tenses, use the exercises on the next two pages.

Action and Linking Verbs
Know the Rule

An **action verb** shows action.
> Example: Marian Anderson's voice **enchanted** everyone who **heard** her singing.

A **linking verb** does not show action. Instead, a linking verb connects the subject of a sentence to one or more words that describe or rename the subject.
Linking verbs are usually forms of *be;* some of these are *am*, *is*, *are*, *was*, *were*, and *will be*. *Become*, *seem*, *appear*, and *look* can also be used as linking verbs.
> Examples: She **was** a serious music student. She **became** a famous singer.

Practice the Rule

Number a separate sheet of paper 1–10. Write the verb or verbs in each sentence, adding the letter **A** for action verbs and the letter **L** for linking verbs.

1. Woody Guthrie was a singer and songwriter who lived from 1912 to 1967.
2. At his birth in Oklahoma, his parents named him Woodrow Wilson Guthrie.
3. Woody was not a trained musician, but he learned guitar from a family friend.
4. His mother's illness, a dear sister's death, and a disastrous fire were some of the many difficulties of his childhood.
5. Woody had little formal education, but he loved reading, writing, drawing, and singing.
6. From library books, he learned many subjects.
7. Woody became very creative with the sounds, rhythms, and feelings of words.
8. As a young man, he traveled to different parts of the country on foot and in freight cars.
9. "This Land is Your Land" is one of his best-known songs.
10. Woody wrote more than three thousand songs, including many for and about his children.

Verb Tense

Know the Rule

All words in a sentence must work together to give an accurate sense of time. Make sure each **verb** is in the proper **tense** for the time period being discussed. Use dates, time, and other **time expressions** such as *last week, next week, yesterday, later,* or *during* to help show time.

> **Example: Last year,** I **wrote** a short biography of George Washington Carver, who **lived** from 1864 to 1943.

> **Example: Next week,** we **will write** biographies of friends or family members after we **interview** them about their lives.

Practice the Rule

Number a separate sheet of paper 1–10. Write the correct verb or verbs in parentheses to complete each sentence.

1. Cesar Chavez (was/is) born in Arizona on March 31, 1927, and died in 1993.

2. Since 2001 in California, his birthday (has been/will be) a state holiday called Cesar Chavez Day.

3. Arizona, Texas, and Colorado (are/were) some other states that now honor Cesar Chavez on this date.

4. After circulating petitions around the country, some groups hope that Cesar Chavez Day (became/will become) a national holiday.

5. Cesar Chavez (is/was) a farm worker, labor leader, and civil rights activist.

6. In 1962, he (founds/founded) the National Farm Workers Association that later (becomes/became) the United Farm Workers.

7. Besides organizing farm workers to strike against the unfair conditions of grape pickers, he (gets/got) people around the country to stop buying grapes until conditions improved.

8. Based on his childhood and adult experience as a farm worker, Cesar Chavez (was/is) deeply committed to ending unfair, unsafe, and unrewarding conditions.

9. Through nonviolent actions such as fasts and marches, Cesar Chavez (inspired/inspires) others to support the causes he stood for.

10. On the next Cesar Chavez Day, students in our school (participated/will participate) in community service projects.

Publish

+Presentation

Publishing Strategy — Present your biography as a slide show.

Presentation Strategy — Use visuals that illustrate the life and times of the subject.

I've written and revised my biography, but I still have to plan how to present it in social studies class. Our teacher expects us to present a slide show and include visuals. Luckily there are many photos of Will Rogers because he was a performer and film star. I even found a website with videos of Will Rogers performing rope tricks. I would like to show a few minutes of that video clip as part of my presentation because it shows his skill and humor and gives us an idea of film technology in his time. I'll need to plan and time it to fit it in with my text and other visuals. I'll also want to use my final checklist to make sure I haven't overlooked anything.

My Final Checklist

Did I—

✔ check my spelling, punctuation, and capitalization carefully?

✔ use verb tenses correctly?

✔ find visuals that go with my subject?

✔ practice my presentation and the timing of my visuals?

Apply

Find visuals to go with the subject of your biography and plan an effective way to fit them in with the words of your presentation.

Will Rogers
Rider, Roper, Writer, Actor

by Marco

Will Rogers, famous film star, humorist, writer, and stage performer, was born in 1879 on a ranch in a part of Indian Territory that would later become the state of Oklahoma. His parents, both proud of their Native American heritage, named him after a Cherokee leader, William Penn Adair. Will's father, Clement Rogers, was a military and government leader who tried to stand up for Cherokee rights within the laws of the United States.

Growing up on the family ranch, Will loved to ride horses and rope cattle. He learned and practiced many tricks with the lariat, or rope, and he dreamed of winning rodeo prizes. In contrast, he did not do well in most school subjects, and teachers called him a class clown. Yet Will Rogers became nationally known for his writing and wise sayings, as well as his acting and humor. His many talents developed at different times in his life.

One exciting time in his life began in 1901 when he set out from home for Argentina to find work on a cattle ranch. Though he did not find ranch work in Argentina, he got a job tending cattle and other animals on a big ship bound for South Africa. In South Africa Will was hired to perform rope tricks and other cowboy skills in a traveling Wild West show, where he gained confidence as a performer. After that he sailed to Australia, where he used his talents in a traveling circus. During his travels, he wrote letters that entertained his friends and family with humorous but thoughtful observations.

Will Rogers, sometimes called the Cherokee Kid, returned to Oklahoma in 1904, with skills that gave him opportunities to perform in other parts of the United States. In New York City, Will's quick action in one cowboy show made big news when he expertly roped a steer that had accidentally gotten loose into the audience. As his career in show business became more solid, he married a woman he had met in Oklahoma. They settled in New York to raise a family.

For many years, Will Rogers continued to be a popular performer in major New York stage shows, where he perfected an act that included cowboy rope tricks and his own funny, clever comments on the daily news. Will began his act each time by saying, "All I know is what I read in the papers." Later on, he used a similar approach to news of the day and conditions of the times when he spoke on the radio or wrote a regular newspaper column. In his writing, he could sum up the problems and progress of the nation in a few simple words. Over the years, he compiled his thoughts in books that sold very well.

In writing and on the radio, Will Rogers made fun of politics and government, but he also expressed his belief in American democracy and in ordinary human beings. Especially during the Great Depression, when large numbers of people were out of work and very poor, his words helped many laugh and somehow feel hopeful. He was critical of Republican presidents Calvin Coolidge and Herbert Hoover and much more upbeat about Democrat Franklin D. Roosevelt. All three presidents paid close attention to what he said.

Besides newspaper and radio, film was another medium that suited Will Rogers. He began as a cowboy star in silent films that were made in the New York area. When the film industry shifted location to California, Will eventually moved there with his wife and children. After

sound films became possible in 1929, Will's movie career soared. His voice, along with good looks, comic style, and warm personality, won countless fans. As the star of 21 feature films in a period of six years, he was often allowed to make up lines on the spot rather than stick to a script as most actors did.

Though he gained wealth and stardom, Will Rogers never seemed to change his modest, friendly manner. One of his famous quotes was "No man is great if he thinks he is." Will never seemed to think he was great. Others thought he was. When his life ended in a plane crash on August 15, 1935, the sudden loss stunned people around the country. In remembering and honoring Will Rogers long after his death, people confirmed the greatness of his gentle humor, sensible words, and memorable performances.

Will Rogers ~
Showing his children what he can do with his lasso.

Reflect

Which traits in this biography seemed strongest to you? After checking the biography against the rubric, do the same with the biography you have written.

Narrative test writing

Read the Writing Prompt

When you take a writing test, you'll get a writing prompt. Most writing prompts have three parts:

Setup This part of the writing prompt gives you the background information you need to get ready to write.

Task This part of the writing prompt tells you exactly what you are supposed to write: an eyewitness account about a newsworthy event that you observed.

Scoring Guide This section tells how your writing will be scored. To do well on the test, you should make sure you do everything on the list.

Remember the rubrics you used earlier in the unit? When you take a writing test, you don't always have all of the information that's on a rubric. But the scoring guide is a lot like a rubric. It lists everything you need to think about to write a good paper. Like the rubrics you've used in this unit, many scoring guides are based on these important traits of writing:

  Conventions

Think about a newsworthy event, one that might make the local news. It can be something you saw or heard about or something you made up yourself.

Then write an eyewitness account telling about the event.

Be sure your writing
- uses descriptive details to develop the events.
- tells the event in a logical order and uses transition words to convey sequence.
- has a voice that matches audience and purpose.
- uses precise words and phrases to convey the events.
- contains sentences that flow smoothly.
- contains correct grammar, punctuation, capitalization, and spelling.

Writing Traits in the Scoring Guide

The scoring guide in the prompt on page 103 has been made into this chart. Does it remind you of the rubrics you've used? Not all prompts include all of the writing traits, but this one does. Use them to do your best writing. Remember to work neatly and put your name on each page.

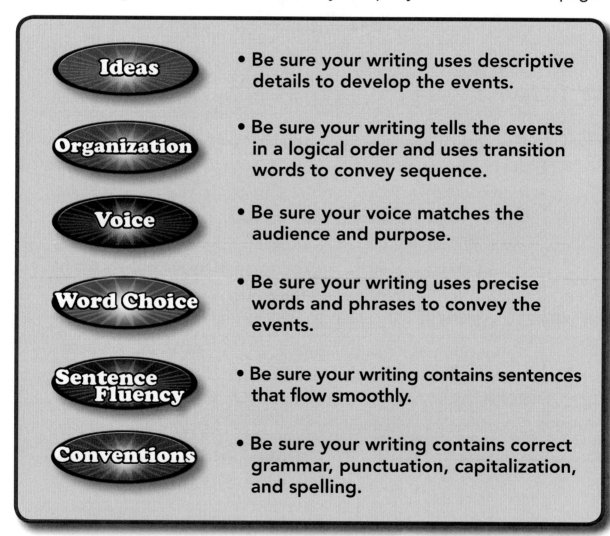

Ideas
- Be sure your writing uses descriptive details to develop the events.

Organization
- Be sure your writing tells the events in a logical order and uses transition words to convey sequence.

Voice
- Be sure your voice matches the audience and purpose.

Word Choice
- Be sure your writing uses precise words and phrases to convey the events.

Sentence Fluency
- Be sure your writing contains sentences that flow smoothly.

Conventions
- Be sure your writing contains correct grammar, punctuation, capitalization, and spelling.

Look at Olivia Mayes's story on the next page. Did she follow the scoring guide?

Bucky's Big Break

by Olivia Mayes

I knew something was wrong the moment my mom turned onto our street Monday afternoon. Several of our neighbors were standing outside and so, I noticed, was another resident of Shelton Lane. Bucky, the 1,000-pound longhorn who lived in a field across the street from us, had escaped once again. The neighbors were banding together to bring him back home.

My mom rolled down her window. "Looks like Bucky is up to his old tricks again," she told Mr. Thatcher, Bucky's owner. Bucky had been known in the past to break through the fence of the Thatchers' yard in order to take a stroll through the neighborhood. Mr. Thatcher just shook his head.

Slowly, we drove by Bucky, who was standing in the Garcias' front yard, happily chomping on Mrs. Garcia's flowers, or what was left of her flowers! Bucky gazed up at us, oblivious to what was about to happen.

After we parked in our driveway, mom and I walked back to the front yard to witness the action. Kenny, Mr. Thatcher's teenage son, was hammering away at the fence, repairing the break that Bucky had used for his escape. "Okay, ready!" he called to his dad and the other neighbors. Lassoing this wandering longhorn and guiding him back to the field was a four-person effort!

Although Bucky was a gentle animal who mainly stayed in the yard, lazily eating and observing the neighborly goings-on, he was still a big animal. The men approached him cautiously.

"Okay, boy," Mr. Thatcher said, "time to come home."

Pausing from his afternoon snack, Bucky turned his head toward the men and seemed to realize the party was about to end. Quickly, he started to move away. The men trailed him, ready with the lasso. Bucky picked up his pace.

Then the men tossed the lasso over his head and tugged. Bucky stopped, appearing quite annoyed that his play time was ending. The men led him back to the open gate. Without missing a beat, Bucky resumed his eating, and the neighbors returned home knowing this wouldn't be the last time they'd have to bring Mr. Thatcher's wayward longhorn home again.

Using the Scoring Guide to Study the Model

Now let's use the scoring guide to check Olivia's writing test, "Bucky's Big Break." We'll see how well her eyewitness account meets each of the six writing traits.

 **Ideas**

- **The writing uses descriptive details to develop the events.**

Olivia's narrative is full of vivid description that helps develop the events for me in my mind. In the paragraph below, I can really picture the size and usual gentleness of the longhorn, as well as the men walking up to him—very carefully.

> Although Bucky was a gentle animal who mainly stayed in the yard, lazily eating and observing the neighborly goings-on, he was still a big animal. The men approached him cautiously.

 **Organization**

- **The writing tells the event in a logical order and uses transition words to convey sequence.**

I found Olivia's story easy to follow because she tells what happens in chronological order. Notice how she uses the transition words *After* and *Then* in the sentences below to move the action along.

> After we parked in our driveway, Mom and I walked back to the front yard to witness the action. . . .
>
> Then the men tossed the lasso over his head and tugged.

Voice

• **The voice matches the audience and purpose.**

Right from the beginning, Olivia's voice appeals to the reader and creates interest. You know that her purpose is to tell a story. Look at these sentences that draw you into the event and make you want to read more.

Bucky, the 1,000-pound longhorn who lived in a field across the street, had escaped once again. The neighbors were banding together to bring him back home.

Word Choice

• **The writing uses precise words and phrases to convey the events.**

I can tell when I read Olivia's story that she made careful and specific word choices to describe what happened. Olivia could have said the longhorn was *eating* flowers, but instead she used the word *chomping*. I think that's a much more precise way to describe how a 1,000-pound animal eats. She also says he *gazed up* at the men, instead of *looked up*. I'd say she definitely made the right word choices!

Slowly, we drove by Bucky, who was standing in the Garcias' front yard, happily chomping on Mrs. Garcia's flowers, or what was left of her flowers! Bucky gazed up at us, oblivious to what was about to happen.

Using the Scoring Guide to Study the Model

- **The writing contains sentences that flow smoothly.**

The story really flowed naturally as I read it. I think it helps that Olivia uses a variety of sentences, including dialogue. In the last paragraph, she starts off with the transition *Then*. She also starts sentences with clauses and adverbs.

Then the men tossed the lasso over his head and tugged. Bucky stopped, appearing quite annoyed that his play time was ending. The men led him back to the open gate. Without missing a beat, Bucky resumed his eating, and the neighbors returned home knowing this wouldn't be the last time they'd have to bring Mr. Thatcher's wayward longhorn home again.

- **The writing contains correct grammar, punctuation, capitalization, and spelling.**

It looks as though Olivia didn't make any grammar or spelling mistakes. I know that's really important when you take a test. That's why it's a good idea to check for mistakes in your own work. Throughout the writing process, you should edit for correct grammar, punctuation, capitalization, and spelling. That way, you won't have any errors on your final test.

Planning My Time

Before giving us a writing test prompt, my teacher tells us how much time we'll have to complete the test. Since I'm already familiar with the writing process, I can think about how much total time I need and then divide it up into the different parts of the writing process. If the test takes an hour, here's how I can organize my time. Planning your time will help you, too!

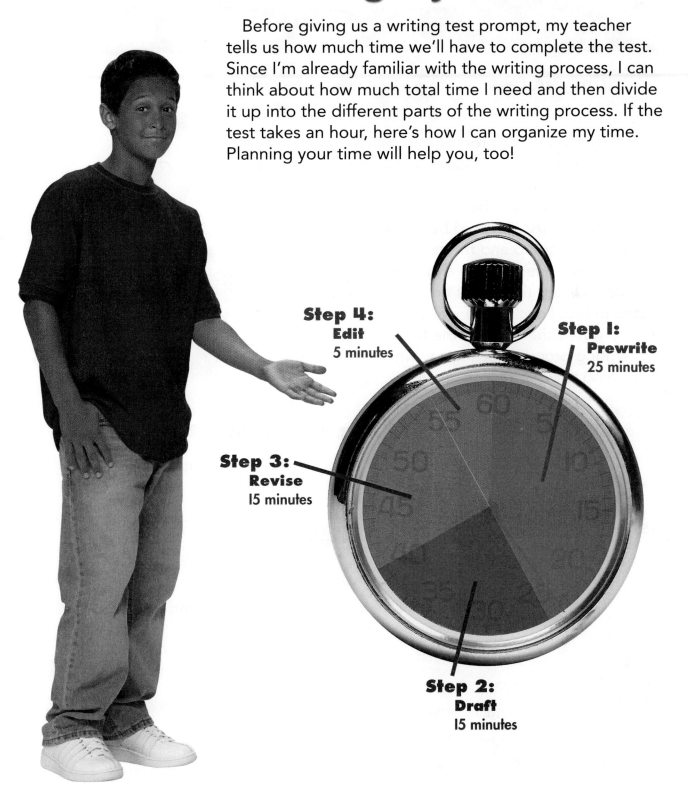

Step 4:
Edit
5 minutes

Step 1:
Prewrite
25 minutes

Step 3:
Revise
15 minutes

Step 2:
Draft
15 minutes

Prewrite

Focus on **Ideas**

Writing Strategy   Study the writing prompt to find out what to do.

I study the writing prompt as soon as I get it so that I know exactly what I'm supposed to do. The writing prompt usually has three parts. Since the parts aren't always labeled, you'll have to find and label them on your own, just like I did below. Then circle key words in the setup and the task that tell what kind of writing you need to do and who your audience will be. I circled the words *newsworthy event* in the setup in red. I circled the words *eyewitness account telling about the event* in the task in purple. Since my writing prompt doesn't say who the audience is, I'm going to write for my teacher.

My Writing Test Prompt

Setup — Think about a (newsworthy event,) one that might make the local news. It can be something you saw or heard about or something you made up yourself.

Task — Then write an (eyewitness account telling about the event.)

Scoring Guide — Be sure your writing

- has description that develops the events.
- tells the event in a logical order and uses transition words to convey sequence.
- has a voice that matches audience and purpose.
- uses precise words and phrases to convey the events.
- contains sentences that flow smoothly.
- contains correct grammar, punctuation, capitalization, and spelling.

You'll want to think about how the scoring guide relates to the writing traits you've studied in the rubrics. All of the traits might not be included in every scoring guide, but you need to remember them all to write a good essay.

Ideas

- Be sure your writing uses descriptive details to develop the events.

I want my reader to fully understand my account, so I'll use lots of descriptive details to develop the events.

Organization

- Be sure your writing tells the event in a logical order and uses transition words to convey sequence.

To make the story easy to follow, I'll tell what happens in chronological order and use transitions to move my story along.

Voice

- Be sure your voice matches the audience and purpose.

My voice should connect to my audience and create interest. My reader should know that my purpose is to tell a story.

Word Choice

- Be sure your writing uses precise words and phrases to convey the events.

My writing will be much more interesting if I make careful and precise word choices to describe what happened.

Sentence Fluency

- Be sure your writing contains sentences that flow smoothly.

I can use a variety of sentences with clauses or adverbs, as well as dialogue, to help my writing flow smoothly.

Conventions

- Be sure your writing contains correct grammar, punctuation, capitalization, and spelling.

It's really important to edit my story for correct grammar and mechanics!

Prewrite

Focus on **Ideas**

Writing Strategy **Respond to the task.**

Before I start writing, I'm going to gather some information and take notes. In a writing test, you can gather a lot of information right from the writing prompt. Look at the task to find out what you are supposed to write. Then think about how you'll respond to the task. That'll help save time since you won't have much time during a test!

The writing prompt for my test says to write an eyewitness account of a newsworthy event. I decided to write about the time I saw a construction crew lift a new pedestrian overpass over the freeway with a huge crane. I quickly jotted down some notes.

Task ——— Then write an eyewitness account telling about the event.

Notes

✔ Crews used a huge crane to move the overpass over the freeway.

✔ They had to shut down traffic on both sides.

✔ A bunch of people stopped to watch it.

Apply

Be sure to think about how you are going to respond to the task before you start writing. Then write down notes that will help you gather information.

Writing Strategy   Choose a graphic organizer.

The writing prompt says my event should be told in a logical order. Using a 5 W's chart in the past has been helpful in ordering details or events, so I'll use one now.

First, I wrote down *who* was there. Then I wrote *what* I saw. I also included some interesting details, since the scoring guide says I should include details that help make the narrative real. Next, I wrote *when* it happened, *where* it happened, and *why* it happened.

Who **was there?** My cousin and I were watching the action.

What **happened?** The construction crew used a crane to put a pedestrian bridge across a freeway.
  • They closed the freeway. There were no cars!
  • The bridge was in two parts. The crane operator moved one part over the freeway. They put one side of it in the middle where the cement support was. Then they did the same thing with the other side.
  • Then the crew went on to finish installing and connecting it.

When **did it happen?** Last summer. It was really early on a Saturday morning.

Where **did it happen?** On a freeway near Denver, where my cousin lives.

Why **did it happen?** They're putting in a new rail system near the freeway and had to put in a pedestrian bridge so people could cross the road.

Reflect

Does the chart answer *who, what, when, where,* and *why*?

Apply

Choose a graphic organizer that fits the type of writing you're doing. Here a 5 W's Chart worked best.

Prewrite

Focus on Organization

Writing Strategy Check the graphic organizer against the scoring guide.

You won't have much time, if any, to revise when you take some tests. That's why prewriting is important! Before I start to write, I'll check my 5 W's Chart against the scoring guide in the writing prompt.

Who **was there?** My cousin and I were watching the action.

What **happened?** The construction crew used a crane to put a pedestrian bridge across a freeway.
- They closed the freeway. There were no cars!
- The bridge was in two parts. The crane operator moved one part over the freeway. They put one side of it in the middle where the cement support was. Then they did the same thing with the other side.
- Then the crew went on to finish installing and connecting it.

When **did it happen?** Last summer. It was really early on a Saturday morning.

Where **did it happen?** On a freeway near Denver, where my cousin lives.

Why **did it happen?** They're putting in a new rail system near the freeway and had to put in a pedestrian bridge so people could cross the road.

Ideas

• Be sure your writing uses descriptive details to develop the events.

I think the details in my chart will help me describe the events in a realistic and engaging way.

Organization

• Be sure your writing tells the event in a logical order and uses transition words to convey sequence.

I'll arrange the information from my chart to tell the story in chronological order, with the help of transition words.

Voice

• Be sure your writing voice matches the audience and purpose.

My voice should connect to my reader and create interest so he or she knows that my purpose is to tell a story.

Word Choice

• Be sure your writing uses precise words and phrases to convey the events.

Even though I have the details written down, I'll need to use precise, descriptive language and vocabulary as I write.

Sentence Fluency

• Be sure your writing contains sentences that flow smoothly.

As I write my draft, I'll use dialogue and pay attention to how my sentences are flowing.

Conventions

• Be sure your writing contains correct grammar, punctuation, capitalization, and spelling.

I'll check my writing closely for errors when I go back and edit my draft.

Reflect

The 5 W's Chart covers a lot of the points from the scoring guide. How will the chart help Marco write an engaging account?

Apply

You'll want to go back and reread the writing prompt one more time so you know just what to do when you start writing your draft.

Draft

Focus on (**Ideas**)

Writing Strategy   Use specific, related details.

The scoring guide says to use description to develop the events. I need to create scenes for the reader that sound like they really happened, even if the reader has never seen what I am describing. I also need to do it in a way that's not dull and boring. All the details have to be related to my topic. I'll bet not many people have seen a bridge being installed across a freeway.

[DRAFT]

The Day the Freeway Closed

by Marco

Have you ever wondered how contruction crews build a bridge across the top of a freeway. Well, I got to see it firsthand, and it was the coolest, most amazing thing to watch! You would not believe how they install a bridge it's almost unreal. Here's what happened one early morning last summer.

I got to go to visit my cousin. Xavier lives in Denver, where they are building a new rail system alongside a freeway that it will take people to and from downtown Denver. Xavier and his family lives near the freeway, and early one Saturday morning, his dad told us the freeway had been shut down. Imagine a whole freeway being closed? We had to go see it, so we took off on bikes to an open lot by the freeway.

When we got there, there wasn't a single car on the road, just a bunch of constructions workers and heavy equipment. Then we saw the crane start to move. Hanging from it was a bridge. "they're putting in a pedestrian bridge so people can walk to the new train station, Xavier told me.

The crane operator moved the bridge to the support structures that had been built on the side and in the middle of the freeway. I could tell now that this was only have of the bridge. The other half was still lying on the other side of the road.

The construction crew moved in to check things. They moved to the other bridge to help secure the crane to it. This took quite some time. The crane started moving again slowly. This part seemed even trickier, having to match up one part of the bridge with the other without crashing into it! There was man now standing on the part of the bridge that had been placed, watching closely as the crane moved.

Soon, the other half of the bridge was in place The crew on the ground moved in again, ready to begin checking and securing the new bridge. With the heavy loading and moving done Xavier and I decided to leave.

Reflect

Do the details help develop the events? Do they sound real and related to the topic?

Apply

You'll want to draw your readers in from the very beginning, so be sure your first paragraph is interesting and exciting.

Revise

Focus on **Organization**

Writing Strategy Use transition words to guide the reader.

Now that I have written my draft, I reread it to see if I missed anything. The scoring guide says to use transition words to help my reader see the sequence of events. I can move smoothly from one paragraph to the next by repeating a word. I see where I can do that in the beginning of this paragraph. I'll also use the transition word *During* to show that my summer vacation and my visit to Xavier happened at the same time.

[DRAFT]

[Added transition words]

Here's what happened one early morning last summer.
During my summer vacation,
I got to visit my cousin. Xavier lives in Denver, where they are building

a new rail system alongside a freeway that it will take people to and

from downtown Denver.

Apply

When you're writing a story, use transition words to move smoothly from one paragraph to the next.

Revise

Writing Strategy   Use a casual tone.

Now to check my paper for voice. Since the purpose of writing a story is to share a personal experience, my tone can be casual and informal. I have already addressed the reader directly by using *you*. Look at how I added a more appealing ending to my story. Using the word *but* is not a typical way to start a sentence, but it fits the casual tone.

[DRAFT]

The crew on the ground moved in again, ready to begin checking and

securing the new bridge. With the heavy loading and moving done

~~But we sure had a story to tell.~~

Xavier and I decided to leave.
        ∧

Reflect
Does the story appeal to the reader with a casual tone?

Apply
When you share a personal experience, add words that have a casual and informal tone.

Revise

Focus on Word Choice

Writing Strategy   Use precise words and phrases.

The scoring guide says that I should use precise words and phrases to convey the events. I don't want my writing to seem dull or confusing! I found a few places where changing a word or adding a phrase would make a huge difference in how my story reads. I'll make my changes as neatly and carefully as I can.

[DRAFT]

———— [added precise words and phrases] ————

When we got there, there wasn't a single car on the road, just a

bunch of constructions workers and heavy equipment. Then we saw the **huge**

, slowly and cautiously   **what looked like a long metal cage.**

crane start to move. Hanging from it was ~~a bridge~~ "they're putting in a

pedestrian bridge so people can walk to the new train station, Xavier

told me.

Reflect

Does Marco use the best words to describe things in his account?

Apply

Your word choices can make a huge difference. Replace dull and ordinary words with more precise words that fit your writing.

Writing Strategy   Check the grammar, punctuation, capitalization, and spelling.

I'm almost done—just one more step! The scoring guide says to use correct grammar, punctuation, capitalization, and spelling. That's very important, so I made sure to leave enough time.

[FINAL DRAFT]

The Day the Freeway Closed

by Marco

Have you ever wondered how ~~contruction~~ construction crews build a bridge across the top of a freeway? Well, I got to see it firsthand, and it was the coolest, most amazing thing to watch! You would not believe how they install a bridge; it's almost unreal. Here's what happened one early morning last summer.

During my summer vacation,
I got to go to visit my cousin. Xavier lives in Denver, where they are building a new rail system alongside a freeway that it will take people to and from downtown Denver. Xavier and his family lives near the freeway, and early one Saturday morning, his dad told us the freeway had been shut down. Imagine a whole freeway being closed? We had to go see it, so we took off on bikes to an open lot by the freeway.

Don't forget to check your grammar, punctuation, capitalization, and spelling every time you write for a test.

FINAL DRAFT

When we got there, there wasn't a single car on the road, just a bunch of construction workers and heavy equipment. Then we saw the huge crane start to move, slowly and cautiously. Hanging from it was what looked like a long metal cage. "they're putting in a pedestrian bridge so people can walk to the new train station," Xavier told me.

The bridge was huge—three lanes long. It must have weighed tons! The crane operator moved the bridge to the cement support structures that had been built on the side and in the middle of the freeway. I could tell now that this was only half of the bridge. The other half was still lying on top of what appeared to be part of a flat-bed truck on the other side of the road.

With the bridge in place, The construction crew moved in to check things. Then They moved to the other bridge to help secure the crane to it. This took quite some time, but we weren't about to leave!

Finally, The crane started moving again slowly. This part seemed even trickier, having to match up one part of the bridge with the other without crashing into it! There was a man now standing on the part of the bridge that had been placed, watching closely as the crane moved.

Soon, the other half of the bridge was in place. The crew on the ground moved in again, ready to begin checking and securing the new bridge. With the heavy loading and moving done, Xavier and I decided to leave. But we sure had a story to tell.

Reflect

Is anything missing? Check Marco's draft against the scoring guide one last time. It's important to use the writing prompt's scoring guide to check your writing any time you take a test!

Well, we're done. And it wasn't so bad, was it? Here are some helpful tips for when you write for a test.

TEST TIPS

1. **Study the writing prompt before you start to write.** Most writing prompts have three parts: the setup, the task, and the scoring guide. The parts probably won't be labeled. You'll have to figure them out for yourself!

2. **Make sure you understand the task before you start to write.**
   - Read all three parts of the writing prompt carefully.
   - Circle key words in the task part of the writing prompt that tell what kind of writing you need to do. The task might also identify your audience.
   - Make sure you know how you'll be graded.
   - Say the assignment in your own words to yourself.

3. **Keep an eye on the clock.** Decide how much time you will spend on each part of the writing process and try to stick to your schedule. Don't spend so much time prewriting that you don't have enough time left to write.

4. **Reread your writing. Compare it to the scoring guide at least twice.** Remember the rubrics you have used all year? A scoring guide on a writing test is like a rubric. It can help you keep what's important in mind.

5. **Plan, plan, plan!** You don't get much time to revise during a test, so planning is more important than ever.

6. **Write neatly.** Remember: If the people who score your test can't read your writing, it doesn't matter how good your essay is!

Informative/ Explanatory writing explains something to the reader.

Hello! I'm Justin. I'm learning about informative/explanatory writing in school. I think I'll really like this kind of writing. Studying real-life people and things is fun, and I think I'll be good at explaining them. Can I inform my readers and make my writing interesting, too? Here's my chance to find out!

IN THIS UNIT

- ☐ **Summary**
- ☐ **Cause-and-Effect Report**
- ☐ **Research Report**
- MATH CONNECTION ▷ **Explanatory Essay**
- ☐ **Writing for a Test**

Name: Justin
Home: Connecticut
Hobbies: coin collecting,
planting trees,
Connecticut history
Favorite Tree: white oak
(Connecticut's
state tree)
Favorite Foods: Mexican and Indian

What's a Summary?

A summary is a short piece of writing that tells the main points of a longer piece. I think explaining the main ideas of another piece of writing in as few words as possible will be an interesting challenge. It reminds me of packing only what I need when I go on a trip!

What's in a Summary?

Length
The point of a summary is to condense information, and that's not always easy to do. I'll have to decide what's important enough to be included and what I should leave out.

Organization
I can't waste a word in my summary, so I'm going to organize things very carefully. I'll focus on just the main ideas and organize my points logically. I'll use only relevant details that support the main ideas.

A Clear Beginning
My readers need to know right away what I'm writing about. I'll start my summary with a clear and interesting topic sentence.

Interest
Sometimes nonfiction writing can sound a bit dull. To keep my audience reading, I'm going to bring out interesting points about my subject.

Why write a Summary?

I've been thinking about some good reasons to write a summary. Here are a few of my ideas. Can you think of any more?

Information

Everybody can't read everything! I can use a summary to inform other people about a piece of writing they haven't read.

Clarification

When there's a lot of information in a written piece, summarizing can help me be clear about what's important. I can also make sure I really understand the author's explanations and main points.

Research

Summarizing could be really useful when I'm doing research. When I'm starting a project, I read a lot of different reference materials before I focus on my topic. If I write a summary of each reference article, I can keep track of things.

Linking Informative/Explanatory Writing Traits to a Summary

In this chapter, you will write a brief account of an article you have read. This type of informative/explanatory writing is called a summary. Justin will guide you through the stages of the writing process: Prewrite, Draft, Revise, Edit, and Publish. In each stage, Justin will show you important writing strategies that are linked to the Informative/Explanatory Writing Traits below.

Informative/Explanatory Writing Traits

Ideas
- a clear, focused topic
- credible, engaging facts and details that support and develop the topic

Organization
- information that is organized logically into a strong introduction, body, and conclusion
- transitions that clarify relationships between ideas

Voice
- a voice and tone that are appropriate for the purpose and audience

Word Choice
- language that is precise and concise
- domain-specific vocabulary that is used correctly and explained as necessary

Sentence Fluency
- sentences that vary in length and flow smoothly

Conventions
- no or few errors in grammar, usage, mechanics, and spelling

Before you write, read Keesha Kane's summary of the article "A Touch of Genius." Then use the summary rubric on pages 132–133 to decide how well she did. (You might want to look back at What's in a Summary? on page 126, too!)

"A Touch of Genius"

by Patricia Millman
Summary by Keesha Kane

Organization   Clear beginning ⤸   Short length ⤵

Michael Naranjo is a Native American sculptor in Santa Fe, New Mexico. He chose his career when he was a boy helping his mother make pottery in the pueblo. At age 23, however, Naranjo was wounded in the Vietnam War. He was blinded and left without the complete use of one hand.

⤶ Interesting point ⤴

Naranjo was unsure if he would still be able to sculpt. While recovering in the hospital, he molded several clay sculptures of animals. One was so good that it was photographed for the newspaper. That convinced him to pursue his dream.

Although he cannot see, he can remember images from his past. His mind carries the images to his fingertips.

Interesting point

Naranjo has won awards for his work and leads sculpture ⤶ workshops. His sculptures are displayed in museums and public buildings around the world. Private collectors also seek his art.

Michael A. Naranjo

A Touch of Genius

by Patricia Millman

Michael Naranjo is a Native American, a Vietnam War veteran, and "a sculptor who happens to be blind." Behind this statement lies a remarkable story.

Michael grew up in the Tewa Indian pueblo of Santa Clara, New Mexico. As a boy, he roamed the scenic foothills west of the pueblo community and explored the Rio Grande, a river to the south and east. His world was enriched by the beautiful sights and sounds of the desert country.

This artist sees with his hands.

Michael's love of sculpting was born at the pueblo, too. "My mother was a potter, and I would help her fix clay," he recalls. "She gathered her clay in a place in the hills that only she knew about. Every potter has their own source of clay, and when they find that clay, they're very secretive about it.

"My mother would bring in the clay and screen it to get out anything that didn't belong, and then she would soak it in tubs. After that, she'd put the clay into a square of canvas cloth, and she'd sprinkle a different white kind of clay on top. Then she would fold this square of canvas and press on it this way and that way, and when she unfolded the canvas I could see this little log of clay inside.

"Then I would take off my shoes and perform a little dance with the clay. I would sidestep on this log of clay. I could feel the moist clay on the side of my foot and between my toes. And when I reached the other end, I'd step off the square of canvas, and she'd fold it and push it this way and that way and refold it, and I would have this little log of clay again. And once again I would perform my little dance."

Michael's dance served a very important purpose. He was blending the white clay and the brown clay to make it stronger. With this strong clay, his mother could make pots that would last a long time.

"That's probably how I started sculpting. . . playing with clay," Michael says. "Not long after that, I wanted to make figures of animals. And as they became more detailed, they became sculptures. So even way back then, I knew that what I wanted to do was be an artist someday."

One More by
Michael A. Naranjo

Seeing with His Hands

Michael's goal would not be reached easily. While serving with the Army in Vietnam, Michael was badly wounded in battle. He lost his sight and partial use of one hand. For the first time, Michael wondered if he could ever be a sculptor.

One day, while recovering in the hospital, Michael asked if he could have a small piece of clay. From it he made an inchworm.

The next sculpture Michael made, an Indian on a horse, was so good it was photographed by the newspapers. Lucky thing! Because when

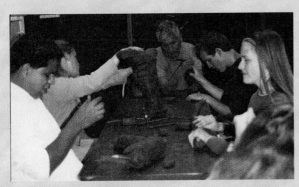

Michael enjoys teaching sculpting workshops. "One step at a time and you can do it," he reminds his students.

Michael decided to make his next sculpture, he found that the hospital didn't have any more clay. So he reshaped the Indian on a horse into a bear with a fish in its mouth.

Today, Michael has lots of material to use to make his memories come to life. "I was able to see until I was twenty-three years old, so I have a very good idea of what most things look like," he said. "So I sit, and I think about it, and I get a picture in my mind. If you close your eyes and think of. . . well, if you have a cat or a dog, you can picture this pet. The same process happens with me.

"Once you have the material in your hand that you can mold and shape, then you can carry it over from your mind to your fingertips; and your mind tells your fingers, 'Make that bigger or smaller. . .' until this whole process slowly starts happening.

"Nowadays, when I make animals, I sit there and think about the days when I'd take a moment sitting on a cliff side and look down and see a deer down there or watch some turkeys walk through the forest. Or the time I followed a mountain stream and a deer stopped in this pool of water and looked at me with his huge brown eyes. It lasted just a few moments, but it's one of those moments that I draw on for inspiration."

Michael inspires others by leading sculpture workshops for children and adults, veterans and seniors, both sighted and visually impaired.

In 1999, Michael was named the Outstanding Disabled Veteran of the Year and received the LIFE Presidential Unsung Hero Award. His sculptures can be seen in museums and public buildings across the United States, in the Vatican, and in the White House.

A Special Fan

Many people like to collect Michael's work, but Michael fondly remembers one special young "collector."

"It was maybe twenty years ago at the Indian Market in Santa Fe. One day there was this little boy who came, and he was looking at my work and I was telling him about it. Next year, he came back and said, 'I was here last year. Do you remember me?' And I said, 'Yes.' He said, 'I want to buy that little buffalo.' And I said, 'OK.' I told him how much it was.

"As he paid for it, he said, 'I worked all last summer and this summer, and saved my money.' I had no words to describe the emotion I felt. I still can't describe what a moment like that feels like."

Does Michael have one piece of sculpture that is his very favorite? Could it be the buffalo from the Santa Fe Indian Market? Or the bear with a fish in its mouth?

"You know, it's the same as with children," Michael said. "If you have more than one, you love them all equally. That's how I feel about my sculptures."

Rubric

Use this 6-point rubric to plan and score a summary.

	6	5	4
Ideas	Relevant facts and concrete details focus on the main points. There are no unnecessary details.	Facts and details focus on the main points. There are no unnecessary details.	Most facts and details focus on the main points. There are a few unnecessary details.
Organization	Details are organized logically and are connected in a thoughtful way. The beginning introduces the topic and grabs the reader's attention.	Details are arranged in order. The beginning works well.	Some of the details are out of order or poorly connected. The beginning is unexciting but clear.
Voice	The writer establishes and maintains a formal style.	The writer uses a formal style throughout most of the summary.	The writer uses a formal style, but there are a few moments where the tone is too casual or lacks confidence.
Word Choice	The language is concise and clear. No unnecessary words are used.	Most words and phrases are clear and used correctly. One or two could be cut.	A few vague or unnecessary words are used, but most of the language is concise.
Sentence Fluency	Sentences flow smoothly. There is striking variety in sentence lengths and structures.	Sentences flow smoothly. There is noticeable variety in lengths and structures. The writing is easy to read aloud.	There is some variety in sentence lengths and structures. The writing is not difficult to read.
Conventions	Subjects and verbs agree. There are no dangling or misplaced modifiers. Conventions are used skillfully.	The writing contains a few minor errors with subject-verb agreement or modifiers.	The writing has some noticeable errors with subject-verb agreement and modifiers. They do not interfere with meaning.

✚ Presentation Paragraphs are indented.

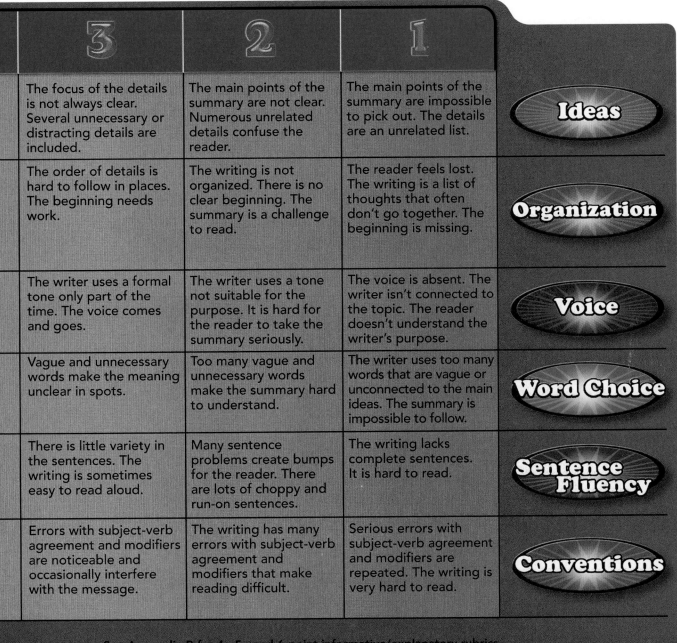

3	2	1	
The focus of the details is not always clear. Several unnecessary or distracting details are included.	The main points of the summary are not clear. Numerous unrelated details confuse the reader.	The main points of the summary are impossible to pick out. The details are an unrelated list.	**Ideas**
The order of details is hard to follow in places. The beginning needs work.	The writing is not organized. There is no clear beginning. The summary is a challenge to read.	The reader feels lost. The writing is a list of thoughts that often don't go together. The beginning is missing.	**Organization**
The writer uses a formal tone only part of the time. The voice comes and goes.	The writer uses a tone not suitable for the purpose. It is hard for the reader to take the summary seriously.	The voice is absent. The writer isn't connected to the topic. The reader doesn't understand the writer's purpose.	**Voice**
Vague and unnecessary words make the meaning unclear in spots.	Too many vague and unnecessary words make the summary hard to understand.	The writer uses too many words that are vague or unconnected to the main ideas. The summary is impossible to follow.	**Word Choice**
There is little variety in the sentences. The writing is sometimes easy to read aloud.	Many sentence problems create bumps for the reader. There are lots of choppy and run-on sentences.	The writing lacks complete sentences. It is hard to read.	**Sentence Fluency**
Errors with subject-verb agreement and modifiers are noticeable and occasionally interfere with the message.	The writing has many errors with subject-verb agreement and modifiers that make reading difficult.	Serious errors with subject-verb agreement and modifiers are repeated. The writing is very hard to read.	**Conventions**

See Appendix B for 4-, 5-, and 6-point informative/explanatory rubrics.

Using the ^Summary Rubric to Study the Model

Did you notice that the model on page 129 points out some key elements of a summary? As she wrote the summary of "A Touch of Genius," Keesha Kane used these elements to help her. She also used the 6-point rubric on pages 132–133 to plan, draft, revise, and edit the writing. A rubric is a great tool to evaluate writing during the writing process.

Now let's use the same rubric to score the model. To do this, we'll focus on each trait separately, starting with Ideas. We'll use the top descriptor for each trait (column 6) along with examples from the model, to help us understand how the traits work together. How would you score Keesha on each trait?

Ideas

- Relevant facts and concrete details focus on the main points.
- There are no unnecessary details.

The writer states the main points in a clear and focused way. She gives just enough relevant and concrete details to support the main points. For example, the paragraph below tells how successful the sculptor is, without a lot of unnecessary detail.

[from the writing model]

Naranjo has won awards for his work and leads sculpture workshops. His sculptures are displayed in museums and public buildings around the world. Private collectors also seek his art.

Organization

- Details are organized logically and are connected in a thoughtful way.
- The beginning introduces the topic and grabs the reader's attention.

In each paragraph, Keesha's details are well organized and all related to each other. In her opening paragraph, the first sentence gives clear, identifying information to pull the reader in. Then she includes important details about Naranjo's early life.

[from the writing model]

Michael Naranjo is a Native American sculptor in Santa Fe, New Mexico. He chose his career when he was a boy helping his mother make pottery in the pueblo. At age 23, however, Naranjo was wounded in the Vietnam War. He was blinded and left without the complete use of one hand.

Voice

- The writer establishes and maintains a formal style.

In a summary, it's important for the writer to establish a knowledgeable and formal tone. Keesha does just that, which helps me take her writing seriously and feel confident that she has written an accurate and thorough summary.

[from the writing model]

While recovering in the hospital, he molded several clay sculptures of animals. One was so good that it was photographed for the newspaper. That convinced him to pursue his dream.

Word Choice

- The language is concise and clear.
- No unnecessary words are used.

Keesha knows that a summary needs to be as short as possible, so she makes sure her writing is not wordy. For the second sentence below, she might have written *He sits and thinks about the image in his mind. After he gets a picture of it, the image goes to his fingertips.* Instead she carefully chooses her words and uses as few of them as possible.

[from the writing model]

Although he cannot see, he can remember images from his past. His mind carries the images to his fingertips.

Sentence Fluency

- Sentences flow smoothly.
- There is striking variety in sentence lengths and structures.

Keesha did a great job using a variety of sentence lengths and structures. She avoids short, choppy sentences. In some places, she combines ideas and uses longer sentences. For example, Keesha could have written her last paragraph this way: *Naranjo has won awards for his work. He leads sculpture workshops. His sculptures are displayed in museums. They are also displayed in public buildings around the world. Private collectors also seek his art.* You can read below how she really wrote the paragraph.

[from the writing model]

Naranjo has won awards for his work and leads sculpture workshops. His sculptures are displayed in museums and public buildings around the world. Private collectors also seek his art.

Conventions

- Subjects and verbs agree.
- There are no dangling or misplaced modifiers.
- Conventions are used skillfully.

I checked Keesha's summary for mistakes, but I couldn't find any. She did a great job on spelling, punctuation, and capitalization. All verbs agree with their subjects, and there are no dangling modifiers. For example, look at the sentence below. *His mind* is a singular subject, so it needs the singular verb *carries*. She wrote it correctly.

[from the writing model]	

His mind carries the images to his fingertips.

This sentence contains a perfectly placed modifier.

[from the writing model]

Although he cannot see, he can remember images from his past.

✚Presentation Paragraphs are indented.

My Turn!

I'm going to write a summary using good writing strategies. I'll also use what I learned from the rubric and good writing strategies. Follow along and see how I do it.

Prewrite

Focus on **Ideas**

The Rubric Says Relevant facts and concrete details focus on the main points.

Writing Strategy Read an article and take notes on the main points.

My teacher asked us to write a summary of an article. I chose the article below because it combines my interests in trees, the history of my state, and coins. As I read the article, I found the main points in it. On page 140, you can see the notes I took as I read.

The Tree That Saved History

by Jane Sutcliffe

An unusual funeral took place in Hartford, Connecticut, on August 21, 1856. The city's bells tolled in mourning, and a band played funeral hymns. It was an outpouring of grief fit for a hero—except that this hero was a tree, a white oak to be exact.

For nearly 169 years this special tree had been known simply as the Charter Oak in honor of the part it played in the history of colonial America.

The Charter Oak was an old and respected tree even before colonial times. Native Americans of the area held meetings under its branches. And when the tree's new leaves were as big as a mouse's ear, they knew that it was time to plant corn.

In time, the English came to the valley surrounding the big oak. They settled there and founded the colony of Connecticut. Every colony had to obtain a contract, called a charter, from the king of England. The charter helped to protect the colony's rights. The charter given to Connecticut by King Charles II in 1662 was the pride of the colony. It allowed the colonists to govern themselves by their own constitution. More than a century before the Declaration of Independence, the charter treated Connecticut almost as if it were an independent country.

Then, in 1685, King Charles died. The new English ruler, King James II, not only disapproved of Connecticut's charter but he also disliked having so many colonies. He thought it would be better to combine the colonies of the northeast into one big colony.

King James ordered Sir Edmund Andros, the governor of the Dominion of New England, to seize any documents recognizing the colonies' old rights. Most colonies felt they had no choice and turned over their charters. Only Connecticut delayed. Again and again, Andros demanded that Connecticut give up its charter to him. Again and again, the colonists politely but firmly refused. Finally, Andros had had enough. On All Hallow's Eve, 1687, Andros and more than sixty British soldiers marched into Hartford.

Connecticut Governor Robert Treat was waiting for Andros at the door of the meetinghouse, where leaders of the colony were assembled. Politely he escorted Andros inside. Andros wasted no time. He demanded that Connecticut obey the king and surrender its charter.

By now a crowd of townspeople had gathered outside. As they strained to hear every word, Governor Treat spoke passionately about the struggles of the people to build their colony, and about their love of freedom. Giving up the charter, he said, would be like giving up his life. Andros was unmoved. At dark, candles were lit so that the meeting could continue, but Andros had heard enough. He demanded to see the charter. The colonists could delay no longer. They brought out the charter and placed it on the table before him.

Suddenly all the candles in the room went out. In the darkness, a young patriot, Captain Joseph Wadsworth, snatched the charter and jumped out an open window. Carefully wrapping the document in his cloak, he placed it in the hollow of the great white oak. Had the brave captain simply seized the opportunity provided by the sudden darkness, or had it all been a clever plan? No one would ever know. By the

Captain Joseph Wadsworth carefully placed Connecticut's charter in the hollow of the great white oak.

time the candles were lit again, Andros was looking at nothing but innocent faces.

If Andros was furious at being outsmarted, he did not show it. With or without the charter, he said that the government of the colony was over. Fortunately, King James was soon overthrown. Andros was imprisoned and then sent back to England. The new rulers, King William III and Queen Mary II, agreed that since Connecticut had never surrendered its charter, the colony could take up its old freedoms again.

The Charter Oak became a beloved symbol of freedom throughout the land. After it was blown down in a storm on August 21, 1856, people requested keepsakes of its wood. There was plenty to go around—so much, in fact, that author Mark Twain said there was enough "to build a plank road from here (Hartford) to Great Salt Lake City."

Craftsmen fashioned pianos, chairs, and even a cradle of Charter Oak wood. One of the fanciest pieces was an elaborately carved chair that is still used in the Senate Chamber in the State Capitol Building in Hartford. It occupies a place of honor in memory of the Charter Oak, one of the most unusual heroes in our country's struggle for liberty.

The Charter Oak appears on the Connecticut quarter, issued in 1999 by the U.S. Mint. Connecticut became a state in 1788.

There are tons of details that make learning about the Charter Oak interesting. My assignment, however, is to summarize the information in the article so only the most important facts stand out. I have to use as few words as possible, so using only relevant and concrete details is critical. Here are my notes from the article. Would you choose the same main points?

Notes on "The Tree That Saved History"

✔ Charter Oak grew in Hartford, CT. Important in CT's history. Funeral held for tree.

✔ English settlers who founded CT colony got charter (contract) from King Charles II to govern themselves. King Charles II died. New king (James II) wanted to take charter away.

✔ Edmund Andros (gov. of New England) tried to collect CT charter. Met with CT gov. and other leaders in Hartford. When candles went out, Captain Joseph Wadsworth grabbed charter and jumped through window. He hid the charter in a huge white oak.

✔ King James took away CT's freedom anyway. New king and queen said CT didn't give up charter so it got its freedom back.

✔ Tree became symbol of freedom: Wood made into fancy chair. Tree is on CT state quarter.

Apply

Choose an article about an interesting topic. Read the article and take notes on the main points.

The Rubric Says	Details are organized logically and are connected in a thoughtful way.
Writing Strategy	Make a Spider Map from your notes.

✏️ Writer's Term___

Spider Map
A **Spider Map** organizes information about a topic. The subject is written in the body, and a main point is written on each leg.

Now, to organize and connect my details in a logical way, I'll organize my notes into a Spider Map. Each leg of my spider will be a main point about the Charter Oak. You can see my Spider Map below.

Spider Map

King James tried to take away CT's charter.

The old white oak was important in history of CT.

The King took away CT's freedom anyway, but CT got it back.

Charter Oak of CT

The charter was hidden in an old oak tree.

The Charter Oak symbolizes freedom; a chair made from it is still in CT capitol.

Reflect

Think about it. Are all the main points from Justin's notes on the Spider Map?

Apply

Organize your notes using a Spider Map.

Draft

Focus on Ideas

The Rubric Says	There are no unnecessary details.
Writing Strategy	Include only the most important ideas and details.

It's time to start writing! The rubric reminds me to use only necessary details. That means I need to be clear and concise. I'll start with the topic of my article. My teacher said that most summaries are about one-third as long as the original article. This guideline will help me keep my summary short.

As I write my draft, I will do my best with spelling, punctuation, capitalization, and grammar. I can correct any errors I make later.

[DRAFT]

The Charter Oak

The Charter Oak was important in the history of Connecticut. This tree has an interesting history.

← [clear topic sentence]

[DRAFT]

The Charter Oak

In colonal times, England's King Charles II granted charters to the American colonies that he ruled in those days before they became the United States. The charters from the king was contracts that gave the colonies the freedom to govern themselves instead of having Great Britain govern them. Connecticut had the privilege of receiving its charter in 1662. In 1685, 23 years later, after King Charles II died, King James II gave orders to go and take away the charters and join all the New England colonies into one. Edmund Andros, the govenor of New England, got all the charters except Connecticut's.

[main points]

Andros went to Hartford, Connecticut, to ask for the charter. He brought 60 British soldiers and met with the colony's governor, Robert Treat, on All Hallow's Eve. Other leaders of the colony was there, too. Before Andros could take the charter, however, the candles in the room blew out. A patriot named Captain Joseph Wadsworth grabbed the charter and leeped out the window. He wrapped the charter in his cloak and hid it in an old white oak tree.

Reflect

What do you think of the beginning of Justin's draft? Is this part of the draft clear and concise?

Apply

Write a draft using the main points from your Spider Map. Include only the most important ideas and details.

Revise

Focus on Organization

The Rubric Says — The beginning introduces the topic and grabs the reader's attention.

Writing Strategy — Include an interesting detail in the opening paragraph.

Writer's Term

Details

The **details** are the words used to describe a person, convince an audience, explain a process, or in some way support a main idea.

The rubric says the beginning of my summary should introduce the topic and grab my reader's attention. Well, I know my topic's clear in the first sentence, but maybe the beginning could be more engaging. I decided to use an interesting detail to draw the reader in. What do you think of my revision?

[DRAFT]

The Charter Oak

The Charter Oak was important in the history of Connecticut. This even had a funeral ← tree ~~has an interesting history.~~

[included interesting detail]

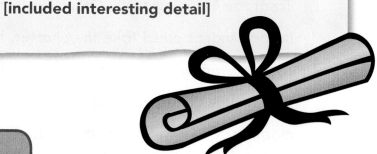

Apply

Check your summary to make sure the beginning clearly introduces the topic and grabs the reader's attention.

Revise

The Rubric Says The writer establishes and maintains a formal style.

Writing Strategy Use third-person point of view plus facts.

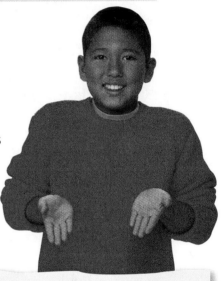

When summarizing anything written by someone else, third-person point of view is most appropriate. Using third person helps me establish a formal style, which is necessary if I want my reader to take me seriously. Including facts about my topic strengthens my voice and gives my writing credibility.

When I reread my draft, I found a place where I forgot to use third person. I'll fix that now to maintain a formal style throughout my summary.

[DRAFT]   [maintained third person]

~~I learned that~~ King James II didn't get the charter, but he took away Connecticut's freedom anyway. ~~As you might expect,~~ Soon another English king and queen came into power.

Reflect

What do you think? How have Justin's revisions strengthened his writing?

Apply

Look for any first- or second-person point of view pronouns, and replace them with third-person pronouns.

Summary 145

Revise

Focus on Word Choice

The Rubric Says	The language is concise and clear. No unnecessary words are used.
Writing Strategy	Choose words carefully and replace wordy phrases with succinct language.

Writer's Term

Succinct Language
Succinct language is brief and to the point; there are no wasted words.

A summary has to be concise and clear. There should be no extra words. I read my paper aloud to listen for wordy phrases and sentences, and I heard a lot of unnecessary words! To fix this problem, I replaced unnecessary words with language that is to the point, or succinct. What do you think?

[removed unnecessary words]   **[DRAFT]**

In colonal times, England's King Charles II granted charters to the American colonies ~~that he ruled in those days before they became the United States.~~ The charters from the king was contracts that gave the colonies the freedom to govern themselves ~~instead of having Great Britain govern them.~~ Connecticut ~~had the privilege of receiving~~ **gained** its charter in 1662. In 1685, ~~23 years later,~~ after King Charles II died, King James II gave orders to ~~go and take away~~ **seize** the charters and join all the New England colonies into one.

[used succinct words]

Apply

Take out any wordy phrases in your summary and use succinct language instead.

Edit

The Rubric Says   Subjects and verbs agree. There are no dangling or misplaced modifiers. Conventions are used skillfully.

Writing Strategy   Be sure all subjects and verbs agree. Check that all modifiers are clear.

Writer's Term

Subject-Verb Agreement
Every sentence must have a subject and a verb. A **singular subject** requires a **singular verb,** and a **plural subject** requires a **plural verb**.

Now I need to fix any mistakes. I'll check my spelling, punctuation, and capitalization. The rubric also says to check subject-verb agreement and look for dangling or misplaced modifiers.

[DRAFT]

colonial

In ~~colonial~~ times, England's King Charles II granted charters to the

American colonies ~~that he ruled in those days before they became the~~

were

~~United States~~. The charters from the king ~~was~~ contracts that gave the

colonies the freedom to govern themselves ~~instead of having Great~~

gained

~~Britain govern them.~~ Connecticut ~~had the privilege of receiving~~ its

[corrected subject-verb agreement]

charter in 1662.

Reflect

How do the edits make the summary easier to read?

Apply   Conventions

Edit your draft for spelling, punctuation, and capitalization. Be sure to fix any problems with subject-verb agreement and modifiers.

For more practice fixing errors in subject-verb agreement and modifiers, use the exercises on the next two pages.

Subject-Verb Agreement
Know the Rule

Every sentence must have a subject and a verb. A **singular subject** requires a **singular verb,** and a **plural subject** requires a **plural verb**.

In many sentences, a prepositional phrase comes between the subject and the verb. A prepositional phrase is a group of words that begins with a preposition and ends with an object. Do not mistake the object of the preposition for the subject of the sentence. The verb in every sentence must agree with its subject, not the object of the preposition (op).

                    s   op v
Incorrect: The charters from the king was contracts.

                   s   op v
Correct: The charters from the king were contracts.

               s   op   v
Incorrect: One of the patriots were named Joseph Wadsworth.

               s   op   v
Correct: One of the patriots was named Joseph Wadsworth.

Practice the Rule

Number a separate sheet of paper 1–10. Write the correct verb form for each sentence.

1. Connecticut (is/are/am) one of six New England states.
2. Maine (was/were) the last New England colony to become a state.
3. The U.S. Mint (has/have) issued a quarter for each state.
4. The first quarter for the New England states (was/were) for Connecticut.
5. Many people in this country (collect/collects) state quarters.
6. The distinctive design for each state (is/are) on the reverse side of the coin.
7. People often (buy/buys) bags of quarters from coin dealers.
8. A few places for keeping coins (is/are) folders, coin envelopes, and special plastic bags.
9. Rhode Island (is/are) the smallest New England state.
10. Rhode Island and Connecticut (share/shares) a border.

Dangling and Misplaced Modifiers

Know the Rule

A **dangling modifier** is a phrase that does not clearly refer to any particular word in the sentence. When you begin a sentence with a verbal phrase, be sure the noun or pronoun that follows is correct. In the sentence below, who is freezing?

> **Example:** Freezing from the cold wind, a scarf can help you keep warm. (not clear)
>
> When you are freezing from the cold wind, a scarf can help you keep warm. (clear)

A **misplaced modifier** is a word that is in the wrong place and can cause confusion for the reader.

> **Example:** The stolen student's backpack was left on the playground. (incorrect)
>
> The student's stolen backpack was left on the playground. (correct)

Practice the Rule

Number a separate sheet of paper 1–8. Read each sentence and decide whether the modifying word or phrase clearly describes the intended noun or pronoun. If it does, write **yes**. If it does not, write **no**. Rewrite two of the unclear sentences correctly.

1. Stacked in a pile on the desk, Mr. Hamilton handed out our new textbooks.
2. Mr. Hamilton told us to read chapter five, which is about the Pilgrims' voyage.
3. We read about how the Wampanoag grew squash and beans in our textbook.
4. Only Mr. Hamilton said to answer questions 1, 3, and 4.
5. Tika almost did all of her social studies homework.
6. While I was reading a book in the library, the fire alarm went off.
7. Kent left the library just about ten minutes ago, so he should be here soon.
8. Keeping an eye on the clock, I found that time passed slowly.

Publish

✛ Presentation

Publishing Strategy   Read your summary to the class.

Presentation Strategy   Indent each paragraph.

There are different ways I could publish my summary. For example, I could include it in my scrapbook about Connecticut. First, though, my classmates and I are going to read our summaries aloud so we can all learn about the articles we've read. Before I read my summary aloud, I want to make sure it is neat and easy to read. Whether I handwrite or type my summary, indenting each paragraph will visually group related information. I'll also use this final checklist to check my summary one last time.

My Final Checklist

Did I—

✔ make sure all the subjects and verbs agree?

✔ correct any dangling or misplaced modifiers?

✔ make sure my paragraphs are indented?

✔ proofread carefully for spelling, grammar, and punctuation?

Apply

Make a checklist to help you check your summary. How did you do?

"The Tree That Saved History" by Jane Sutcliffe

Summary by Justin

The Charter Oak was important in the history of Connecticut. This tree even had a funeral.

In colonial times, England's King Charles II granted charters to the American colonies. The charters from the king were contracts that gave the colonies the freedom to govern themselves. Connecticut gained its charter in 1662. In 1685, after King Charles II died, King James II gave orders to seize the charters and join all the New England colonies into one. Edmund Andros, the governor of New England, collected all the charters except Connecticut's.

Andros went to Hartford, Connecticut, to ask for the charter. He met with the colony's governor and other leaders. Before Andros could take the charter, however, the candles in the room blew out. A patriot named Joseph Wadsworth grabbed the charter and leaped out the window. He hid the charter in the hollow of an old white oak tree.

King James II didn't get the charter, but he took away Connecticut's freedom anyway. Soon another English king and queen came into power. They ruled that the colony could have its freedom back because it never surrendered its charter.

In 1856 a storm blew down the tree. After a funeral for the Charter Oak, its wood was carved into many things. A beautiful chair made from the Charter Oak now sits in the state capitol. The Charter Oak also appears on the 1999 Connecticut state quarter. The famous tree still symbolizes our freedom.

Reflect

Think about Justin's summary. Does the writing contain all the traits of a good summary? Check it against the rubric. Don't forget to use the rubric to check your own summary.

What's a Cause-and-Effect Report?

A cause-and-effect report tells how a cause or causes produce certain effects. It might also describe certain effects and trace them back to their causes. This kind of writing really makes you think!

What's in a Cause-and-Effect Report?

Connections
Cause-and-effect writing is about showing connections. I really have to understand the cause-and-effect relationships and make them clear to my readers. So it's important to organize my report well and to include plenty of supporting details.

Interest
To capture my audience's attention from the start, I'll begin my report with a fascinating fact. Once I have them interested, I'll keep them reading with good reasoning and smooth writing.

Research
A cause-and-effect report isn't based on opinions. I'll have to do some research to find facts that support the cause-and-effect relationships. I'll use a variety of references to get the whole story on my topic. And I won't use just any source—I need reliable references I can trust!

Why write a Cause-and-Effect Report?

I can think of a lot of reasons for writing a cause-and-effect report, and I've listed some of them below. What's my reason? I'm still thinking about that!

Reasoning Skills

To write a cause-and-effect report, I have to really think things through. Looking at causes and figuring out their effects, or looking at effects and examining their causes, makes me use my reasoning skills. I have to think logically and make sure all my points are valid. This is the kind of thinking I need in all my subjects—and in life!

Information

A cause-and-effect report is a good way to inform other people about our world—and about why things happen the way they do. I can help others learn about nature, current events, historical happenings, and many other things with this kind of writing.

Practice

I've had to write cause-and-effect reports in social studies, science, and English. I'm sure I'll be assigned more of this kind of writing in the future, so I can use the practice!

Linking Informative/Explanatory Writing Traits to a **Cause-and-Effect Report**

In this chapter, you will write a report about how one thing can cause another. This type of informative/explanatory writing is called a cause-and-effect report. Justin will guide you through the stages of the writing process: Prewrite, Draft, Revise, Edit, and Publish. In each stage, Justin will show you important writing strategies that are linked to the Informative/Explanatory Writing Traits below.

Informative/Explanatory Writing Traits

	• a clear, focused topic • credible, engaging facts and details that support and develop the topic
	• information that is organized logically into a strong introduction, body, and conclusion • transitions that clarify relationships between ideas
	• a voice and tone that are appropriate for the purpose and audience
	• language that is precise and concise • domain-specific vocabulary that is used correctly and explained as necessary
	• sentences that vary in length and flow smoothly
	• no or few errors in grammar, usage, mechanics, and spelling

Before you write, read Julia Tazzi's cause-and-effect report on the next page. After you read, use the cause-and-effect rubric on pages 156–157 to decide how well she did. (You might want to look back at What's in a Cause-and-Effect Report? on page 152, too!)

Understanding the Barrier Islands

by Julia Tazzi

Interesting beginning ↴   Research

The barrier islands are called the "children of the sea." Born after the last ice age, they stretch along the Atlantic coast in long, narrow chains. Some of these chains extend for 100 miles or more. The islands have been around for nearly 18 centuries, but did you know they may not last forever?

Cause

What caused the islands to form? At the end of the ice age, the air warmed and the glaciers melted. The melting ice caused rivers and streams to rise. As they flooded over the beaches, they carried sand and sediment to shallow areas just off the Atlantic coast. Ridges formed there. Then waves deposited more sand on the ridges. The ridges slowly became islands. Ocean currents pushed the sand up and down the islands. That caused them to lengthen into narrow strips.

Effects

Connections

The barrier islands have broad beaches and dunes on the ocean side. They have mud flats and salt marshes on the mainland side. This low, sandy structure is vulnerable to erosion. However, plants in the dunes, flats, and marshes help stabilize the islands. The plants and the dunes themselves slow the wind. As the wind slows down, it is not strong enough to pick up sand and carry it away. Plant roots also hold the sand in place.

Natural erosion isn't the only danger to these islands. People who enjoy the beach love to vacation on the barrier islands. To build houses, hotels, and roads for them, developers flatten the dunes. As they fill in mud flats and marshes, they bury the plants growing there. As they change the islands, developers increase the erosion that occurs.

Since communities want to save their islands, they try to stop the erosion with "beach nourishment." This involves dumping many truckloads of sand on eroding beaches. However, this helps only for a while. The erosion starts up again because there are no dunes to break the wind or plants to hold the sand in place. The new sand is soon washed away. As a result, the islands continue to be in danger.

Research

Erosion has caused many changes in the islands. For example, the Cape Hatteras Lighthouse had to be moved. The beach had eroded, so in 1999, the lighthouse was moved about one-half mile inland.

We need to learn ways to deal with the relentless force of erosion so we can preserve these sandy national treasures.

Rubric

Use this 6-point rubric to plan and score a cause-and-effect report.

	6	5	4
Ideas	The topic is focused and supported by credible sources. Relevant facts support and explain causes and effects.	The topic is clear and supported. One or two facts are not related to the causes and effects.	The topic is clear, but parts are not well supported by credible sources. Most of the facts explain causes and effects.
Organization	The report is organized in a clear cause-and-effect pattern. Transitions clarify relationships among causes and effects.	The writing is organized in a cause-and-effect pattern. Transitions work well.	The cause-and-effect organization of the writing works most of the time. Transitions are present.
Voice	Second-person voice connects immediately and consistently with the reader. The voice enhances the writing.	Second-person voice is appealing to the reader. The writing stands out from other writing.	Second-person voice is used inconsistently. It engages the reader from time to time.
Word Choice	Precise language and specific vocabulary are used and, where necessary, defined.	The writer's language is clear and precise. Most unfamiliar words are defined.	Most of the writing is clear. A few words or phrases are inaccurate or need to be defined.
Sentence Fluency	All sentences are clearly written and logically structured. They flow smoothly.	Most sentences are clearly written and well structured. They are easy to read aloud.	Some sentences are poorly structured and hard to follow. They interrupt the flow of the writing.
Conventions	Correct forms of pronouns and verbs are used. The writer's strong knowledge of conventions strengthens the writing.	Correct forms of pronouns and verbs are used. There are a few convention errors, but they are hard to find.	Some pronouns and verbs in the wrong form cause confusion. Noticeable errors do not interfere with reading.

✚ **Presentation**   The cause-and-effect report is neat and legible.

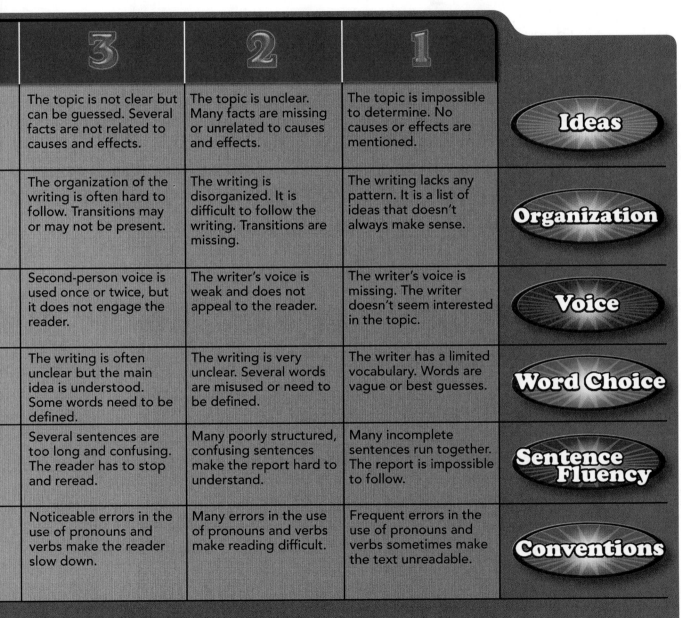

3	2	1	
The topic is not clear but can be guessed. Several facts are not related to causes and effects.	The topic is unclear. Many facts are missing or unrelated to causes and effects.	The topic is impossible to determine. No causes or effects are mentioned.	Ideas
The organization of the writing is often hard to follow. Transitions may or may not be present.	The writing is disorganized. It is difficult to follow the writing. Transitions are missing.	The writing lacks any pattern. It is a list of ideas that doesn't always make sense.	Organization
Second-person voice is used once or twice, but it does not engage the reader.	The writer's voice is weak and does not appeal to the reader.	The writer's voice is missing. The writer doesn't seem interested in the topic.	Voice
The writing is often unclear but the main idea is understood. Some words need to be defined.	The writing is very unclear. Several words are misused or need to be defined.	The writer has a limited vocabulary. Words are vague or best guesses.	Word Choice
Several sentences are too long and confusing. The reader has to stop and reread.	Many poorly structured, confusing sentences make the report hard to understand.	Many incomplete sentences run together. The report is impossible to follow.	Sentence Fluency
Noticeable errors in the use of pronouns and verbs make the reader slow down.	Many errors in the use of pronouns and verbs make reading difficult.	Frequent errors in the use of pronouns and verbs sometimes make the text unreadable.	Conventions

See Appendix B for 4-, 5-, and 6-point informative/explanatory rubrics.

Cause-and-Effect Report

Using the Rubric to Study the Model

Did you notice that the model on page 155 points out some key elements of a cause-and-effect report? As she wrote "Understanding the Barrier Islands," Julia Tazzi used these elements to help with her report. She also used the 6-point rubric on pages 156–157 to plan, draft, revise, and edit her writing. A rubric is a great tool for evaluating writing during the writing process.

Now let's use the same rubric to score the model. To do this, we'll focus on each trait separately, starting with Ideas. We'll use the top descriptor for each trait (column 6), along with examples from the model, to help us understand how the traits work together. How would you score Julia on each trait?

- **The topic is focused and supported by credible sources.**
- **Relevant facts support and explain causes and effects.**

Julia stays with one topic throughout the essay and uses relevant facts to explain the cause-and-effect relationships. One fact that stood out for me was the need to move the Cape Hatteras Lighthouse. Erosion must have really washed away the beach around it! I bet the lighthouse was hard to move, too!

[from the writing model]

Erosion has caused many changes in the islands. For example, the Cape Hatteras Lighthouse had to be moved. The beach had eroded, so in 1999, the lighthouse was moved about one-half mile inland.

Organization

- The report is organized in a clear cause-and-effect pattern.
- Transitions clarify relationships among causes and effects.

Julia uses a logical pattern for cause and effect, stating the causes first and then the effects. Transitions, such as *As they flooded over the beaches*, help me understand how the causes and effects are related.

[from the writing model]

At the end of the ice age, the air warmed and the glaciers melted. The melting ice caused rivers and streams to rise. As they flooded over the beaches, they carried sand and sediment to shallow areas just off the Atlantic coast.

Voice

- Second-person voice connects immediately and consistently with the reader.
- The voice enhances the writing.

Julia begins with fascinating information about the barrier islands. She ends her first paragraph with a question in second-person point of view. I felt like she was addressing me directly, which helped me feel involved with her topic.

[from the writing model]

The barrier islands are called the "children of the sea." Born after the last ice age, they stretch along the Atlantic coast in long, narrow chains. Some of these chains extend for 100 miles or more. The islands have been around for nearly 18 centuries, but did you know they may not last forever?

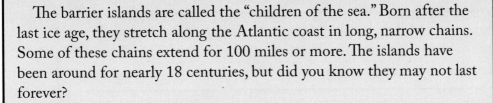

Word Choice

- **Precise language and specific vocabulary are used and, where necessary, defined.**

Julia makes sure she is precise in her word choice, using the vocabulary that best describes the barrier islands and what is happening to them. She even defines words her readers might not be familiar with, which helps me fully understand her report.

[from the writing model]

Since communities want to save their islands, they try to stop the erosion with "beach nourishment." This involves dumping many truckloads of sand on eroding beaches. However, this helps only for a while. The erosion starts up again because there are no dunes to break the wind or plants to hold the sand in place. The new sand is soon washed away. As a result, the islands continue to be in danger.

Sentence Fluency

- **All sentences are clearly written and logically structured. They flow smoothly.**

Julia uses easy-to-understand sentences, not long, confusing ones. If she had connected each sentence below with *and,* I would have quit reading before I got to the end. The shorter, clearer sentences are much easier to read, and they keep me interested.

[from the writing model]

The barrier islands have broad beaches and dunes on the ocean side. They have mud flats and salt marshes on the mainland side. This low, sandy structure is vulnerable to erosion.

Conventions

- **Correct forms of pronouns and verbs are used.**
- **The writer's strong knowledge of conventions strengthens the writing.**

The spelling, punctuation, and capitalization are all correct in this report. Notice how Julia chooses the correct pronouns—*who* and *them*—and uses the correct verb forms.

[from the writing model]

Natural erosion isn't the only danger to these islands. People who enjoy the beach love to vacation on the barrier islands.
To build houses, hotels, and roads for them, developers flatten the dunes.

✛Presentation The cause-and-effect report is neat and legible.

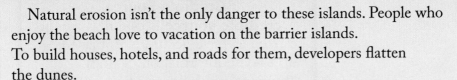

Now I'm going to write a cause-and-effect report! I'll use the rubric and good writing strategies to help me. Follow along and learn with me.

Prewrite

Focus on **Ideas**

The Rubric Says　The topic is focused and supported by credible sources.

Writing Strategy　Use the Internet to find credible sources of information on the topic.

Writer's Term

Credible Source
A **credible source** is one that can be trusted to have accurate, unbiased, up-to-date information. School librarians can help you find credible sources if you need guidance.

When our teacher asked us to write a cause-and-effect report, I thought about what I wanted to do. Then I zeroed in on the topic of irrigation in Nevada. I got interested in that subject last year when I visited my cousins, who live in Nevada. It was fun to stay on their farm and learn about a completely different way of life!

I wanted to do some of my research on the Internet. My teacher told us that some websites might not be good. Some sites are too complicated for me to understand. Other sites are out of date. Our librarian says we can trust a website run by a government agency, most news organizations, an encyclopedia, or an educational organization (like a university or a museum).

I found two credible sources for my topic on the Internet.

Then I carefully took notes from my sources. I put the notes for each source on a separate sheet of paper. You can see some of my notes below. I found other sources, too, so I will have more pages of notes for my report.

I might not use all the facts in these notes. I will choose the ones that best explain the causes and effects in my report.

Notes From the US Geological Survey—Water Science for Schools: Irrigation Water Use

http://www.usgs.gov

1. About 60 percent of the world's fresh water is used for irrigation.
2. About 40 percent of the fresh water used in the United States is used to irrigate crops.
3. Farms could not feed the world without irrigation from rivers, lakes, reservoirs, and wells.
4. Of the water used for flood irrigation, one half is lost through evaporation or in transit (leaking pipes).

Notes From Colorado River Water Users Association: Nevada

http://www.crwua.org/ColoradoRiver/MemberStates/Nevada.aspx

1. Nevada gets less rainfall than any other state, an average of 9 inches a year.
2. Building Hoover Dam on the Colorado River helped Nevada with water supply and hydroelectric power.
3. Agriculture uses 75 percent of the water in Nevada.
4. Water conservation is common and necessary in Nevada.

Apply

Choose a topic that interests you and gather information about it from credible sources, including the Internet. Take notes on what you read.

Prewrite

Focus on Organization

The Rubric Says The report is organized in a clear cause-and-effect pattern.

Writing Strategy Make a Cause-and-Effect Chain to organize your notes.

As I looked over my notes, I noticed how some things cause other things. For example, Nevada gets little rain, so the farmers have to use irrigation.

The rubric reminds me to organize my report into a cause-and-effect pattern. This will help me show what causes what. I know that sometimes one cause has several effects, like when a storm blows down trees, causes rivers to overflow, and brings lightning.

Other times, several causes lead to the same effect. One example I can think of is when you pay attention in class, read the assigned chapters, and do your homework. What's the effect? You get good grades! (You also learn more, of course!)

A Cause-and-Effect Chain shows how events connect. The effect of one event can become the cause of the next event. The events link together in a chain.

You can see part of my chain on the next page.

Writer's Term

Cause-and-Effect Chain
A **Cause-and-Effect Chain** shows actions and their results. One effect can have several causes, and one cause can have several effects.

Cause-and-Effect Chain

Cause

Not enough rain falls in the U.S. where many crops are grown.

Effect/Cause

About 40% of fresh water in the U.S. is used for irrigation.

Effect/Cause

About half of the water used in flood irrigation is lost.

Effect/Cause

Farmers in Nevada and other states are turning to more efficient irrigation methods.

Effect

Drip irrigation is being used for fruits and vegetables.

Effect

Spray irrigation is being used on large farms.

Reflect

Did Justin include enough cause-and-effect relationships to write a logical report?

Apply

Organize your notes into a Cause-and-Effect Chain. Make sure you show the relationships between causes and effects.

Draft

The Rubric Says The report is organized in a clear cause-and-effect pattern.

Writing Strategy Introduce the topic and present causes and effects in a logical order.

Now it's time to start writing. I'll use my Cause-and-Effect Chain to show how each cause leads to an effect. I'll add facts and details along the way.

I'll also think of a way to begin that grabs the attention of my audience— my classmates, in this case. They may not have to irrigate crops, but natural resources like water are important to everyone. I'll start with an introduction that gets them thinking about how we use our water. Then I'll include interesting facts that will keep them reading.

I'll do my best with spelling, punctuation, and grammar now and check for mistakes when I edit my draft.

You can read the beginning of my draft on the next page.

[DRAFT]

[interesting introduction] Almost 40 percent of the fresh water in the United States is used in a special way. It's not used for drinking or baths or swimming pools. It's used for irrigation! Many areas in the United States don't get enough rainfall to grow crops, so the land must be irrigated.

[cause] Most irrigation is in the western states. Water is scarce there. Nevada gets less rainfall than any other state. Farmers in nevada must depend on irrigation to grow their crops. [effect]

The oldest and cheapest type of irrigation is flood irrigation. However, about half of the water used in this type of irrigation evaporates or runs off the feelds. To keep water from running off there fields, farmers whom live in hilly areas make their feelds as level as possible. They also release water at intervals. This reduces runoff, too. In addition, some farmers capture the runoff in ponds. There it is stored for they to use again. [cause]

To conserve water, farmers across the West have experimented with irrigation. Many of they now use more efficient methods. [effect]

Reflect

What do you think? How has the Cause-and-Effect Chain helped Justin draft his report? Does the order in which he presents his facts make sense to you?

Apply

Write a draft of your report using your Cause-and-Effect Chain as a guide. Grab your reader's attention with an interesting fact right at the beginning.

Revise

Focus on **Voice**

The Rubric Says   Second-person voice connects immediately and consistently with the reader. The voice enhances the writing.

Writing Strategy   Speak directly to the reader.

When you write a report, you want to pull the reader right in. The rubric reminds me that this is easy to do by addressing the reader directly with *you*—the second-person point of view. But I need to remember to write most of my report in third-person point of view to present the information that I researched. Look at the first paragraph where I added a second-person point of view. Does it sound like I'm talking directly to my reader now?

[DRAFT]

Do you know how ← [added second-person point of view]

∧Almost 40 percent of the fresh water in the United States is used ~~in a special way~~. It's not used for drinking or baths or swimming pools. It's used for irrigation! Many areas in the United States don't get enough rainfall to grow crops, so the land must be irrigated.

Apply

Try adding second-person point of view to connect directly with your reader.

The Rubric Says	Precise language and specific vocabulary are used and, where necessary, defined.
Writing Strategy	Use specific words. Define them, if necessary.

When you write a report, you have to make sure all of your explanations are clear so the reader understands exactly what you are talking about. The rubric tells me that I should use precise language. Sometimes vocabulary is very specific to the topic and may be unfamiliar to the audience. If I have words like that, I should be sure to define them in my writing. Notice that I added a sentence to explain flood irrigation.

[DRAFT]

The oldest and cheapest type of irrigation is flood irrigation. In this method, water is allowed to flow along rows of plants.

However, about half of the water used in this type of irrigation evaporates or runs off the feelds.

[defined specific language]

Reflect

How does using precise language strengthen Justin's writing? How does adding a definition improve the report?

Apply

Add more precise language to your report and define any new terms for the reader.

Revise

Focus on Sentence Fluency

The Rubric Says All sentences are clearly written and logically structured. They flow smoothly.

Writing Strategy Rewrite long, confusing sentences.

I read my draft to my friend, Eric. He can always tell when something isn't quite clear. He pointed out the long, confusing sentence in this paragraph. So I divided it into three sentences! Now it's easier to read and understand, don't you think? Long sentences can confuse readers, so I'm glad I revised this section for clarity.

[DRAFT]

Many farmers, including those in Nevada, now uses drip irrigation for fruits and vegetables. The water runs through plastic pipes laid along crop rows or buried in the soil and holes in the pipes allow the water to drip directly into the soil and the water soaks into the ground instead of running off or evaporating.

[rewrote long sentence]

Apply

Do you have any long, confusing sentences in your report? If you do, rewrite them to make them clearer and easier to understand.

The Rubric Says	Correct forms of pronouns and verbs are used.
Writing Strategy	Make sure subject and object pronouns are used correctly and that irregular verbs are in the correct form.

Writer's Term

Subject and Object Pronouns
A **subject pronoun** takes the place of the subject in a sentence. An **object pronoun** replaces the object of a verb or a preposition.

This is the time to check spelling, capitalization, punctuation, and grammar. I'll also make sure I used irregular verbs and subject and object pronouns correctly. When to use *who* and *whom* can be confusing, so I'll look for those errors, too.

[DRAFT]

[changed to a subject pronoun]

or runs off the ~~feelds~~ fields. To keep water from running off ~~there~~ their fields, farmers ~~whom~~ who live in hilly areas make their ~~feelds~~ fields as level as possible. They also release water at intervals. This reduces runoff, too. In addition, some farmers capture the runoff in ponds. There it is stored for ~~they~~ them to use again.

[changed to an object pronoun]

Reflect

Is Justin's report clear and interesting? Are the sentences easy to read and understand? Are the subject and object pronouns and irregular verbs correct?

Apply

Conventions

Edit your draft for spelling, punctuation, and capitalization errors. Correct any problems with subject and object pronouns and irregular verbs.

For more practice fixing subject and object pronouns and irregular verbs, use the exercises on the next two pages.

Subject and Object Pronouns

Know the Rule

A **subject pronoun** takes the place of the subject in a sentence.
> **Example: Leanne** lives near Hoover Dam.
> **She** lives near Hoover Dam.

An **object pronoun** replaces the object of a verb or a preposition.
> **Example:** The dam helps **farmers** irrigate.
> The dam helps **them** irrigate.

Use *who* as a subject pronoun. Use *whom* as an object pronoun.
> **Example:** Herbert Hoover, **who** was president then, made a speech.
> He talked to farmers for **whom** the dam would make a huge difference. (*Who* is the subject of the verb *was. Whom* is the object of the preposition *for.*)

Practice the Rule

Number a separate piece of paper 1–10. Choose the correct pronoun for each sentence and write it on your paper. Add **S** if you chose a subject pronoun or **O** if you chose an object pronoun.

1. People (who/whom) live in the desert value water.
2. (I/me) grew up in the Mojave Desert in Nevada.
3. Hoover Dam was built near (us/we) in the early 1930s.
4. For (who/whom) was Hoover Dam built?
5. It was built for all of (we/us) in the Southwest.
6. My family and (I/me) went to see Hoover Dam last year.
7. The tour guide told (we/us) that the dam is a National Historic Landmark.
8. The Colorado River runs through the turbines in the dam, and (they/them) can handle all that water.
9. The people of Nevada benefit from the dam as it creates power for (them/they).
10. (Whom/Who) knew moving water could be so powerful and helpful?

Irregular Verbs

Know the Rule

Many verbs are **irregular;** they do not add *-ed* in the past tense. Here are some irregular verbs:

Present	Past	With *has, had,* or *have*
eat	ate	eaten
hear	heard	heard
teach	taught	taught
read	read	read
write	wrote	written

Example: We **eat** the same pizza every Friday night.
We now have **eaten** mushroom pizza ten weeks in a row!

Practice the Rule

On a separate piece of paper, rewrite the following sentences using the correct form of the verb in parentheses.

1. Last year, Mr. Li (read) a lot of books about Earth's water supply.
2. He had (hear) that the water supply is very limited in some places.
3. Water was on his mind because during last year's flood we only (drink) water after we had boiled it.
4. The author of Mr. Li's book (write) that of all the water on Earth, more than 97 percent is salt water.
5. My science teacher (teach) us that salt water is poisonous if you drink too much of it.
6. I have (swim) in salt water, but I didn't know that humans can't survive by drinking it.
7. Since he read the book, Mr. Li has (write) some letters to the newspaper about the world's water supply.
8. It's a topic he has (think) about a lot.
9. When we (eat) dinner at his house, he talked about it at great length.
10. I've (read) some books about the subject myself.

Publish + Presentation

Publishing Strategy   Add your cause-and-effect report to the class binder.

Presentation Strategy   Neatly handwrite or type the report.

Now it's time to publish my cause-and-effect report! I could submit it to a science website. But I think I'll add my report to the science binder my class is putting together. Other people will read my report, so it has to be neatly handwritten, or, better yet, neatly word-processed. I'll keep in mind, too, that the margins have to be wide enough for the three-ring binder. Before I publish my work, I'll check it one more time using this final checklist.

My Final Checklist

Did I—

✔ make sure all the subject and object pronouns are correct?

✔ check that I used the correct forms of irregular verbs?

✔ make sure my report is neat and legible?

✔ make sure I used appropriate margins?

Apply

Make a checklist to check your own cause-and-effect report. Then make a final copy to publish.

Why Are Nevada's Crops Irrigated?

by Justin

Do you know how almost 40 percent of the fresh water in the United States is used? It's not used for drinking or baths or swimming pools. It's used for irrigation! Many areas in the United States don't get enough rainfall to grow crops. That land must be irrigated.

Most irrigation is in the Western states because water is scarce there. Nevada gets less rainfall than any other state, so farmers in Nevada must depend on irrigation to grow their crops. In Nevada, 67 percent of all cropland requires irrigation. In fact, the U.S. government's first irrigation project was in Nevada.

The oldest and cheapest type of irrigation is flood irrigation. In this method, water is allowed to flow along rows of plants. However, about half of the water used in this type of irrigation evaporates or runs off the fields. To keep water from running off their fields, farmers who live in hilly areas make their fields as level as possible. They also release water at intervals. This reduces runoff, too. In addition, some farmers capture the runoff in ponds. There it is stored for them to use again.

To conserve water, farmers across the West have experimented with other methods of irrigation. Many of them now use more efficient methods. Farmers who have to deal with the Nevada desert must be especially careful. Nevada potato farmers, in particular, need to irrigate their fields. Potatoes need seven times more water than crops like wheat!

Many farmers, including those in Nevada, now use drip irrigation for fruits and vegetables. The water runs through plastic pipes laid along crop rows or buried in the soil. Holes in the pipes allow the water to drip directly into the soil. The water soaks into the ground instead of running off or evaporating.

Spray irrigation is used on many large farms. When older machinery is used, most of the water evaporates into the air because water shoots through the air to the ground. Newer machinery gently sprays water from a hanging pipe onto the ground. Little of it evaporates. Farmers who use the newer machinery conserve water. They can increase their irrigation efficiency from 60 percent to 90 percent.

In Nevada, if you want to grow crops, you must irrigate!

Reflect

How does Justin's report look? Check the writing against the rubric. Be sure to use the rubric to check your own writing, too!

What's a Research Report?

To write a research report, a writer gathers information from multiple credible and reliable sources, organizes it, and explains the main points to readers. This kind of writing is a challenge, but I like the idea of gathering facts from different sources and putting them together like a puzzle!

What's in a Research Report?

Multiple and Credible Sources
Hey, there's a reason they call it a research report! I need to do plenty of research to really understand my topic. And I should mix up my sources instead of relying on just one type of information, such as encyclopedia articles.

Organization
With all the information I'll be gathering, organization will be very important. I have to focus on the topic and organize all the main points in a logical way. I'll need good supporting details and a strong conclusion to pull it all together.

Lively Writing
It's easy to slip into dull language when you're writing something factual. I'm going to watch out for that! I want to use a variety of interesting and strong sentences to keep my writing lively.

Fully Cited Sources
It's important that I fully cite the sources for my research report. After all, I'm presenting factual information. Using another person's words or information without giving credit is plagiarism, a serious offense.

Why write a Research Report?

There are many good reasons to write a research report. I'm still thinking about why I want to do this kind of writing. Here are some possible reasons.

Information

A good research report contains tons of valuable information. Readers can learn a lot from this kind of report.

Mastery

I can learn a lot by reading an article or a chapter about a subject, but researching a topic myself is even better! Gathering facts and putting everything together helps me really absorb the information and make it my own.

Going Deeper

Sometimes I'm interested in a topic, but I don't really know much about it. Writing a research report can help me get deeper into a subject. I might find out new things about that particular topic. My research could help me understand a subject better or lead me to other fascinating topics.

Linking Informative/Explanatory Writing Traits to a Research Report

In this chapter, you will choose a topic to research thoroughly, and then explain what you have learned. This type of informative/explanatory writing is called a research report. Justin will guide you through the stages of the writing process: Prewrite, Draft, Revise, Edit, and Publish. In each stage, Justin will show you important writing strategies that are linked to the Informative/Explanatory Writing Traits below.

Informative/Explanatory Writing Traits

- a clear, focused topic
- credible, engaging facts and details that support and develop the topic

- information that is organized logically into a strong introduction, body, and conclusion
- transitions that clarify relationships between ideas

- a voice and tone that are appropriate for the purpose and audience

- language that is precise and concise
- domain-specific vocabulary that is used correctly and explained as necessary

- sentences that vary in length and flow smoothly

- no or few errors in grammar, usage, mechanics, and spelling

Before you write, read Peter Nuan's research report on the next three pages. Then use the research report rubric on pages 182–183 to decide how well he did. (You might want to look back at What's in a Research Report? on page 176, too!)

Digging Into Backyard Archaeology

by Peter Nuan

Lively writing

With a toothbrush, Jan Haas carefully removed dirt from a little lump in her hand. The object under the dirt glinted in the sunlight. Was it a piece of gold jewelry? She continued to brush off the soil hiding the object. The shape became clear. It was round and fairly flat. Then she saw a design. Soon it was clear that the object was a tarnished brass button.

It had been buried six inches deep in Jan's backyard in Baltimore, Maryland. She dug it up near an old washhouse. The washhouse had been built in the mid-1700s. Later, Jan learned the button was from the Colonial period.

As a backyard archaeologist, Jan was pleased with her find. Backyard archaeologists are amateurs. Like the professionals, they search for and study objects made by people long ago.

Organization—main point

Across America, people like Jan Haas are digging up their backyards. They hope to find treasures. These treasures will probably not be gold or diamonds. More likely, they will be old buttons or chipped glass. They are still valuable, though. They tell about an area's history and culture. A dig in the backyards of Alexandria, Virginia, uncovered items from more than a century ago. They included marbles, medicine bottles, and pottery shards. Before the Civil War, free African American people lived in the area. "By studying these artifacts, we were able to trace the development of this neighborhood and the lifestyles of its inhabitants," said the city's archaeologist, Pamela J. Cressey, Ph.D.

Archaeologists urge people who dig as a hobby to follow a few guidelines. If amateurs just start digging, they may destroy valuable old objects.

First, property owners should research their site. Town records may provide facts about former owners. Many libraries and museums may have collections of news clippings and photos. Information about early Native American groups living in the region is usually available at history museums.

Organization—supporting details

Organization—main point

Backyard archaeologists should then contact authorities and explain what they have learned about the site. The state archaeologist is a good person to contact. Other possible contacts are historical societies and college archaeology departments. An expert will often arrange a survey of the site.

Some backyard sites contain valuable objects. Unless such a site is in danger of being destroyed, archaeologists usually ask property owners not to dig there. They believe the past should be left untouched so it will be preserved for the future. If the site is in danger, the archaeologists may conduct a dig. They often ask the property owner to help.

Whatever diggers find at the site belongs to the property owners. Some backyard archaeologists donate the items to a historical society or museum. There, trained professionals can catalog and care for the items. Objects removed from the ground may dry out, rot, or get moldy. Professionals know how to preserve these objects. They can keep them safe for study and display.

Lively writing

Some backyard archaeologists get started by volunteering at a dig site. Several government agencies offer a chance to work in the field. For example, Passport in Time (PIT) is a volunteer program of the U.S. Forest Service. Its aim is to preserve landmarks and historical sites in national forests. PIT volunteers work with archaeologists on sites around the country. Linda Ruys volunteered at a PIT site in Idaho. She learned a lot about the people of the past—and made friends in the present! "The words 'kindred spirits' and 'family' were repeated often in a group that had just met," she said. She found joy in working with these people. "We understood our connectedness as human beings—a life lesson worth learning."

Organization—main point

School programs are another place to learn the basics of archaeology. Sixth-grade students at Blake Middle School in Medfield, Massachusetts, learn through a hands-on experience. Each fall they work in teams on an old trash heap owned by a local family. They have found old nails, jars, and pieces of an old toy bank.

Organization—supporting details

The students learn to use the correct tools and methods. They are shown how to mark the site into square plots. They learn how to properly dig with a trowel. They also practice sifting buckets of soil through screens. Any objects in the soil remain on the screen while the dirt falls through. Finally, they learn to record what they find and where they find it.

Another place to learn about archaeology is a website called "Dr. Dig." This Web site is about archaeology in general, but the advice on the site can help backyard archaeologists, too. For example, Dr. Dig suggests using tools that fit the location and the job in order to avoid damaging artifacts. Dr. Dig once used a tongue depressor to excavate some flint! "As a general rule," says Dr. Dig, "small tools are used to uncover small artifacts, large-scale tools for large artifacts." He also cautions amateurs to contact their local utility companies before starting to dig. This will protect any buried wires on their property.

Archaeology requires patience and attention to detail. It requires caring about the past and the future. Many backyard archaeologists love their hobby for these reasons. Some professional archaeologists worry about what might be lost if the amateurs are not careful. However, amateurs can learn how to dig the right way by consulting experts and working as volunteers in the field. As Dr. Dig might say to backyard archaeologists, every tarnished button counts, so be careful!

Organization—strong conclusion

Works Consulted

"Archaeology." *Encyclopedia Britannica*. 2007 ed.

Ask Dr. Dig. DIG Magazine. 2006, accessed April 5, 2012, http://www.digonsite.com/drdig.

Atkin, Ross. "Kids dig history." *Christian Science Monitor*. 23 Nov. 1999: 22.

Haas, Jan. Personal interview. 12 Sept. 2001.

Kersting, Jane. "The PIT Experience: Life Lessons and So Much More." *Passport in Time*. 6 Dec. 2006, accessed April 6, 2012, http://www.passportintime.com.

Proeller, Marie. "Backyard Archaeology." *Country Living*. Aug. 1998: 40.

Multiple and varied sources, fully cited

Rubric

Use this 6-point rubric to plan and score a research report.

	6	5	4
Ideas	The report focuses on one clearly defined, well-researched topic. Relevant facts and concrete details develop the topic thoroughly.	The report focuses on one topic. Most details and facts are relevant to the topic.	The report focuses on one topic, but it may be too narrow or broad. Some details are irrelevant or lacking.
Organization	The structure of the writing is perfect for the topic and enhances the reader's understanding. A thoughtful conclusion follows from the information presented.	The structure of the writing works well. The conclusion follows logically from the information presented.	The structure of the writing is easy to follow. The conclusion works.
Voice	Active voice connects to the reader. It is clear the writer cares about the topic.	The writer's knowledge of the topic engages the reader. Active voice is used throughout.	Active voice is used inconsistently at times. The writer occasionally sounds indifferent to the topic.
Word Choice	Domain-specific content vocabulary informs the reader about the topic and is clearly defined.	Some domain-specific content vocabulary words are used and defined.	Domain-specific content vocabulary words are used, but several are not defined.
Sentence Fluency	Sentences are lively and highly varied in length and structure. They move the reader along.	There is noticeable variety in sentence length and style. The writing is easy to read.	There is some variety in sentence length and style. The writing is easy to read.
Conventions	The report uses a variety of nouns correctly. It is well edited and ready to publish.	A variety of nouns are used correctly. A few errors are present, but they are hard to spot.	Noticeable errors with nouns may distract the reader.
✚ Presentation	Media, such as illustrations and sound, are all well integrated into the report.		

3	2	1	
The topic is not clearly stated and has to be guessed. Several details are irrelevant or poorly researched.	The topic is unclear and hard to guess. Most details are irrelevant or poorly researched.	The report is not focused on a topic. Facts and details read like an unconnected list.	**Ideas**
Parts of the report are hard to follow. The conclusion could be improved.	The reader often feels lost. The writing is out of order. The conclusion is missing or needs work.	The writing is extremely difficult to follow. The report lacks an opening or a conclusion.	**Organization**
The writer's voice fades in and out. Active voice is used inconsistently.	The writer's interest in the topic rarely comes through. Many sentences should be in the active voice.	It sounds like the writer doesn't care about the topic. Sentences are incorrect or in the passive voice.	**Voice**
A lack of domain-specific words makes it difficult for the reader to understand the topic. Many unfamiliar words are not defined.	Many words are unclear. Poorly defined terms make it hard for the reader to understand the report.	The writer's words are vague and confusing. The reader cannot understand the report.	**Word Choice**
Too many sentences are similar in length and structure. Some are fragments or run-on sentences.	Many sentences are poorly written and repetitious. Fragments, run-ons, and incomplete sentences are present.	The writing lacks complete sentences. Sentences run together and are hard to read.	**Sentence Fluency**
Several noticeable errors with nouns may affect the meaning.	Many errors with nouns interfere with the meaning. Reading takes effort.	The writer struggles with the correct use of nouns. The errors continually interfere with reading.	**Conventions**

See Appendix B for 4-, 5-, and 6-point informative/explanatory rubrics.

Research Report
Using the Rubric to Study the Model

Did you notice that the model on pages 179–181 points out some key elements of a research report? As he wrote "Digging Into Backyard Archaeology," Peter Nuan used these elements to help him write a report. He also used the 6-point rubric on pages 182–183 to plan, draft, revise, and edit the writing. A rubric is a great tool for evaluating writing during the writing process.

Now let's use the same rubric to score the model. To do this, we'll focus on each trait separately, starting with Ideas. We'll use the top descriptor for each trait (column 6), along with examples from the model, to help us understand how the traits work together. How would you score Peter on each trait?

Ideas

- **The report focuses on one clearly defined, well-researched topic.**
- **Relevant facts and concrete details develop the topic thoroughly.**

Peter sticks to one very clear topic: amateur archeologists. The facts and details he includes are accurate and relevant to his topic. In these sentences, he gives some tips for amateur archaeologists.

[from the writing model]

First, property owners should research their site. Town records may provide facts about former owners. Many libraries and museums may have collections of news clippings and photos. Information about early Native American groups living in the region is usually available at history museums.

Organization

- The structure of the writing is perfect for the topic and enhances the reader's understanding.
- A thoughtful conclusion follows from the information presented.

Peter organizes his writing perfectly. He opens with an attention-grabbing introduction, includes one or two paragraphs about each of his main points, and then neatly wraps up his report with a strong conclusion. Notice how his conclusion picks up the ideas of his report and wraps them up in an engaging way.

[from the writing model]

However, amateurs can learn how to dig the right way by consulting experts and working as volunteers in the field. As Dr. Dig might say to backyard archaeologists, every tarnished button counts, so be careful!

Voice

- Active voice connects to the reader.
- It is clear the writer cares about the topic.

Peter uses active voice to make the reader feel connected to the information. He could have said, "Patience and attention to detail are required for archaeology. Caring about the past and future are also required." Instead, he chose to make stronger statements in the active voice. You can see, too, that he cares about his topic and about amateur archaeologists learning to do it right.

[from the writing model]

Archaeology requires patience and attention to detail. It requires caring about the past and the future. Many backyard archaeologists love their hobby for these reasons. Some professional archaeologists worry about what might be lost if the amateurs are not careful. However, amateurs can learn how to dig the right way by consulting experts and working as volunteers in the field. As Dr. Dig might say to backyard archaeologists, every tarnished button counts, so be careful!

Word Choice

- Domain-specific content vocabulary informs the reader about the topic and is clearly defined.

For the report to offer clear explanations to the reader, the language has to be accurate and describe the details well. When Peter uses a domain-specific word, he gives a detailed explanation to make sure the reader knows what it means.

[from the writing model]

Several government agencies offer a chance to work in the field. For example, Passport in Time (PIT) is a volunteer program of the U.S. Forest Service. Its aim is to preserve landmarks and historical sites in national forests. PIT volunteers work with archaeologists on sites around the country.

Sentence Fluency

- Sentences are lively and highly varied in length and structure. They move the reader along.

Peter does a good job of making his sentences lively. Look at how he does it in the following paragraphs. He uses short sentences and long sentences. Some sentences start with dependent clauses; some do not. Peter mixes up the structure of his sentences, too, using different patterns throughout the report.

[from the writing model]

It had been buried six inches deep in Jan's backyard in Baltimore, Maryland. She dug it up near an old washhouse. The washhouse had been built in the mid-1700s. Later, Jan learned the button was from the Colonial period.

As a backyard archaeologist, Jan was pleased with her find. Backyard archaeologists are amateurs. Like the professionals, they search for and study objects made by people long ago.

Conventions

- The report uses a variety of nouns correctly.
- It is well edited and ready to publish.

I couldn't find any mistakes in spelling, punctuation, or capitalization in Peter's report. He even wrote all the proper nouns and proper adjectives correctly!

[from the writing model]

A dig in the backyards of Alexandria, Virginia, uncovered items from more than a century ago. They included marbles, medicine bottles, and pottery shards. Before the Civil War, free African American people lived in the area. "By studying these artifacts, we were able to trace the development of this neighborhood and the lifestyles of its inhabitants," said the city's archaeologist, Pamela J. Cressey, Ph.D.

✛Presentation Media, such as illustrations and sound, are all well integrated into the report.

My Turn!

I'm going to write a research report on my own topic. With the help of the rubric and good writing strategies, I think I'll write a good one. Follow along and see how I do it!

Prewrite

Focus on Ideas

The Rubric Says	The report focuses on one clearly defined, well-researched topic.
Writing Strategy	Use an encyclopedia and at least two other sources to research the topic.

As soon as I heard we were going to write research reports, I thought of India because I love Indian food! I figured there was a lot about India that would be interesting to my classmates. They will be my audience.

When I looked up the word *India* in an encyclopedia, I found a long list of topics. They included India's people, geography, climate, natural resources, religions, history, government—the list went on and on. I needed to narrow my topic!

I noticed there was a section about Indian food. Maybe I could focus on just that area. But then I realized that even Indian food was too broad a topic for my report. There are so many kinds!

I learned from the encyclopedia that people in different parts of India eat different dishes. I decided to narrow my topic to regional foods of India. I think my classmates will find that interesting. They love anything that has to do with food!

In addition to the encyclopedia, I checked two other credible sources. As I read, I took notes on note cards. Each card had one piece of information and its source. Here are two of my note cards.

Regional Food in India—South India

source: Voros, Sharon. "Fare of the Country; The Vegetarian Snacks of South India." http://query.nytimes.com (April 19, 2012)

foods made from rice:

"Idlis, which resemble spongy dumplings, are always served in pairs. Dosas are crepelike pancakes served neatly rolled."

Regional Food in India—Introduction

source: Kanitkar, V. P. Indian Food and Drink. New York: The Bookwright Press, 1987.

Religion and climate are two things that determine food habits in each region.

Apply

Choose a topic and look it up in the encyclopedia. Narrow the topic. Then check two more reliable sources and start making note cards.

Prewrite

The Rubric Says   The structure of the writing is perfect for the topic and enhances the reader's understanding.

Writing Strategy   Make an outline to organize your notes.

The best way to organize my report is to organize my notes, right? I considered several different graphic organizers and decided to use an Outline to organize the body of my report. That way, I can put details under the main points. Then I'll write one or two paragraphs about each main point and its details. I'll write the introduction and conclusion of my report later.

To get started, I made a separate pile of note cards for each main point. Then I wrote the Outline you see on the next page.

Writer's Term

Outline

An **Outline** organizes notes by main points and supporting details. Each main point has a Roman numeral. The supporting details under each main point have capital letters. Any information listed under a supporting detail gets a number.

Outline

Regional Food in India

I. Regional foods are determined by many things.
  A. One main influence is religion.
    1. Most people are vegetarian Hindus.
    2. Immigrants from other religions who eat meat influence the Hindu diet.
  B. India's many different climates also affect food production.
II. The North has a strong Muslim influence.
  A. Muslims live in the North.
    1. They eat lamb, chicken, beef, and fish.
    2. Many do not eat pork.
  B. Dates, nuts, and milk are used in sweets (desserts).
  C. Hindu bread and vegetarian dishes are also common.
III. Food in the South has a more traditional Hindu style.
  A. Rice is cooked in many ways.
  B. Two popular dishes are dosas and idlis.
  C. Vegetables served with rice include soupy dishes made from peas or beans.
IV. Coastal Indian food has many influences.
  A. Fish dishes are common and varied.
  B. They include carp with chilies, prawns with mustard seed, and fish curry.
  C. Some foods are made with coconut.

Reflect

How will the Outline help Justin write his research report?

Apply

Look through your note cards. Then organize your notes into an Outline.

Draft

Focus on **Voice**

The Rubric Says	Active voice connects to the reader. It is clear the writer cares about the topic.
Writing Strategy	Use active voice.

Writer's Term

Active Voice and Passive Voice
A verb is in **active voice** if the subject of the sentence is doing the action. A verb is in **passive voice** if the subject is being acted upon.
Active Voice: **George ate his lunch.**
Passive Voice: **The lunch was eaten by George.**

Now I'll write one or two paragraphs for each point in my Outline. This will be the body of my report. I'll make sure there's plenty of good information to interest my audience.

I know this is a draft and I will be revising it. But I can start now to think about how I want my voice to sound. In a report, I want my information to sound strong, like I know what I'm talking about. Active voice will help me do that.

Later I'll add an engaging introduction and a strong conclusion. I'll also watch out for subject-verb agreement. Look at the start of my draft on the next page.

[DRAFT]

The foods people eat in each region of India are determined by [active voice] many things. Religion is a major factor. In India, 80 percent of the population is hindu, and strict hindus are vegetarians and do not eat meat. Over the centuries, Immigrants whom practice other religions have come to India. Many of these people do eat meat. They have influenced the traditional hindu diet in some places.

Another big thing is climate. The type of food production of a region is affected by the climate there. For example, rice is grown mostly in the tropical south and the rainy northeast (I heard that people's personalities can change during the long monsoon season), and wheat is an important crop in the dry northern plains.

[active voice] The North has a strong muslim influence. Muslims eat lamb, chicken, beef, and fish but not pork. One favorite dish is lamb kebab. Lamb kebab is pieces of mildly spiced meat roasted on skewers. Another favorite is tandoori chicken, spiced chicken cooked in a clay oven. Dates, nuts, and milk are in many deserts called milk sweets. The milk comes from water buffalos. They are the main source of milk in India. Kheer is a milk sweet similar to rice pudding.

Reflect

Read the beginning of Justin's draft. Do the details hold the reader's interest? How does the active voice strengthen the writing?

Apply

Use your Outline to write a draft. Include concrete details and use active voice to keep your writing strong.

Revise

Focus on **Ideas**

The Rubric Says	Relevant facts and concrete details develop the topic thoroughly.
Writing Strategy	Take out unrelated details or facts.

I used my outline to write a draft of my report. As I wrote, I tried to keep my readers in mind and explain all my points clearly, using only relevant, solid details and facts that are related to what I am saying. I know that my message will be weakened if I include information that isn't necessary. I see in this section that I have some extra information. Does the paragraph sound better without it?

[DRAFT]

Another big thing is climate. The type of food production of a region is affected by the climate there. For example, rice is grown mostly in the tropical south and the rainy northeast (~~I heard that people's personalities can change during the long monsoon season~~), and wheat is an important crop in the dry northern plains.

[removed unrelated detail]

Apply

Are there any places where you included unnecessary information? Be sure to take out any details or facts that are not relevant to the topic.

Focus on **Word Choice**

The Rubric Says	Domain-specific content vocabulary informs the reader about the topic and is clearly defined.
Writing Strategy	Define all domain-specific words.

The rubric says to use and define domain-specific content vocabulary. *Domain-specific words* are words that relate to a specialized area of knowledge, such as cooking. I understand that some of my readers may not be familiar with the food-related terms I include. If I don't properly explain the terms, my readers won't fully understand my report. Look how I added a definition of *dahl*. Does it help you better understand what dahl is?

[DRAFT]

Two popular South Indian foods are made from rice. Dosas are thin rice-flour pancakes. Idlis are steamed rice dumplings. Vegetables , which is a soupy dish made from split peas or beans. served with rice include dahl

[defined domain-specific word]

Reflect

How does Justin's revision help you connect to his writing?

Apply

Define any terms that you think readers may not understand.

Revise

Focus on Sentence Fluency

The Rubric Says Sentences are lively and highly varied in length and structure. They move the reader along.

Writing Strategy Use sentences of different lengths and structures.

According to the rubric, I should use lively sentences that vary in length and structure. When I reread this section of my report, I realized I wasn't doing that at all. Many of my sentences are the same length, and they follow the same pattern. Look at how I rewrote this part of my report to spice up the sentences!

[DRAFT]

[changed sentences for variety]

Coastal indian food has many influences. ~~People on the coast of~~
Naturally, people there
indiá eat a lot of fish. The residents of west Bengal ~~eat fish from the~~ ~~live near rivers and the bay of Bengal~~
enjoy
~~rivers, too~~. They ~~like~~ carp cooked with chilies. ~~They also like~~ prawns, Another favorite Bengali recipe is

which are large shrimp, spiced with mustard seeds.

[changed sentences for variety]

Apply

Do a lot of your sentences sound alike? Are too many of them a similar length? Vary your sentences, and make your writing more lively!

Focus on **Conventions**

The Rubric Says	The report uses a variety of nouns correctly. It is well edited and ready to publish.
Writing Strategy	Make sure proper nouns and proper adjectives are capitalized correctly.

Writer's Term

Proper Nouns and Proper Adjectives
Proper nouns name a specific person, place, thing, or idea. **Proper adjectives** are formed from proper nouns.

Now I'll check my spelling, grammar, and punctuation. I'll make sure I capitalized and punctuated proper nouns and proper adjectives correctly.

[DRAFT]

[capitalized proper noun]

[capitalized proper adjective]

Food in the south has a more traditional hindu style. Rice is prepared in many ways. Vopo Kanitkar, author of Indian Food and Drink, says, "Rice grains simply boiled may appear to us to be a poor meal, but different processes like grinding, pounding, steaming, and frying transform rice and other cereals into tasty dishes."

[capitalized proper initials]

Reflect

Do Justin's sentence revisions make his writing more enjoyable to read? Has he corrected every error?

Apply

Conventions

Edit your draft for grammar, spelling, punctuation, and capitalization. Be sure to check proper nouns and proper adjectives.

For more practice capitalizing and punctuating proper nouns and adjectives, use the exercises on the next two pages.

Kinds of Nouns

Know the Rule

A **noun** names a person, a place, a thing, or an idea.
Common Noun: names any person, place, thing, or idea (*sister, museum, dream*)
Proper Noun: names a specific person, place, thing, or idea (*Antoine, Chicago, Presidents' Day*)
Singular Noun: names one person, place, thing, or idea (*bus, library, mouse*)
Plural Noun: names more than one (*buses, libraries, mice*)
Possessive Noun: shows ownership (*bus's, buses', mice's*)

Practice the Rule

Number a separate sheet of paper 1–10. Write the noun(s) in each sentence. Write the type of each noun as well. The number after each sentence tells you how many nouns to look for.

1. Italian cuisine is very popular. (1)
2. Many meals take little time to prepare. (2)
3. My aunt's husband is Italian. (2)
4. Uncle Tony is from Lombardy. (2)
5. This region is also known for its cheeses. (2)
6. White truffles grow in Tuscany. (2)
7. Parts of the coast are known for seafood. (3)
8. Of the three pasta dishes, I prefer my uncle's. (2)
9. Water buffalo's milk is common in some regions. (3)
10. The food of Sicily includes many fruits and vegetables. (4)

Proper Nouns and Proper Adjectives

Know the Rule

1. Capitalize **proper nouns**.
   Example: My family immigrated to the **United States** from **India**.

2. Capitalize **proper adjectives**.
   Example: Have you ever tasted **Indian** food?

3. Capitalize **titles of respect** before a person's name.
   Example: **Mr.** Raj Chopra gave a presentation to our class.

4. Capitalize **proper abbreviations** (words in addresses, such as *street* and *avenue*, days, months, and parts of business names in informal notes). End the abbreviations with a period.
   Example: Sakthi's address is 247 Fourteenth **St**.

5. Capitalize an **initial** when it replaces the name of a person or place. Follow the initial with a period.
   Example: Our new neighbor's name is **P. R.** Phalke.

Practice the Rule

Number a sheet of paper 1–8. Write the proper nouns and proper adjectives correctly.

1. The indian film industry is over 100 years old.
2. The French Lumière brothers showed six short silent films at a bombay hotel in 1886.
3. Shortly afterwards, Hiralal Sen and H S Bhatavdekar started making films.
4. india's first talkie, *Alam Ara,* was released in march 1931.
5. Imperial Film Co was the producer of that film.
6. Years later, mr. S. k. Patil saw the commercial value in many of India's films.
7. In 1995, director Satyajit Ray, from the region of bengal, made the film *pather Panchali.*
8. The hollywood influence on Indian cinema is apparent in the musical *Bombay* from 1995.

Publish +Presentation

Publishing Strategy	Include my written report as part of a multimedia presentation to the class.
Presentation Strategy	Choose video, photos, and sound to enhance the report.

Publishing with multimedia doesn't mean you have to use a computer, although I plan to. It just means that you present information in more than one way. For example, you could use pictures, video, and sound.

I need to choose additional resources that support my report and that don't contradict any information or make it confusing. If I use too many resources, my audience will not know where to look! Because my report will be on cards, I should be able to read them while I am presenting other media. But first I want to check over my report one more time. I'll use this final checklist to help me make sure my report is ready for publication.

My Final Checklist

Did I—

✔ make sure all the proper nouns and proper adjectives are capitalized?

✔ use all the different kinds of nouns correctly?

✔ choose media that support and enhance my report?

✔ proofread my report for grammar, spelling, and punctuation?

Apply

Check your research report against your own checklist. Then make a final copy to publish.

Variety Is the Spice of Indian Food

by Justin

WARNING: This report may cause an uncontrollable craving for Indian food, such as samosas. A samosa is a deep-fried, triangular pastry stuffed with potatoes and other vegetables. Spices, such as chili powder and garlic, give it zing. Samosas are a common dish in Gujarat, one of India's many regions. People eat different types of foods in different regions of India.

Many factors determine the foods people eat in each region of India. Religion is a major factor. In India, 80 percent of the population is Hindu, and strict Hindus are vegetarians and do not eat meat. Over the centuries, immigrants who practice other religions have come to India. Many of these people do eat meat. They have influenced the traditional Hindu diet in some places.

Another major factor is climate. The climate of a region affects the food production there. For example, people grow rice mostly in the tropical South and the rainy Northeast. Wheat is an important crop in the dry northern plains.

The North has a strong Muslim influence. Muslims eat lamb, chicken, beef, and fish, but not pork. One favorite dish is lamb kebab. Lamb kebab is pieces of mildly spiced meat roasted on skewers. Another favorite is tandoori chicken, spiced chicken cooked in a clay oven. Dates, nuts, and milk are in many desserts called milk sweets. The milk comes from water buffalo. They are the main source of milk in India. Kheer is a milk sweet similar to rice pudding.

Bread and vegetarian dishes from the Hindu tradition are also common in the North. Most breads don't have any yeast, so they don't rise. Parathas are flat cakes of wheat dough baked on a hot stone and then pan-fried. Purees are flat circles of wheat dough deep-fried in oil until they puff up like balloons. A dish of spiced rice and vegetables called pullao is also popular. In the North, the pullao vegetables are usually cauliflower and peas.

Food in the South has a more traditional Hindu style. Rice is prepared in many ways. V. P. Kanitkar, author of *Indian Food and Drink,* says, "Rice grains simply boiled may appear to us to be a poor meal, but different processes like grinding, pounding, steaming, and frying transform rice and other cereals into tasty dishes."

Two popular South Indian foods are made from rice. Dosas are thin rice-flour pancakes. Idlis are steamed rice dumplings. Vegetables served with rice include dahl, which is a soupy dish made from split peas or beans.

Coastal Indian food has many influences. Naturally, people there eat a lot of fish. The residents of West Bengal live near rivers and the Bay of Bengal. They enjoy carp cooked with chilies. Another favorite Bengali recipe is prawns, which are large shrimp, spiced with mustard seeds.

Goa has a strong Portuguese influence. Its fish curries are well known. A curry is a general term for a dish cooked with crushed spices and turmeric. Turmeric is an herb that adds a yellow color. Coconuts are plentiful in Kerala. Coconut milk is used in fish, rice, and vegetable curries.

Because of the influence of religion and climate, the many regions of India offer a huge range of foods. Variety is the spice of Indian food. Anyone who ignored the warning at the beginning of this report will now probably be ready to sample the many types of Indian food.

Works Consulted

"India." *The World Book Encyclopedia*. 2007 ed.

Kanitkar, V. P. *Indian Food and Drink*. New York: The Bookwright Press, 1987.

Voros, Sharon. "Fare of the Country; The Vegetarian Snacks of South India." http://query.nytimes.com (April 19, 2012)

Reflect

Check Justin's report. Does the writing show all the traits of a good research report? Check it against the rubric. Don't forget to use the rubric to check your own research report.

What's an **Explanatory Essay?**

An explanatory essay explains or describes something. It might tell the reader where an idea came from, or why something is the way it is. This kind of writing is informative and helps the reader better understand the topic.

What's in an **Explanatory Essay?**

Introduction
The introduction is where I clearly state what my essay is about in the form of a well-written thesis statement. This is also where I need to grab my readers' attention and prepare them for the rest of my essay.

Body
The body consists of several well-sequenced paragraphs where I actually explain the subject. This is where I'll put all supporting details, examples, and facts to help my reader understand the topic.

Conclusion
This is the last section of my essay. Here's where I neatly wrap up my subject in a way that my reader will remember. My conclusion should be brief and to the point.

Precise Language
It's important that I use the most accurate words possible when explaining my topic. The more precise my language, the better my reader will understand the idea.

Why write an Explanatory Essay?

There are many reasons to write an explanatory essay, and below I've mentioned a few. Why am I writing one? I need to explain a math concept to my teacher.

Understanding

To write a good explanatory essay, I have to really understand the topic. Maybe my purpose is to prove how well I grasp the subject. Maybe I'll be writing about something that will require me to do a little research. Either way, in the end, my understanding of the topic will be deeper than when I started.

Information

Another great reason for writing an explanatory essay is to share knowledge with the reader. Everyone wants to understand the world around them. If I have information about a specific idea or topic, sharing what I know is a fun and logical step to take.

Explanation

So many small ideas can be used to understand larger concepts in our world. When I explain my topic, I can help both myself and my reader see the relationship between my subject and the larger world.

Linking Informative/Explanatory Writing Traits to an Explanatory Essay

In this chapter, you will provide a written explanation about an idea or a topic. This type of writing is called an explanatory essay. Justin will guide you through the stages of the writing process: Prewrite, Draft, Revise, Edit, and Publish. In each stage, Justin will show you important writing strategies that are linked to the Informative/Explanatory Writing Traits below.

Informative/Explanatory Writing Traits

Ideas	• a clear, focused topic • credible, engaging facts and details that support and develop the topic
Organization	• information that is organized logically into a strong introduction, body, and conclusion • transitions that clarify relationships between ideas
Voice	• a voice and tone that are appropriate for the purpose and audience
Word Choice	• language that is precise and concise • domain-specific vocabulary that is used correctly and explained as necessary
Sentence Fluency	• sentences that vary in length and flow smoothly
Conventions	• no or few errors in grammar, usage, mechanics, and spelling

Before you write, read Zoya Petrovich's explanatory essay on the next page. Then use the explanatory essay rubric on pages 208–209 to decide how well she did. (You might want to look back at What's in an Explanatory Essay? on page 204, too!)

Parallel or Perpendicular?

by Zoya Petrovich

Introduction

I've always had a hard time remembering just what *parallel* and *perpendicular* mean. Both words start with the letter *p*. Both refer to concepts regarding lines and shapes that I've studied in math class. It was easy to confuse the two. But then I took the ideas of parallel and perpendicular and applied them to real-life examples, and I have not struggled since.

Precise language

The definition of *parallel* seems easy enough to understand. Parallel lines can extend in both directions forever, but never intersect. However, when I have had to identify parallel lines in two- or three-dimensional shapes, I struggled with applying the definition to the example. That's when I decided that if I could find examples of parallel lines in the concrete world around me, the definition would be so much easier to fully comprehend. I began to look for parallel lines everywhere I went. Let me say that once you start looking, they really are everywhere!

For example, railroad tracks are parallel. They extend mile after mile, and yet the two rails never cross each other. Most buildings have parallel edges, too. Skyscrapers may reach dizzying heights, but the vertical lines at each corner of the building still never intersect. Even the most common objects in our world, such as a television set, have parallel lines.

Body

Then I decided to search the world around me for examples of *perpendicular*. Perpendicular lines meet or intersect at a right angle. A right angle measures 90 degrees. Again, I understood the idea but would sometimes have a hard time applying that understanding in homework assignments or on quizzes.

One of the most common examples of perpendicular lines is street intersections. The next time you are waiting at a red light, take a moment and look at the street that runs to the left and right. That street is perpendicular to the street you are on. There are also many perpendicular lines in our homes. Walls and floors are perpendicular to each other, as are walls and most ceilings.

Conclusion

As you can see, these mathematical concepts do not have to be things we only think about. Parallel and perpendicular lines are everywhere and play critical roles in the physical world. Once that everyday connection was made, I never had to ask the question, "Is this parallel or perpendicular?" again.

Rubric

Use this 6-point rubric to plan and score an explanatory essay.

	6	5	4
Ideas	The thesis is clearly stated. Relevant facts and concrete details support and develop the thesis.	The thesis is clearly stated. One or two more details would help to develop the thesis.	The thesis is stated. The facts are mostly relevant, and the details are mostly concrete.
Organization	The introduction presents the topic, strong body paragraphs explain the examples, and a conclusion follows from the explanation. Appropriate transitions clarify relationships among ideas.	The essay has an introduction, a body, and a conclusion. One or two transitions are needed.	The essay has an introduction, a body, and a conclusion. More or better transitions are needed to clarify ideas.
Voice	The writer establishes and maintains a formal style. The tone is ideal for the audience.	The writer uses a formal style most of the time. The tone is mostly appropriate for audience.	The writer uses a formal style inconsistently. The tone is somewhat appropriate.
Word Choice	Domain-specific content vocabulary is used correctly and defined as appropriate.	Domain-specific content vocabulary words are used. One or two definitions or explanations could be clearer.	Domain-specific content vocabulary words are used. Definitions or explanations are needed or are unclear.
Sentence Fluency	The writer varies sentence beginnings and structures. The sentences are interesting and enjoyable to read.	The writer varies most of the sentence structures. Several in a row share the same length.	The writer varies some of the sentence structures. Several in a row share the same beginning.
Conventions	The writing has been carefully edited. Prepositions and prepositional phrases are used correctly.	Minor errors are present but do not interfere with meaning. Prepositions and phrases are used correctly.	A few errors cause confusion. One or two prepositional phrases may be misplaced.

✛ Presentation   The format helps readers access the information.

3	2	1	
A thesis is stated but needs clarification. A few details are not relevant, and some details are not specific.	A thesis is not stated. Details and facts are unrelated or unimportant.	A thesis is not stated. Details are randomly listed.	**Ideas**
The introduction or conclusion is weak or missing. Transitions clarifying ideas may be confusing or missing.	The paragraphs are not in order. Transitions are used incorrectly or not used.	The writing is not organized into paragraphs. Transitions are not used.	**Organization**
The writer's style is too casual in places. The tone is inconsistent.	The writer's style is too casual and does not connect with the audience. An appropriate tone is not established.	The voice is very weak or absent. The reader cannot determine who is writing, or why.	**Voice**
A few domain-specific content vocabulary words are used. Definitions are not provided.	Domain-specific content vocabulary words are not used. Many words are ordinary or overused.	Domain-specific content vocabulary words are not used. Many words are used incorrectly.	**Word Choice**
Most sentences share the same structure. The writing becomes dull and predictable in spots.	Most sentences share the same structure. Many sentences are short and choppy.	Too many sentences are incomplete, run on, or incorrect.	**Sentence Fluency**
Many errors are repeated and cause confusion. Prepositions may be confused. (Ex. uses *by* for *to*)	Serious errors interfere with meaning. Prepositions may be confused; phrases may be unclear.	The writing has not been edited.	**Conventions**

See Appendix B for 4-, 5-, and 6-point informative/explanatory rubrics.

Explanatory Essay
Using the Rubric to Study the Model

Did you notice that the model on page 207 points out some key elements of an explanatory essay? As she wrote "Parallel or Perpendicular?" Zoya Petrovich used these elements to help her describe two math concepts. She also used the 6-point rubric on pages 208–209 to plan, draft, revise, and edit the writing. A rubric is a great tool to evaluate writing during the writing process.

Now let's use the same rubric to score the model. To do this, we'll focus on each trait separately, starting with Ideas. We'll use the top descriptor for each trait (column 6), along with examples from the model, to help us understand how the traits work together. How would you score Zoya on each trait?

Ideas

- The thesis is clearly stated.
- Relevant facts and concrete details support and develop the thesis.

Zoya lets me know exactly what her essay is about right away. I like that. Her thesis statement is clear and easy to understand. She also includes lots of solid supporting details to explain her ideas.

[from the writing model]

For example, railroad tracks are parallel. They extend mile after mile, and yet the two rails never cross each other. Most buildings have parallel edges, too. Skyscrapers may reach dizzying heights, but the vertical lines at each corner of the building still never intersect.

Organization

- The introduction presents the topic, strong body paragraphs explain the examples, and a conclusion follows from the explanation.
- Appropriate transitions clarify relationships among ideas.

Zoya grabs my attention right away with her interesting and honest introduction. I have also struggled with these concepts, and I wanted to learn how she helped herself. Several body paragraphs and transitions make her ideas easy to follow. She wraps it all up with a neat and strong conclusion, too. I also like how she used transitions such as *But then* to link ideas.

[from the writing model]

I've always had a hard time remembering just what *parallel* and *perpendicular* mean. Both words start with the letter *p*. Both refer to concepts regarding lines and shapes that I've studied in math class. It was easy to confuse the two. But then I took the ideas of parallel and perpendicular and applied them to real-life examples, and I have not struggled since.

Voice

- The writer establishes and maintains a formal style.
- The tone is ideal for the audience.

Reading Zoya's essay feels effortless because she really knows how to connect with the reader—me! She uses words and phrases I understand, as well as a tone that's formal but friendly. She even includes imagery that's easy for me to visualize, such as city streets and the inside of my home.

[from the writing model]

One of the most common examples of perpendicular lines is street intersections. The next time you are waiting at a red light, take a moment and look at the street that runs to the left and right. That street is perpendicular to the street you are on.

Explanatory Essay 211

Word Choice

- Domain-specific content vocabulary is used correctly and defined as appropriate.

Whenever Zoya uses a vocabulary word related to her topic, she takes the time to define it. I appreciate that. It's clear that she really wants her reader to understand her ideas as thoroughly as possible.

[from the writing model]

Then I decided to search the world around me for examples of *perpendicular*. Perpendicular lines meet or intersect at a right angle. A right angle measures 90 degrees.

Sentence Fluency

- The writer varies sentence beginnings and structures.
- The sentences are interesting and enjoyable to read.

Zoya uses a variety of sentences throughout her essay. She also keeps things interesting by using all kinds of sentence beginnings. Reading the same sentence structures over and over is boring and tiring. I'm glad Zoya avoided that trap.

[from the writing model]

The definition of *parallel* seems easy enough to understand. Parallel lines can extend in both directions forever, but never intersect. However, when I have had to identify parallel lines in two- or three-dimensional shapes, I struggled with applying the definition to the example.

Conventions

- The writing has been carefully edited.
- Prepositions and prepositional phrases are used correctly.

Zoya worked hard at editing and it shows. I can't find a single spelling, grammar, or punctuation error! She even uses all prepositions and prepositional phrases correctly. I want to be just as careful when I edit my own essay.

[from the writing model]

Again, I understood the idea but would sometimes have a hard time applying that understanding in homework assignments or on quizzes.

✚Presentation   The format helps readers access the information.

My Turn!

Now it's my turn to write an explanatory essay. I'll use the rubric and good writing strategies to help me. Read on to see how I do it.

Prewrite

Focus on **Ideas**

The Rubric Says   The thesis is clearly stated.

Writing Strategy   Choose and narrow a topic that can be explained in an essay. Take notes.

My math teacher just gave me an interesting assignment. She wants me to write an essay explaining some of the most common 3-dimensional shapes. My essay will show her how well I understand the topic and help any classmates who read it understand the subject better, too. Writing an explanatory essay for math sounds like fun. Time to get started!

First I'll take some notes. I want to get all the details down on paper before I start writing. That way I can organize all the facts, and I won't forget any important details. Once I have my facts in order, I can start writing my draft.

Notes on 3-Dimensional Shapes

✔ 3-D shapes have length, width, and depth
✔ 3-D shapes in real world can hold stuff, like liquid
✔ spheres—like a ball or an orange, similar to a circle
✔ cones—an ice cream cone—top opening is round
✔ cubes—like a box, sides (faces) are all square
✔ pyramids—base is either a triangle or square, think Egypt!

Apply

Takes notes on your subject. Include all the important facts and information.

The Rubric Says	The introduction presents the topic, strong body paragraphs explain the examples, and a conclusion follows from the explanation.
Writing Strategy	Make a Fact Web to organize my notes.

Writer's Term

Fact Web

Use a **Fact Web** to organize several categories and facts about a given topic. Write the main topic in the center circle. Write your categories in circles around the main topic circle. Then write your facts in the circles around each category.

I decided that creating a Fact Web for three-dimensional shapes was the best way to organize my notes. When I go to write my draft, I can then use each category circle for a new paragraph. This will really help me write strong body paragraphs and keep all my information in order. Check out my Fact Web below. What do you think?

Fact Web

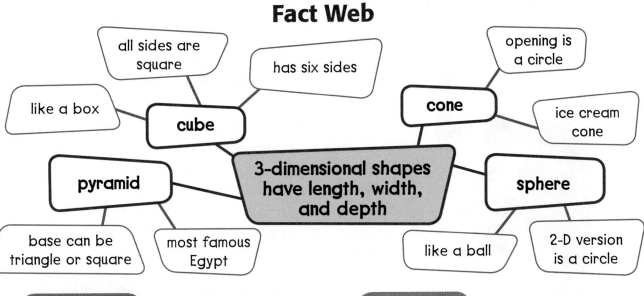

Reflect

How will Justin's Fact Web help him write the body of his essay?

Apply

Make a Fact Web about your topic. Use it to guide you when writing your body paragraphs.

Draft

Focus on Word Choice

The Rubric Says — Domain-specific content vocabulary is used correctly and defined as appropriate.

Writing Strategy — Make sure unfamiliar words are defined.

Now that my Fact Web is done, writing my draft will be easier. All the information I need is organized, so I just need to get started.

The rubric says I should use domain-specific content vocabulary words. I'll make sure I use words specific to the 3-dimensional shapes I'm describing. The more accurate my language, the better my reader will understand the topic.

The rubric also says I should define any words my reader might not understand. That makes sense. I want my reader to learn more about 3-dimensional shapes. It won't help if I use unfamiliar words without defining them. I want to show I really know what I'm talking about. I might even look up a few terms in a reference source, like a dictionary, but I'll be sure to use my own words when I write.

Time to get started! I won't worry too much about spelling and grammar at first. I can go back later to fix any mistakes. Right now the most important goal is to get my ideas written down. Check out the beginning of my draft on the next page. What do you think?

[DRAFT]

Everyday 3-Dimensional Shapes Explained

by Justin

We all live in a 3-dimensional world, but most of us probably never think about it that way. Two-dimensional shapes have only length and width. Shapes like circles, squares, and triangles are great on paper, but they are flat and cannot hold substances, such as liquids, solids, or gases. In fact, our world, our entire universe, could not exist in only two dimensions. However, 3-dimensional shapes have not only length and width, but they also have depth. This third dimension makes all the difference and is a crucial—absolutely necessary—element of life as we know it. Circles become spheres, squares transform into cubes, and triangles can morph into either cones or pyramids. It's cool! Check it out!

[used and defined domain-specific words]

Spheres are everywhere! In fact, the universe is full of spheres. Planets, moons, stars, even our own sun, all are spheres. The easiest way to envision a sphere is to imagine a ball. That ball has a length and width, but it also has depth. It can hold a substance, like the water in a water balloon.

Reflect

How did Justin do? Does he include and define enough domain-specific content words to help his reader better understand the essay?

Apply

Use your Fact Web as a guide and write a draft of your essay. Use and define domain-specific words to explain your subject.

Revise

Focus on **Ideas**

The Rubric Says   Relevant facts and concrete details support and develop the thesis.

Writing Strategy   Replace unnecessary or weak details with strong facts and details.

Writer's Term

Concrete Details

A **concrete detail** is a specific detail that can be verified by more than one reliable source. Examples of reliable sources are textbooks, reliable websites, magazine and newspaper articles, or an encyclopedia.

Now that my draft is done, I can start revising. The rubric says I should include relevant facts and concrete details about my topic. All details must be related to my subject, or my reader will become confused. Also, the details I include should be concrete, not vague. Vague details don't really provide much information and will weaken my writing. As I read my draft, I found a weak detail that needed revision. I'll go and fix that now.

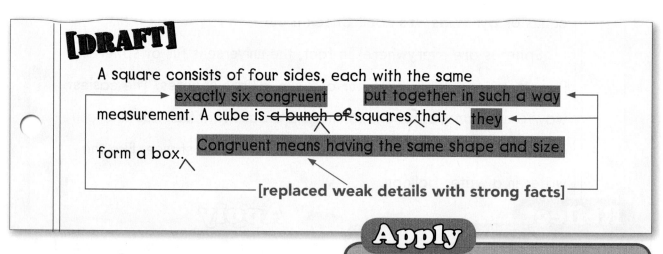

[DRAFT]

A square consists of four sides, each with the same
                          exactly six congruent   put together in such a way
measurement. A cube is a bunch of squares that   they
form a box.   Congruent means having the same shape and size.

[replaced weak details with strong facts]

Apply

To strengthen your essay, replace weak, vague details with strong, concrete details.

Revise

The Rubric Says	Appropriate transitions clarify relationships among ideas.
Writing Strategy	Use transition words or phrases to connect sentences and paragraphs.

Revising is easy when I tackle one aspect of my writing at a time. The rubric says that using transitions will clarify how my ideas are related. I can use transitions like *however*, *but*, and *in addition* to show how several points made about one idea are related. Also, repeating certain words can show how sentences are connected. I read over my draft, looking for places where transitions would help clarify an idea. My paragraph on cones could really use some clarification. I'll take care of that now.

[DRAFT]

[used transitions to connect ideas]

Cones are interesting 3-dimensional shapes. First, Imagine an ice cream cone. When you look straight down at a cone, You'll notice that the top, or opening, is a circle. Then again, When you view a cone from the side, you'll see a triangle. A cone is kind of like a triangle that has been wrapped around so two edges meet.

Reflect

What do you think? How do Justin's revisions clarify and strengthen this paragraph?

Apply

Use transitions or repeat certain key words to show how sentences or ideas are related.

Revise

Focus on Sentence Fluency

The Rubric Says   The writer varies sentence beginnings and structures. The sentences are interesting and enjoyable to read.

Writing Strategy   Add prepositional phrases to sentences.

Now the rubric says to vary sentence beginnings to add variety. I know that prepositional phrases add more information in a sentence, but they can also be used to change how sentences begin. When several sentences in a row start the same way, the writing seems stiff and uninteresting. I'll use some introductory prepositional phrases to mix things up, while at the same time adding more information to the sentences.

[DRAFT]

Triangles also appear in another 3-dimensional shape: the

Throughout this year, I've learned about

pyramid. ~~There are~~ two kinds of pyramids. One has a square base

In math class, we also discussed

and four triangular faces, which all meet in a point at the top.

that

Another version has a triangle for a base and three more

[used prepositional phrases for variety]

triangles for the sides.

Apply

Use introductory prepositional phrases to add information and variety, and keep your writing interesting.

The Rubric Says   The writing has been carefully edited. Prepositions and prepositional phrases are used correctly.

Writing Strategy   Make sure all prepositions are correct.

Writer's Term

Prepositional Phrases

A **prepositional phrase** begins with a preposition (**about, around, from, on**) and ends with the object of the preposition. It is placed near the noun or verb it describes. Use prepositional phrases to add information to a sentence, but make sure you use the right preposition.

The rubric reminds me to make sure I've used each prepositional phrase correctly. Prepositional phrases are a great way to provide the reader with more information. But if a preposition is used incorrectly, the reader will just be confused.

[DRAFT]

as you can see, these common 3-dimensional shapes are

everywhere. It's important to remember how rare it is to find perfect

in ← [used correct preposition]

mathematical examples of these shapes at our everyday world.

Reflect

How will Justin's edits make his essay easier to read? How does the fixed prepositional phrase clarify his idea?

Apply   Conventions

Edit your draft for spelling, punctuation, and capitalization errors. Be sure that all of your prepositions are used correctly.

For more practice using prepositions and prepositional phrases, do the activities on the next two pages.

Prepositional Phrases

Know the Rule

A **prepositional phrase** can tell *how, what kind, when, how much,* or *where.* A prepositional phrase begins with a **preposition** such as *about, around, at, by, from, in, into, of, on, over, to,* or *with.* It ends with a noun or pronoun that is the **object of the preposition.** The words between the preposition and its object are part of the prepositional phrase. A prepositional phrase can appear at the beginning, middle, or end of a sentence.

> **Example:** The best bakery (in) the city is right next door.

Practice the Rule

Number a piece of paper 1–10. Copy each of the prepositional phrases in the following sentences. Then circle each preposition.

1. Preparing for a math test is important.
2. First, be sure to sleep well the night before the exam.
3. Without a healthy breakfast, you won't have the energy you need.
4. Look at your notes one more time when you get to school.
5. Keep your work area tidy—don't let clutter gather on your desk.
6. Don't let any worries or doubts about your math abilities trouble you.
7. Between problems, mentally encourage yourself—you're doing great!
8. Try not to work over the allotted time.
9. Place the pages of the exam into a neat stack and turn them in.
10. Remember—doing well starts with a positive attitude.

Prepositional Phrases

Know the Rule

A **prepositional phrase** can be used to add information to a sentence. Be sure to use the correct preposition so as not to confuse the reader.

Practice the Rule

Number a piece of paper 1–10. Copy the following sentences, choosing the correct preposition for each.

1. Write the percent sign (before/after) the number.
2. Parallel lines can extend forever (in/on) both directions, but they never intersect.
3. A circle's diameter extends (across/below) its center.
4. All octagons consist (in/of) eight sides.
5. If two lines intersect (at/around) a 90-degree angle, they are perpendicular to each other.
6. (Before/Between) reducing a fraction, you must first determine the greatest common factor for both the numerator and the denominator.
7. When you multiply a number by ½, you'll get the same answer as if you divided the number (on/by) 2.
8. When we subtract the *subtrahend* (into/from) the *minuend,* we are left with the *difference*.
9. When discussing circles, it's important to remember that all radii extend (toward/beyond) the center and meet at the circle's central point.
10. All angles fall (upon/into) one of three major categories—acute, right, or obtuse.

Publish
✚ Presentation

Publishing Strategy — Present the essay as a slide show.

Presentation Strategy — Display information clearly.

I'm done! I can't wait to share my work with my class . . . but how? I know. I'll create a slide show featuring the main points and 3-dimensional shapes from my essay. I won't clutter the slides, and I'll use a clear font so even the students in the back of the room can easily read them. First, though, I'll make sure I've done everything on my final checklist.

My Final Checklist

Did I—

✔ use the correct prepositions?

✔ use prepositional phrases accurately in my writing?

✔ create informative slides, using an easy-to-read font?

✔ include only the main points on my slides?

✔ use appropriate and topic-related visuals on my slides?

Apply

Make a checklist to check your own explanatory essay. Then make a final copy to publish.

Everyday 3-Dimensional Shapes Explained

by Justin

We all live in a 3-dimensional world, but most of us probably never think about it that way. Two-dimensional shapes have only length and width. Shapes like circles, squares, and triangles are great on paper, but they are flat and cannot hold substances, such as liquids, solids, or gases. In fact, our world, our entire universe, could not exist in only two dimensions. However, 3-dimensional shapes have not only length and width, but they also have depth. This third dimension makes all the difference and is a crucial—absolutely necessary—element of life as we know it. Circles become spheres, squares transform into cubes, and triangles can morph into either cones or pyramids. Let's take a closer look at these shapes commonly found throughout our world.

Spheres are everywhere! In fact, the universe is full of spheres. Planets, moons, stars, even our own sun, all are spheres. The easiest way to envision a sphere is to imagine a ball. That ball has a length and width, but it also has depth. It can hold a substance, like the water in a water balloon. A multitude of fruits and vegetables are sphere-like. For instance, oranges, tomatoes, grapes, apples, and pomegranates are all delicious examples of sphere-like foods.

To understand cubes, you need to first understand the 2-dimensional square. A square consists of four sides, each with the same measurement. A cube is exactly six congruent squares put together in such a way that they form a box. Congruent means having the same shape and size. Just think of dice! A die is a cube. It has six faces, or sides. Some gift boxes are cubes. My grandmother even uses cubes made of sugar in her tea.

Cones are interesting 3-dimensional shapes. First, imagine an ice cream cone. When you look straight down at a cone, you'll notice that the top, or opening, is a circle. Then again, when you view a cone from the side, you'll see a triangle. A cone is kind of like a triangle that has been wrapped around so two edges meet. Other common examples of cones are party hats, megaphones, and Victorian Christmas candy cones.

Triangles also appear in another 3-dimensional shape: the pyramid. Throughout this year, I've learned about two kinds of pyramids. One has a square base and four triangular faces, which all meet in a point at the top. In math class, we also discussed another version that has a triangle for a base and three more triangles for the sides. Perhaps the most identifiable pyramids in the world are the Egyptian pyramids in Giza. Other everyday examples are some church steeples and the food pyramid.

As you can see, these common 3-dimensional shapes are everywhere. It's important to remember how rare it is to find perfect mathematical examples of these shapes in our everyday world. A church steeple is not a perfect pyramid, for example, but the general shape is there. Take a moment and look around. You just might be surprised at how many of these shapes you will find.

3-Dimensional Shapes

- 3-dimensional objects have length, width, and depth.
- 3-dimensional objects can hold substances.
- Our universe and world are full of common 3-dimensional shapes such as the sphere, cube, cone, and pyramid.

A sphere is basically a ball.

Reflect

How did Justin do? Check his writing against the rubric. Be sure to check your own writing against the rubric, too!

Informative/ Explanatory test writing

Read the Writing Prompt

Every writing test starts with a writing prompt. Most writing prompts have three parts:

Setup This part of the writing prompt gives you the background information you need to get ready to write.

Task This part of the writing prompt tells you exactly what you are supposed to write: an explanation of a problem in your school or community with ideas on how to fix it.

Scoring Guide This section tells how your writing will be scored. To do well on the test, you should make sure your writing does everything on the list.

Remember the rubrics you used earlier in this unit? When you take a writing test, you don't always have all of the information that's on a rubric. But the scoring guide is a lot like a rubric. It lists everything you need to think about to write a good paper. Like the rubrics you've used in this unit, many scoring guides are based upon these important traits of writing:

Think about a problem in your school or community that should be fixed.

Explain what the problem is, why it needs to be corrected, and how you would go about fixing it.

Be sure your writing

- has a topic that is clear and includes relevant, credible details that appeal to your audience.

- is well organized and uses transitions to clarify relationships among ideas.

- uses active voice and first-person point of view to engage your readers.

- uses specific words to explain the topic.

- has a variety of sentence patterns.

- contains correct grammar, punctuation, capitalization, and spelling.

Writing Traits
in the Scoring Guide

The scoring guide in the prompt on page 229 has been made into this chart. Does it remind you of the rubrics you've used? Not all prompts include all of the writing traits, but this one does. Use them to do your best writing. Remember to work neatly and put your name on each page.

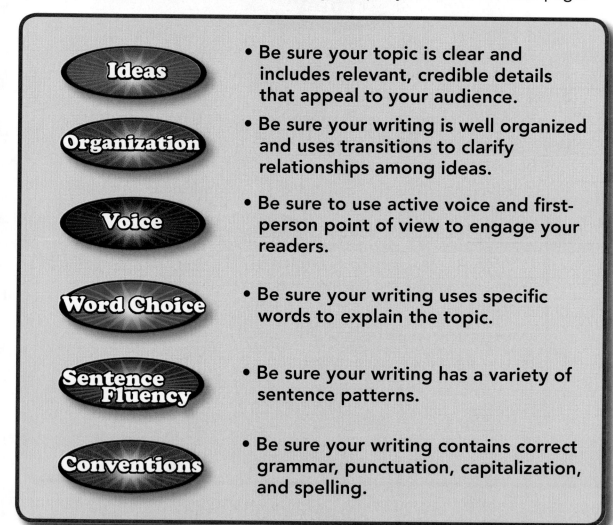

Ideas
- Be sure your topic is clear and includes relevant, credible details that appeal to your audience.

Organization
- Be sure your writing is well organized and uses transitions to clarify relationships among ideas.

Voice
- Be sure to use active voice and first-person point of view to engage your readers.

Word Choice
- Be sure your writing uses specific words to explain the topic.

Sentence Fluency
- Be sure your writing has a variety of sentence patterns.

Conventions
- Be sure your writing contains correct grammar, punctuation, capitalization, and spelling.

Look at Bonnie Campbell's essay on the next page. Did she follow the scoring guide?

A Place for Us

by Bonnie Campbell

A big problem in our community is that many middle school students have nowhere to go after school. I would like to explain my solution to this problem.

There are many kids in our town who would like to spend time together after school. I'm not talking about kids who play sports. I'm concerned about a whole group of other kids like me who have nothing to do after school. Our parents don't like us to get together at our homes when no adults are there, so where can we go?

There is no place for us to hang out without getting in trouble. If we go to the diner for a snack, we can't stay there very long. The servers complain that we don't spend enough money to take up the tables. If we go to the library, people complain that we are too noisy. If we get together outside the shops downtown, sometimes adults tell us to move. They say we're blocking the sidewalk.

Now that I've explained the problem, I'd like to explain my solution to it. There is an empty store on Main Street. If we could make this a drop-in center, it would keep students off the street. We could play table tennis and air hockey. There could also be quiet areas for kids to do their homework. In addition, it would be great if we had a little kitchen or some machines with snacks. I also know kids would like it if we could listen to music there and maybe watch some videos.

This way, kids would not have to go home to empty houses or apartments after school. They would not be on the street. Kids with no place else to go would not be bored and would stay out of trouble. There could be one or two adults at the center to make sure everyone behaves. We kids could even help out. We could keep the place clean and do other jobs like making snacks. We could help pay for the center by having fundraisers, such as car washes or bake sales.

With a special place for kids to go after school, everybody wins! Kids stay busy and have fun, and parents don't have to worry about them.

Using the Scoring Guide to Study the Model

Let's use the scoring guide to check Bonnie's writing test, "A Place for Us." How well does her explanation meet each of the six writing traits?

- **The topic is clear.**
- **The writing includes relevant, credible details that appeal to the audience.**

Bonnie's first paragraph announces the topic: the middle school kids need a place to hang out. She then begins to give relevant, credible details that sound authoritative and reach out to the reader in a friendly way.

> A big problem in our community is that many middle school students have nowhere to go after school.

> There are many kids in our town who would like to spend time together after school. . . . I'm concerned about a whole group of other kids like me who have nothing to do after school. Our parents don't like us to get together at our homes when no adults are there, so where can we go?

- **The writing is well organized.**
- **The writing uses transitions to clarify relationships among ideas.**

In the body, Bonnie explains the problem, offers a solution, and explains the solution. Transitions help move the reader easily from one idea to the next. This example contains a smooth transition from describing the problem to introducing the next topic: the solution.

> If we get together outside the shops downtown, sometimes adults tell us to move. They say we're blocking the sidewalk.

> Now that I've explained the problem, I'd like to explain my solution to it.

Voice

- **The writing uses active voice and first-person point of view to engage the reader.**

Bonnie uses first person—*we* and *I*—to make the reader feel part of the discussion. She also uses active voice to keep her writing engaging. Instead of using dull sentences such as *The adults could be helped by us,* or *The place could be cleaned by kids,* she writes active sentences like these.

We kids could even help out. We could keep the place clean and do other jobs like making snacks. We could help pay for the center by having fundraisers, such as car washes or bake sales.

Word Choice

- **The writing uses specific words to explain the topic.**

Specific and precise words help make the writer's meaning clear. Bonnie uses words like *snacks, fundraisers,* and *car washes* so the reader knows exactly what she is suggesting.

We kids could help out. We could keep the place clean and do other jobs like making snacks. We could help pay for the center by having fundraisers, such as car washes or bake sales.

Using the Scoring Guide to Study the Model

- **The writing has a variety of sentence patterns.**

Bonnie uses a variety of sentence patterns. She begins by stating that there's no place to go, and then she follows up with several *if* clauses that further explain her original statement. The clauses connect one sentence to the next, which makes the writing flow.

There is no place for us to hang out without getting in trouble. If we go to the diner for a snack, we can't stay there very long. The servers complain that we don't spend enough money to take up the tables. If we go to the library, people complain that we are too noisy. If we get together outside the shops downtown, sometimes adults tell us to move. They say we're blocking the sidewalk.

- **The writing contains correct grammar, punctuation, capitalization, and spelling.**

As far as I can tell, Bonnie didn't make any mistakes in capitalization, punctuation, spelling, or grammar. But don't forget to check for mistakes in your own work. For example, if you know you often misspell words, you should pay close attention to spelling. Editing for grammar and mechanics at every step of the writing process will help you to avoid errors on your final test!

Planning My Time

Before giving us a writing test prompt, my teacher tells us how much time we'll have to complete the test. Since I'm already familiar with the writing process, I can think about how much total time I need and then divide it up into the different parts of the writing process. If the test takes an hour, here's how I can organize my time. Planning your time will help you, too!

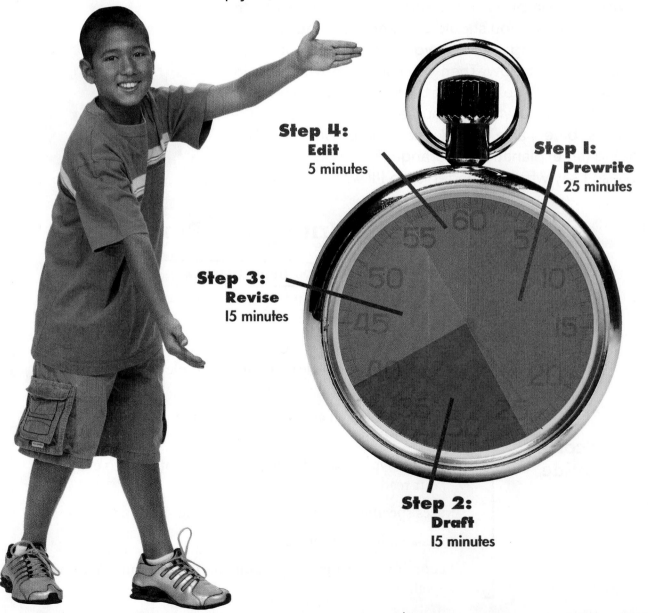

Step 4:
Edit
5 minutes

Step 1:
Prewrite
25 minutes

Step 3:
Revise
15 minutes

Step 2:
Draft
15 minutes

Prewrite

Focus on **Ideas**

Writing Strategy Study the writing prompt to find out what to do.

Once I have my writing prompt, I study it and make sure I know exactly what I'm supposed to do. Usually a writing prompt has three parts, but the parts aren't always labeled. You should find and label the setup, task, and scoring guide on your writing prompt, just like I did on mine below. Then you can circle key words in the setup and the task that tell what kind of writing you need to do and who your audience will be. I circled my topic in blue. I also circled what kind of writing I'll be doing (an explanation) in orange. The writing prompt doesn't say who the reader is, so I'll write for my teacher.

My Writing Test Prompt

Setup — Suppose you have (an opportunity to travel on a space shuttle.)

Task — Write (an essay explaining why) you would or would not want to go on a space shuttle.

Scoring Guide — Be sure your writing

- has a topic that is clear and includes relevant, credible details that appeal to your audience.

- is well organized and uses transitions to clarify relationships among ideas.

- uses active voice and first-person point of view to engage your readers.

- uses specific words to explain the topic.

- has a variety of sentence patterns.

- contains correct grammar, punctuation, capitalization, and spelling.

Think about how the scoring guide relates to the writing traits you've studied in the rubrics. All of the traits might not be included in every scoring guide, but you need to remember them all to write a good essay!

Ideas
- Be sure your topic is clear and includes relevant, credible details that appeal to your audience.

I want my reader to know right away what my topic is, believe the details I give, and feel drawn into the writing.

Organization
- Be sure your writing is well organized and uses transitions to clarify relationships among ideas.

My reader will have an easier time following my explanation if I use transition words to identify how ideas connect.

Voice
- Be sure to use active voice and first-person point of view to engage your readers.

Strong, active-voice verbs and the first-person pronouns *I* and *we* will help keep my reader engaged.

Word Choice
- Be sure your writing uses specific words to explain the topic

My reader will understand the information better if I use specific words to express what I mean.

Sentence Fluency
- Be sure your writing has a variety of sentence patterns.

I can add liveliness to my writing by using different kinds of sentences. This will keep my reader interested and help make my writing flow.

Conventions
- Be sure your writing contains correct grammar, punctuation, capitalization, and spelling.

I should always remember to check my grammar and mechanics any time I write!

Prewrite

Focus on **Ideas**

Writing Strategy   Respond to the task.

I've learned that good writers always gather information before they begin writing. When you write to take a test, you can gather information from the writing prompt. Let's take another look at the task, since this is the part of the writing prompt that explains what I'm supposed to write. Remember, you won't have much time when writing for a test! That's why it's really important to think about how you'll respond before you begin to write.

I see that first I have to decide whether I want to take a ride on a space shuttle. I think blasting off into space would be fun, but now I have to explain why. I think jotting down some notes will help, but I have to do it quickly because the clock is ticking!

Task — Write an essay explaining why you would or would not want to go on a space shuttle.

Notes

- ✔ I'd do well in space, and I'm not afraid to go.
- ✔ I would like the feeling.
- ✔ It would be fun.

Apply

Make sure you think about how you'll respond to the task in your writing prompt before you write. Then you can jot down some notes to help you gather information.

Writing Strategy   Choose a graphic organizer.

I don't have much time, so I'll begin organizing my ideas. First, I'll choose a useful graphic organizer. I'm writing an explanation, so a Spider Map will help me remember the important ideas I want to include. The map will help me keep track of main ideas and details. Some of the information comes right out of the setup and the task.

I've decided I would like to fly on a space shuttle. I'll write that in the center circle of my Spider Map. Next, I'll identify the reasons why and write the main ones on each leg.

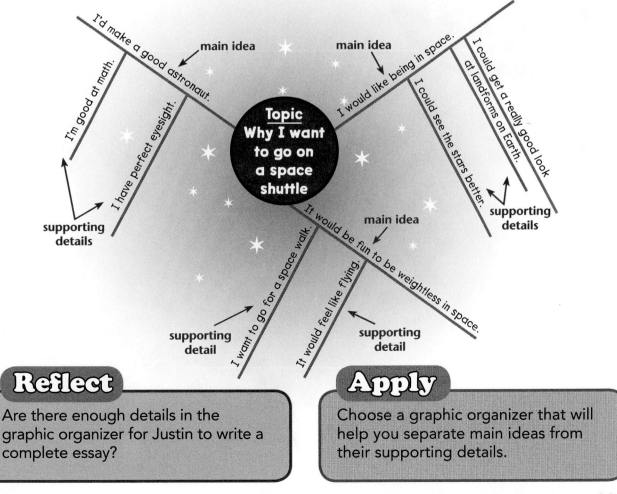

Reflect

Are there enough details in the graphic organizer for Justin to write a complete essay?

Apply

Choose a graphic organizer that will help you separate main ideas from their supporting details.

Prewrite

Focus on Organization

Writing Strategy Check the graphic organizer against the scoring guide.

In a test, you don't always get much time to revise. That makes prewriting more important than ever! So before I write, I'll check my Spider Map against the scoring guide in the writing prompt.

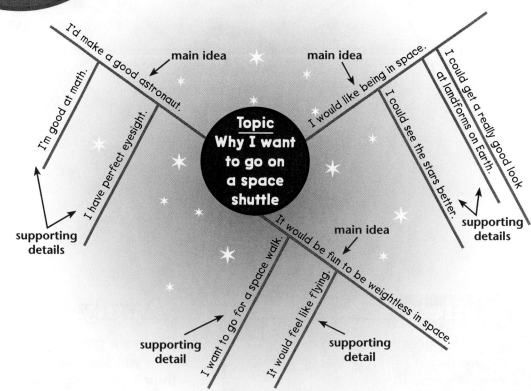

main idea

main idea

I'd make a good astronaut.

I would like being in space.

I'm good at math.

I could see the stars better.

I could get a really good look at landforms on Earth.

I have perfect eyesight.

Topic
Why I want to go on a space shuttle

supporting details

supporting details

It would be fun to be weightless in space.

main idea

I want to go for a space walk.

It would feel like flying.

supporting detail

supporting detail

Ideas

- Be sure your topic is clear and includes relevant, credible details that appeal to your audience.

The Spider Map clearly states my topic and includes details that are relevant and credible. I'll use those in my writing.

Organization

- Be sure your writing is well organized and uses transitions to clarify relationships among ideas.

My Spider Map doesn't show connecting sentences yet, but as I write, I'll use transition words to connect my ideas.

Voice

- Be sure to use active voice and first-person point of view to engage your readers.

Since my topic is why I want to go on a space shuttle, it should be easy to use the first-person pronoun *I*. I'll also use active voice to keep the discussion engaging.

Word Choice

- Be sure your writing uses specific words to explain the topic.

My Spider Map already includes some specific words, such as *eyesight, space walk*, and *landforms*, that I will talk about.

Sentence Fluency

- Be sure your writing has a variety of sentence patterns.

I'll need to remember to do this when I start writing!

Conventions

- Be sure your writing contains correct grammar, punctuation, capitalization, and spelling.

I'll check for proper grammar and mechanics when I edit my draft.

Reflect

The Spider Map doesn't include every point in the scoring guide, but it covers most of them. Is anything else missing?

Apply

Before you start to write, reread the scoring guide in the writing prompt to be sure you know what to do.

Draft

Focus on   **Ideas**

Writing Strategy   State the topic clearly.

I can use the information in my Spider Map to start drafting. As I look back at the scoring guide, I can see that it's important to identify my topic early in the paper. I think I'll use my opening sentence to do this. This way my reader will know right away what I am writing about. In later paragraphs, I'll add relevant, interesting details.

[DRAFT]

The Sky's the Limit!

by Justin

[clear topic]

If I ever had an opportunity to go on the Space Shuttle, I would jump at the chance. Actually, maybe I should say I would fly at the chance! There are several reasons why I think this would be the experience of a lifetime.

First of all, being an astronaut would be fun. I like all of the rides at amusement parks, even the ones where you turn upside down. I'm also good in math, and I have perfect eyesight, so those are two more things in my favor.

I would be fascinated by the whole experience of being in space. I love looking at the stars from here on Earth. I can only imagine how

Proofreading Marks

⌐ Indent   ℓ Take out something
≡ Make uppercase   ⊙ Add a period
/ Make lowercase   ⁋ New paragraph
∧ Add something   (SP) Spelling error

[relevant, credible details]

much better stargazing would be up in the sky. The other astronauts and me could look down at Earth when we got tired of stargazing. I've read that you can see Rivers, Mountains, and other landforms from space.

I think that moving around without gravity wood be fun. My greatest dream is to be free in space. Walking in space would be just about the best thing I can imagine. Some people might be afraid of floating into space forever I don't think that would be a problem. The people who designed the space shuttle and all of it's equipment is very careful about everything they do.

I know that not many people would enjoy eating and drinking food from tubes especially while being cooped up with other people in such a small space. Those things wouldn't bother me, though. Instead, being in space would make me really appreciate what I have here on earth.

Reflect

Think about the draft. Is the topic in a good place, and is it stated clearly?

Apply

The topic should be identified in the introduction so that the reader will know right away what the writing is about. Then add believable details that are appealing to the reader.

Revise

Focus on Organization

Writing Strategy   Use transition words to clarify connecting ideas.

I'll read my paper again and see if any parts could be clearer. The scoring guide says that I should use transition words to clarify how ideas are related. I see some places where I can add transition words that will make my writing clearer.

[DRAFT]

[added transition words]

Second,
I would be fascinated by the whole experience of being in space.
, so
I love looking at the stars from here on Earth. I can only imagine how
What's more,
much better stargazing would be up in the sky. The other astronauts
and me could look down at Earth when we got tired of stargazing.
In fact,
I've read that you can see Rivers, Mountains, and other landforms
from space.

Apply

Make sure your writing is clear. Use transition words to clarify relationships among ideas.

Writing Strategy   Use active voice and first-person point of view.

I know I'm really interested in my topic—it's very exciting to me! But I need to connect with my readers and get them interested in what I have to say as well. Active voice will help with that. Since this is my personal experience, I'll use first-person point of view to draw readers in. Look where I found two more places to use first person and active voice.

[DRAFT]

[added first person]

I think I would make a good astronaut.

First of all, ~~being an astronaut would be fun.~~ I like all of the rides at amusement parks, even the ones where you turn upside down. I'm also good in math, and I have perfect eyesight, so those are two more things in my favor.

Second,

~~I would be fascinated by~~ the whole experience of being in space. fascinates me

Reflect

What do you think of the revisions? Do first person and active voice help you connect with what Justin is saying?

Apply

Find places to use first-person point of view and active voice to engage your reader.

Revise

Focus on Word Choice

Writing Strategy   Use specific words.

The scoring guide says I should use specific words to explain my topic. Choosing just the right words makes my meaning clear and helps the reader quickly grasp what I'm trying to say. I'll check for vague words that I can replace with specific words to make my writing clearer. I think I found one or two in this section.

[DRAFT]

[replaced vague words with specific words]

just like flying

I think that moving around without gravity wood be ~~fun~~. My greatest

go for a space walk

dream is to ~~be free in space~~. Walking in space would be just about the

best thing I can imagine.

Apply

Vague words make your writing sound weak and harder to understand. Replace those words with more specific words to create a sharp picture in the reader's mind.

Writing Strategy   Check the grammar, punctuation, capitalization, and spelling.

Now there's just one last step! The scoring guide says to use correct grammar and mechanics. I always leave plenty of time to check for errors in these important areas.

The Sky's the Limit!

by Justin

If I ever had an opportunity to go on the Space Shuttle, I would jump at the chance. Actually, maybe I should say I would fly at the chance! There are several reasons why I think this would be the experience of a lifetime.

I think I would make a good astronaut.
First of all, ~~being an astronaut would be fun~~, I like all of the rides at amusement parks, even the ones where you turn upside down. I'm also good in math, and I have perfect eyesight, so those are two more
          Plus, I like working on a team with other people,
things in my favor. and I have a knack for helping others get along.
Second,
      the whole experience of being in space fascinates me. I love looking at the stars from here on Earth, so I can only imagine how

Apply

Check your grammar, punctuation, capitalization, and spelling every time you write for a test.

[FINAL DRAFT]

much better stargazing would be up in the sky. **What's more,** The other astronauts and ~~me~~ (I) could look down at Earth when we got tired of stargazing. **In fact,** I've read that you can see Rivers, Mountains, and other landforms from space.

I think that moving around without gravity ~~wood~~ **would** be ~~fun~~ **just like flying.** My greatest dream is to ~~be free in space~~ **, however,** **go for a space walk.** Walking in space would be just about the best thing I can imagine. Some people might be afraid of floating into space forever **, but** I don't think that would be a problem. The people who designed the space shuttle and all of it's equipment ~~is~~ **are** very careful about everything they do.

I know that not many people would enjoy eating and drinking food from tubes, especially while being cooped up with other people in such a small space. Those things wouldn't bother me, though. Instead, being in space would make me really appreciate what I have here on earth.

With my skills, my interest in space, and my lack of fear, I think I would be a good person to travel in a shuttle. Now, I'd like to sign up **! I wonder where I can do that, don't you?**

Reflect

Is the writing missing anything? Check it against the scoring guide. Remember to use your writing prompt's scoring guide to check your writing any time you take a test!

We're finished! That wasn't so bad! Remember these important tips when you write for a test.

TEST TIPS

1. **Study the writing prompt before you start to write.** Most writing prompts have three parts: the setup, the task, and the scoring guide. The parts probably won't be labeled. You'll have to figure them out for yourself!

2. **Make sure you understand the task before you start to write.**

   - Read all three parts of the writing prompt carefully.

   - Circle key words in the task part of the writing prompt that tell what kind of writing you need to do. The task might also identify your audience.

   - Make sure you know how you'll be graded.

   - Say the assignment in your own words to yourself.

3. **Keep an eye on the clock.** Decide how much time you will spend on each part of the writing process and try to stick to your schedule. Don't spend so much time prewriting that you don't have enough time left to write.

4. **Reread your writing. Compare it to the scoring guide at least twice.** Remember the rubrics you have used all year? A scoring guide on a writing test is like a rubric. It can help you keep what's important in mind.

5. **Plan, plan, plan!** You don't get much time to revise during a test, so planning is more important than ever.

6. **Write neatly.** Remember: If the people who score your test can't read your writing, it doesn't matter how good your essay is!

Argument

writing convinces the reader of something.

Hi, there! I'm Leila. I'm learning about argument writing in school. I really like to share my opinions with other people and get them to understand my point of view. I want to convince people through good reasoning, and this kind of writing should help me learn to do that better.

IN THIS UNIT

☐ **Response to Literature**

☐ **Argument Essay**

☐ **Business Letter**

SCIENCE CONNECTION ▶ **Speech**

☐ **Writing for a Test**

Name: Leila
Home: Tennessee
Hobbies: watching old movies, playing blues guitar, reading
Favorite Blues Song: "Crossroad Blues" by Robert Johnson
Favorite Book: *The Diary of Anne Frank*

What's a Response to Literature?

A response to literature is a way to express my opinions and ideas about what I have read. I am going to write a book review, in which my opinion will be supported with facts and details from the book. In a book review, I can convince other people to read a book I like.

What's in a Response to Literature?

Thesis Statement
This expresses the writer's opinion. I'll make my thesis statement very clear, and I'll put it right in the first paragraph so my audience knows where I stand.

Organization
One effective way to organize a response to literature is to use a compare-and-contrast pattern. I'm going to do that in my review. That will make my comparisons very clear to my readers.

Supporting Evidence
If I want to convince my readers of my opinion, I have to have some evidence supporting my point of view. Quoting directly from the book can help support my opinions, and so can adding facts about what happens in the book.

Clear Writing
Since I'll have to leave a lot of the details out of my response, I need to be careful that things don't get confusing. All my sentences must be complete and clear, smooth and interesting.

Why write a Response to Literature?

I've never written a book review before, but I can think of all sorts of reasons to write one. I've listed some of my ideas below—and I'm still thinking!

Encouragement

A book review can encourage other people to read. After reading a review, they may decide to read the same book, another book by the same author, or a book on a similar topic or theme.

Personal Reflection

Sometimes I get in a big rush because I can't wait to finish one book and start another! Writing a book review can help me stop and really think about what I've read and what it means to me.

Sharing My Opinion

My friends and family know this is one of my favorite things to do! Writing a book review gives me the chance to express my opinions about something I really love—books!

Responding to Literature

When you respond to literature, you analyze it by looking at the parts of the work, their relationship to each other, and their relationship to the whole. This is an important kind of thinking that I'll need in other subjects and in real life. Responding to literature takes analytical thinking, so this will be good practice.

Linking Argument Writing Traits to a Response to Literature

In this chapter, you will write an opinion about a book you have read. This type of argument writing is called a book review. Leila will guide you through the stages of the writing process: Prewrite, Draft, Revise, Edit, and Publish. In each stage, Leila will show you important writing strategies that are linked to the Argument Writing Traits below.

Argument Writing Traits

Ideas
- clearly stated claims, often balanced by alternate or opposing claims
- supporting evidence from accurate and credible sources

Organization
- a strong introduction that presents the writer's position
- reasons and evidence that are organized logically
- a conclusion that restates the thesis and possibly provides a call to action
- transitions that clarify the relationships between ideas

Voice
- a voice that supports the writer's purpose

Word Choice
- language that is compelling

Sentence Fluency
- sentences that vary in length and begin in different ways

Conventions
- no or few errors in grammar, usage, mechanics, and spelling

Before you write, read Juan Cepeda's book review on the next page. Then use the response to literature rubric on pages 256–257 to decide how well he did. (You might want to look back at What's in a Response to Literature? on page 252, too!)

Two Books by One Excellent Author

by Juan Cepeda

Virginia Hamilton has written a wide range of stories. *The House of Dies Drear,* for example, is a spellbinding mystery. In contrast, *Cousins* is an emotional story of love and betrayal. Although different, both books are ideal for middle graders.   **Thesis statement**

Organization—comparing characters

These readers can easily identify with the young main characters in these two books. While these characters are both independent, they love their families. In *The House of Dies Drear,* Thomas Small attempts to unravel the dark secrets of his new house by himself. Thomas wants to prove that he is brave and smart, like his father. He also wants to protect his family from dangers in the house. In *Cousins,* on the other hand, young Cammy loves being her mother's "baby." Like Thomas, though, she also enjoys freedom. She wants to visit her grandmother whenever she pleases. Unlike Thomas, Cammy rarely sees her father. Instead, she looks up to her big brother. Sometimes she feels "like she would burst with love" for him.

Clear writing

Supporting evidence

Organization—comparing settings

The settings of both books combine the familiar and the unfamiliar. Thomas's new home is a mysterious old house. The huge mansion had been a stop on the Underground Railroad. It has a homey kitchen, but it also has secret passages. The house looms over the story, creating a dark mood. In contrast, the pleasant little town in *Cousins* creates a sunny mood. As in *The House of Dies Drear,* however, that setting can turn threatening. In *Cousins,* a river swallows one of Cammy's cousins.

Organization— comparing themes

Each book addresses the theme of dealing with changes. Many middle-grade readers can identify with this theme, as they are also dealing with changes. Thomas has to overcome his fears about moving to a new place. Similarly, Cammy copes with her grief over the death of her cousin.

Virginia Hamilton tells stories that middle graders can understand and enjoy. Read *The House of Dies Drear, Cousins,* or any of Hamilton's other novels. You will see how the characters, settings, and themes make her stories so appealing.   **Clear writing**

Rubric

Use this 6-point rubric to plan and score a response to literature.

	6	5	4	
Ideas	A clear thesis statement states the writer's opinion. Comparisons are well supported with relevant facts and quotations from reliable sources.	The thesis statement includes the writer's opinion. Relevant facts and quotations support the thesis.	The thesis statement is present but may be unclear. The writer may focus the review on only one book. Facts or quotations are used.	
Organization	A clear compare-contrast pattern organizes the information. Transition words effectively clarify similarities and differences.	A compare-contrast pattern is used well. Transitions clarify ideas.	A compare-contrast pattern is used and is fairly easy to follow. Transitions are often helpful.	
Voice	The writer establishes and consistently maintains a formal style.	The writer establishes a formal style and maintains it most of the time.	The writer establishes a formal style but does not maintain it consistently.	
Word Choice	Neutral language presents the writer's opinion fairly. Precise words clarify and enhance opinions.	The writer uses neutral language well. Precise words clarify and enhance comparisons.	The writer uses neutral language. Most comparisons are clear and easy to understand.	
Sentence Fluency	Great variety in sentence patterns and lengths makes the writing flow smoothly.	Variety in sentence patterns and lengths makes the writing flow smoothly.	Some variety in sentence patterns and lengths makes the writing easy to read.	
Conventions	The writing has been thoroughly edited. Complex sentences are punctuated correctly.	A few hard-to-find errors are present. Most complex sentences are punctuated correctly.	Some errors are present but don't take away from the meaning. Some complex sentences are punctuated correctly.	

✚ **Presentation**   White space organizes the text for easy reading.

3	2	1	
The thesis statement takes work to discover. Facts and quotations are limited and may be irrelevant or unreliable. The reader is left with questions.	The topic is not clear. The writer's opinion is not shared. Vague information lacks relevant facts or quotations.	The writing is not clear and contains no thesis statement. It lacks information.	**Ideas**
The writing is not organized in a compare-contrast pattern. Sometimes transitions are missing or do not make the ideas clear.	The writing is hard to follow, and transitions are unclear or missing.	Transitions are missing, and the reader feels lost. The writing lacks any organization.	**Organization**
The style wavers between formal and informal throughout the writing.	The style is mainly informal, with occasional moments of formality.	The writing has no clear voice and is too casual throughout.	**Voice**
The writer uses some biased words. Some comparisons are hard to follow because vague words are used.	Much of the writer's language is biased or too general. Comparisons are hard to understand.	Words simply fill the page. The reader feels lost.	**Word Choice**
Some sentences are choppy. Sentence beginnings and lengths are often the same.	Sentences are either too short or too long. Sentences are incomplete, run-on, or choppy.	The writing is difficult to read. Sentences are incomplete or incorrect.	**Sentence Fluency**
Errors in complex sentences are noticeable and may take away from the meaning.	Writing contains frequent errors in complex sentences that take away from the meaning.	The writing is not edited. Many serious errors in complex sentences make the reading hard or impossible to read.	**Conventions**

See Appendix B for 4-, 5-, and 6-point argument rubrics.

Using the Rubric to Study the Model

Response to Literature

Did you notice that the model on page 255 points out some key elements of a response to literature? As he wrote "Two Books by One Excellent Author," Juan Cepeda used these elements to help him write his opinion. He also used the 6-point rubric on pages 256–257 to plan, draft, revise, and edit the writing. A rubric is a great tool for evaluating writing during the writing process.

Now let's use the same rubric to score the model. To do this, we'll focus on each trait separately, starting with Ideas. We'll use the top descriptor for each trait (column 6), along with examples from the model, to help us understand how the traits work together. How would you score Juan on each trait?

- A clear thesis statement states the writer's opinion.
- Comparisons are well supported with relevant facts and quotations from reliable sources.

Juan gives his opinion in the first paragraph. He points out that Virginia Hamilton has written many books and names two of them. Then he clearly states that middle graders should read these two books.

[from the writing model]

Virginia Hamilton has written a wide range of stories. *The House of Dies Drear*, for example, is a spellbinding mystery. In contrast, *Cousins* is an emotional story of love and betrayal. Although different, both books are ideal for middle graders.

Organization

- A clear compare-contrast pattern organizes the information.
- Transition words effectively clarify similarities and differences.

Juan writes a paragraph each on the characters, settings, and themes of the books. Juan first states a way both books appeal to readers. Then he demonstrates how each book does that. Notice the transition word *Similarly* that tells readers the author is making a comparison.

[from the writing model]

Each book addresses the theme of dealing with changes. Many middle-grade readers can identify with this theme, as they are also dealing with changes. Thomas has to overcome his fears about moving to a new place. Similarly, Cammy copes with her grief over the death of her cousin.

Voice

- The writer establishes and consistently maintains a formal style.

Juan's writing style is appropriate for a book review; he keeps his language formal. That doesn't mean he sounds stuffy or dull. It does mean he avoids casual, slangy language. Juan's formal, direct style encourages the reader to take him seriously.

[from the writing model]

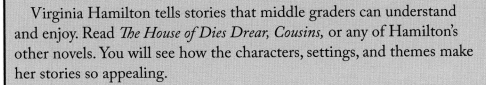

Virginia Hamilton tells stories that middle graders can understand and enjoy. Read *The House of Dies Drear*, *Cousins*, or any of Hamilton's other novels. You will see how the characters, settings, and themes make her stories so appealing.

Word Choice

- Neutral language presents the writer's opinion fairly.
- Precise words clarify and enhance opinions.

Juan is careful to be fair in presenting his opinions. He doesn't use biased or negative words. In the example below, he uses precise words like *mysterious, looms, pleasant* and *little* to contrast the dark mood in one book with the sunny mood in the other book. Words like these gave me a very clear picture of how the two books are different.

[from the writing model]

Thomas's new home is a mysterious old house. The huge mansion had been a stop on the Underground Railroad. It has a homey kitchen, but it also has secret passages. The house looms over the story, creating a dark mood. In contrast, the pleasant little town in *Cousins* creates a sunny mood.

Sentence Fluency

- Great variety in sentence patterns and lengths makes the writing flow smoothly.

Juan uses a variety of sentences throughout his review to keep things flowing smoothly, but I especially like this paragraph. The sentences are well written and clear, and none of them follow the same pattern. There's even a command in there!

[from the writing model]

Virginia Hamilton tells stories that middle graders can understand and enjoy. Read *The House of Dies Drear, Cousins,* or any of Hamilton's other novels. You will see how the characters, settings, and themes make her stories so appealing.

Conventions

- **The writing has been thoroughly edited.**
- **Complex sentences are punctuated correctly.**

Juan seems to have edited his book review well—I didn't find any mistakes. He was even careful to correctly put a comma after the introductory clause in this complex sentence.

[from the writing model]

While these characters are both independent, they love their families.

✚ Presentation   White space organizes the text for easy reading.

Now it's my turn to write! How can I apply good writing strategies in my own response to literature? Just watch! I'm going to use what I learned from the rubric and some good writing strategies.

Prewrite

Focus on **Ideas**

The Rubric Says	A clear thesis statement states the writer's opinion. Comparisons are well supported with relevant facts and quotations from reliable sources.
Writing Strategy	Find two similar books. Take notes in a response journal.

Recently I read *Number the Stars* by Lois Lowry. I chose it because it was about my Jewish heritage. I'll use it for my next writing assignment: a book review that compares two books.

The review on page 255 compares two books by the same author. I decided to compare two fiction books on the same topic. *Good Night, Maman* is a fiction book like *Number the Stars*, but it's by a different author, Norma Fox Mazer.

I need to take good notes so the thesis statement and supporting evidence I write later are clear and complete.

I wrote these notes from memory about *Number the Stars* before I read *Good Night, Maman*.

My Notes on Number the Stars

✔ World War II: Nazi soldiers all over Copenhagen, Denmark

✔ 1943: Nazis begin arresting Jews. Jewish Rosens leave their daughter Ellen with her friend Annemarie Johansen and her family. Johansens pretend Ellen is their daughter.

✔ Annemarie and her mom take Ellen to Uncle Henrik's house at the coast. Ellen's parents come there. They have a fake funeral so Jews can gather at the house disguised as mourners. Nazis investigate; girls are terrified, but brave.

✔ Annemarie's parents, Uncle Henrik, and others help Jews hide on fishing boats to escape to Sweden.

✔ Annemarie meets Nazis in woods; she is frightened, but brave. Rosens get to Sweden safely.

Instead of taking notes as I read my second book, I'm keeping a response journal. That way, I can write down my thoughts as I read the book. This book is also about a Jewish girl and her family hiding from the Nazis during World War II. I included my own reactions and lots of quotations (with the page numbers where I found them). See what I've written so far?

✒ **Writer's Term**

Response Journal

A **response journal** is a notebook or other place where someone jots down his or her impressions about an experience, such as reading a book.

My Response Journal for <u>Good Night, Maman</u>
(page 1)

I couldn't stay quiet for a year like Karin Levi did in that attic closet. I guess she just had to.

Maman is strict but sweet. You can see why Karin loves her so much. Marc acts so mature. He's trying to be the man since his dad was shot.

It must have been terrible to run from your home, begging for food, with no place to live. Karin said, "It had been weeks since I'd slept on a real bed, in a real room." (p. 31) She said, "We were free and unfree. We were in our own beloved land, but it was not ours." (p. 36)

It was so sad when Karin kissed Maman goodbye. Karin was worried Maman wouldn't find them after she got better. "How was she going to do that? Find us where?" Karin said. (p. 58)

I thought everyone who helped the Jews was nice to them, but Madame Zetain wasn't. The farmer and Maria Theresa were. Maria Theresa even told them about a ship that could take them to America.

Apply

Choose a book you've already read and liked, and make notes on it. Then keep a response journal as you read a second book that you plan to compare with it.

Prewrite

The Rubric Says   A clear compare-contrast pattern organizes the information.

Writing Strategy   Make a Venn Diagram from the notes and response journal.

The rubric stresses the importance of organizing my book review. I'll review my notes and my response journal and organize the important points into a Venn Diagram. This diagram will help me keep track of the ways that the books are similar and different.

Writer's Term____

Venn Diagram

A **Venn Diagram** is two overlapping circles that show how two things are similar and different. Ways the things are similar are described in the overlapping section. Ways they are different are described in the outside part of each circle.

One of the first things I notice is that *Number the Stars* is set in Denmark, but *Good Night, Maman* is set in France and other countries. That's one way the two books are different. I'll put that information in each outside circle.

However, both books take place during World War II. That's one way they are the same. I'll write that in the overlapping part of the circles. I already have a good start on my Venn Diagram!

Here is my completed Venn Diagram. Besides the settings, I compared the characters, the main events, and the themes. I decided that the theme is the same in both books: Hope and bravery help the children survive.

VENN DIAGRAM
Comparing My Books

Number the Stars
- set in Denmark
- Annemarie and Ellen are warm and fed.
- Rosens are together and safe.
- Rosens escape to Sweden.

Both Books
- 10-year-old girls
- set in WWII
- Nazis are searching for Jews.
- People help Jews escape.
- Hope and bravery help the children survive.

Good Night, Maman
- set in France, Italy, USA
- Karin and Marc are homeless and hungry.
- Levi family splits up; mother dies later.
- Karin and Marc escape to USA.

Reflect

How does Leila's Venn Diagram look? Does it make the major similarities and differences clear?

Apply

Organize your ideas by using a Venn Diagram.

Draft

Focus on **Ideas**

The Rubric Says   A clear thesis statement states the writer's opinion.

Writing Strategy   Write a clear thesis statement and include relevant supporting evidence.

The rubric reminds me that my thesis statement should be very clear. It should prepare the reader for what's coming in my book review, so I need to put it in my first paragraph.

After looking at my notes and response journal, I think I like *Good Night, Maman* better than *Number the Stars*. That will be my thesis statement!

Next I'll summarize the plot of each book. I'll support my thesis with relevant facts and quotations from both stories and show why I think *Good Night, Maman* is better in some ways. The first part of my draft is on the next page.

Writer's Term___

Thesis Statement

A **thesis statement** is the opinion the writer is attempting to prove. The writer tries to convince readers to accept or believe his or her opinion or thesis statement.

[DRAFT]

Bravery and Hope

by Leila

Number the Stars, by Lois Lowry, and Good Night, Maman, by Norma Fox Mazer, tell about brave young girls during World War II. I prefer Good Night, Maman. It shows better than Number the Stars that children needed both hope and bravery to get through terrible experiences during the war. **[thesis statement]**

In Number the Stars, Annemarie Johansen and Ellen Rosen are friends. They are 10 years old and live in Copenhagen, Denmark. It is 1943, and the Nazis have started arresting Jews in Copenhagen. The Rosens are Jewish. **[relevant facts]**

Ellen stays with Annemarie and pretends to be her sister. Although scared, Annemarie and Ellen face the Nazis when they come to the Johansens' apartment.

Reflect

What do you think? Is Leila's thesis statement clear? How do the facts support her thesis?

Apply

Write a draft using your Venn Diagram. Write a clear thesis statement and use relevant facts and quotations to support it.

Revise

Focus on Organization

The Rubric Says	Transition words effectively clarify similarities and differences.
Writing Strategy	Link ideas with transitions, such as *same, similarly, however, yet,* and *on one hand.*

The rubric points out that transition words can help make comparisons clearer. Useful transition words for comparing and contrasting include *in the same way, similarly, likewise, like, as, also, on the other hand, in contrast, unlike, although, more/less, yet,* and *but.* I added a few transition words to this paragraph. Read what I wrote to see if it's clearer.

Writer's Term

Transition Words

Transition words show how ideas are linked to one another. In argument writing, transition words can help tell the reader that two ideas are similar or different.

[DRAFT]

[added transition words]

Danish people help the Jews in <u>Number the Stars</u>. Similarly, French and Italian people help them in <u>Good Night, Maman</u>. In <u>Number the Stars</u>, Ellen is separated from her parents for only a few days. In contrast, Karin and Marc are separated from Maman for months.

Apply

Add transition words to clarify the similarities and differences in your review.

Focus on Voice

The Rubric Says The writer establishes and consistently maintains a formal style.

Writing Strategy Use a formal style throughout.

The rubric points out that I need to keep my style formal throughout my review. After all, I want my readers to take me and my opinions seriously. I can't let my voice fade and become too casual halfway through my writing. I also need to show that I've read the books carefully and that I know my topic. I see a place in this paragraph where I can make my voice sound more appropriate.

[DRAFT]

[used more formal language]

The separation becomes

I realized the separation was wider when Karen and Marc board a
taking
ship that takes lots of Jewish refugees to the United States. Annemarie
has only
and Ellen can depend on their parents for help, but Karin doesn't have
anybody but Marc.

Reflect

How did Leila make the style of her writing more formal?

Apply

Read over your draft. Make sure you maintain a formal style throughout your paper. Revise for voice where necessary.

Revise

Focus on Word Choice

The Rubric Says Neutral language presents the writer's opinion fairly. Precise words clarify and enhance opinions.

Writing Strategy Avoid loaded words that cause a strong negative reaction.

The rubric cautions me about using language that is loaded—words that show my bias. Language like this won't convince my readers and can actually push them away. In addition, using vague or too-general words can confuse readers. I need to share my opinions by using neutral words and precise language.

[DRAFT]

[used precise language]

Both of these books are about 10-year-old Jewish girls coping with
~~occupied by the~~
life in countries ~~where there are~~ Nazis. While I enjoyed reading both of
them, ~~I thought the ending of Number the Stars was kind of dumb.~~

I liked *Good Night, Maman* a little better because I thought the ending
 more realistic
was ~~so much cooler~~. [used neutral, more precise language]

Apply

Is your language neutral so it presents your opinion fairly? Are your words precise? Look for loaded words that might cause a negative reaction and vague words that could confuse your readers.

The Rubric Says	The writing has been thoroughly edited. Complex sentences are punctuated correctly.
Writing Strategy	Check that all dependent clauses are part of complex sentences and are punctuated correctly.

Writer's Term

Complex Sentence and Dependent Clause

A **complex sentence** contains an independent clause and a **dependent clause**. An independent clause has a subject and a verb. It is also a simple sentence. A dependent clause has a subject and a verb but does not make sense by itself. It is a sentence fragment.

Now it's time to check my draft for mistakes in spelling, capitalization, and punctuation. I also need to check my use of dependent clauses. By themselves, they are sentence fragments. I'll make sure they are part of complex sentences and punctuated correctly.

[DRAFT]

[made dependent clause part of a complex sentence]

"It had been years since I'd had friends my own age. I hardly even remembered how to act like a friend, but I pretended I did. Karin

, Karin does well

says. Although it's not easy being in a new country. Perhaps Ellen does well in Sweden, too, but Number the Stars does not discuss that.

Reflect

It takes hard work to select the best words and to make sure all the sentences are complete. How have Leila's revisions and edits strengthened her book review?

Apply   Conventions

Edit your draft for spelling, punctuation, and capitalization. Be sure that any dependent clauses are contained within complex sentences.

For more practice with complex sentences and dependent clauses, use the exercises on the next two pages.

Complex Sentences

Know the Rule

A **complex sentence** contains an independent clause and a dependent clause. An **independent clause** has a subject and a verb. It is also a simple sentence. A **dependent clause** has a subject and a verb but does not make sense by itself. It is one kind of **sentence fragment**. Dependent clauses begin with **subordinating conjunctions** such as *although, because, if, as, before,* or *when.*

> **Example:**
> **(independent clause)**
> You will make wise decisions.
> **(dependent clause)**
> If you think carefully.
> **(dependent clause + independent clause = complex sentence)**
> If you think carefully, you will make wise decisions.

Practice the Rule

Number a separate sheet of paper from 1–8. Read each group of words and write **CX** if it is a complex sentence or **F** (fragment) if it is a dependent clause.

1. Although Lois Lowry has written many books, *Number the Stars* was her first to win the Newbery Award.
2. When Lowry learned about the World War II rescue of Jews in Denmark.
3. After the Nazis began to threaten the Danish Jews, the Danish Resistance smuggled nearly 7,000 Jews to safety.
4. If you were a Jew in Denmark during the early 1940s.
5. A resistance is a secret organization because it works against a government.
6. Although most European Jews had to wear a yellow star on their clothing during World War II.
7. Because Norma Fox Mazer wanted to write both fiction and history, she wrote the historical novel *Good Night, Maman.*
8. When Mazer prepared to write her book.

Commas After Introductory Clauses

Know the Rule

When a complex sentence begins with a dependent clause, a **comma** separates it from the rest of the sentence.

Example:
After you finish your homework, we can go out to eat. (Sentence begins with a dependent clause.)
We can go out to eat after you finish your homework. (Sentence begins with an independent clause.)

Practice the Rule

Number a separate sheet of paper from 1–10. Rewrite and correctly punctuate the sentences that require a comma. Write **Correct** if the sentence does not need a comma.

1. Before the bell rang our teacher assigned our book review.
2. Because Jenna likes animals she looked for a book about animals to read and review.
3. After I talked to my teacher I decided on a book about the Underground Railroad.
4. I started to read the book before I went to bed.
5. Dan didn't read his book in time because he started it too late.
6. While we read our books the teacher asked us to make notes in our response journals about the story.
7. When we give our opinions we use neutral language and a formal tone.
8. Although Pietro finished his book review he is proofreading it again.
9. If Lisette reads her book review aloud the whole class will listen.
10. I think my book review is excellent because I worked hard on it.

Publish

+Presentation

Publishing Strategy	Publish the review in the school newspaper.
Presentation Strategy	Use white space to organize the information.

I like to share my opinions about what I read. A lot of people can read my review in the school newspaper! As I prepare my review, I need to include enough white space to make it easy to read and understand. I'll check to make sure my title is centered, the margins are wide enough, my paragraphs are indented, and the line spacing is appropriate. If I prepare my final copy on the computer, this will be easy to do. Then I'll check my review over one last time using this checklist to help me.

My Final Checklist

Did I—

✔ make sure all the dependent clauses are connected to independent clauses?

✔ use commas after dependent clauses at the beginnings of sentences?

✔ use white space to help organize my information and make it easy to read?

✔ proofread for spelling, capitalization, grammar, and punctuation?

Apply

Make a final checklist to check your book review. Then make a final copy to publish.

Bravery and Hope

by Leila

Number the Stars by Lois Lowry and *Good Night, Maman* by Norma Fox Mazer tell about brave young girls during World War II. I prefer *Good Night, Maman.* It shows better than *Number the Stars* that children needed both hope and bravery to get through terrible experiences during the war.

In *Number the Stars,* Annemarie Johansen and Ellen Rosen are friends. They are 10 years old and live in Copenhagen, Denmark. It is 1943, and the Nazis have started arresting Jews in Copenhagen. The Rosens are Jewish.

Ellen stays with Annemarie and pretends to be her sister. Although scared, Annemarie and Ellen face the Nazis when they come to the Johansens' apartment.

The Johansens then take Ellen to Uncle Henrik's house by the sea. There Ellen is reunited with her parents. Annemarie realizes her family and friends are in danger, but she is unsure that she is brave enough to help them. Uncle Henrik says, "I think you are like your mama, and your papa, and like me. Frightened, but determined, and if the time came to be brave, I am quite sure you would be very, very brave."

Later, Annemarie proves she is brave by delivering an important package to Uncle Henrik. It contains a handkerchief treated to make the Nazi dogs lose their sense of smell. Because the dogs can't smell the people hidden on Uncle Henrik's boat, the Rosens make it safely to Sweden.

The main character in *Good Night, Maman* is also a 10-year-old girl. Karin Levi lives in Paris, France, with her mother (Maman) and her brother, Marc. The Nazis have also occupied this country and have been searching for Jewish people like the Levis. They have shot Karin's father already. Her family must hide in a tiny attic closet for a year. This is worse than anything Annemarie or Ellen goes through, but Karin stays hopeful.

Suddenly the Levis must flee Paris. Annemarie and Ellen see Nazis. Karin's family doesn't. On the other hand, the threat of capture out in the open is always there for the Levis. They must travel at night and hide during the day. Karin is frightened and puzzled. As they walk, she says, "We were free and unfree. We were in our own beloved land, but it was not ours."

Karin's journey to freedom is rough. She does not have food and shelter the way Ellen did. When Karin's family stops to beg for food at a farmhouse and she sees a cot in the corner, she says, "It had been weeks since I'd slept on a real bed, in a real room."

Danish people help the Jews in *Number the Stars*. Similarly, French and Italian people help them in *Good Night, Maman*. In *Number the Stars,* Ellen is separated from her parents for only a few days. In contrast, Karin and Marc are separated from Maman for months.

The separation becomes wider when Karin and Marc board a ship taking Jewish refugees to the United States. Annemarie and Ellen can depend on their parents for help, but Karin has only Marc. She begins writing letters to Maman. The letters show how brave and strong she is. In her first letter, she writes, "I never wanted to go so far away from you. I didn't want to get on this boat. But Marc said we wouldn't be safe anywhere in Europe until the war was over, and that you would absolutely want us to do this."

In the United States, Karin and Marc stay in a refugee camp and learn American ways. Karin still writes to Maman, but she also is determined to make new friends. "It had been years since I'd had friends my own age. I hardly even remembered how to act like a friend, but I pretended I did," Karin says. Although it's not easy being in a new country, Karin does well. Perhaps

Ellen does well in Sweden, too, but *Number the Stars* does not discuss that.

Finally Karin learns the truth: her mother is dead. Marc has known about it for a few months. He helps Karin handle her grief.

When the war ends, Annemarie waits for Ellen to come back to Copenhagen. Karin plans to live in California with her aunt. Although Karin has no parents, she has bravery and hope. Karin says, "I thought about everything I had learned about people—some bad, some good. And I had learned that you can't look back for too long. You just have to keep going."

Both of these books are about 10-year-old Jewish girls coping with life in countries occupied by the Nazis. While I enjoyed reading both of them, I liked *Good Night, Maman* a little better because I thought the ending was more realistic. Many Jewish families were separated forever by that war, and *Good Night, Maman* showed that clearly.

Reflect

What do you think? Does Leila's paper have all the traits of a good book review? Check it against the rubric. Then use the rubric to check your own book review.

What's an Argument Essay?

An argument essay expresses a writer's opinion on a topic. It tries to convince readers to agree with the writer and maybe even act in a certain way. For example, an argument essay might try to convince readers to conserve energy in specific ways.

I think I'll like writing an argument essay. I get to act like a lawyer and present a case for my opinion!

What's in an Argument Essay?

Clear Opinion
I need to decide exactly what I think of the issue I'm writing about. Then I have to make that opinion clear to my readers. That means stating the opinion convincingly so my audience knows just where I stand.

Good Reasoning
Readers aren't going to be convinced that my opinion is right just because I say so. I need to write a well-organized essay with plenty of supportive, relevant facts and good, logical reasons for my opinions.

Neutral Language
When you're expressing an opinion on something you care about, it's easy to get emotional. But negative language or emotionally loaded words just turn readers off. I'll use neutral language in my essay so my audience will be willing to consider my opinion.

Question-and-Answer Pattern
Facts are important in this kind of writing, but I don't want my essay to be boring! I'm going to use a question-and-answer pattern to keep things interesting.

Why write an Argument Essay?

I enjoy convincing people of an opinion I think is right, but there are other reasons to write an argument essay. I've listed a few suggestions here to give you some ideas.

Changing Lives

Maybe that sounds a bit dramatic, but I really think an argument essay can do this! A good essay can change someone's point of view—and even encourage him or her to do something differently.

Reasoning Skills

You really have to think things through to write an argument essay. So this kind of writing gives me some good practice in reasoning skills, such as organizing my thoughts, backing up a point, and following a logical train of thought.

Informing

Even if an argument essay doesn't change a reader's opinion, it gives him or her more information on the topic. He or she might learn something completely new—or develop a deeper understanding of the issue.

Keeping Calm

Writing an argument essay helps make a disagreement about an issue less emotional and personal. This kind of writing turns things into a debate instead of a fight!

Linking Argument Writing Traits to an **Argument Essay**

In this chapter, you will write an essay that expresses your opinion about a topic. This type of argument writing is called an argument essay. Leila will guide you through the stages of the writing process: Prewrite, Draft, Revise, Edit, and Publish. In each stage, Leila will show you important writing strategies that are linked to the Argument Writing Traits below.

Argument Writing Traits

- clearly stated claims, often balanced by alternate or opposing claims
- supporting evidence from accurate and credible sources

- a strong introduction that presents the writer's position
- reasons and evidence that are organized logically
- a conclusion that restates the thesis and possibly provides a call to action
- transitions that clarify the relationships between ideas

- a voice that supports the writer's purpose

- language that is compelling

- sentences that vary in length and begin in different ways

- no or few errors in grammar, usage, mechanics, and spelling

Before you write, read Arina Zubatova's argument essay on the next page. Then use the argument essay rubric on pages 282–283 to decide how well she did. (You might want to look back at What's in an Argument Essay? on page 278, too!)

The Right Angle on the Triangle
by Arina Zubatova

Question →

When you think about the Bermuda Triangle, what comes to your mind? Do you picture mysterious forces, time warps, and the underwater city of Atlantis? That is how some people explain the disappearances of boats and planes in the Bermuda Triangle. However, the dangers there are natural, not supernatural.

Answer

↳ Clear opinion

The corners of the Bermuda Triangle are Bermuda, Puerto Rico, and Fort Lauderdale, Florida. About 100 boats and planes have disappeared in this region. About 1,000 people have died there in the past century. However, that is only ten people a year, not a high number for such a large area. If this region were especially dangerous, insurance companies would charge higher rates for crafts that pass through it. They do not.

Logical reasoning

Question →

Why did those 100 boats and planes disappear in the Triangle? The causes were natural, not supernatural. In the tropics, sudden storms—even giant waterspouts—can destroy ships and aircraft. The Gulf Stream, a strong ocean current, can pull amateur sailors far off course. In addition, the region has trenches thousands of feet deep. In fact, the deepest trench in the Atlantic Ocean is in the Bermuda Triangle. Remains of boats and planes may be buried in these trenches.

Answer

↳ Neutral language

Despite these facts, many accidents in the Bermuda Triangle have been described as mysterious. The 1945 disappearance of five Navy bombers off the coast of Florida was one of them. The planes disappeared during a training flight for rookies. The flight was led by an experienced pilot. However, radio transcripts show that his compass was not working. It caused him to lead the group out to sea instead of toward Florida. Then a storm blew in. The planes vanished, and no wreckage was ever found.

What happened to those Navy bombers? The planes probably ended up far out in the Atlantic. There they ran out of gas and fell into the sea. Sharks took the pilots. A trench swallowed the wreckage. In spite of this logical explanation, this and many other disappearances have been blamed on mysterious forces in the Triangle.

↳ Neutral language

People like a good story. Still, we must not ignore the facts about the Bermuda Triangle. The dangers are real, not supernatural.

↳ Clear opinion

Rubric

Use this 6-point rubric to plan and score an argument essay.

	6	5	4
Ideas	The topic is clearly presented. Clear reasons and relevant facts support the opinion and show an understanding of the topic.	The topic is stated. Reasons and facts support the opinion and show some understanding of the topic.	The topic can be identified. Several reasons and facts are included, but some may not be relevant.
Organization	The essay is organized into an introduction, body, and conclusion that work together to promote the argument.	The essay has a clear introduction, body, and conclusion. All parts relate clearly to the argument.	The essay has an introduction, body, and conclusion, but parts may be unclear or do not support the argument.
Voice	The writer establishes and consistently maintains a direct, formal style.	The writer's style is direct and formal most of the time.	Occasionally the writer's voice becomes vague or too informal, but overall the style is appropriate.
Word Choice	Neutral words create a balanced and fair tone. The writer avoids loaded or negative words.	The writer's words are fair. The writer avoids loaded or negative words.	Some words are loaded or negative in tone. The reader may question the writer's opinion.
Sentence Fluency	Varied sentences hold the reader's interest. Thoughtful questions move the reader along.	Most sentences use varied patterns. Questions move the reader along.	Some variety in sentence patterns is present. The writing could use another question or two.
Conventions	The writing has been thoughtfully edited. Pronouns are correct, and their antecedents are clear.	The writing is edited well. Just a few errors are present. Most pronouns are correct and antecedents are clear.	A few noticeable errors in pronoun use and unclear antecedents don't confuse the reader.
✚Presentation	The essay is neatly prepared and legible.		

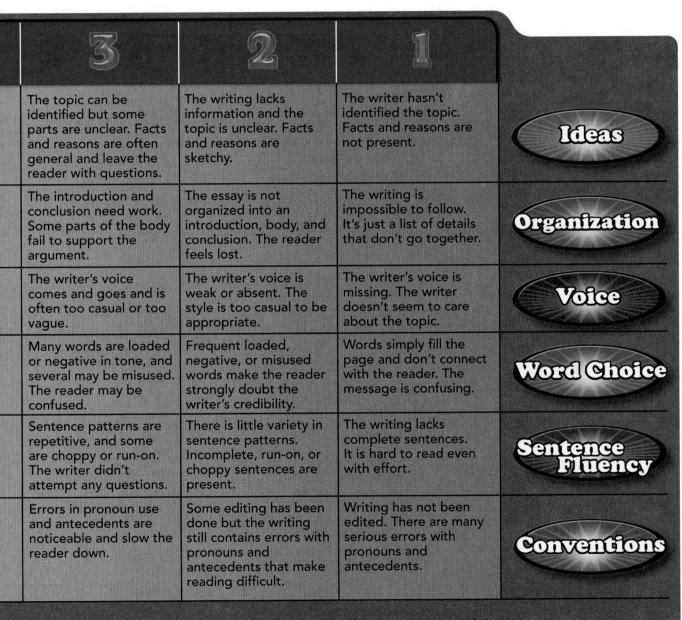

3	2	1	
The topic can be identified but some parts are unclear. Facts and reasons are often general and leave the reader with questions.	The writing lacks information and the topic is unclear. Facts and reasons are sketchy.	The writer hasn't identified the topic. Facts and reasons are not present.	**Ideas**
The introduction and conclusion need work. Some parts of the body fail to support the argument.	The essay is not organized into an introduction, body, and conclusion. The reader feels lost.	The writing is impossible to follow. It's just a list of details that don't go together.	**Organization**
The writer's voice comes and goes and is often too casual or too vague.	The writer's voice is weak or absent. The style is too casual to be appropriate.	The writer's voice is missing. The writer doesn't seem to care about the topic.	**Voice**
Many words are loaded or negative in tone, and several may be misused. The reader may be confused.	Frequent loaded, negative, or misused words make the reader strongly doubt the writer's credibility.	Words simply fill the page and don't connect with the reader. The message is confusing.	**Word Choice**
Sentence patterns are repetitive, and some are choppy or run-on. The writer didn't attempt any questions.	There is little variety in sentence patterns. Incomplete, run-on, or choppy sentences are present.	The writing lacks complete sentences. It is hard to read even with effort.	**Sentence Fluency**
Errors in pronoun use and antecedents are noticeable and slow the reader down.	Some editing has been done but the writing still contains errors with pronouns and antecedents that make reading difficult.	Writing has not been edited. There are many serious errors with pronouns and antecedents.	**Conventions**

See Appendix B for 4-, 5-, and 6-point argument rubrics.

Argument Essay
Using the Rubric to Study the Model

Did you notice that the model on page 281 points out some key elements of an argument essay? As she wrote "The Right Angle on the Triangle," Arina Zubatova used these elements to help her express her opinion persuasively. She also used the 6-point rubric on pages 282–283 to plan, draft, revise, and edit the writing. A rubric is a great tool for evaluating writing during the writing process.

Now let's use the same rubric to score the model. To do this, we'll focus on each trait separately, starting with Ideas. We'll use the top descriptor for each trait (column 6), along with examples from the model, to help us understand how the traits work together. How would you score Arina on each trait?

Ideas

- **The topic is clearly presented.**
- **Clear reasons and relevant facts support the opinion and show an understanding of the topic.**

Arina clearly states her topic in the first paragraph. Then she carefully lays out her reasons and facts to support her opinion. For example, she lists the natural hazards within the Bermuda Triangle that can endanger ships and planes alike. I must admit, her facts are pretty convincing, and it's clear Arina knows what she's talking about!

[from the writing model]

In the tropics, sudden storms—even giant waterspouts—can destroy ships and aircraft. The Gulf Stream, a strong ocean current, can pull amateur sailors far off course.

Organization

- **The essay is organized into an introduction, body, and conclusion that work together to promote the argument.**

The introduction clearly states Arina's topic: strange disappearances in the Bermuda Triangle. The body presents her supporting facts, and the conclusion neatly sums up her opinion. Notice how clearly she presents her facts in the body.

[from the writing model]

The corners of the Bermuda Triangle are Bermuda, Puerto Rico, and Fort Lauderdale, Florida. About 100 boats and planes have disappeared in this region. About 1,000 people have died there in the past century. However, that is only ten people a year, not a high number for such a large area.

Voice

- **The writer establishes and consistently maintains a direct, formal style.**

Arina establishes a direct style right away by addressing the reader as *you* in the introduction. This helps her make a solid connection with the reader while maintaining a formal, serious style.

[from the writing model]

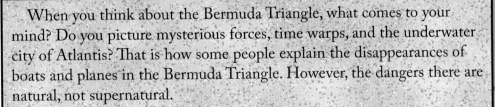

When you think about the Bermuda Triangle, what comes to your mind? Do you picture mysterious forces, time warps, and the underwater city of Atlantis? That is how some people explain the disappearances of boats and planes in the Bermuda Triangle. However, the dangers there are natural, not supernatural.

- Neutral words create a balanced and fair tone.
- The writer avoids loaded or negative words.

Arina might have used loaded, negative words, like *fool*, to show that she is amazed that some people believe there are mysterious forces in the Bermuda Triangle. However, she doesn't say, "Some fools will believe anything." Instead, her language is balanced and fair, like this:

[from the writing model]

People like a good story. Still, we must not ignore the facts about the Bermuda Triangle. The dangers are real, not supernatural.

- Varied sentences hold the reader's interest.
- Thoughtful questions move the reader along.

To help keep the reader interested, Arina varies her sentence patterns. For example, she includes a few questions to keep the reader moving through the essay. Here, she really got my attention by using a question and then answering it with details.

[from the writing model]

What happened to those Navy bombers? The planes probably ended up far out in the Atlantic. There they ran out of gas and fell into the sea. Sharks took the pilots. A trench swallowed the wreckage.

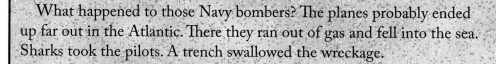

Conventions

- The writing has been thoughtfully edited.
- Pronouns are correct, and their antecedents are clear.

I didn't find a single mistake in spelling, punctuation, or capitalization. The writer was also careful with pronouns. Can you tell what the pronoun *it* refers to in the first sentence below? It refers to *region*, right? *It* and *region* are both singular, so they agree. In the second sentence, it's clear that *They* refers to *companies*. These words are both plural, so they agree.

[from the writing model]

If this region were especially dangerous, insurance companies would charge higher rates for crafts that pass through it. They do not.

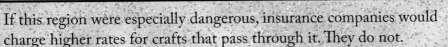

Presentation   The essay is neatly prepared and legible.

My Turn!

Now it's my turn to write an argument essay. I'll use what I learned from the rubric and good writing strategies. Follow along with me to see how I do it.

Prewrite

Focus on **Ideas**

The Rubric Says

The topic is clearly presented. Clear reasons and relevant facts support the opinion and show an understanding of the topic.

Writing Strategy

Choose an issue and find information to support the opinion.

I live in Tennessee, but California is the main location of one of my hobbies—old movies. My favorite aunt lives in California, too, and I visit her whenever I can.

Some people think that all Californians care only about how they look and what the latest fads are. That upsets me.

When our teacher asked us to write an argument essay, I decided to try to convince my classmates not to stereotype people based on where they live. I read some articles about California and took these notes.

Notes on Californians

CA's population grew 50 percent between 1970 and 1990.

CA has more immigrants from other countries than any other state.

Californians come in all shapes and sizes.

One in four Californians is Hispanic.

In 1990 census, nearly 5 million Californians had German ancestors; 3.5 million were from Irish families.

1990 census: more than half of the people living in CA were not born there.

Migrants come from all over the nation, especially the South and Northeast.

Apply

Choose an issue about which you have an opinion. Do some research and find facts to support your opinion.

The Rubric Says   The essay is organized into an introduction, body, and conclusion that work together to promote the argument.

Writing Strategy   Use a Network Tree to organize the ideas.

Writer's Term

Network Tree

A **Network Tree** organizes information about a topic. The topic or opinion goes at the top, with main ideas or reasons on the next level. The bottom level contains facts to support the main ideas or reasons.

A Network Tree can help me get my ideas in order. I'll put my opinion at the top, the reasons for my opinion under that, and supportive facts underneath each reason. The Network Tree will help me state my topic in the introduction and organize my facts for the body of my essay.

Network Tree

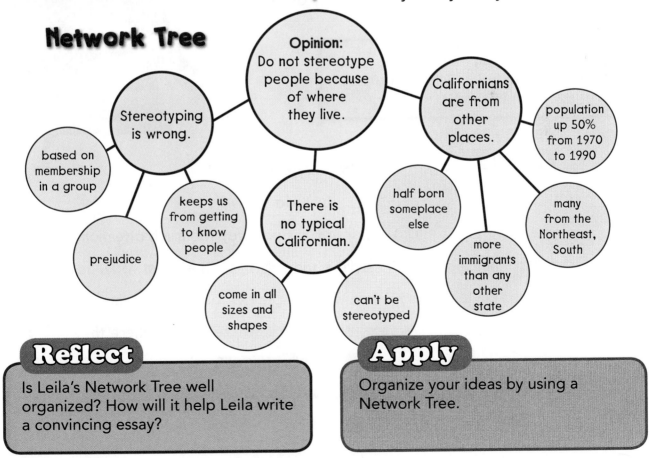

Reflect

Is Leila's Network Tree well organized? How will it help Leila write a convincing essay?

Apply

Organize your ideas by using a Network Tree.

Draft

Focus on Organization

The Rubric Says The essay is organized into an introduction, body, and conclusion that work together to promote the argument.

Writing Strategy Write well-organized paragraphs.

Now I'm ready to write my draft. Well-organized paragraphs will promote my argument. I'll use my Network Tree as a guide. The information in the middle-sized circles will be the main ideas in my body paragraphs. The small circles contain the details for the paragraphs. I know I can fix any mistakes later, so for now I'll just focus on getting my ideas down on paper. Here's a part of my draft.

Writer's Term

Opinion
An **opinion** is a belief, often strong, that cannot be proven to be true.

[DRAFT]

Don't Stereotype by State!

by Leila

Some people think all Californiains pay way too much attention to how they look. Others believe they all follow the latest fads, no matter how temporary. When we lump people together like this. In this case, we are forming an opinion about them based on where they live. That's wrong! The people who live in California are as different from one another as the people who live in every other state. We must stop stereotyping them!

[opinion/thesis]

[fact]

[DRAFT]

[reason]

Stereotyping is wrong. It's a kind of prejudice. Some ignorant people use stereotypes to jump to decisions. They decide whether they like people because of the group they belong to. They don't bother to get to know him. It's like being prejudiced against people because of the shabby clothes they wear or the strange language she speaks. You could miss meeting good friends if you make decisions based on stereotypes.

[fact]

It's really a dumb mistake to stereotype Californians. In the 1990 census, California had more than 29 million residents. More than half of Californians were born someplace else, and he moved there. Between 1970 and 1990, the poplulation of california grew by 50 percent. Many of these new residents came from the northeastern and southern states. California also has more imigrants from other countries than any other state. They can't really be grouped together because they are not the same.

Reflect

Is Leila's thesis or opinion clearly stated in the introduction? Are the reasons and the supporting facts clear?

Apply

Write a draft using your Network Tree to help you. Remember to state your opinion at the beginning, support it in the body, and sum it up in the conclusion.

Revise

Focus on **Voice**

The Rubric Says	The writer establishes and consistently maintains a direct, formal style.
Writing Strategy	Use second-person point of view, as appropriate.

I need to convince my reader that I believe passionately in my opinion. I know that second-person point of view will help me sound like I am speaking directly to the reader. If I do this immediately in my essay, my reader will be involved right away. Then I'll continue addressing my readers in a formal style, so that they'll take my views seriously.

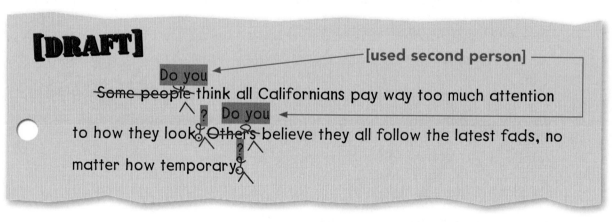

[DRAFT]

[used second person]

Do you
~~Some people~~ think all Californians pay way too much attention

Do you
to how they look? ~~Others~~ believe they all follow the latest fads, no

matter how temporary?

Apply

Try adding second-person point of view to speak directly to the reader.

Revise

Focus on Word Choice

The Rubric Says	Neutral words create a balanced and fair tone. The writer avoids loaded or negative words.
Writing Strategy	Replace loaded words with neutral words.

Writer's Term

Loaded Word

A **loaded word** has an emotional meaning. It can be a positive meaning or a negative one. For example, **shack** is a negatively loaded word for **house**. **Mansion** is a positively loaded word. Loaded words can influence a reader's thinking unfairly.

I feel strongly about my opinion, and I want to make it clear. Yet when I read my argument essay to myself, I realized that I might be using loaded words to sway readers unfairly. I replaced those words with more objective words. Now my essay seems more reasonable than emotional. You can see how it helped in this paragraph.

[DRAFT]

Stereotyping is wrong. It's a kind of prejudice. Some ~~ignorant~~

make

people use stereotypes to ~~jump to~~ decisions. They decide whether

[replaced loaded words]

they like people because of the group they belong to. They don't

take the time

~~bother~~ to get to know him. It's like being prejudiced against people

kind of

because of the ~~shabby~~ clothes they wear or the ~~strange~~ language

[deleted loaded words]

she speaks.

Reflect

Did changing the loaded words make Leila's essay seem more objective?

Apply

Replace any loaded words with neutral words.

Revise

Focus on Sentence Fluency

The Rubric Says　Varied sentences hold the reader's interest. Thoughtful questions move the reader along.

Writing Strategy　Choose punctuation for effect.

The rubric says that if I vary the types of sentences in my writing, I create more interest for my reader. Most of my sentences are statements, but I can include exclamations to show my passion about the topic and thoughtful questions to keep the reader moving along. You can see where I changed some statements to an exclamation and questions to make the writing more interesting.

[DRAFT]

How could you group all these people together? How could you say they are all the same?

Between 1970 and 1990, the poplulation of california grew by 50 percent. Many of these new residents came from the northeastern and southern states. California also has more imigrants from other countries than any other state. ~~They can't really be grouped together because they are not the same.~~

[varied punctuation for effect]　　　　[added thoughtful questions]

Apply

Look over your writing and insert a question or two to engage the reader. Vary punctuation when appropriate for effect, too.

The Rubric Says	The writing has been thoughtfully edited. Pronouns are correct, and their antecedents are clear.
Writing Strategy	Recognize and correct inappropriate shifts in pronoun number and person.

Now I have to fix my mistakes in spelling, grammar, and punctuation. I also need to make sure that my pronouns and antecedents match and that each pronoun has a clear antecedent. If I'm not careful with my pronouns, my audience will wonder whom or what I'm talking about.

Here's some of my draft, so you can see the kinds of errors I corrected.

[DRAFT]

[corrected pronoun]

census, California had more than 29 million residents. More than half

they

of Californians were born someplace else, and he moved there.

population

Between 1970 and 1990, the population of california grew by 50

percent. Many of these new residents came from the northeastern

m

and southern states. California also has more imigrants from

Reflect

Did adding questions make the writing more interesting? Are all the pronouns and antecedents clear? How have Leila's revisions and edits strengthened her essay?

Apply

Conventions

Edit your draft for spelling, punctuation, and capitalization. Be sure that all pronouns have clear antecedents that match.

For more practice with antecedents and relative pronouns, use the exercises on the next two pages.

Pronouns and Antecedents

Know the Rule

A **pronoun** must agree with its **antecedent** in two ways:
- The pronoun is singular if its antecedent is singular. The pronoun is plural if its antecedent is plural.
- The pronoun is female if its antecedent is female—or male if its antecedent is male.

> **Example:** Stereotyping might lead a girl to choose **her** friends based on the clothes **they** wear. (*Her* is singular and female, so it agrees with its singular antecedent, *girl. They* is plural and agrees with its plural antecedent, *friends.*)

When you use a pronoun, make sure its antecedent is clear.

> **Example:** Mark's friend is named Jamal. **He** lives down the street. (It is unclear whether *He* refers to *Mark* or *Jamal.*)
>
> Mark's friend Jamal lives down the street. (Sometimes the best way to correct an unclear antecedent is not to use a pronoun at all!)

Practice the Rule

Number a sheet of paper 1–8. Identify the antecedent for the underlined pronoun in each sentence.

1. Stereotyping is a part of our culture. <u>It</u> is something we should try to change.

2. Stereotyping occurs when people are grouped together. Perhaps <u>they</u> are grouped because they all play football or chess.

3. We make poor judgments when we stereotype individuals. We do not respect <u>them</u>.

4. Stereotypes can be positive or negative, but <u>they</u> are almost always unfair.

5. Victims of stereotyping often do not know what to do about <u>it</u>.

6. When we don't see people as individuals, it is easy to stereotype <u>them</u>.

7. We may feel good about ourselves if we belong to a group that people value and other people do not belong to <u>it</u>.

8. In literature and drama, stereotypes are common. <u>They</u> are often referred to as stock characters.

Relative Pronouns

Know the Rule

> When the pronouns *who, whom, whose, which,* and *that* are used to introduce
> an adjective clause, they are called **relative pronouns**. A relative pronoun always
> follows the noun described by the adjective clause it begins.
> **Example:** I have several cousins **who** live in California.

Practice the Rule

Number a sheet of paper 1–10. Write the pronoun that correctly completes the sentence. Choose from the pronouns *who, whom, whose, which,* and *that.*

1. Many places _____ have stereotypes are viewed unfairly.
2. New Yorkers _____ enjoy nature can go to Central Park to take a break from the urban environment.
3. New York workers, _____ people stereotype as moving too fast, are just like workers everywhere.
4. Bad drivers _____ live in Massachusetts are stereotypes of that state.
5. Massachusetts, _____ was a common destination for immigrants from Europe, took in many Irish immigrants.
6. Southerners, _____ love of country music is well known, may also like classical or pop music.
7. Not all people _____ live in Florida spend most of their time on the beach.
8. States _____ have the most open space have stereotypes of cowboys and ranchers.
9. Football, _____ people all over the country watch, isn't necessarily more popular in one region than another.
10. The farmers in Nebraska, _____ many people stereotype as having immense farms, work both large and small farms.

Publish
+ Presentation

Publishing Strategy   Post the essay on a class bulletin board.

Presentation Strategy   The essay is neatly prepared and legible.

Now it's time to publish my argument essay! I think I'll post it on the class bulletin board so all my classmates can read it. Before that, I want to make sure my writing is neat and legible. If my classmates can't even read my work they'll never be convinced by it! I'll either use my very best handwriting or choose a couple of readable fonts on the computer—not fancy or italic fonts. Then I'll read over my essay one more time, using the items on this final checklist.

My Final Checklist

Did I—

✔ make sure all my pronouns and antecedents agree?

✔ use relative pronouns correctly?

✔ make sure the essay looks neat and is legible?

✔ check to make sure my name is on the paper?

Apply

Make a final checklist and use it to check your argument essay. Then make a final copy to publish.

Don't Stereotype by State!

by Leila

Do you think all Californians pay too much attention to how they look? Do you believe they all follow the latest fads, no matter how temporary? When we group people together like this, we are stereotyping them. In this case, we are forming an opinion about them based on where they live. That's wrong! The people who live in California are as different from one another as the people who live in every other state. We must stop stereotyping Californians!

Stereotyping is wrong. It's a kind of prejudice. Some people use stereotypes to make decisions. They decide whether they like people because of the group those people belong to. They don't take the time to get to know them. It's like being prejudiced against people because of the kind of clothes they wear or the language they speak. You could miss meeting good friends if you make decisions based on stereotypes.

It's really unwise to stereotype Californians. More than half of Californians were born someplace else. Then they moved to California. Between 1970 and 1990, the population of California grew by 50 percent! Many of these new residents came from the northeastern and southern states. Between 1990 and 1999, more than 233,000 people moved to California from Oregon! California also has more immigrants from other countries than any other state. How could you group all these people together? How could you say they are all the same?

There is no typical Californian. One in four Californians is Hispanic. In the 1990 census, nearly 5 million Californians said they had German ancestors. Another 3.5 million Californians had Irish ancestors.

Californians have different backgrounds, customs, likes, and dislikes. Aren't they just like people everywhere? Sure, a few pay too much attention to how they look. A few people in our state do, too. Let's treat Californians like the individuals they are!

Reflect

What do you think? Are all the traits of a good argument essay in the writing? Check it against the rubric. Then check your own argument essay against the rubric.

What's a Business Letter?

You can write a business letter to express an opinion and to convince readers to consider that opinion. This isn't just a note for fun—it's a professional communication. I like the idea of writing something meaningful that I can mail to a real person!

What's in a Business Letter?

Organization
A business letter isn't very long, so my writing needs to be organized and efficient! I'll make my opinion clear at the start, and I'll stay focused on my topic and list my reasons in a logical order.

Correct Form
An effective business letter has a six-part format: the heading, inside address, salutation (or greeting), body, closing, and signature. I want to stick to the proper form so my readers will see that I care enough to do things the right way.

Formal Style
If I want my audience to consider my opinion, I have to be businesslike. A business letter is not the place for personal comments. The way I sound and the sentences I write should be consistently formal and direct.

Supporting Details
Just expressing my opinion won't be enough to convince readers. I need to show I have reasoned my way to that opinion. That's why I'll be including relevant details that clearly support my point of view.

Why write a Business Letter?

I haven't yet decided the reason for my business letter, but I have a lot of ideas about why someone might do this kind of writing. I've listed some of my ideas below.

Expressing an Opinion

I have a lot of opinions about a lot of things! A business letter gives me a good way to share those opinions with the appropriate people.

Information

Sometimes a company may not know about a problem. If I write a business letter, I can inform the company about the trouble and explain how at least one customer feels about it.

Business Skills

This kind of writing is part of many jobs. In my career, I'll probably need to know how to use the six-part format correctly and how to write in a professional way. This assignment should be good practice for that!

Encouraging Change

Sometimes more than one person will write a business letter about the same issue. If company presidents, politicians, and other decision-makers receive a lot of these letters, they might be convinced to change things. Sometimes even just one powerfully written letter can have a positive impact!

Linking Argument Writing Traits to a Business Letter

In this chapter, you will write a letter expressing your opinion to the owner or manager of a business you use. This type of argument writing is called a business letter. Leila will guide you through the stages of the writing process: Prewrite, Draft, Revise, Edit, and Publish. In each stage, Leila will show you important writing strategies that are linked to the Argument Writing Traits below.

Argument Writing Traits

	• clearly stated claims, often balanced by alternate or opposing claims • supporting evidence from accurate and credible sources
	• a strong introduction that presents the writer's position • reasons and evidence that are organized logically • a conclusion that restates the thesis and possibly provides a call to action • transitions that clarify the relationships between ideas
	• a voice that supports the writer's purpose
	• language that is compelling
	• sentences that vary in length and begin in different ways
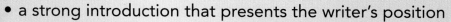	• no or few errors in grammar, usage, mechanics, and spelling

Before you write, read Jean Silverstone's business letter on the next page. Then use the business letter rubric on pages 304–305 to decide how well she did. (You might want to look back at What's in a Business Letter? on page 300, too!)

Tiny Tikes Daycare Center
333 Willow Park Road
Lexington, KY 40509
May 4, 2012

Heading

Customer Service Manager
Real Cereal, Inc.
2128 N. Jarvis St.
Trenton, NJ 08620

Inside address

Dear Customer Service Manager: **Salutation**

Businesslike tone

I own a daycare center that serves breakfast cereal to children in the morning. I am usually pleased with Real Cereal products. However, the "new and improved" Oaty Boats is not satisfactory. I refuse to continue to buy Oaty Boats until Real Cereal addresses its problems. **Clear opinion**

The boats now have little taste, and they sink instead of floating. Furthermore, the food dye in the new boats turns the milk in the bowl greenish brown.

Supporting details

In addition, I do not like a recent commercial that shows Oaty Boats as destroyers in a battle. What does your ad tell children about the uses of a boat? It tells them only that a boat is used to fight.

Body

There are sailboats, tugboats, and freighters in Oaty Boats, too. It would be more positive and educational to show children a range of boats and a range of uses. You're as responsible for molding their young minds as I am. I would like to see more thoughtful advertising from Real Cereal. Remember, it takes a community to raise a child. Please change the cereal back to its original flavor and natural color. Also, think more carefully about how you use boats in your advertising. Until Oaty Boats is returned to its original form, I will no longer purchase it for the children in my daycare center. **Clear opinion**

Sincerely, **Closing**

Jean Silverstone **Signature**

Jean Silverstone, Director

Rubric

Use this 6-point rubric to plan and score a business letter.

	6	5	4
Ideas	The purpose is clearly stated. Clear reasons and relevant, important evidence support the writer's opinion.	The purpose is clearly stated. The details are clear and most are supported with relevant evidence.	The reader can tell what the purpose of the writing is. Some details are unclear or poorly supported.
Organization	Reasons and supporting evidence are organized in order of importance. The purpose is strongly restated in the conclusion.	Most of the reasons and evidence are organized in order of importance. The purpose is restated in the conclusion.	Some reasons and evidence may be out of order, but the reader is not confused. The purpose is stated in the conclusion but may not be clear.
Voice	The writer's tone is respectful and business-like and fits the purpose well. The writer speaks directly to the reader.	The writer speaks to the reader. The tone fits the purpose and the audience.	The tone is acceptable for the audience and purpose. The writer sometimes speaks directly to the reader.
Word Choice	Specific nouns and strong verbs make the writing lively and informative.	The writing is clear and informative. Specific nouns and verbs help with the meaning.	The writing is usually clear, but some verbs are weak or overused. Some nouns are too general.
Sentence Fluency	Sentences are well written, smooth, and easy to read. They reflect the purpose of the letter.	Sentences are well written and reflect the writer's purpose.	There is some variety in sentences. The writing is easy to read silently, but harder to read aloud.
Conventions	The writing has been thoughtfully edited. Homophones are used correctly.	A few errors can be found if you look for them. Most homophones are used correctly.	Errors with homophones or other conventions are present but don't confuse the reader.
✛ Presentation	The business letter is in the proper format.		

3	2	1	
Some parts of the writing are unclear. Details are often general.	The purpose of the writing is unclear. The details are sketchy and leave the reader with questions.	The purpose in writing the letter is not stated. Details are confusing.	**Ideas**
Some reasons and evidence are not in order. The reader may be confused. The purpose is not restated in the conclusion.	The organization is not clear. The conclusion is missing or lacks any focus.	The writing is just a list of random details that don't fit together. The reader can't follow the writing.	**Organization**
The voice is hesitant or distant. The writer does not connect with the reader.	The voice is very weak or absent. The reader does not know the writer's purpose.	The writer's voice is absent. It does not connect with the reader at all.	**Voice**
Several words are weak, too general, or over-used. The words do not convince the reader.	Many words and phrases are misused or vague. It is hard to picture what the writer means.	The words are vague and confusing. The meaning is not clear.	**Word Choice**
Sentence beginnings and lengths are alike. There are some choppy sentences, and the writing takes practice to read aloud.	There is no variety in sentence beginnings. Sentences are choppy and hard to read aloud.	Sentences are incomplete. It is hard to tell where sentences begin and end. The writing is hard to read, even silently.	**Sentence Fluency**
Some errors with homophones or other conventions slow down reading.	The writing has many errors with homophones and other conventions that get in the way of the message.	The writing is filled with many different kinds of mistakes. Reading is difficult even with effort.	**Conventions**

See Appendix B for 4-, 5-, and 6-point argument rubrics.

Business Letter

Using the Rubric to Study the Model

Did you notice that the model on page 303 points out some key elements of a business letter? As she wrote it, Jean Silverstone used these elements to help her write her letter. She also used the 6-point rubric on pages 304–305 to plan, draft, revise, and edit the writing. A rubric is a great tool for evaluating writing during the writing process.

Now let's use the same rubric to score the model. To do this, we'll focus on each trait separately, starting with Ideas. We'll use the top descriptor for each trait (column 6), along with examples from the model, to help us understand how the traits work together. How would you score Jean on each trait?

Ideas

- The purpose is clearly stated.
- Clear reasons and relevant, important evidence support the writer's opinion.

Jean's purpose of complaining about the cereal is very clear in the first paragraph. In addition, she does a good job of supporting her opinion. She uses enough details to prove her point, but she doesn't distract her reader with details that aren't important. In this paragraph, she gives some relevant details about why the cereal is unsatisfactory.

[from the writing model]

The boats now have little taste, and they sink instead of floating. Furthermore, the food dye in the new boats turns the milk in the bowl greenish brown.

Organization

- **Reasons and supporting evidence are organized in order of importance.**
- **The purpose is strongly restated in the conclusion.**

Jean is very clear about what she doesn't like about the new Oaty Boats, and she states her complaints in order of importance. I like the way she lists her reasons in this paragraph.

| [from the writing model] | |

The boats now have little taste, and they sink instead of floating. Furthermore, the food dye in the new boats turns the milk in the bowl greenish brown.

In her conclusion, Jean repeats her purpose in different words.

| [from the writing model] | |

Until Oaty Boats is returned to its original form, I will no longer purchase it for the children in my daycare center.

Voice

- **The writer's tone is respectful and businesslike and fits the purpose well.**
- **The writer speaks directly to the reader.**

Jean uses a businesslike tone to express her thoughts in a direct way. For example, she is angry about the commercial, but she doesn't use angry words. Instead, she uses a tone that is polite and formal.

| [from the writing model] | |

There are sailboats, tugboats, and freighters in Oaty Boats, too. It would be more positive and educational to show children a range of boats and a range of uses.

Word Choice

- **Specific nouns and strong verbs make the writing lively and informative.**

Jean wants to convince the customer service manager that she is not pleased with the product. Specific nouns, like *sailboats* and *tugboats*, and strong verbs, such as *molding*, help make the writing lively. If she had simply written "There are other kinds of boats" or "You're as responsible for helping to form their young minds," her writing would have been weaker and less gripping.

[from the writing model]

There are sailboats, tugboats, and freighters in Oaty Boats, too. It would be more positive and educational to show children a range of boats and a range of uses. You're as responsible for molding their young minds as I am.

Sentence Fluency

- **Sentences are well written, smooth, and easy to read. They reflect the purpose of the letter.**

Jean doesn't waste the time of the busy customer service manager at the cereal company. She makes sure that each and every sentence of her letter relates to the business at hand. For example, in the section of the letter shown below, the writer could have started talking about how difficult it is to be responsible for young children, but that would not have reflected the purpose of her letter. Take a look.

[from the writing model]

You're as responsible for molding their young minds as I am.
I would like to see more thoughtful advertising from Real Cereal.
Remember, it takes a community to raise a child.

Conventions
- **The writing has been thoughtfully edited.**
- **Homophones are used correctly.**

I went back and checked the letter to see if there were any mistakes, but I couldn't find any. Spelling, punctuation, and capitalization are all correct. The writer also used homophones correctly. When she had to choose among words such as *to/too/two* and *your/you're*, she chose the right word every time.

[from the writing model]

There are sailboats, tugboats, and freighters in Oaty Boats, too.

⊕ Presentation The business letter is in the proper format.

My Turn!

I'm going to write a business letter about a change I'd like a business to make. Follow along and see how I use the rubric and good writing strategies to do it!

Prewrite

Focus on **Ideas**

The Rubric Says The purpose is clearly stated.

Writing Strategy Pick something you would like a business to change. List reasons for the change.

I love music, especially the blues. One of our local radio stations, KTNT, used to have a great blues show called "Down to the Blues." A few weeks ago, they decided to cancel it! When my teacher said we were going to write a business letter, I decided to write to KTNT to ask the station to put "Down to the Blues" back on the air. Here are my reasons.

Reasons To Bring Back "Down to the Blues"

- It was the only radio program in the area that educated listeners about the blues.
- The program played songs by classic blues artists like Robert Johnson, Blind Lemon Jefferson, and Ma Rainey. It also played songs by modern blues artists like B. B. King, Luther Allison, and Koko Taylor. It was a good show for fans of both styles of the blues.
- I was learning a lot about the blues from the show. One night a week, it had a guest musician. I learned all about the guest artists and their music. Once a month, a blues guitarist taught listeners a new blues song.
- My dog, Muddy, loves to howl the blues, and he misses the show, too! He's named after Muddy Waters.
- The show was on from 7 to 9 P.M. on two weeknights, so kids could listen to it after finishing their homework and before going to bed.

Apply

Think of a change you would like a business to make. Jot down some notes about why the change is a good idea.

Focus on Organization

The Rubric Says	Reasons and supporting evidence are organized in order of importance.
Writing Strategy	Use an Order-of-Importance Organizer to organize the reasons.

According to the rubric, I should organize the reasons in my letter by order of importance. I'll start with the most important and end with the least important.

I'll use an Order-of-Importance Organizer. The upside-down triangle shows my points from most to least important.

> **Writer's Term**
>
> **Order-of-Importance Organizer**
> An **Order-of-Importance Organizer** shows the main points in order of importance. The points can be ordered from most to least important or from least to most important.

Order-of-Importance Organizer

It was the only show that educated listeners about the blues.

The program played songs by classic and modern blues artists.

The show was on at a good time for kids.

Reflect

Will the Order-of-Importance Organizer give Leila's letter a useful structure?

Apply

Organize your ideas by using an Order-of-Importance Organizer.

Draft

Focus on **Voice**

The Rubric Says	The writer's tone is respectful and businesslike and fits the purpose well.
Writing Strategy	Use formal language.

If my letter is going to get results, I have to send it to someone who might be able to make the change I want. I think the KTNT station manager will be my audience.

The rubric says to use a businesslike tone, and using the proper format is part of that. Business letters have six parts and are commonly in block style.

Writer's Term

The Six Parts of a Business Letter

- The **heading** is about an inch from the top and on the left-hand side of the page. It has the sender's complete address and the date.
- The **inside address** is below the heading. It has the reader's complete address. The reader's title is below his or her name.
- The **salutation** (greeting) is below the inside address, followed by a colon.
- The **body** of the letter is below the salutation.
- The **closing** is below the body. It begins with *Yours truly* or *Sincerely* and ends with a comma.
- Type full name below the closing. Leave enough space for the **signature** between the closing and your typed name.

As I write my letter using this form, I'll use language that sounds like I'm talking to my reader, but with an appropriate formal tone. I want to sound businesslike and respectful so my reader will pay attention to what I have to say. Part of my letter is on the next page.

Proofreading Marks

⌐ Indent
≡ Make uppercase
/ Make lowercase
∧ Add something

ℓ Take out something
⊙ Add a period
¶ New paragraph
SP Spelling error

[DRAFT]

4922 Tinley Drive
Nashville, TN 37201   ◄── [heading]
October 16, 2012

Station Manager
KTNT Radio Station
1148 W. Filmore Road   ◄── [inside address]
Nashville, TN 37203

Dear Station Manager, ◄── [salutation]

[body]

Blues superstar Luther Allison said, "If you don't like the blues, you've got a whole in your soul." I have a passion for the blues, and you're program "Down to the Blues" taught me more about it every week. When KTNT canceled this excellent show, I couldn't believe it! I'm writing to ask you to please put you're blues program back on the air. Please! Please! Please!   ◄── [formal language]

There's a lot to learn from the blues. "down to the Blues was a cool radio program that taught blues songs on the air. I learned a lot about varius blues musicians. And there stories and music inspired me!

Reflect

Did Leila use the correct business letter format? How does she make her voice sound respectful and businesslike?

Apply

Write a draft using your Order-of-Importance Organizer as a guide. Be sure to use a formal tone and format!

Revise

Focus on **Ideas**

The Rubric Says Clear reasons and relevant, important evidence support the writer's opinion.

Writing Strategy Add details to support the opinion.

After I read over my draft, I looked at the rubric again. It says I should include clear reasons and relevant details to support my opinion. I think I stated my reasons quite plainly, but I found a part of my letter that didn't have enough details. So I added a piece of information that's both relevant and important to my argument. Also, I took out a detail that wasn't relevant at all.

[DRAFT]

songs by classic blues artists and modern blues artists, too ◄— [added detail]

I really liked it that the show played ~~different songs by different blues artists.~~ They made "Down to the Blues" entertaining four any blues fan.

The timing of the program was perfect for me and other kids, to. The 7 P.M. time slot was late enough that I could finish my homework before the program started, but it didnt keep me up to late. ~~I have to get up at six o'clock in the morning.~~

◄— [took out irrelevant detail]

Apply

Try adding some relevant details to support your opinions. Take out any details that aren't relevant.

The Rubric Says	Specific nouns and strong verbs make the writing lively and informative.
Writing Strategy	Replace vague nouns and verbs.

When I checked the rubric, I realized that not all my nouns and verbs are strong enough. If they are vague and weak, it will be harder to get my opinion across. Look at where I revised a noun and a verb. Do you agree that my message is stronger now?

[DRAFT]

[added specific words]

blues fans   enjoy

I really miss "Down to the Blues." All kinds of ~~people like~~ the program and learn so much from listening, especially us kids!

Reflect

Do the stronger, more specific nouns and verbs make the writing more interesting to read?

Apply

Make your writing more lively by replacing vague nouns and verbs with specific and strong ones.

Revise

Focus on Sentence Fluency

The Rubric Says   Sentences are well written, smooth, and easy to read. They reflect the purpose of the letter.

Writing Strategy   Make sure each sentence reflects the purpose of the letter.

Now to check my sentence fluency. The rubric says that each sentence of my letter should reflect why I'm writing, but I see some sentences that don't. I need to clearly state my feelings about my favorite radio show being canceled. And that last sentence interrupts the smooth flow of my sentences without adding anything to my argument.

[DRAFT]

[changed sentence to better reflect purpose]

Blues superstar Luther Allison said, "If you don't like the blues, you've got a whole in your soul." I have a passion for the blues, and you're program "Down to the Blues" taught me more about it every week. When KTNT canceled this excellent show, ~~I couldn't believe it!~~ I was very disappointed. I'm writing to ask you to please put you're blues program back on the air. ~~Please! Please! Please!~~ [deleted sentence that didn't reflect purpose]

Apply

Does every sentence in your letter reflect your purpose for writing? Take out or rewrite any sentences that don't.

The Rubric Says	The writing has been thoughtfully edited. Homophones are used correctly.
Writing Strategy	Check the use of homophones.

Writer's Term

Homophones

Homophones are words that are pronounced the same but have different spellings and meanings.

Now I need to check my spelling, punctuation, and capitalization. The rubric also says to be sure I've used homophones correctly. Sometimes I get confused with homophones because those words sound alike but are spelled differently. I'll really have to check carefully!

[DRAFT]

~~There's a lot~~ There is so much to learn from the blues. "down to the Blues" was a cool radio program that taught blues songs on the air. I learned a lot about ~~varius~~ various blues musicians. And ~~there~~ their stories and music inspired me!

[corrected homophone]

Reflect

Are all the homophones correct now? The spell checker on the computer won't catch homophone mistakes, so they need to be checked carefully.

Apply   Conventions

Edit your draft for spelling, punctuation, and capitalization. Be sure to check that any homophones are correct.

For more practice with homophones, use the exercises on the next two pages.

Homophones

Know the Rule

Homophones are words that are pronounced the same but have different spellings and meanings.

Here are some examples of homophones and their meanings. Make sure you are using the correct word.

its—possessive pronoun meaning "belonging to it"
it's—contraction of *it is* or *it has*

there—adverb meaning "in that place"
their—possessive pronoun meaning "belonging to them"
they're—contraction of *they are*

your—possessive pronoun meaning "belonging to you"
you're—contraction of *you are*

whose—possessive pronoun meaning "belonging to someone"
who's—contraction of *who is* or *who has*

Practice the Rule

Number your paper 1–10. Write the correct word to complete each sentence.

1. Three chords and a simple pattern give the blues (its/it's) unique form.
2. (It's/Its) one of the oldest forms of American music.
3. (There/Their/They're) are several views about the origins of the blues.
4. The songs are called the blues because (there/their/they're) often sad.
5. At first, only people in the South sang or listened (two/to/too) the blues.
6. By the 1920s, people in the North were enjoying the blues, (two/to/too).
7. Today, (your/you're) likely to hear blues mixed with other styles of music.
8. If you could play blues-style piano, (would/wood) you?
9. There are many famous musicians (who's/whose) first love in music was the blues.
10. What's (your/you're) favorite blues song?

More Homophones

Know the Rule

know—verb meaning "to have information about something in your mind"
no—adverb that indicates the negative

theirs—adjective meaning "belonging to them"
there's—contraction of *there is*

too—adverb meaning "more, in addition, also"
two—adjective meaning the number 2
to—preposition meaning "in order to be in a certain place"

vary—verb meaning "to be different from each other"
very—adverb used for emphasis

weak—adjective meaning "not strong"
week—noun meaning "the seven days from Sunday through Saturday"

whether—conjunction that indicates a choice
weather—noun that refers to the temperature and other conditions, like rain, snow, wind, sun, clouds

Practice the Rule

Number a sheet of paper 1–10. Write the correct word to complete each sentence.

1. (Theirs/There's) nothing more joyful than moving to the beat of music you love.
2. Do you (no/know) a lot about the folk music of Ireland?
3. Most people like at least (to/two/too) kinds of music.
4. (Whether/Weather) you like rock or blues, pop or rap, classical or reggae, you can find a music festival that features your favorite music.
5. Next (week/weak) there is a concert I want to go to.
6. My cousins were here for the weekend, and these CDs are (there's/theirs).
7. Country music is (vary/very) popular in the South.
8. Since my brother came back from New Orleans, he likes (to/two/too) listen to jazz.
9. Jin likes to (vary/very) the kind of music she downloads.
10. On any given day, she might listen (to/two/too) country or dance music.

Publish +Presentation

Publishing Strategy   Mail the business letter.

Presentation Strategy   Include all the parts of a business letter.

Now that I've finished my business letter, I can't wait to mail it to the station manager! Before I do that, I'm going to make sure my letter is in proper business letter format. The six parts of a business letter are listed on page 312. I'll refer to that list to make sure I've included all the parts and written them correctly. Then I'll check over my letter one last time, using the items in the final checklist below. Finally I'll carefully handwrite or type a copy on the computer and mail it.

My Final Checklist

Did I—

✔ make sure all the homophones are correct?

✔ use correct business letter format?

✔ check for all six parts of a business letter?

✔ make sure my grammar, punctuation, and spelling are correct?

Apply

Make a final checklist to check your business letter. Then make a final copy to publish.

4922 Tinley Drive
Nashville, TN 37201
October 16, 2012

Station Manager
KTNT Radio Station
1148 W. Filmore Road
Nashville, TN 37203

Dear Station Manager:

Blues superstar Luther Allison said, "If you don't like the blues, you've got a hole in your soul." I have a passion for the blues, and your program "Down to the Blues" taught me more about it every week. When KTNT canceled this excellent show, I was very disappointed. I'm writing to ask you to please put your blues program back on the air.

There is so much to learn about the blues. "Down to the Blues" was the only radio program that taught blues songs on the air. I learned a lot about various blues musicians. And their stories and music inspired me!

I really liked it that the show played songs by classic blues artists and modern blues artists, too. The good mix made "Down to the Blues" entertaining for any blues fan.

The timing of the program was perfect for me and other kids, too. The 7 P.M. time slot was late enough that I could finish my homework before the program started, but it didn't keep me up too late.

I hope KTNT will return "Down to the Blues" to its evening programming. All kinds of blues fans enjoy the program and learn so much from listening, especially us kids!

Yours truly,

Leila Hirsch

Leila Hirsch

Reflect

What did you think? Does Leila's letter have all the traits of a good business letter that makes an argument? Check it against the rubric. Then use the rubric to check your own business letter.

What's a Speech?

A speech is a spoken expression of a writer's opinion. In an argument speech, a presenter speaks to convince an audience of listeners to believe in and support a message or cause. Writing a speech will be fun. What better way to have your actual voice be heard?

What's in a Speech?

Claim
The main idea of my speech is the claim that I will be making. It must be something that can be argued, or something that has at least two sides to it, so I can build an argument that will convince people to be on my side!

Supporting Evidence
I'll need details and facts that support my main idea, or claim, to make my view believable. I'll use information and facts from credible and trusted sources so that my points are valid.

Plagiarism
Plagiarism is using someone else's words and ideas without giving them credit. It is a serious offense. I'll provide a full reference for the source of the facts and details I use in my speech. I'll also put ideas into my own words.

Why write a Speech?

I've never given a speech before, but it sounds like a good way to express my opinions. Here are some more reasons to write an argument speech.

Argument

A good speech can convince others to agree with your opinion. This kind of writing can give readers (or listeners) the information they need to make up their minds—or change their minds—about an issue.

Information

Because an argument speech is on a topic about which the writer feels strongly, the writer really wants you to agree with his or her side. So a good speech is filled with important facts and details. An audience can learn a lot from a speech.

Understanding

To give a speech, you have to become an expert on the topic. To become an expert, you need to find out as much as you can about the subject matter. Giving a speech is like being a teacher, in a way, because you are making others aware of something. You know you understand something when you can teach it to others.

Linking Argument Writing Traits to a Speech

In this chapter, you will write about something you believe in strongly and then try to convince listeners to agree with your argument. This type of argument writing is called a speech. Leila will guide you through the stages of the writing process: Prewrite, Draft, Revise, Edit, and Publish. In each stage, Leila will show you important writing strategies that are linked to the Argument Writing Traits below.

Argument Writing Traits

- clearly stated claims, often balanced by alternate or opposing claims
- supporting evidence from accurate and credible sources

- a strong introduction that presents the writer's position
- reasons and evidence that are organized logically
- a conclusion that restates the thesis and possibly provides a call to action
- transitions that clarify the relationships between ideas

- a voice that supports the writer's purpose

- language that is compelling

- sentences that vary in length and begin in different ways

- no or few errors in grammar, usage, mechanics, and spelling

Before you write, read Linnea Moore's speech on the next page. Then use the speech rubric on pages 326–327 to decide how well she did. (You might want to look back at What's in a Speech? on page 322, too!)

The Mother of Modern Physics

by Linnea Moore

She won two Nobel Prizes, coined the term *radioactivity,* and discovered the elements radium and polonium. She believed in working for the betterment of humanity. Her name is Marie Curie, and she is the most influential woman in the history of science. **Claim**

Marie Curie (born Maria Sklodowska) was born in Poland in 1867. Marie was a curious child with a gift for learning. She excelled in high school, graduating ahead of schedule and at the head of her class.

Marie had hopes for a higher education. She was interested in mathematics, physics, and chemistry, but because she was female, she could not go to a university at home. To overcome this discrimination, Marie and her sister promised to put each other through school where women were welcome. Marie helped put her sister through medical school in Paris, France. Then her sister, as promised, returned the favor, and off Marie went to the University of Paris, the Sorbonne. **Supporting evidence**

At the University, Marie immersed herself in the studies she loved. She earned Master's degrees in physics and mathematics. She also married Pierre Curie. Together, they studied what Marie called radioactivity, or how certain substances spontaneously react, and they discovered the elements radium and polonium. For their discovery, which would lead to aiding cancer treatments, the Curies won the Nobel Prize in physics in 1903. That same year, Marie became the first woman in France to earn her doctorate degree in physics.

Marie did not stop at one Nobel Prize. She went on to earn another in chemistry in 1911 for her work with radium. She was the first person in history to win two such prizes. Marie also became the first female professor at the Sorbonne. With all of her fame, Marie remained committed to science and humanity. She said, "You cannot hope to build a better world without improving the individuals." To show her humanitarianism, she decided to help World War I casualties. By using x-rays, she assisted doctors in locating bullets and shrapnel to aid treatment.

Marie Curie's contributions to society are numerous, and her love of learning and desire to discover are unmatched. As a woman, she forged ahead, breaking down barriers. Marie Curie's achievements are unsurpassed by any other scientist in history. **used quotes to avoid plagiarism**

Rubric

Use this 6-point rubric to plan and score a speech.

	6	5	4
Ideas	The writer's claim is clear and compelling. Supporting evidence is accurate. Credible sources are cited.	The writer's claim is clear. Most supporting evidence is accurate and taken from credible sources.	The writer's claim is stated. Some evidence is lacking. Some sources are not credible or are incorrectly cited.
Organization	The introduction, body, and conclusion are strong and compelling. Appropriate transitions clarify relationships among ideas.	The introduction, body, and conclusion are strong. Transitions show how ideas are related.	The introduction, body, and conclusion are fairly strong. Only one or two transitions are used.
Voice	The voice is lively and direct. Active voice provides energy.	The voice is lively and direct most of the time. Active voice is used.	The voice could sound more lively and direct in parts. Active voice is used.
Word Choice	Domain-specific content words are used correctly and defined clearly.	Domain-specific content words are used correctly. One or two words need definitions.	Most domain-specific content words are used correctly. The definitions could be clearer.
Sentence Fluency	A variety of sentence patterns makes the text flow smoothly.	A variety of sentence patterns is used.	Some variety of sentence patterns is present. The flow is interrupted in a few places.
Conventions	The writing has been carefully edited. All forms of verbs are used correctly and effectively.	Minor errors are present but do not interfere with meaning. Forms of be are used correctly.	A few errors cause confusion. Forms of be are used correctly.
✚ **Presentation**	Visuals support and enhance the meaning of the text.		

3	2	1	
The writer's claim is not clear. More evidence is needed. Sources are not credible or not cited.	The writer's claim is not supported. Evidence or citations are skimpy or inaccurate.	The writer does not present a claim. No evidence is given.	**Ideas**
The introduction, body, and conclusion are weak. Transitions, if used, are not effective or correct.	There is no introduction or conclusion. The writing just starts and stops. No transition words are used.	The writing is not organized as a speech.	**Organization**
The voice is not engaging enough. Active voice fades in parts as passive voice takes over.	The voice does not engage the audience. Passive voice is used more often than active.	The voice is inconsistent or absent. The audience does not know who is speaking, or why.	**Voice**
Few domain-specific content words are used and they lack definitions.	Domain-specific content words, if used, are used incorrectly.	Domain-specific content words are not used.	**Word Choice**
Many sentences share the same pattern. There is no flow.	The sentences all sound the same. They are repetitive and dull.	Many sentences are incomplete or incorrect. The audience cannot follow the ideas.	**Sentence Fluency**
Many errors are repeated and cause confusion. Several verbs are used incorrectly.	Serious errors interfere with meaning. Forms of the verb *be* are frequently used incorrectly.	Many errors confuse the meaning. Forms of common verbs are inconsistent or incorrect.	**Conventions**

See Appendix B for 4-, 5-, and 6-point argument rubrics.

Using the Speech Rubric to Study the Model

Did you notice that the model on page 325 points out some key elements of a speech? As she wrote "The Mother of Modern Physics," Linnea Moore used these elements to help express her opinion through a speech. She also used the 6-point rubric on pages 326–327 to plan, draft, revise, and edit the writing. A rubric is a great tool for evaluating writing during the writing process.

Now let's use the same rubric to score the model. To do this, we'll focus on each trait separately, starting with Ideas. We'll use the top descriptor for each trait (column 6), along with examples from the model, to help us understand how the traits work together. How would you score Linnea on each trait?

Ideas

- The writer's claim is clear and compelling.
- Supporting evidence is accurate.
- Credible sources are cited.

Linnea opens her speech with a clear and convincing claim. She also supports her claim with accurate facts about Marie Curie. For her quote she cites the most credible source about Marie Curie—the scientist herself.

[from the writing model]

She won two Nobel Prizes, coined the term *radioactivity*, and discovered the elements radium and polonium. She believed in working for the betterment of humanity. Her name is Marie Curie, and she is the most influential woman in the history of science.

[from the writing model]

With all of her fame, Marie remained committed to science and humanity. She said, "You cannot hope to build a better world without improving the individuals."

Organization

- The introduction, body, and conclusion are strong and compelling.
- Appropriate transitions clarify relationships among ideas.

This writer grabs my attention right from the first paragraph. I am interested to find out who this "she" is, who has so many great achievements. Then the body describes Marie's achievements in greater detail, and the conclusion strongly restates the claim, tying everything together.

Transitional phrases such as *At the University* link ideas and helped me follow the story of Marie's life.

[from the writing model]

Marie helped put her sister through medical school in Paris, France. Then her sister, as promised, returned the favor, and off Marie went to the University of Paris, the Sorbonne.

At the University, Marie immersed herself in the studies she loved. She earned Master's degrees in physics and mathematics.

Voice

- The voice is lively and direct.
- Active voice provides energy.

Linnea uses direct, energetic language to talk about Marie's achievements. Notice the strong, direct statement at the start of the excerpt below. Similarly, Linnea avoids boring phrases such as "she was named to be a professor." Instead she uses active voice to state, "Marie also became the first female professor at the Sorbonne."

[from the writing model]

Marie did not stop at one Nobel Prize. She went on to earn another in chemistry in 1911 for her work with radium. She was the first person in history to win two such prizes. Marie also became the first female professor at the Sorbonne.

• **Domain-specific content words are used correctly and defined clearly.**

Linnea clearly defines *radioactivity*, a term closely related to the topic of this speech.

[from the writing model]

Together, they studied what Marie called radioactivity, or how certain substances spontaneously react, and they discovered the elements radium and polonium.

• **A variety of sentence patterns makes the text flow smoothly.**

Linnea uses a variety of sentence patterns to make the text flow smoothly. She uses simple sentences, as well as compound, complex, and compound complex sentences. Can you identify them all? The varied sentence structure gives her speech a nice flow. Read the following paragraph aloud to hear for yourself.

[from the writing model]

Marie had hopes for a higher education. She was interested in mathematics, physics, and chemistry, but because she was female, she could not go to a university at home. To overcome this discrimination, Marie and her sister promised to put each other through school where women were welcome. Marie helped put her sister through medical school in Paris, France. Then her sister, as promised, returned the favor, and off Marie went to the University of Paris, the Sorbonne.

Conventions

- **The writing has been carefully edited.**
- **All forms of verbs are used correctly and effectively.**

The writing has been carefully edited because I didn't find a single mistake. Also, all forms of verbs are used correctly. In the first sentence below, do you see how the verb *be* takes its singular form (*was*) to agree with the singular subject (*Marie*)? In the next sentence, the plural form (*were*) agrees with the plural subject (*women*).

[from the writing model]

Marie was a curious child with a gift for learning.

To overcome this discrimination, Marie and her sister promised to put each other through school where women were welcome.

✚ Presentation
Visuals support and enhance the meaning of the text.

My Turn!

Now it's my turn to write an argument speech. I'll use the rubric and good writing strategies to help me. Read on to see how I do it.

Prewrite

Focus on **Ideas**

The Rubric Says The writer's claim is clear and compelling. Supporting evidence is accurate. Credible sources are cited.

Writing Strategy Decide on a position and do some research.

I'm excited about writing an argument speech because I like to have my voice heard. Linnea's speech got me thinking about important women in science, so I thought it would be interesting to learn more about the first African American woman in space, Dr. Mae Jemison. I'll need to find lots of good facts and details about her to make my writing clear and convincing, and I'll have my teacher approve my sources. As I do my research, I'll be sure to keep track of the source information, so I can give credit accordingly.

Notes on Mae Jemison

Source

- Jemison, Mae. *Where the Wind Goes: Moments from My Life.* New York: Scholastic Press: 2001.
- Dejoie, Joyce, and Elizabeth Truelove. "Dr. Mae Jemison." http://starchild.gsfc.nasa.gov/docs/StarChild/whos_who_level2/jemison.html.

Note

- Mae Jemison worked as a medical officer in the Peace Corps.
- Mae Jemison went into space in September of 1992 as a mission specialist.

Apply

Choose a topic and find some sources on it that you can trust to be accurate. Do some research and take some notes of your own.

The Rubric Says The introduction, body, and conclusion are strong and compelling.

Writing Strategy Use an Argument Map to plan the speech.

Writer's Term

Argument Map
An **Argument Map** organizes reasons and supporting evidence that support a claim.

An Argument Map can help me organize my thoughts. I'll put my claim at the left and connect my reasons to that. Then I'll connect supporting evidence to my reasons.

Argument Map

Claim:
Mae Jemison is the most driven and accomplished woman in astronautic history.

Reason:
She doesn't let anything hold her back.

Supporting Evidence: She graduated high school at age 16.

Supporting Evidence: She applied to NASA a second time to be admitted.

Supporting Evidence: She lived out her dreams regardless of her gender and ethnicity.

Reason:
She holds multiple degrees.

Supporting Evidence: She has Bachelor's degrees in chemical engineering and African and Afro-American Studies, and a Doctorate degree in medicine.

Reason:
She has many varied experiences.

Supporting Evidence: She has worked as a medical officer and teacher in the Peace Corps.

Supporting Evidence: She has worked in a Cambodian refugee camp and had her own practice in L.A.

Supporting Evidence: After becoming a doctor, she became an astronaut.

Reflect

How will the Argument Map help Leila organize her writing?

Apply

Organize your notes for your speech in an Argument Map.

Draft

Focus on Word Choice

The Rubric Says   Domain-specific content words are used correctly and defined clearly.

Writing Strategy   Define unfamiliar words.

As I write my draft, I'll use my Argument Map to get all of the important details down and to make sure I state my claim. I want to be accurate in my writing, so I'll use the correct domain-specific content words to describe my topic. Domain-specific content words are words that apply to a certain field, such as medicine or space exploration. If I use a word I don't think my readers will know, I'll be sure to explain its meaning. I may need to check the definitions in a dictionary or other resource. If I do, I will be sure to rewrite the definition in my own words.

Sometimes it's hard to avoid making mistakes in grammar, punctuation, and spelling when I'm getting my ideas on paper. That's OK. I know I can fix my mistakes later when I edit my writing. Part of my draft is on the next page.

[DRAFT]

Mae Jemison

by Leila

On September 12, 1992, the Shuttle *Endeavor* hurtled off the launch pad, carrying the first African American woman into space. Mae Jemison had years of education and experience behind her. This space mission would add yet another achievement to her list of successes. She did not let her ethnicity, or cultural makeup, or the fact she was a woman hold her back. Mae Jemison is the most driven and accomplished woman in astronautic (having to do with astronauts) history. ⟵ [claim]

Born in Decatur, Alabama, in 1956 and raised in Chicago, Illinois, Mae Jemison became interested in science at an early age. A gifted student, she finished high school at age 16, won a scholarship, and attended college, where she earned Bachelor's degrees in chemical engineering and African and Afro-American Studies. She went on to earn a Doctorate of Medicine.

[domain-specific content word]

Reflect

How does Leila make her writing clear? What details help you agree with her claim?

Apply

Using your Argument Map as a guide, write a draft. Don't forget to clearly state your claim.

Revise

Focus on **Ideas**

The Rubric Says Supporting evidence is accurate. Credible sources are cited.

Writing Strategy Use credible sources.

Writer's Term

Credible Websites
Credible means "believable" or "trusted." Websites should always be evaluated to make sure they are credible and reliable.

I know from the rubric that the evidence I use has to be accurate. I'll get this kind of information from sources I can trust. Because websites vary in their reliability, or how much you can trust their information, my teacher has given me a checklist to evaluate sites. I'll look at who runs the website, whether there are advertisements (and, if so, who advertises), and whether the links are good and work. I'll also be sure to double-check my facts and details across several sources to make sure each source provides the same information about a certain fact. That way I'll know that the facts I use in my speech are true.

[DRAFT]

[checked facts in more than one source]

Born in Decatur, Alabama, in 1956 and raised in Chicago, Illinois, Mae Jemison became interested in science at an early age. A gifted student, she finished high school at age 16, won a scholarship, and attended college, where she earned Bachelor's degrees in chemical engineering and African and Afro-American Studies. She went on to earn a Doctorate of Medicine.

Apply

Check your sources to make sure they are reliable. Check your facts across multiple sources to see if the sources agree on similar facts.

Focus on Organization

The Rubric Says	Appropriate transitions clarify relationships among ideas.
Writing Strategy	Use effective transitions to show how ideas are connected.

✎ Writer's Term

Transitions

Transitions help readers move smoothly through a piece of writing. They show how ideas are connected. Transitions such as **first, next,** and **last** show sequence. Transitions such as **not only . . . but also** and **as a result** show how ideas relate.

Because my main audience will be listening to my speech, I want to make sure my ideas flow smoothly. My audience won't be able to go back and reread if they miss a connection! Using appropriate transitions will help me show how my ideas are related.

[DRAFT]

Not only has

∧Mae Jemison practiced medicine in the United States, in Los

, but she also has   In addition,

Angeles. ~~She also~~ practiced in a Cambodian refugee camp. ∧She

served as a medical officer in the Peace Corps in West Africa.

[inserted transitions to show relationships]

Reflect

How do transitions help Leila's speech?

Apply

Insert appropriate transitions to show your readers how your ideas relate to each other.

Revise

Focus on Sentence Fluency

The Rubric Says A variety of sentence patterns makes the text flow smoothly.

Writing Strategy Use phrases and clauses to vary sentences.

Writer's Term

Clauses and Phrases

A **clause** is a group of words that has a subject and verb. A **phrase** is a group of words that has no subject or verb separate from those in the main part of the sentence.

As you know, my speech has to flow smoothly when I read it to an audience of listeners. Inserting some clauses and phrases will vary the sentence patterns to make for easy listening. Added clauses and phrases will also be a way to include more information about my opinion. Here's some of my draft with a clause and a phrase that I added. Read it aloud to hear how the writing becomes less choppy and how the added text adds helpful information.

[DRAFT]

In addition,
She served as medical officer in the Peace Corps in where she also did some teaching West Africa.

[added clause]

After pursuing engineering and medicine,
It were time to look to space. She applied to NASA's training program. Her first application did not go through, so she applied again and was accepted.

[inserted phrase]

Apply

Use clauses and phrases to vary your sentences, add information, and make for easy listening.

Focus on Conventions

The Rubric Says	The writing has been carefully edited. All forms of verbs are used correctly and effectively.
Writing Strategy	Check forms of *be* and change passive voice to active.

Writer's Term

Active and Passive Voice

A sentence in which the subject performs an action is in **active voice**. A sentence in which the subject is acted upon by something else is said to be in **passive voice**.

Now is the time for me to make sure that spelling, grammar, capitalization, and punctuation are all correct. I will check forms of the verb *be*, making sure the forms agree with their subjects. I will also change any instances of passive voice to active voice for a more direct and lively speech.

[DRAFT]

After pursuing engineering and medicine, **[corrected form of verb *be*]**

~~It were~~ time to look to space. She applied to NASA's training
    ∧   ∧ was

program. Her first application did not go through, so she applied

NASA accepted her
again and ~~was accepted~~.
    ∧

[changed passive voice to active voice]

Reflect

How does editing help Leila's speech? Do these edits make her writing more engaging?

Apply   Conventions

Edit your draft for spelling, grammar, capitalization, and punctuation.
Check for correct use of the verb *be*, and make sure you've avoided using passive sentences.
For more practice with the verb *be* and active voice, use the exercises on the next two pages.

Forms of *Be*

Know the Rule

Am, is, was, are, and **were** are forms of the verb **be**. They often serve as linking verbs, connecting the subject of a sentence to a word or words in the predicate that tell about the subject.

First Person		Second Person	Third Person	
Singular	**Plural**	**Singular and Plural**	**Singular**	**Plural**
am	are, were	are, were	is, was	are, were

Practice the Rule

Number a sheet of paper from 1–10. Choose a verb from the list above to complete each sentence.

1. Right now, we _____ studying space exploration at school.
2. I _____ excited to learn more about outer space this week.
3. Some students _____ starting to think up space project ideas.
4. Starting at a young age, Mae Jemison _____ motivated to become an astronaut.
5. As she went through school, she _____ always drawn to the sciences.
6. Her family _____ a great support to her and encouraged her love of science.
7. They _____ always there to cheer her on with each new challenge.
8. Mae _____ the first African American woman to enter space.
9. Becoming an astronaut _____ a commendable achievement.
10. I _____ hopeful that one day I will be an astronaut.

Active and Passive Voice

Know the Rule

If the subject performs an action, the verb is said to be in **active voice**. If the subject is acted upon by something else, the verb is said to be in **passive voice**. Many sentences in passive voice have a phrase beginning with the word *by*. Both are correct. However, active voice makes writing more interesting for the reader.

Practice the Rule

Number a sheet of paper 1–10. Write **passive** for each sentence that is in passive voice. Write **active** for each sentence that is in active voice.

1. School was taken seriously by Mae Jemison.
2. She had a variety of interests and excelled at each.
3. It is important to follow your dreams.
4. Dr. Jemison was accepted into NASA's astronaut training program.
5. Final tests on the space unit were passed out to us.
6. Many people find the requirements to be an astronaut difficult to meet.
7. We were taken to the spacesuit fitting room.
8. Envelopes were handed out, revealing who would be the next science mission specialist.
9. She intends to fly to the moon.
10. Mistakes were made that delayed the launch of the spacecraft.

Publish +Presentation

Publishing Strategy Give the speech to the class.

Presentation Strategy Choose visuals that support the claim.

Now I am ready to publish my speech. One way to publish a piece of writing is to read it aloud to an audience, and that is just what a speech is meant for! To add to my speech, I will use visuals that support my claim. I could project images from a computer, but I have decided to make a poster with photos of Mae Jemison.

My pictures show Mae's many achievements: graduating from Cornell Medical College, working in the Peace Corps, Mae's NASA head shot, and floating in zero gravity on her monumental space flight. Before I give my final speech, I'll read it one more time, going through this final checklist.

My Final Checklist

Did I—

- ✔ make sure all verb forms are used correctly, especially the verb *be*?
- ✔ replace passive voice with active voice, as appropriate?
- ✔ check all spelling, grammar, punctuation, and capitalization?
- ✔ create presentation visuals that support my claim?

Apply

Make a final checklist and use it to finalize your speech. Then get ready to give your speech!

Mae Jemison

by Leila

On September 12, 1992, the Shuttle *Endeavor* hurtled off the launch pad, carrying the first African American woman into space. Mae Jemison had years of education and experience behind her. This space mission would add yet another achievement to her list of successes. She did not let her ethnicity, or cultural makeup, or the fact she was a woman hold her back. Mae Jemison is the most driven and accomplished woman in astronautic (having to do with astronauts) history.

Born in Decatur, Alabama, in 1956 and raised in Chicago, Illinois, Mae Jemison became interested in science at an early age. A gifted student, she finished high school at age 16, won a scholarship, and attended college, where she earned Bachelor's degrees in chemical engineering and African and Afro-American Studies. She went on to earn a Doctorate of Medicine.

Not only has Mae Jemison practiced medicine in the United States, in Los Angeles, but she also has practiced in a Cambodian refugee camp. In addition, she served as a medical officer in the Peace Corps in West Africa, where she also did some teaching.

After pursuing engineering and medicine, it was time to look to space. She applied to NASA's training program. Her first application did not go through, so she applied again and NASA accepted her. She went through astronaut training, became an astronaut, and flew into space as a science mission specialist on the Shuttle *Endeavor*. A mission specialist is someone who performs specific experiments on a space mission.

Mae Jemison's achievements in school and her experiences outside of school have paved her way to greatness. Her accomplishments have set her apart from all other astronauts of her time.

Works Consulted:

Dejoie, Joyce, and Elizabeth Truelove. "Dr. Mae Jemison." http://starchild.gsfc
.nasa.gov/docs/StarChild/whos_who_level2/jemison.html.

Jemison, Mae. *Where the Wind Goes: Moments from My Life.* New York: Scholastic
Press: 2001.

"Mae Jemison." http://www.notablebiographies.com/Ho-Jo/Jemison-Mae.html.

Reflect

How well do you think Leila did as she brought her speech through the writing process?

Argument
test writing

Read the Writing Prompt

When you take a writing test, you'll be given a writing prompt. Most writing prompts have three parts:

Setup This part of the writing prompt gives you the background information you need to get ready to write.

Task This part of the writing prompt tells you exactly what you are supposed to write: an argument essay.

Scoring Guide This section tells how your writing will be scored. To do well on the test, you should make sure your writing does everything on the list.

Remember the rubrics you have been using? When you take a writing test, you don't always have all of the information that's on a rubric. However, the scoring guide is a lot like a rubric. It lists everything you need to think about to write a good paper. Like the rubrics you've used in this unit, many scoring guides are based upon the six important traits of writing:

Ideas Organization Voice

Word Choice Sentence Fluency Conventions

Your community is trying to decide between adding a skateboard park in the empty lot adjacent to the city park or putting in more picnic tables. Some of the members of the community feel a skateboard park would be too dangerous, but others say there are plenty of picnic tables and a skateboard park would provide a safer alternative for all the kids in the community who like to skateboard.

Write an argument essay for members of your community stating your support for either the skateboard park or the new picnic tables.

Be sure your writing

- clearly identifies your position and contains supporting facts and reasons.

- is well organized and contains an introduction, body, and conclusion.

- establishes and maintains a formal style.

- uses precise language.

- has varied sentence structures.

- contains correct grammar, punctuation, capitalization, and spelling.

Writing Traits
in the Scoring Guide

The scoring guide in the prompt on page 345 has been made into this chart. Does it remind you of the rubrics you've used? Not all prompts include all of the writing traits, but this one does. Use them to do your best writing. Remember to work neatly and put your name on each page.

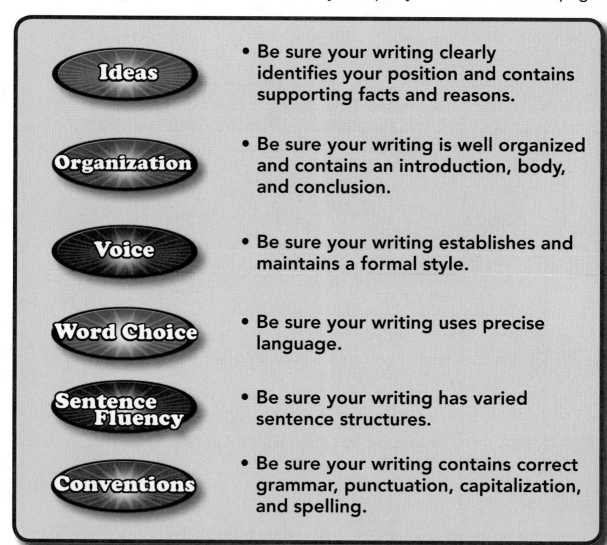

Ideas
• Be sure your writing clearly identifies your position and contains supporting facts and reasons.

Organization
• Be sure your writing is well organized and contains an introduction, body, and conclusion.

Voice
• Be sure your writing establishes and maintains a formal style.

Word Choice
• Be sure your writing uses precise language.

Sentence Fluency
• Be sure your writing has varied sentence structures.

Conventions
• Be sure your writing contains correct grammar, punctuation, capitalization, and spelling.

Look at Sam Patel's essay on the next page. Did he follow the scoring guide?

A Safe Place to Skate

by Sam Patel

By proposing a skateboard park to be built next to the city park, it's clear that members of our community realize that the large number of skateboarders who live here need a safe and accessible place to practice their sport. Although there are many people opposed to the skateboard park, I'd like to explain to you why I think this is a good idea.

First of all, our community's parks are there to provide enjoyment for the community and to promote the safety and welfare of the residents, and that should include skateboarders, too. Already, the park contains places to enjoy baseball, soccer, football, basketball, and tennis. But these days, skateboarding is just as popular. There is even a skateboard club in the community. These skateboarders need a place to go, yet there is not a place within our entire community that welcomes them.

Next, without a place that they can go to skateboard, many skateboarders use the street, which is not a safe alternative. I see many skateboarders riding along the streets and using curbs and stairways to practice their jumps. They also use plywood and other materials to build their own ramps, which do not look very safe at all. A skateboard park, though, would provide jumps that have been built with skateboarders' safety in mind. The many skateboarders who live in the community would not have to ride in the street and potentially get hit by cars.

Finally, although there are people in our town who want to add more benches, our park already contains enough benches and picnic tables. On the days that I have been to the park, including weekends, weekdays, and during the summer (when it is usually busiest) there have always been open benches and tables. It is clear to me that at this time we do not need additional benches.

Let's remember what our parks are here for, and let's put in something that will keep our skateboarders safe and address the needs of the many people enjoying this popular sport.

Using the Scoring Guide to Study the Model

Now let's use the scoring guide to check Sam's writing test, "A Safe Place to Skate." Let's see how well his essay meets each of the six writing traits.

- **The writing clearly identifies your position and contains supporting facts and reasons.**

There is no doubt in the reader's mind that Sam is in favor of a skateboard park. In the first paragraph, he states this position clearly. He also offers a supporting reason that adults in the community agree with.

By proposing a skateboard park to be built next to the city park, it's clear that members of our community realize that the large number of skateboarders who live here need a safe and accessible place to practice their sport. . . . I'd like to explain to you why I think this is a good idea.

- **The writing is well organized and contains an introduction, body, and conclusion.**

Sam's essay is well organized. He includes an introductory paragraph, three paragraphs to support his opinion, and a conclusion paragraph to wrap things up. Here is Sam's conclusion.

Let's remember what our parks are here for, and let's put in something that will keep our skateboarders safe and address the needs of the many people enjoying this popular sport.

Voice

- **The writer establishes and maintains a formal style.**

Sam's audience is adults who make decisions about public spaces. He speaks directly to them in a respectful and formal tone. His purpose is to convince them that a skateboard park is needed, and he stays focused on that with supporting reasons.

I see many skateboarders riding along the streets and using curbs and stairways to practice their jumps. They also use plywood and other materials to build their own ramps, which do not look very safe at all. A skateboard park, though, would provide jumps that have been built with skateboarders' safety in mind.

Word Choice

- **The writing uses precise language.**

Sam uses precise words to make a strong impression on the reader. Here he specifies which sports are already accommodated in the parks. He also uses the specific words *entire* and *welcomes* rather than using a more general phrase such as "there isn't a place for them to go."

Already, the park contains places to enjoy baseball, soccer, football, basketball, and tennis. But these days, skateboarding is just as popular. There is even a skateboard club in the community. These skateboarders need a place to go, yet there is not a place within our entire community that welcomes them.

Using the Scoring Guide to Study the Model

Sentence Fluency

- **The writing has varied sentence structures.**

In the paragraph below, Sam's sentences are varied. He includes introductory phrases, transition words, and a compound sentence. This variety helps keep the reader's interest.

First of all, our community's parks are there to provide enjoyment for the community and to promote the safety and welfare of the residents, and that should include skateboarders, too. Already, the park contains places to enjoy baseball, soccer, football, basketball, and tennis. But these days, skateboarding is just as popular. There is even a skateboard club in the community. These skateboarders need a place to go, yet there is not a place within our entire community that welcomes them.

Conventions

- **The essay contains correct grammar, punctuation, capitalization, and spelling.**

I think Sam did a great job with his grammar and mechanics. From what I can see, he did not make any serious mistakes in capitalization, punctuation, sentence structure, or spelling. Look at the section below. See any mistakes? Neither did I.

By proposing a skateboard park to be built next to the city park, it's clear that members of our community realize that the large number of skateboarders who live here need a safe and accessible place to practice their sport. Although there are many people opposed to the skateboard park, I'd like to explain to you why I think this is a good idea.

Planning My Time

Before giving us a writing test prompt, my teacher tells us how much time we'll have to complete the test. Since I'm already familiar with the writing process, I can think about how much total time I need and then divide it up into the different parts of the writing process. If the test takes an hour, here's how I can organize my time. Planning your time will help you, too!

Step 4:
Edit
5 minutes

Step 1:
Prewrite
25 minutes

Step 3:
Revise
15 minutes

Step 2:
Draft
15 minutes

Prewrite

Focus on **Ideas**

Writing Strategy   Study the writing prompt to find out what to do.

When you take a writing test, study the writing prompt so you know just what you need to do. The writing prompt usually has three parts. Although the parts may not be labeled, you should be able to find them and label them on your own. Take a look at how I marked my writing prompt. First I found the setup, task, and scoring guide in the writing prompt. Then I circled key words in the setup and the task that tell what kind of writing I need to do. I circled the setup in purple and the task in red.

My Writing Test Prompt

Setup — Your school is trying to decide on a cover image and saying for this year's school yearbook. They want an image that will be visually appealing and a saying that will represent the school well.

Task — Come up with an idea for the cover of your school's yearbook and write an argument essay to convince the other students to agree with your choice.

Scoring Guide — Be sure your writing

- clearly identifies your position and contains supporting facts and reasons.

- is well organized and contains an introduction, body, and conclusion.

- establishes and maintains a formal style.

- uses precise language.

- has varied sentence structures.

- contains correct grammar, punctuation, capitalization, and spelling.

Think about how the scoring guide relates to the six writing traits you've studied in the rubrics. All of the traits might not be included in every scoring guide, but you need to remember them all to write a good argument test.

Ideas

- Be sure your writing clearly identifies your position and contains supporting facts and reasons.

I'll state my position clearly in the first paragraph. Then I'll include relevant supporting facts and reasons in each paragraph.

Organization

- Be sure your writing is well organized and contains an introduction, body, and conclusion.

I'll begin my essay with an introductory paragraph. Then I'll write the body and finish with a concluding statement that sums up my argument.

Voice

- Be sure your writing establishes and maintains a formal style.

As I write, I'll stay focused on my purpose and be convincing. I'll keep my language formal and respectful to my audience.

Word Choice

- Be sure your writing uses precise language.

Precise language that sticks to my topic will help me sound like I know what I'm talking about—and help convince my reader of my opinion.

Sentence Fluency

- Be sure your writing has varied sentence structures.

I don't want my reader to lose interest, so I'll be sure to use a variety of sentence types, including questions and exclamations.

Conventions

- Be sure your writing contains correct grammar, punctuation, capitalization, and spelling.

I'll read my essay once I have completed it to find and fix any spelling and grammar mistakes.

Prewrite

Focus on **Ideas**

Writing Strategy   Respond to the task.

When you write for a test, it's important to prepare before you begin writing. I'm going to gather some information and jot down notes before I start writing. The writing prompt is a good place to start gathering information. First, look at the task to find out what you are supposed to write. Think about how you'll respond to the task before you start writing. Even though you don't have a lot of time when you are writing for a test, prewriting can actually save you time by helping you get your ideas organized up front.

Since the task says to write an argument essay about my choice for this year's yearbook, I'll start jotting down some ideas.

Task — Come up with an idea for the cover of your school's yearbook and write an argument essay to convince the other students to agree with your choice.

Notes

✔ We did a lot of great things this year.

✔ Test scores were higher.

✔ Higher. . . what about something to do with that?

Apply

Jotting down notes about a topic can help you hone in on exactly what you are going to write.

Writing Strategy   Choose a graphic organizer.

Now that I have decided what to write about (thanks to my notes!), I am going to arrange my ideas. A graphic organizer will help me organize my ideas. Since I am writing an argument essay, I think a Network Tree will be the best organizer to help me remember and organize all the details and ideas I want to include.

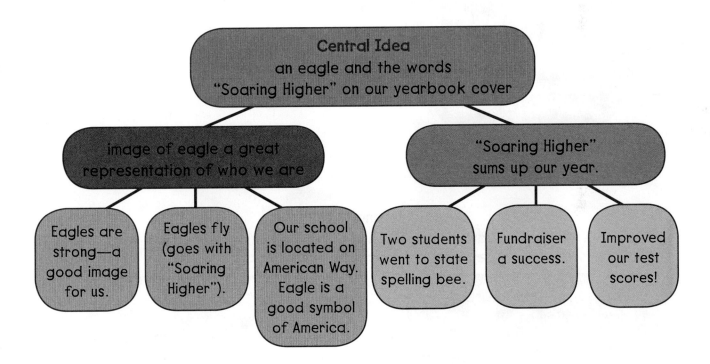

Central Idea
an eagle and the words "Soaring Higher" on our yearbook cover

image of eagle a great representation of who we are

"Soaring Higher" sums up our year.

Eagles are strong—a good image for us.

Eagles fly (goes with "Soaring Higher").

Our school is located on American Way. Eagle is a good symbol of America.

Two students went to state spelling bee.

Fundraiser a success.

Improved our test scores!

Reflect

Are there enough good reasons in Leila's Network Tree to convince readers?

Apply

A graphic organizer helps you arrange all the information you need to include in your essay.

Prewrite

Focus on Organization

Writing Strategy   Check the graphic organizer against the scoring guide.

Since you won't get a lot of time to revise during a test, prewriting is super important. Before I dive in and start writing my essay, I'll take another look at my Network Tree and compare it to the scoring guide from my writing prompt.

Central Idea
an eagle and the words "Soaring Higher" on our yearbook cover

image of eagle a great representation of who we are

- Eagles are strong—a good image for us.
- Eagles fly (goes with "Soaring Higher").
- Our school is located on American Way. Eagle is a good symbol of America.

"Soaring Higher" sums up our year.

- Two students went to state spelling bee.
- Fundraiser a success.
- Improved our test scores!

Ideas

- Be sure your writing clearly identifies your position and contains supporting facts and reasons.

My position is clearly stated in the Central Idea space. I've also written down some good supporting explanations for why "Soaring Higher" and an eagle would make a great yearbook cover.

Organization

- Be sure your writing is well organized and contains an introduction, body, and conclusion.

My introductory paragraph will state my Central Idea. Then I'll use information from the rest of the Network Tree for the body. My conclusion will be a summary.

Voice

- Be sure your writing establishes and maintains a formal style.

I'll use appropriate formal language right from the beginning, and I'll be careful not to let casual words creep in as I write.

Word Choice

- Be sure your writing uses precise language.

I'll be sure to use precise, specific words to make my points. I'll avoid vague or general language that might bore or confuse my readers.

Sentence Fluency

- Be sure your writing has varied sentence structures.

I'm going to keep my reader interested by using different types of sentences.

Conventions

- Be sure your writing contains correct grammar, punctuation, capitalization, and spelling.

I don't want to leave any mistakes in my paper, so I will be sure to check my work carefully.

Reflect

There is good information in Leila's Network Tree. Now it all needs to be worked into a great essay!

Apply

Check your graphic organizer against the scoring guide.

Draft

Focus on Ideas

Writing Strategy State the position clearly.

My position is that this year the school yearbook should feature an eagle along with the words "Soaring Higher." I'll state that in my opening sentence. Then I can use the rest of the essay to tell the readers why.

[DRAFT]

Let's Soar This Year!
by Leila

[my position]

If you want to feature a picture and words that really express our school on the cover of this years yearbook, then theres no better choice than using an eagle along with the words "Soaring Higher" to represent us. Here is while I feel so strongly about it.

First, the image of the eagle is a great representation of who we are. The school is located on American Way. Eagles are really cool animals, and having an animal on the cover with such a good, strong image will be uplifting for the students and teachers and will let everyone no that we are just awesome! Btw, the eagle is also an animal that flys, which would go nicely with the saying I am proposing we use, "Soaring Higher"

Why "Soaring Higher" on the cover. This year we have truly been doing just that. Our overall test scores have improved. This gave us one of the top rankings in the area. We had not one, but two students go to the state spelling bee to represent our school. Last year we did not send any students. In addition, we did so well for our annual fundraiser that we were able to get a new Gym Floor. This will benfit the school for year's to come. If anyone has soared high this year, I would say it was us!

There is a final reason why I think this would be a good image and saying for our yearbook. And that is because you want your yearbook to be good. When you see an image of a bold and strong eagle next to the words "Soaring Higher," you will be happy.

So when you decide on what goes on this year's yearbook, think strength, think soring, and chose an eagle and the words "Soaring Higher." It will be a cover image the students won't soon forget.

Reflect

How good a job did Leila do with writing a convincing essay?

Apply

Your draft is your first attempt at getting all your ideas down on paper. Be thorough, but remember that you will have the opportunity to go back and do edits.

Revise

Focus on Organization

Writing Strategy   Use transitions to organize the writing.

Now is the time to read my essay and be sure that my reasons are organized clearly. I know that transition words are like signposts that guide the reader. Since I am listing several reasons, I can use transitions to signal to the reader when I am moving from one reason to the next. I already used *First* and *final reason*. Here is a place in the middle where I can add another transition.

[DRAFT]   [added transition]

Next, why should we put
~~Why~~ "Soaring Higher" on the cover? This year we have truly been
doing just that. Our overall test scores have improved. This gave us
one of the top rankings in the area.

Apply

Good writers give the reader a clear guide to follow, using transitions to organize the writing.

Revise

Focus on Voice

The scoring guide says I should establish and maintain a formal style in my writing. Even though I'm addressing my fellow students, I don't want to sound too casual. They won't take me seriously if I sound like I'm just standing around chatting in the hallway.

[DRAFT]

[replaced casual language]

strong and powerful →

Eagles are ~~really cool~~ animals, and having an animal on the cover

with such a good, strong image will be uplifting for the students and

strong ←

teachers and will let everyone no that we are ~~just awesome~~! ~~Btw~~, the

eagle is also an animal that flys, which would go nicely with the saying

I am proposing we use, "Soaring Higher"

Reflect

Is the language appropriately formal now that it's been revised?

Apply

Use formal and direct language throughout your essay.

Revise

Focus on Word Choice

Writing Strategy   Choose words and phrases to convey ideas precisely.

Now is my chance to reread my essay and be sure that I have included only strong, precise words. After all, if I use weak words, my essay just won't fly! When I went back and read it again, I noticed that my final reason for wanting to use an eagle and "Soaring Higher" isn't that strong. Look at how I strengthened my sentences by using precise words!

[DRAFT]

powerful

There is a final reason why I think this would be a ~~good~~ image and saying for our yearbook. And that is because you want your yearbook

memorable

to be ~~good~~. When you see an image of a bold and strong eagle next

feel a thrill

to the words "Soaring Higher," you will ~~be happy~~.

[used precise words]

Apply

Good writers use strong and precise words to sound more convincing.

Writing Strategy   Check my grammar, punctuation, capitalization, and spelling.

Always check your paper one last time. The scoring guide says to use correct grammar, punctuation, capitalization, and spelling. I always leave plenty of time to check for errors in these important areas.

Let's Soar This Year!

by Leila

If you want to feature a picture and words that really express our school on the cover of this year's yearbook, then there's no better choice than using an eagle along with the words "Soaring Higher" to represent us. Here is ~~while~~ why I feel so strongly about it.

First, the image of the eagle is a great representation of who we , and the eagle just happens to be one of the symbols of the United States government.   strong and powerful are. The school is located on American Way. Eagles are ~~really cool~~ animals, and having an animal on the cover with such a good, strong image will be uplifting for the students and teachers and will let everyone ~~no~~ know that we are ~~just awesome~~ strong! ~~Btw,~~ the eagle is also an animal that ~~flys,~~ flies which would go nicely with the saying I am proposing we use, "Soaring Higher."

Apply

Even though you have read and reread your essay, you want to look at it carefully at this point to find and correct any mistakes.

[FINAL DRAFT]

Next, why should we put

^Why "Soaring Higher" on the cover? This year we have truly been

doing just that. Our overall test scores have improved, giving us

~~This gave~~ us one of the top rankings in the area. We had not one, but two students

go to the state spelling bee to represent our school. Last year we

did not send any students. In addition, we did so well for our annual

fundraiser that we were able to get a new Gym Floor, something that ~~This~~ will benefite

the school for years to come. If anyone has soared high this year, I

would say it was us!

There is a final reason why I think this would be a ~~good~~ powerful image and

saying for our yearbook. And that is because you want your yearbook

to be ~~good~~ memorable. When you see an image of a bold and strong eagle next

to the words "Soaring Higher," you will ~~be happy~~ feel a thrill.

So when you decide on what goes on this year's yearbook, think

strength, think ~~soring~~ soaring, and chose an eagle and the words "Soaring

Higher." It will be a cover image the students won't soon forget.

Reflect

Has Leila missed anything? Make sure you use your last few minutes to check your writing for grammar, punctuation, or spelling errors.

The test is complete! When you follow the right steps, it's not that difficult at all. Here are some helpful tips to remember when you write for a test.

TEST TIPS

1. **Study the writing prompt before you start to write.** Most writing prompts have three parts: the setup, the task, and the scoring guide. The parts probably won't be labeled. You'll have to figure them out for yourself!

2. **Make sure you understand the task before you start to write.**

   • Read all three parts of the writing prompt carefully.

   • Circle key words in the task part of the writing prompt that tell what kind of writing you need to do. The task might also identify your audience.

   • Make sure you know how you'll be graded.

   • Say the assignment in your own words to yourself.

3. **Keep an eye on the clock.** Decide how much time you will spend on each part of the writing process and try to stick to your schedule. Don't spend so much time prewriting that you don't have enough time left to write.

4. **Reread your writing. Compare it to the scoring guide at least twice.** Remember the rubrics you have used all year? A scoring guide on a writing test is like a rubric. It can help you keep what's important in mind.

5. **Plan, plan, plan!** You don't get much time to revise during a test, so planning is more important than ever.

6. **Write neatly.** Remember: If the people who score your test can't read your writing, it doesn't matter how good your essay is!

Descriptive writing describes something to the reader.

Hi! I'm Denise. I'm learning about descriptive writing in school. I like this kind of writing because it's so real. When you read a good description, you feel as if you're actually experiencing something right at that moment. I want to learn how to write like that!

IN THIS UNIT

- ☐ Descriptive Essay
- ☐ Observation Report
- ☐ Descriptive Article
- LITERATURE CONNECTION ▷ Poem
- ☐ Writing for a Test

Name: Denise
Home: Minnesota
Hobbies: modeling, cooking,
and photography

What's a Descriptive Essay?

A descriptive essay gives a clear, detailed picture of a person, a place, a thing, or an event. You have to be really observant to do this kind of writing. And you have to communicate what you've observed to your readers.

What's in a Descriptive Essay?

Vivid Imagery
A descriptive essay doesn't just give readers an idea of what something or someone is like—it makes the subject come alive! Powerful images in the essay help the audience clearly visualize the subject.

Precise Language
A descriptive essay needs precise language. Instead of vague, overused words, I'll use specific, interesting ones. Good metaphors will really strengthen my ideas.

Point of View
A descriptive essay can be written in either third person or first person. I'll have to decide which point of view fits my subject the best. Sometimes an essay is more powerful when I don't place myself inside it. At other times, I can breathe more life into a subject by making it personal. This will be a tough decision!

Organization
It's easy to ramble when you're writing a description. I'm going to organize my essay into paragraphs with topic sentences and supporting detail sentences. Each paragraph will tell about one main idea.

Why write a Descriptive Essay?

I've been thinking about why I want to write a descriptive essay.
I've listed a few ideas below. Do you have some ideas of your own?

Observation Skills
Writing a descriptive essay can really help me improve my powers of observation. After all, to be able to describe something, you first have to observe it carefully!

Appreciation
Often I just glance at something and move on. Writing a description can make me stop and really reflect on what I'm seeing and appreciate what's interesting or beautiful or strange about it.

Sharing an Experience
If I do a really good job describing something, my readers will feel as if they experienced it, too. That's a great way to share my life with other people!

Language Skills
I have to choose my words carefully and use strong, effective language to write a good essay. I think descriptive writing is going to be a good experience for me.

Linking Descriptive Writing Traits to a Descriptive Essay

In this chapter, you will describe a person, a place, a thing, or an event. This type of descriptive writing is called a descriptive essay. Denise will guide you through the stages of the writing process: Prewrite, Draft, Revise, Edit, and Publish. In each stage, Denise will show you important writing strategies that are linked to the Descriptive Writing Traits below.

Descriptive Writing Traits

Ideas
- a clear topic that is supported and enhanced by specific sensory details

Organization
- well-organized paragraphs that follow the order of the description, whether by time, location, or another order

Voice
- a voice and tone that are appropriate for the purpose and audience

Word Choice
- precise, descriptive words, possibly with figurative language, that create an accurate picture for the reader

Sentence Fluency
- sentences that vary in length and type to add flow to the writing

Conventions
- no or few errors in grammar, usage, mechanics, and spelling

Before you write, read Anna Yuishmal's descriptive essay on the next page. Then use the descriptive essay rubric on pages 372–373 to decide how well she did. (You might want to look back at What's in a Descriptive Essay? on page 368, too!)

A STRIKING IMAGE

by Anna Yuishmal

Vivid imagery **Point of view—first person**

I was leisurely thumbing through a book about weather recently when I was suddenly struck by lightning—in a photograph. Filling the page was a lightning storm, a monstrous fire in the sky. Against an inky black sky, mounds of angry clouds piled on top of each other. A charred, smoky-gray mass smoldered near the bottom of the photo. A raging orange cloud exploded like lava. Looming above was a brilliant yellow cloudburst, singed red at its edges. The lightning bolts were a tangle of glowing white wires that sliced the night into jagged pieces.

Lightning is a split-second show, a glimpse of nature's awesome energy. Zing! Steely fingers reach out to snatch a piece of the sky. Poof! They are gone. The photographer captured the brief moment. As the lightning flashed, the shutter snapped.   **Precise language**

The image reminded me of what comes after a lightning strike. The metallic odor of burnt oxygen, or ozone, follows the flash. Then comes thunder, a distant rolling rumble or a sudden echoing boom. To me, thunder is the delicious dessert after the lightning.

As I closed the book, I could still feel the high-voltage force of the fleeting event caught in the photo. A shiver like a lightning bolt ran down my spine and stayed there.

Organization—supporting details

Organization—topic sentence

Rubric

Use this 6-point rubric to plan and score a descriptive essay.

	6	5	4
Ideas	The topic is clear and focused. Vivid sensory details create a picture for the reader.	The topic is clear and focused. Strong sensory details create a picture for the reader.	The topic is often clear and focused. Solid sensory details are used.
Organization	The description is organized so that the topic is introduced at the beginning and the details are organized into logical paragraphs.	The topic is introduced at the beginning. Most details are organized into logical paragraphs.	The topic is mentioned at the beginning. The paragraphs are easy to follow, but some details are not logically organized.
Voice	The voice connects directly with the reader in a friendly way.	The writer's voice connects with the reader throughout most of the essay.	The writer's voice is sincere but sometimes fails to connect with the reader.
Word Choice	Precise words and phrases help the reader form a visual image.	Most words and phrases are precise and help the reader visualize the topic.	In a few places, the words are too general and do not create an image for the reader.
Sentence Fluency	The writer effectively uses repeated sentence structures to highlight related ideas.	The writer uses repeated sentence structures for related ideas with some effectiveness.	The writer attempts repeated sentence structures for related ideas but is not always effective.
Conventions	Appositives, predicate nouns, and predicate adjectives are used correctly and add style to the writing.	There are one or two minor errors with predicate nouns, predicate adjectives, and appositives.	Some appositives are not punctuated correctly. One or two predicate nouns or adjectives are used incorrectly.

✚ **Presentation**   White space organizes the text for easy reading.

3	2	1	
Some of the writing is clear and focused. Many details are too general to create a picture.	The topic is not clear. The details are too vague to help the reader create a picture.	The topic cannot be guessed. The details are simply an unconnected list.	Ideas
The topic is mentioned at the beginning but is not clear. Some paragraphs are poorly organized or lacking details.	The topic is not introduced at the beginning. Paragraphs are poorly organized and hard to follow.	The topic is never stated. The paragraphs are just unconnected sentences.	Organization
The writer's voice often fades away. It sometimes connects with the audience.	The writer's voice is weak. There is little attempt to connect with the audience.	The writing contains no voice and doesn't connect with the audience.	Voice
Some words and phrases are vague or dull.	Many words and phrases are too general to help the reader form an image of the topic.	The words are so general or poorly used that the reader cannot form any visual images at all.	Word Choice
Repeated sentence structures appear in the writing, but they sometimes do not highlight related ideas.	Repeated sentence structures appear but are not used for related ideas. They make the writing choppy.	There are many choppy and incomplete sentences, making the writing hard to read.	Sentence Fluency
Errors with appositives, predicate nouns, and predicate adjectives slow down reading in spots.	Frequent errors with appositives, predicate nouns, and predicate adjectives make reading a challenge.	Many serious errors with appositives, predicate nouns, and predicate adjectives make the writing very hard to understand.	Conventions

See Appendix B for 4-, 5-, and 6-point descriptive rubrics.

Descriptive Essay

Using the Rubric to Study the Model

Did you notice that the model on page 371 points out some key elements of a descriptive essay? As she wrote "A Striking Image," Anna Yuishmal used these elements to help her describe an event. She also used the 6-point rubric on pages 372–373 to plan, draft, revise, and edit the writing. A rubric is a great tool for evaluating writing during the writing process.

Now let's use the same rubric to score the model. To do this, we'll focus on each trait separately, starting with Ideas. We'll use the top descriptor for each trait (column 6), along with examples from the model, to help us understand how the traits work together. How would you score Anna on each trait?

- **The topic is clear and focused.**
- **Vivid sensory details create a picture for the reader.**

Anna sticks with one topic in her essay—the photo of the lightning storm. She uses vivid and realistic details that make the reader see and hear the lightning storm as if it were really happening. Look at these sensory details.

[from the writing model]

Filling the page was a lightning storm, a monstrous fire in the sky. Against an inky black sky, mounds of angry clouds piled on top of each other. A charred, smoky-gray mass smoldered near the bottom of the photo.

• The description is organized so that the topic is introduced at the beginning and the details are organized into logical paragraphs.

Anna starts her essay with a clear and interesting statement about her topic. Then the essay flows from one well-organized paragraph to the next. Each paragraph has a clear topic sentence, which helps organize the information. See how a supporting detail expands on the topic sentence in this paragraph.

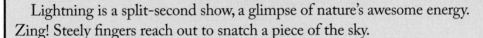

[from the writing model]

Lightning is a split-second show, a glimpse of nature's awesome energy. Zing! Steely fingers reach out to snatch a piece of the sky.

• The voice connects directly with the reader in a friendly way.

This essay uses a tone of voice that the reader can easily relate to. Anna talks about what the photo reminded her of. She also shares her feelings about thunder in a way that sounds friendly, like she is talking directly to us.

[from the writing model]

The image reminded me of what comes after a lightning strike. The metallic odor of burnt oxygen, or ozone, follows the flash. Then comes thunder, a distant rolling rumble or sudden echoing boom. To me, thunder is the delicious dessert after the lightning.

Word Choice

- **Precise words and phrases help the reader form a visual image.**

Talk about great word choice! Anna used exciting words and created lively images of the lightning storm in the photograph. The reader almost doesn't need to see the photograph because Anna's descriptions are so dynamic and precise. Look at these powerful sentences about the colors in the sky.

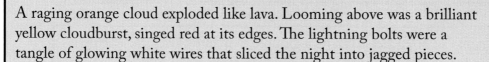

[from the writing model]

A raging orange cloud exploded like lava. Looming above was a brilliant yellow cloudburst, singed red at its edges. The lightning bolts were a tangle of glowing white wires that sliced the night into jagged pieces.

Sentence Fluency

- **The writer effectively uses repeated sentence structures to highlight related ideas.**

Sometimes writers use the same sentence structure in a short space to convey connected ideas. This can add power and depth to the writing. Notice how Anna repeats the dramatic sentence structure she uses to describe lightning's speed and power.

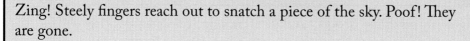

[from the writing model]

Zing! Steely fingers reach out to snatch a piece of the sky. Poof! They are gone.

Conventions

• Appositives, predicate nouns, and predicate adjectives are used correctly and add style to the writing.

I checked over Anna's essay, and I didn't find any mistakes. She even used appositives correctly. In the sentence below, *ozone* is an appositive that provides more information about the burnt oxygen. Anna sets the appositive off with commas.

[from the writing model]

The metallic odor of burnt oxygen, or ozone, follows the flash.

Looming above was a brilliant yellow cloudburst . . .

Lightning is a split-second show . . .

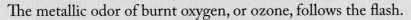

⁺Presentation White space organizes the text for easy reading.

My Turn!

Now I'm ready to write my own descriptive essay. I already have some ideas. Read along and see how I do it. I'm going to use what I learned from the rubric and good writing strategies.

Prewrite

Focus on **Ideas**

The Rubric Says   The topic is clear and focused.

Writing Strategy   Choose a picture and make notes about its sensory details.

While I was looking for a subject for my descriptive essay assignment, I found this photograph of a cat and a fish. It was in a magazine ad, and I couldn't stop looking at it.

I took these notes on the sensory details in the photograph so I could use them in my essay. I had to use my imagination to capture the sight, sound, and feel of things in the picture. I didn't take any notes on smells or tastes, though. I don't think there are any— unless the cat catches the fish!

My Notes on the Picture of the Cat and Fish

✔ **see:** cat looking into fishbowl; looks like cat's face is inside bowl; cat's ears—small pink shark fins; eyes—big baby-blue and black marbles in pink ovals; nose—pale pink; whiskers—white; goldfish—on cat's nose, plump, shiny yellow with bright orange at front, black ink dot for eye, 2 tiny bubbles from open mouth; bowl—open on top, curved edges, water line below cat's ears, white gravel

✔ **feel:** cat's nose—velvety; ears—fluffy inside; whiskers—sharp; fish's tail—gauzy, delicate

✔ **hear:** cat saying, "Mmmm!"; fish saying, "Uh-oh!"

Apply

Choose an interesting subject to describe, and take notes about as many sensory details as possible.

Prewrite

The Rubric Says

The description is organized so that the topic is introduced at the beginning and the details are organized into logical paragraphs.

Writing Strategy

Use a Spider Map to organize the notes.

The rubric stresses that the details of my essay should be organized logically into paragraphs. Since I am describing a picture, I will organize my writing around the senses. I'll start by organizing my notes that way, but I see that most of my details are in the "see" category. I need to break my notes into more categories.

A Spider Map will help me organize my notes better. I can make each leg a different category of details, like what I can see of the cat in the photograph, what I can see of the fish, and so on.

When I get my notes organized into several categories, I will be able to write my essay in logically organized paragraphs. I'll also make sure I introduce my topic clearly right at the start.

Writer's Term

Spider Map

A **Spider Map** organizes information about a topic. The topic is written in the center circle. Each "leg" is one category of details.

SPIDER MAP

see—cat
seems to be inside bowl
ears—pink shark fins
eyes—blue and black marbles in pink ovals
nose—pale pink
whiskers—white

feel
cat's nose—velvety
fish's tail—gauzy, delicate
ears—fluffy inside
whiskers—sharp

see—goldfish
2 tiny bubbles from mouth
black ink dot for eye
plump, shiny yellow
on cat's nose

see—bowl
bubble
open on top
curved edges
white gravel

hear
cat saying, "Mmmm!"
fish saying, "Uh-oh!"

Reflect
Look at the Spider Map. Are the details organized logically? How can Denise use them to write a good descriptive essay?

Apply
Organize your notes by using a Spider Map. Make sure each "leg" of your Spider Map has one category of sensory details.

Draft

Focus on **Ideas**

The Rubric Says   Vivid sensory details create a picture for the reader.

Writing Strategy   Use vivid imagery to help the reader visualize the picture.

According to the rubric, I need to create a picture in my reader's mind. After all, that's the purpose of descriptive writing—to make the reader "see" what I see. I can use sensory details that describe the way the image looks, feels, and sounds. My Spider Map has lots of notes I can use in my detail sentences.

This photograph really got a reaction from me, so I want to make my reader have the same reaction. As I write the draft, I'll do my best with spelling and grammar and check for any mistakes later. Here's the beginning of my essay.

✐ Writer's Term

Detail Sentence

A **detail sentence** supports the paragraph's main idea. The detail sentences in a paragraph should all relate to the main idea.

[DRAFT]

Beware, Little Fishy!

Sometimes people feel like they're in a fishbowl and someone is looking at them. Well, I found a photograph about that idea. A white cat is looking at a goldfish in a bowl. The water changes what you see. It looks like the cat's face is inside the bowl, and the cat's face looks huge.

[detail sentences]

The cat's staring eyes, big blue marbles with black centers, are set in pink ovals. Its ears are like pink shark fins, with tufts of white fluff inside. The ears are above the water line, so they aren't changed. They are much smaller than the eyes and closer together. White whiskers sprowt from the cat's furry cheeks. Its nose is pale pink.

Reflect

Think about the draft. Which sensory details help you picture what the photograph looks like?

Apply

Write a draft using interesting details from your Spider Map. Make sure you use vivid images to write your detail sentences.

Revise

Focus on Organization

The Rubric Says   The description is organized so that the topic is introduced at the beginning and the details are organized into logical paragraphs.

Writing Strategy   Make sure all the detail sentences relate to the topic sentence in every paragraph.

I've introduced my topic in the first paragraph. Now I want to make sure all my paragraphs are logically organized and easy to follow. I'll check that each one has a clear topic sentence and only details that relate to the topic. This paragraph has great details, but it needs a topic sentence to hold it together.

Writer's Term

Topic Sentence
The **topic sentence** states the main idea of a paragraph. It is often the first sentence in the paragraph.

[added topic sentence]

[DRAFT]

The cat's face is scary but sweet.

~~The cat's~~ Its staring eyes, big blue marbles with black centers, are set in pink ovals. Its ears are like pink shark fins, with tufts of white fluff inside. The ears are above the water line, so they aren't changed. They are much smaller than the eyes and closer together.

Apply

Make sure all your paragraphs have topic sentences supported by detail sentences.

Revise

Focus on **Voice**

The Rubric Says   The voice connects directly with the reader in a friendly way.

Writing Strategy   Choose punctuation for effect.

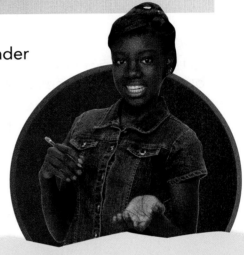

The rubric says to connect with my reader and sound friendly. I can make the paragraph below friendlier by using second person *you*. That will help connect my reader with what I'm describing. I can also use questions and exclamation marks to share my surprise and enthusiasm.

[DRAFT]

[connected with reader by using second person]

~~Sometimes people feel like they're in a fishbowl and someone is~~
Do you ever feel like you're in a fishbowl and someone is looking at you?
~~looking at them.~~ Well, I found a photograph about that idea. A white

cat is looking at a goldfish in a bowl. The water changes what you

see. It looks like the cat's face is inside the bowl, and the cat's face

looks huge.

[added exclamation]

Reflect
Does the writing sound more friendly? Why do you think so?

Apply
Add *you* to make it sound as if you are talking to the reader.

Descriptive Essay 385

Revise

Focus on Word Choice

The Rubric Says   Precise words and phrases help the reader form a visual image.

Writing Strategy   Replace vague words with precise ones.

The rubric says I should use precise words, but I see some places where I don't do that. I'm going to take out some vague words and replace them with precise words that will convey a clearer visual image. This will help my reader picture what I am describing.

[DRAFT]

~~Sometimes people feel like they're in a fishbowl and someone is~~ **watching**
Do you ever feel like you're in a fishbowl and someone is ~~looking at~~ you?
~~looking at them?~~ Well, I found a photograph about that idea. A white
peering intently
cat is ~~looking~~ at a goldfish in a bowl. The water ~~changes~~ **distorts** what you

see. It looks like the cat's face is inside the bowl, and the cat's face

looks huge **!**

———— [replaced vague words] ————

Apply

Replace any vague words with more precise and interesting words.

Edit

The Rubric Says	Appositives, predicate nouns, and predicate adjectives are used correctly and add style to the writing.
Writing Strategy	Check for the correct use of appositives, predicate nouns, and predicate adjectives.

Writer's Term

Appositives

An **appositive** is a word or phrase that follows a noun and helps to identify or describe the noun.

Wow! I'm almost finished! Now I need to make sure my sentence structures are correct. Good structure makes sentences easy to follow. But if I make mistakes, such as forgetting to put commas around appositives, my readers will be confused.

[DRAFT]

[added commas to fix error in appositive]

When you look at the picture, you can imagine what the cat and

the fish are thinking and saying. The cat, a silent and sly hunter, is

                          juicy
thinking about the ~~juicey~~ orange goldfish. The cat murmurs, "Mmmm!"

and the fish replies, "Uh-oh!" Two tiny bubbles float up.

Reflect

What do you think? How have Denise's revisions strengthened her essay? Go back and look over her draft. Can you find any errors she's missed?

Apply   Conventions

Edit your draft for spelling, punctuation, appositives, and predicate nouns and adjectives.

For more practice with appositives and predicate nouns and adjectives, use the exercises on the next two pages.

Appositives

Know the Rule

An **appositive** is a word or phrase that follows a noun or pronoun and helps identify or describe it. Appositives are usually separated from the rest of the sentence by commas.

> **Example:** Dolly, **my cat,** came to our house as a stray.
> My neighbor's dogs, **two boxers,** bark at night.

Practice the Rule

Number your paper 1–10. For the first group of sentences below, write the noun and the appositive that follows.

1. Here are some tips, or guidelines, for getting good photographs of your pets.
2. The first tip, the most important one, is to study your pet.
3. Find your pet's favorite spot, the place where it likes to spend most of its time.
4. For example, Bubba, my shaggy sheepdog, likes to hang out on the braided rug in the den.
5. Observe your pet's typical behavior, what he or she does every day.

In this group of sentences, notice the underlined nouns or pronouns. Write an appositive that you could use for each underlined word.

6. Our <u>neighbor</u>, _____, likes to take pictures of his dog.
7. His best <u>picture</u>, _____, won a prize last year.
8. Our neighbor's <u>daughter</u>, _____, takes the dog for walks.
9. They usually head for their favorite <u>spot</u>, _____.
10. Our neighbor has many pictures of the two of <u>them</u>, _____, at the park.

Predicate Nouns and Adjectives

Know the Rule

A **predicate noun** follows a linking verb and renames the subject.
> **Example:** The cat's tail is a **snake** that can't keep still.

A **predicate adjective** follows a linking verb and describes the subject.
> **Example:** Our dog is **chubby**!

Practice the Rule

Copy the following sentences. Underline the linking verbs. Draw two lines under the predicate nouns and circle the predicate adjectives.

1. Tabby cats are usually good pets.
2. My tabby is small with bright green eyes.
3. When I brush her, she is so relaxed that she almost falls asleep.
4. Our neighbor's dog, a St. Bernard, is a beast!
5. He seems gentle, but he really scares my cat.
6. My tabby feels threatened every time the dog barks.
7. My other cat is a mischievous kitten.
8. His claws and teeth are sharp, and he scratches and bites a lot.
9. The thing he likes least is the cat carrier.
10. When I put him in it, he looks so sad!

Publish

✚Presentation

Publishing Strategy	Read your essay to your classmates. Ask them to draw their own pictures based on the essay.
Presentation Strategy	Adjust margins, line spacing, and paragraph indents for easy reading.

Our class likes to do art projects and discuss them. Reading my essay to my classmates would be a good publishing option. To make reading aloud easier, I need to check for good margins all around. Using generous line spacing and indenting paragraphs will also make the text clear on the page. Before I read my essay, I want to check it over one more time. I'll use the final checklist below.

My Final Checklist

Did I—

- ✔ check for correct use of appositives, including a comma before and after?
- ✔ use predicate nouns and predicate adjectives correctly?
- ✔ create margins, use line spacing, and indent my paragraphs for easy reading?
- ✔ proofread carefully for spelling, punctuation, and grammar?

Apply

Make a checklist to check your descriptive essay. Then make a final copy to publish.

Beware, Little Fishy!

by Denise

Do you ever feel like you're in a fishbowl and someone is watching you? Well, I found a photograph about that idea. A white cat is peering intently at a goldfish in a bowl. The water distorts what you see. So it looks like the cat's face is inside the bowl, and it's huge!

The cat's face is scary but sweet. Its staring eyes, big blue marbles with black centers, are set in pink ovals. Its ears are like pink shark fins, with tufts of white fluff inside. The ears are above the water line, so they aren't changed. They are much smaller than the eyes and set closer together. Spears of white whiskers sprout from the cat's furry cheeks. Its nose is a velvety cushion for the goldfish.

Shimmering in the center of the glass bubble, the goldfish is particularly appealing. Its plump little body is shiny yellow, with a bright orange face and shoulders. Its gauzy, delicate tail is a waving fan that casts a shadow on the cat's cheek.

When you look at the picture, you can imagine what the cat and the fish are thinking and saying. The cat, a silent and sly hunter, is thinking about the juicy orange goldfish. The cat murmurs, "Mmmm!" and the fish replies, "Uh-oh!" Two tiny bubbles float up.

Normally carefree, the goldfish seems to sense the possible danger. Its eye, an inky black dot, glances backward nervously. The curving sides of the bowl frame the tense situation. Beware, little fishy! You may feel safe behind your glass wall, but remember this: The bowl is open on top!

Reflect

Look at Denise's essay. Does it use all the traits of a good descriptive essay? Check it against the rubric. Then use the rubric to check your own descriptive essay.

What's an Observation Report?

An observation report describes in detail an object, a person, an event, or a process. I think I'll enjoy this kind of writing because I like to watch what goes on around me, like my uncle fixing cars. A step-by-step process will be a lot of fun to describe.

What's in an Observation Report?

Point of View
An observation report has a first-person point of view. This makes sense, doesn't it? The writer is involved with the subject of the report and tells what he or she did and observed.

Details
This kind of report should include plenty of vivid details. I want to appeal to all the senses as I write so my readers can imagine every step I'm describing.

Organization
Organization is very important! I'm planning to give my report a short introduction to help readers focus on what's happening. After that, I'll describe the steps in the process, followed by some observations and a clear conclusion.

Clarity
I want to make the process I'm describing as clear as possible to my audience. Using headings and adding a visual aid such as a diagram or a chart can help. I'll also use transition words to make the sequence of events easy to follow.

Why write an Observation Report?

There are tons of reasons for writing an observation report. I listed some here, since I'm still thinking about why I want to write. Do you have some ideas of your own?

Information

This kind of writing contains all kinds of information! Observation reports can educate readers about many different subjects, instruct them in procedures, or help them understand important concepts.

Observation Skills

They're called observation reports for a good reason! To do this kind of writing, you have to observe something well. Writing an observation report really hones your observation skills.

Note-Taking

I'll have to take notes in all kinds of subjects throughout my education. Doing an observation report will give me good practice in this important skill.

Scientific Method

Writing an observation report about an experiment involves following basic scientific methods. I'll have to make a prediction, set up a procedure to test it, evaluate my results, and come to a conclusion.

Linking Descriptive Writing Traits to an Observation Report

In this chapter, you will describe your observations. This type of descriptive writing is called an observation report. Denise will guide you through the stages of the writing process: Prewrite, Draft, Revise, Edit, and Publish. In each stage, Denise will show you important writing strategies that are linked to the Descriptive Writing Traits below.

Descriptive Writing Traits

Ideas
- a clear topic that is supported and enhanced by specific sensory details

Organization
- well-organized paragraphs that follow the order of the description, whether by time, location, or another order

Voice
- a voice and tone that are appropriate for the purpose and audience

Word Choice
- precise, descriptive words, possibly with figurative language, that create an accurate picture for the reader

Sentence Fluency
- sentences that vary in length and type to add flow to the writing

Conventions
- no or few errors in grammar, usage, mechanics, and spelling

Before you write, read Mark Volk's observation report on the next page. Then use the observation report rubric on pages 396–397 to decide how well he did. (You might want to look back at What's in an Observation Report? on page 392, too!)

Growing Paintbrush Mold
by Mark Volk

First-person point of view

    Penicillium notatum is a green mold that grows on cheese, bread, and fruit. This disgusting mold is the source of penicillin, an antibiotic! I already knew that mold grows better in a moist environment. How would temperature affect this mold's growth? My prediction was that the mold would grow better in a warm, moist environment than in a cold, moist environment.

Heading

PROCEDURE

Step 1: First, I rubbed two lemons on the floor to roughen up their skin. Then I left them on the kitchen table overnight. This way, penicillin mold spores, which are in soil and air, would be more likely to stick to the fruit.

Step 2: The next day, I put one of the lemons and one moist cotton ball in a paper bag and closed the bag. I put the bag in the refrigerator. Then I repeated this process with the other lemon and put that paper bag in a warm corner of the kitchen.

Step 3: For the next two weeks, I checked the lemons every day, took notes in my observation log, and made several color sketches.

Step 4: At the end of the two weeks, one lemon was covered with green mold. I scraped a little of this mold into a drop of water on a microscope slide and looked at it. I didn't get too close to the mold or breathe in any of it. Then I sketched the slide for my observation log.

Details

Organization

OBSERVATIONS

    During the whole experiment, the lemon in the refrigerator didn't change much. By the end of the experiment, it was a little drier but still firm and bright yellow. However, on the third day the lemon in the warm corner began to show spots of green powder. By the end of the two weeks, it had turned into a spongy, aqua-colored fuzz ball. It also had a strong smell because it had started to rot.

Vivid details

    What did the mold look like under the microscope? It resembled a cluster of stems with feathery ends—something like a paintbrush. That makes sense because penicillin is named for the Latin word *penicillus,* which means "brush."

Visual aid for clarity

CONCLUSION

    Penicillin grew on the lemon that was kept warm and moist, but not on the one in the refrigerator. A warm, moist environment is better than a cold, moist one for growing penicillin mold.

Rubric

Use this 6-point rubric to plan and score an observation report.

	6	5	4
Ideas	Information is thorough and complete. Details in diagrams or charts enhance information.	Information is thorough. Details in diagrams or charts are useful.	The information may be missing a few details. Diagrams and charts are included.
Organization	Steps are presented in a logical order. A variety of transitions accurately conveys the sequence of events.	The text structure makes sense. Transitions convey the sequence of events.	The organization is easy to follow. Transitions indicate the sequence of events, but some transitions are repetitive.
Voice	First-person point of view is used consistently throughout to connect strongly to the audience.	First-person point of view connects to the audience.	First-person point of view is not used in a few places.
Word Choice	Precise language, such as strong verbs, makes the process clear.	Several strong verbs are used, and precise language describes the process.	Most of the verbs are strong and help the reader follow the process.
Sentence Fluency	Sentence variety is striking. The writing is pleasurable to read.	Sentences are varied in length and beginnings. The writing has a smooth flow.	There is some variety in sentence length and beginnings. A few are choppy or too long.
Conventions	Apostrophes are used correctly to form possessive nouns and contractions.	Apostrophes are used correctly for the most part. There are a few errors that are hard to spot.	Noticeable errors with apostrophes and other conventions don't affect meaning.
✛Presentation	Text features, such as headings, and visuals are integrated thoughtfully.		

3	2	1	
Some information may be inaccurate or missing. Diagrams and charts may be incomplete or unclear.	Information is incomplete or may be inaccurate. Visuals are also incomplete or not included.	The information is inaccurate, and no visuals are included. The writer clearly knows very little about the topic.	**Ideas**
The organization needs attention to follow. Some transitions are missing.	The writing is hard to follow. Transitions are missing or unclear.	Lack of organization is confusing for the reader. No transitions are present.	**Organization**
First-person point of view is used inconsistently, and the writing sometimes fails to connect to the audience.	Point of view switches back and forth often. The reader is confused.	No voice is present in the writing. The writer does not connect with the audience.	**Voice**
Some verbs are weak, making the process harder to follow in places.	Many verbs are weak. The steps are not clearly described.	Verbs are missing. The steps are unclear.	**Word Choice**
Sentence beginnings are the same. There is little variety in length. The writing is readable but choppy.	There is little variety in sentence length and beginnings. Many sentences are incorrect.	Sentences are incomplete or incorrect. The writing takes work to read.	**Sentence Fluency**
Noticeable errors with apostrophes may slow down reading.	Errors with apostrophes and other conventions are distracting and interrupt the message.	The report has not been edited. There are many errors in spelling, grammar, and punctuation.	**Conventions**

See Appendix B for 4-, 5-, and 6-point descriptive rubrics.

Observation Report

Using the Rubric to Study the Model

Did you notice that the model on page 395 points out some key elements of an observation report? As he wrote "Growing Paintbrush Mold," Mark Volk used these elements to help him describe an observation. He also used the 6-point rubric on pages 396–397 to plan, draft, revise, and edit the writing. A rubric is a great tool for evaluating writing during the writing process.

Now let's use the same rubric to score the model. To do this, we'll focus on each trait separately, starting with Ideas. We'll use the top descriptor for each trait (column 6), along with examples from the model, to help us understand how the traits work together. How would you score Mark on each trait?

Ideas

- Information is thorough and complete.
- Details in diagrams or charts enhance information.

The information in Mark's report is complete, from Procedure to Observations to Conclusion. Mark described the mold and included a picture that enhances the reader's understanding of why penicillin is named for the Latin word that means "brush."

[from the writing model]

It resembled a cluster of stems with feathery ends—something like a paintbrush.

Organization

- Steps are presented in a logical order.
- A variety of transitions accurately conveys the sequence of events.

Mark numbers each of the steps and describes them in order. In Step 4, notice how he uses the transition phrase *At the end of the two weeks* to keep the process clear for the reader.

[from the writing model]

Step 3: For the next two weeks, I checked the lemons every day, took notes in my observation log, and made several color sketches.
Step 4: At the end of the two weeks, one lemon was covered with green mold.

Voice

- First-person point of view is used consistently throughout to connect strongly to the audience.

Mark is consistent about using first-person point of view throughout the report. This helps keep the reader focused on following the information in the experiment.

[from the writing model]

Step 1: First, I rubbed two lemons on the floor to roughen up their skin. Then I left them on the kitchen table overnight.

• Precise language, such as strong verbs, makes the process clear.

Several strong verbs describe the action in the experiment and help the reader picture the process in Mark's report. I think the verbs in these sentences are especially good choices for making the process clear.

[from the writing model]

Step 2: . . . Then I repeated this process . . .
Step 3: For the next two weeks, I checked the lemons every day . . .
Step 4: . . . I scraped a little of this mold . . . Then I sketched the slide for my observation log.

• Sentence variety is striking. The writing is pleasurable to read.

Mark's description of his experiment could have sounded dull, but he made sure that didn't happen. He includes interesting questions and exclamations to make the writing flow. See how he does that in his opening paragraph?

[from the writing model]

Penicillium notatum is a green mold that grows on cheese, bread, and fruit. This disgusting mold is the source of penicillin, an antibiotic! I already knew that mold grows better in a moist environment. How would temperature affect this mold's growth? My prediction was that the mold would grow better in a warm, moist environment than in a cold, moist environment.

Conventions

- **Apostrophes are used correctly to form possessive nouns and contractions.**

Mark always uses apostrophes correctly. Read the two sentences below. One shows how he correctly punctuated a contraction. The second sentence includes a possessive noun, with the apostrophe placed correctly.

[from the writing model]

During the whole experiment, the lemon in the refrigerator didn't change much.

[from the writing model]

I already knew that mold grows better in a moist environment. How would temperature affect this mold's growth?

✛ Presentation

Text features, such as headings, and visuals are integrated thoughtfully.

Now it's my turn! I'm going to write an observation report that follows the rubric and good writing strategies. Read along and see how I do it!

Prewrite

The Rubric Says Information is thorough and complete.

Writing Strategy Observe and take notes.

Our teacher asked us to work with partners for this assignment. One partner will do an experiment, and the other one will write an observation report on the experiment. Lisa, my partner, and I found a book in the library that has experiments in speed. One experiment shows how gravity affects acceleration (how fast an object starts to move).

We decided that Lisa would do the experiment, and I would write the report.

My Notes on the Acceleration Experiment

- **Our question:** How would attaching weights to a toy car affect its acceleration?

- **Our prediction:** Each additional weight would increase the car's acceleration.

- **What we did:** attached paper clip hook to car with string; put one weight (washer) on hook and hung it over edge of table; held car 2.5 ft from edge; let car go and started timing with stopwatch; stopped timing when car hit cardboard bumper; recorded time in log; averaged time over 3 runs; repeated with more weights.

- **The results (averages):** 1 weight: car hit bumper in 2.6 seconds; 2 weights: car hit in 1.8 seconds; 3 weights: 1.4 seconds; 4 weights: 1.1 seconds; 5 weights: 0.7 seconds

- **Conclusion:** Our prediction is correct. More weights mean a faster acceleration rate.

Apply

Conduct or observe an experiment. Take notes on what you observed.

Prewrite

Focus on Organization

The Rubric Says   Steps are presented in a logical order.

Writing Strategy   Make a Sequence Chain of the steps in the experiment.

Writer's Term_____

Sequence Chain
A **Sequence Chain** shows steps or events in the order they happen.

According to the rubric, I need to explain the steps in our experiment in the order we did them. A Sequence Chain is a good way to do that.

Sequence Chain

Step 1: To set up the experiment, we
   a) made a paper clip into a hook.
   b) used tape to mark a starting line 2.5 ft from the edge of a table.
   c) taped a cardboard bumper to the edge of the table to stop the car; made a hole at the bottom of the bumper for the string.
   d) cut 3 ft of string; tied one end to the car's axle and the other end to the hook.
   e) pushed the hook through the hole in the bumper.

Step 2: Lisa put one weight on the hook.

Step 3: Next, she held the weight over the edge of the table.

Step 4: With her other hand, she put the car at the starting line.

Step 5: She let the weight fall, and I started the stopwatch.

Step 6: I stopped timing when the car hit the bumper. I recorded the time.

Step 7: We repeated Steps 2–6 two more times. Then we averaged the times.

Step 8: We repeated Steps 2–7 with 2, 3, 4, and 5 weights. We recorded and averaged the times.

Reflect

Is the Sequence Chain logical and complete? How will it help Denise write a well-organized report?

Apply

Organize your notes by using a Sequence Chain.

Observation Report **403**

Draft

The Rubric Says	Steps are presented in a logical order.
Writing Strategy	Introduce the experiment in the introduction and use numbered steps to show the order.

Now it's time to write my report. My parents, my classmates, and their parents are going to read it. The rubric says that the steps have to be in order. Since I am describing something that happened, time (chronological) order makes sense. Just like in the model, I can use headings and numbers to highlight the order of steps in the experiment.

I also have to think about organizing the whole report. It needs an introduction, a body, and a conclusion. I'll tell the steps of the experiment in the body of my report.

As for spelling and grammar, I will do my best now and check for mistakes later. Right now, I need to get my draft on paper. You can read part of my draft on the next page. I still have to write the observations and conclusions sections.

[DRAFT]

[introduction]   **How Gravity Affects Acceleration**

Gravity is one of Earths forces. It keeps everything from floating off into space. Lisa and I did an experiment with a model car to see how gravity affects aceleration—how fast the car starts to move. We decided to attach a weight to one end of a string, tie the other end to the car, and drop the weight over the ege of a table. As gravity pulled the weight down, the weight would pull the car across the table. Lisa and I predickted that as we added more weights, the car would accelerate faster.

PROCEDURE   [heading]

Step 1: Lisa twisted a paper clip into a hook. She used tape to mark

[steps in procedure]

a starting line on a table 2.5 ft from the edge. She taped a bumper, a piece of heavy cardboard, to the edge of the table. This bumper would stop the car from falling off the table. She made a small opening at the bottom of the bumper for the string to slide through. I cut 3 ft of string. Lisa tied one end to the cars axel and the other end to the hook.

Reflect

Think about the draft. Is the report organized so that it's easy to read?

Apply

Write a draft using your Sequence Chain to help you. Be sure to include an introduction, observations, and a conclusion. Use headings to make your report easier to read.

Revise

Focus on **Voice**

The Rubric Says	First-person point of view is used consistently throughout to connect strongly to the audience.
Writing Strategy	Maintain consistency in style and tone.

I was really involved with the gravity experiment I did with Lisa, from setting it up to writing the observation log. In my report, I wanted to show how engaged I was with each step. So I used first person throughout the report. I see one step, however, where the point of view doesn't match up with the rest of the report. I'll revise that now to maintain first person throughout my writing.

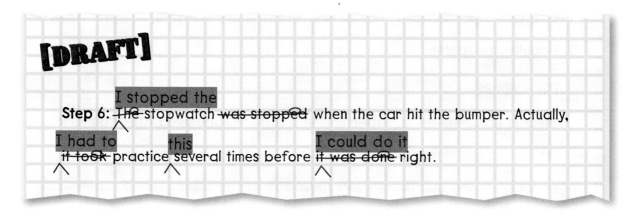

[DRAFT]

Step 6: ~~The~~ I stopped the stopwatch ~~was stopped~~ when the car hit the bumper. Actually, ~~it took~~ I had to practice several times before ~~it was done~~ I could do it this right.

Apply

Make sure you use first-person point of view to show your involvement with your subject.

Focus on Word Choice

The Rubric Says	Precise language, such as strong verbs, makes the process clear.
Writing Strategy	Choose words and phrases to convey ideas precisely.

I want my report to be clear and easy to follow so my reader will understand all the parts of my experiment. The rubric says using precise words—especially strong verbs—will help me make the process clear. I'll look for places where there are weak verbs that I can replace with stronger ones. Look at how I strengthened Step 2 by putting in a stronger, more descriptive verb.

[DRAFT]

Step 2: Lisa ~~put~~ slipped one weight on the hook.

Reflect

How does the stronger verb help you to better follow the process?

Apply

Look for weak verbs and replace them with strong ones to make the process clear.

Revise

Focus on Sentence Fluency

The Rubric Says   Sentence variety is striking. The writing is pleasurable to read.

Writing Strategy   Blend questions and exclamations into the report.

The rubric says I should use different types of sentences to make my writing a pleasure to read. As I read through my report, I noticed that I had used only statements. I also noticed a sentence that was too long and dull. Look at how I changed two sections of my report to make my writing flow better.

[DRAFT]

[added question]

[broke up long, boring sentence]

But how does gravity affect aceleration?

Gravity is one of Earths forces. It keeps everything from floating
about that question, using a   ⊙We wanted
off into space. Lisa and I did an experiment with a model car to see
how gravity affects aceleration—how fast the car starts to move.

[DRAFT]

Step 4: She put the car at the starting line and held it their. Thats when

we figured out that I would have to work the stopwatch since Lisa

Lisa already had her hands full!

was busy with the car.   [added exclamation]

Apply

Are your sentences all statements? Add some questions and exclamations to make your report more enjoyable.

Edit

The Rubric Says	Apostrophes are used correctly to form possessive nouns and contractions.
Writing Strategy	Be sure apostrophes are used correctly in possessive nouns and contractions.

Writer's Term

Apostrophes

Apostrophes are used in possessive nouns and contractions. A possessive noun shows ownership. A contraction is a word formed from two words, such as *I'm (I am)* and *didn't (did not)*.

My last step is to check for spelling, grammar, and punctuation errors. The rubric reminds me to make sure I used apostrophes correctly in possessive nouns and contractions.

[DRAFT]

[apostrophe to show possession]

[apostrophe in a contraction]

Its clear. The numbers say it all. Adding weights increased gravitys pull on the weights. The more weights we added, the faster the car

[no apostrophe for plural]

accelerated across the table. Our prediction was correct.

Reflect

Is the report more interesting with the added questions and exclamations? Do any more errors need to be corrected?

Apply Conventions

Edit your draft for spelling, punctuation, and capitalization. Be sure to fix any errors with apostrophes.

For more practice with apostrophes, use the exercises on the next two pages.

Apostrophes

Know the Rule

To form the **possessive** of a singular noun, add an apostrophe and *s*.
> **Example:** My brother**'s** hobby is racing slot cars.

To form the **possessive** of a plural noun that ends in *s*, just add an apostrophe.
> **Example:** He joined a slot car racer**s'** club.

To form the **possessive** of a plural noun that does not end in *s*, add an apostrophe and *s*.
> **Example:** The club has a large men**'s** group and a small women**'s** group.

To form a **contraction,** use an apostrophe to replace dropped letters.
> **Example: They're** crazy about this hobby.

Practice the Rule

Number a sheet of paper 1–10. Write the correct form of the words in parentheses on your paper.

1. One (dictionary's/dictionarys') definition says a slot car is "an electric toy racing car with a pin underneath that fits into a groove on a track."
2. The (car's/cars') bodies are made of plastic or metal.
3. A slot (car's/cars') power is transmitted through steel rails in the track.
4. My (dad's/dads') oldest track layout is from the 1960s.
5. (It's/Its') a two-lane plastic track that snaps together.
6. (American's/Americans') interest in slot cars grew in the 1960s.
7. Slot cars are (children's/childrens') toys, but adults like Dad enjoy them, too.
8. (I've/Iv'e) played with the slot cars a few times myself.
9. I (do'nt/don't) think I will ever enjoy them as much as Dad and my brother do.
10. (People's/Peoples') interest in slot cars has decreased in the last several decades.

Frequently Confused Words

Know the Rule

Some words are easily confused. Be sure you use these words correctly in your writing.

- **Your** is a possessive pronoun and shows ownership.
  Example: Our teacher said, "**Your** research report is due on Friday."
- **You're** is a contraction made from *you* and *are*.
  Example: You're supposed to be finished with the experiment by now.
- **Their** is a possessive pronoun and means "belonging to them."
  Example: The students keep **their** observation logs on the bookshelf.
- **There** is an adverb and usually means "in that place."
  Example: The moldy lemons are over **there** in the paper bag.
- **They're** is a contraction of *they are*.
  Example: They're ready to do the last step of the experiment.

Practice the Rule

Number a sheet of paper 1–10. Write the correct form of the words in parentheses on your paper.

1. You can feed (your/you're) backyard birds in the winter with sunflower seeds.
2. Some insects leave (their/there/they're) eggs to hibernate under leaves.
3. If you see hibernating spider eggs around your windows, leave them (their/there/they're).
4. When (your/you're) out in the snow, look for animal tracks of birds and deer.
5. Even if skunks and raccoons are hibernating, (their/there/they're) likely to wake up to eat in mild weather.
6. You might see squirrels around (your/you're) house all winter.
7. Many birds migrate to (their/there/they're) nesting grounds in warm climates.
8. Migrating birds may find a flight path because (their/there/they're) using the sun and moon, or possibly Earth's magnetic field.
9. Earthworms move deep into the soil in the winter because it isn't frozen (their/there/they're).
10. If (your/you're) looking at a hibernating animal, it might be in such a deep sleep that it looks dead!

Publish

Publishing Strategy   Display your report on Family Night.

Presentation Strategy   Include headings in dark print and visuals.

Our class decided to display our observation reports during Family Night. We wanted them to look nice for the occasion. Lisa and I used the computer to format headings so the reader will see how we organized our report. To make the steps visually clear and reinforce the information, we also added a diagram. Before Lisa and I turned in our report, we checked it using our final checklist.

My Final Checklist

Did I—

✔ check that apostrophes are used correctly for possessive nouns and contractions?

✔ use the right word—*your* or *you're*, and *there*, *their*, or *they're*?

✔ include headings in dark print and visuals to make the report easier to read and understand?

✔ check my spelling, grammar, and punctuation?

Apply

Check your observation report against your checklist. Then make a final copy to publish.

How Gravity Affects Acceleration

by Lisa and Denise

Gravity is one of Earth's forces. It keeps everything from floating off into space. But how does gravity affect acceleration? Lisa and I did an experiment about that question, using a model car. We wanted to see how gravity affects acceleration—how fast the car starts to move. We decided to attach a weight to one end of a string, tie the other end to the car, and drop the weight over the edge of a table. As gravity pulled the weight down, the weight would pull the car across the table. Lisa and I predicted that as we added more weights, the car would accelerate faster.

PROCEDURE

Step 1: To begin setting up the experiment, Lisa twisted a paper clip into a hook. Next, she used tape to mark a starting line on a table 2.5 feet from the edge of the table. Then she taped a bumper, a piece of heavy cardboard, to the edge of the table. This bumper would stop the car from falling off the table. She made a small opening at the bottom of the bumper for the string to slide through. Meanwhile, I cut 3 feet of string. Lisa tied one end to the car's axle and the other end to the hook. To finish setting up, she pushed the hook through the opening at the bottom of the bumper.

Step 2: Lisa slipped one weight on the hook.

Step 3: Then she held the weight over the edge of the table.

Step 4: She put the car at the starting line and held it there. That's when we figured out that I would have to work the stopwatch. Lisa already had her hands full!

Step 5: Lisa let the weight fall, and I started the stopwatch.

Step 6: I stopped the stopwatch when the car hit the bumper. Actually, I had to practice this several times before I could do it right. That car moved fast!

Step 7: Lisa and I timed the car with one weight on it two more times. Then I added the times and divided by 3 to get the average. I wrote that in our observation log.

Step 8: Then we repeated the whole process with 2, 3, 4, and 5 weights hanging on the hook. We did each number of weights 3 times and averaged the speed.

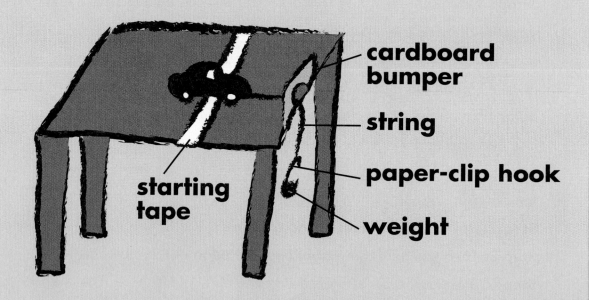

cardboard bumper

string

paper-clip hook

weight

starting tape

OBSERVATIONS

When I looked at our observation log, I didn't see a pattern at first, but Lisa pointed it out. As the number of weights increased, the time decreased.

Observation Log
Time in Seconds to Reach Table's Edge

Number of Weights	Run #1	Run #2	Run #3	Average
1	2.7	2.6	2.6	2.6
2	1.7	1.9	1.8	1.8
3	1.4	1.2	1.6	1.4
4	1.2	1.1	1.0	1.1
5	0.8	0.5	0.9	0.7

CONCLUSION

It's clear. The numbers say it all. Adding weights increased gravity's pull on the weights. The more weights we added, the faster the car accelerated across the table. Our prediction was correct.

Reflect

What do you think? Do all the traits of a good observation report appear in the writing? Check it against the rubric. Then check your own observation report with the rubric.

What's a Descriptive Article?

A descriptive article gives a clear, detailed picture of a person, a place, a thing, or an event. This sounds just like the definition of a descriptive essay, doesn't it? The difference is that a descriptive article is meant to inform the readers of a newspaper, magazine, brochure, or another publication. I think this kind of writing will make me feel like a professional writer!

What's in a Descriptive Article?

Vivid Imagery
I want my readers to see, smell, hear, touch, and taste whatever I'm describing. Using sensory details and clear descriptions will make my subject seem real to my audience!

Point of View
A descriptive article can be written in third person or first person. Either way, it must give a clear picture that shows the writer has actual experience with the subject.

Lively Language
Lively language helps breathe life into a subject. I'll use interesting sentence patterns to keep my audience reading. Instead of clichés, my article will have fresh and appealing phrases!

Audience Appeal
It's always good to think about your audience when you write, but it's especially important with a descriptive article. The article will be published for a specific audience, so it needs to be interesting and informative to those readers!

Why write a Descriptive Article?

I've been thinking about reasons to write a descriptive article. Here are some of my ideas. I'm still trying to decide about my own descriptive article.

Informing

A descriptive article can give readers a lot of information about its subject. Readers get plenty of details, and they can learn about something they haven't experienced personally.

Reflecting

Writing a descriptive article makes me stop and think. Taking time to reflect on the subject I'm describing can help me appreciate it and what it means to me.

Entertaining

A descriptive article is entertaining for me and for my readers! I think it's fun to describe something so clearly that other people can experience it. And my audience can escape awhile with some fun reading!

Sharing

It's a great feeling to share something in my life with other people. A descriptive article gives me a good way to do that.

Linking Descriptive Writing Traits to a Descriptive Article

In this chapter, you will write a detailed description of a person, a place, a thing, or an event. This type of descriptive writing is called a descriptive article. Denise will guide you through the stages of the writing process: Prewrite, Draft, Revise, Edit, and Publish. In each stage, Denise will show you important writing strategies that are linked to the Descriptive Writing Traits below.

Descriptive Writing Traits

- a clear topic that is supported and enhanced by specific sensory details

- well-organized paragraphs that follow the order of the description, whether by time, location, or another order

- a voice and tone that are appropriate for the purpose and audience

- precise, descriptive words, possibly with figurative language, that create an accurate picture for the reader

- sentences that vary in length and type to add flow to the writing

- no or few errors in grammar, usage, mechanics, and spelling

Before you write, read Adam Riley's descriptive article on the next page. Then use the descriptive article rubric on pages 420–421 to decide how well he did. (You might want to look back at What's in a Descriptive Article? on page 416, too!)

Neighborhood Notes

by Adam Riley

Lively language

Growling cars crawl down Main Street. Happy customers swarm the stores. Luscious aromas float out of restaurants. Our little town is bustling as usual. This is a wonderful place to live, but do you ever wish you could slip away to someplace quiet? **Audience appeal**

I do! Luckily, I found the perfect location for a little escape just steps away from Main Street. My family and I love it so much, you'll find us picnicking there almost every weekend.

First-person point of view

To get to our almost-secret spot, we walk behind the town hall and toward the dense patch of woods that borders the lawn. There's a secluded path back there that few people have discovered. As soon as we step onto the path, the sounds of town begin to fade. The leaves above us whisper hushed hellos, and unseen birds warble a friendly welcome. After a short walk, we hear a gurgling noise, like a cheerful baby is playing somewhere nearby. That's Buck Creek, of course! **Lively language**

Suddenly the flickering shadows of the woods give way to the bright sunshine of a large, grassy clearing. The path winds past an old fire pit and down a slope. We see sun sparks dancing on the flowing waters of the creek.

We plop down on the soft grass under the old tree—but only for a moment. In no time, we've stripped off our shoes and socks and raced down to the creek to wade in the cool water. **Vivid imagery**

After playing in the water awhile, we relax under the big oak. Even though we're actually still in town, the air smells fresher here. Sometimes the sharp scent of an evergreen blows our way on a gentle breeze.

There's nothing like the first bite of homemade fried chicken, crisp and warm and juicy! Add the creamy tang of coleslaw and the salty crunch of chips, and you're in picnic heaven! Cold, sweet iced tea washes it all down.

We pack up and head back home feeling like new people. We're relaxed. We're refreshed. We're ready to face our busy lives.

Won't you join us sometime, neighbor? **Audience appeal**

Rubric

Use this 6-point rubric to plan and score a descriptive article.

	6	5	4
Ideas	The writing engages the reader with a clear, focused topic. Relevant, sensory details create a vivid picture for the reader.	The topic is focused. Sensory details are mostly relevant and create strong images for the reader.	The topic is fairly focused. Some details are interesting, but some are irrelevant.
Organization	The structure of the writing enhances the reader's understanding. Each paragraph presents one main idea.	The organization fits the writing and the order makes sense. Most paragraphs are organized around one main idea.	The organization of the writing works most of the time. The focus of some paragraphs is unclear.
Voice	First-person point of view reveals the writer's personality and connects with the reader.	The writer uses first-person point of view and connects with the reader most of the time.	First-person point of view is used inconsistently at times. The writer tries to connect to the audience.
Word Choice	The writer's fresh and interesting phrases make the writing appealing and fun to read.	Some striking words and phrases engage and entertain the reader.	Some of the descriptions are ordinary but convey the writer's message.
Sentence Fluency	Repetitive sentence patterns are used to emphasize a point.	Sentence patterns are repeated for effect.	The writer tries to use repeated sentence patterns for effect but does not always succeed.
Conventions	Verb tenses are consistent throughout. The writing is easy to read and understand.	Verb tenses are consistent. The reader has to hunt to find a few errors.	Verb tenses switch back and forth sometimes, confusing the reader.

✚ Presentation   The page is designed for visual appeal.

3	2	1	
The topic is not clear. The details are general. There are few images for the reader.	The topic is not clear. Details are limited. The reader cannot form images from the details.	The writing lacks details. It reads like a list of thoughts.	**Ideas**
The organizational structure is hard to identify. Several paragraphs are unfocused.	The organization is very hard to follow; the reader feels lost. The paragraphs have no main idea.	The writing has no order. The article is not organized into paragraphs.	**Organization**
Point of view is inconsistent in places. The writer only sometimes connects to the audience.	The voice is weak and point of view is inconsistent throughout the article. The writer does not connect with the reader.	The writing has no voice. The writer is unaware of the reader.	**Voice**
Some of the words and phrases are vague or ordinary. They do not grab the reader.	Many vague and general words confuse the meaning. The writing may be dull to read.	Words are consistently vague and general. The reader has to work to get meaning.	**Word Choice**
Repeated sentence patterns are used, but they may not emphasize a point.	Repeated sentence patterns make the writing choppy and do not help the writer make a point.	There are many sentence problems (incomplete, run-ons), and there is too much repetition.	**Sentence Fluency**
Noticeable verb tense errors slow down the reader.	Many errors with verb tenses make reading this article difficult.	The writing is filled with serious verb-tense errors. It is difficult to read out loud.	**Conventions**

See Appendix B for 4-, 5-, and 6-point descriptive rubrics.

Descriptive Article

Using the ^Rubric to Study the Model

Did you notice that the model on page 419 points out some key elements of a descriptive article? As he wrote "Neighborhood Notes," Adam Riley used these elements to help him describe a special place. He also used the 6-point rubric on pages 420–421 to plan, draft, revise, and edit the writing. A rubric is a great tool for evaluating writing during the writing process.

Now let's use the same rubric to score the model. To do this, we'll focus on each trait separately, starting with Ideas. We'll use the top descriptor for each trait (column 6), along with examples from the model, to help us understand how the traits work together. How would you score Adam on each trait?

- **The writing engages the reader with a clear, focused topic.**
- **Relevant, sensory details create a vivid picture for the reader.**

This article has a focused topic—a secret spot in the neighborhood—and lots of sensory details that make the reader see a vivid picture. I can easily picture myself walking down the path with Adam!

[from the writing model]

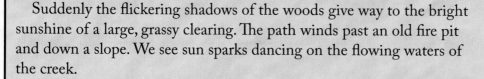

Suddenly the flickering shadows of the woods give way to the bright sunshine of a large, grassy clearing. The path winds past an old fire pit and down a slope. We see sun sparks dancing on the flowing waters of the creek.

**Organization**

- **The structure of the writing enchances the reader's understanding.**
- **Each paragraph presents one main idea.**

Adam has organized his article so that each paragraph focuses on one of the senses. This makes his reading easy to follow. I understand Adam's experience because he leads me through it one sense at a time.

[from the writing model]

After playing in the water awhile, we relax under the big oak. Even though we're actually still in town, the air smells fresher here. Sometimes the sharp scent of an evergreen blows our way on a gentle breeze.

Voice

- **First-person point of view reveals the writer's personality and connects with the reader.**

I can easily relate to Adam's descriptions. Using first-person point of view, he seems to be speaking directly to me. See where he uses the words *I* and *us* to draw the reader in.

[from the writing model]

I do! Luckily, I found the perfect location for a little escape just steps away from Main Street. My family and I love it so much, you'll find us picnicking there almost every weekend.

- **The writer's fresh and interesting phrases make the writing appealing and fun to read.**

Adam could have used worn-out phrases and old clichés in his descriptive article, but he keeps his writing fresh. For example, in the sentences below, he could have said that the leaves rustled, the birds sang, and the creek babbled. Instead, he used fresh ways to describe these things.

[from the writing model]

The leaves above us whisper hushed hellos, and unseen birds warble a friendly welcome. After a short walk, we hear a gurgling noise, like a cheerful baby is playing somewhere nearby.

- **Repetitive sentence patterns are used to emphasize a point.**

It's usually a good idea to vary sentence patterns to keep your writing interesting, but repetition has its place too. Adam sometimes repeats sentence patterns to make a point. For example, he starts his article with repetitive sentences that felt as busy as his little town.

[from the writing model]

Growling cars crawl down Main Street. Happy customers swarm the stores. Luscious aromas float out of restaurants.

Conventions

- Verb tenses are consistent throughout. The writing is easy to read and understand.

Adam does a great job being consistent in his use of verb tenses. All his descriptions are in the present tense, which helps me imagine I'm in his favorite spot right now. When it's appropriate, he does use the past and future tenses.

[from the writing model]

We pack up and head back home feeling like new people. We're relaxed. We're refreshed. We're ready to face our busy lives.

Won't you join us sometime, neighbor?

✛Presentation The page is designed for visual appeal.

My Turn!

I'm going to write a descriptive article about one of my favorite places. I'll follow the rubric and use good writing strategies. Read on to see how I do it!

Prewrite

Focus on **Ideas**

The Rubric Says   The writing engages the reader with a clear, focused topic. Relevant, sensory details create a vivid picture for the reader.

Writing Strategy   Jot down some notes that appeal to the senses.

When I got my assignment, I decided to write about one of my favorite places—my grandmother's kitchen. To get started, I jotted down the sights, sounds, feelings, smells, and tastes of Grandma's kitchen. Here are my notes.

My Notes on Grandma's Kitchen

Family uses back door, goes right into kitchen.
African violets in crusty pots on windowsill
Good smells on back porch, something baking, meat
Kitchen is tiny.
She always fixes me something to eat!
Stuff bubbling on stove
White cabinets, green walls like kiwi
We can sit and be quiet or sit and talk.
Mmmm . . . fresh cookies, melted chocolate chips
Volcano chili—hot as fire!
Grandma tells about old times in low husky voice.
House creaks.
Grandma—big smile, twinkling eyes, strong hands, busy
What she makes is always special.
Refrigerator hums.
Wash dishes in warm, soapy water.
Dry hands on crisp towel.
Can still feel hug after she lets go.

Apply

Choose your favorite spot, and jot down some notes about it. Remember to cover the five senses.

The Rubric Says	The structure of the writing enhances the reader's understanding.
Writing Strategy	Use a Five-Senses Chart to organize the notes.

Writer's Term

Five-Senses Chart
A **Five-Senses Chart** organizes descriptive words according to the five senses.

It looks like I have some good ideas for my article, but I have to get things organized. I can use a Five-Senses Chart to do that. I'll divide a sheet of paper into five parts, one for each sense. Then I'll rewrite my notes in the right spaces. This will help me organize my thoughts and keep me from forgetting anything important.

Five-Senses Chart

Smell: on back porch
something baking
meat
delicious!

Sight:
Kitchen—back door leads to kitchen
tiny, cheery, bright
kiwi-green walls
fresh white cabinets
square wooden table in corner
two purple chairs
deep purple African violets in
crusty pots on windowsill
Grandma—wide smile
twinkling eyes
strong, busy hands

Taste: fresh, homemade cookies, melted
chocolate chips
volcano chili—hot as fire
everything she makes is special

Sound: stuff bubbling on stove
house creaks
refrigerator hums
Grandma's low, husky voice
Grandma's sympathetic sounds

Touch: warm, soapy dishwater
dry hands on crisp, cotton towel
Grandma's arms, soft, warm, strong
can still feel hug when she lets go

Reflect

How does Denise's chart look? Are the notes well organized?

Apply

Organize your notes with a Five-Senses Chart.

Draft

Focus on **Voice**

The Rubric Says   First-person point of view reveals the writer's personality and connects with the reader.

Writing Strategy   Use first-person point of view.

✎ Writer's Term

Point of View

When you write using the pronouns **I, me, my, we,** or **us,** you are writing in the first person. A first-person narration allows the writer to make a personal connection with the reader. However, it limits the action to only what the narrator experiences.

Now I'll use my Five-Senses chart as I write my draft. The rubric says to use first-person point of view, which shows that it's me right there in my description. When I share my thoughts and feelings with my reader that way, my writing sounds personal, and the reader can connect to what I'm saying.

I'll do my best with spelling and grammar, but I know I can check things over later and correct any mistakes. I mostly want to concentrate on getting my description down on paper.

Proofreading Marks

⌐ Indent

≡ Make uppercase

/ Make lowercase

∧ Add something

ℓ Take out something

⊙ Add a period

¶ New paragraph

ⓢⓟ Spelling error

Cooking Up Love   [DRAFT]

Nobody in our family goes to my grandmother's front door. The shed is in the back. We all use the back door, the family entrance. It leads straight to her kitchen—and right into her heart!

It's good to visit often since we live on the same street. Every time you step onto Grandma's porch, something smells wonderful. Sometimes, something is baking. At other times, something chocolate promises a sweet surprise. If it's near suppertime, I'll smell meat or something else delicious!

[first-person point of view]

Grandma greets me with a wide smile and twinkling eyes. Usually her strong hands are chopping or stirring something, so I give her a sideways hug. The kitchen has fresh, white cabinets and green walls that make the place cheery and bright. As soon as I sit down, she fixes me something to eat!

Sometimes she gives me fresh, homemade cookies with melted chocolate chips. Or she might give me a bowl of her volcano chili. It's as hot as fire, but I love it. Whatever she makes is special.

Reflect

How does Denise make you "see" her grandmother's kitchen? How has her Five-Senses Chart guided her writing?

Apply

Write a draft using your Five-Senses Chart. Be sure to make your descriptions vivid!

Writing a Descriptive Article

Revise

Focus on  **Ideas**

The Rubric Says　Relevant, sensory details create a vivid picture for the reader.

Writing Strategy　Add sensory details.

After I wrote my draft, I looked at the rubric again. It says I should use sensory details throughout my article to create a vivid picture for the reader. I tried to do that, but there are places where I didn't appeal to the senses as much as I could. Look at how I improved the paragraph below by adding more sensory details. Can you imagine how the food smells?

[DRAFT]

It's good to visit often since we live on the same street. Every time you step onto Grandma's porch, something smells wonderful. Sometimes, ~~something is baking~~. At other times, ~~something~~ chocolate **mouth-watering** **roasting** promises a sweet surprise. If it's near suppertime, I'll smell meat **zesty spices, or** ~~or~~ something else delicious!

[added sensory details]

the home-baked scents of vanilla and cinnamon welcome me

Apply

Do you see some parts of your article that could use more sensory details? Add some, and make your subject come alive for your readers.

430　Descriptive Writing

The Rubric Says   The writer's fresh and interesting phrases make the writing appealing and fun to read.

Writing Strategy   Replace clichés with interesting phrases.

Writer's Term

Clichés

A **cliché** is a familiar word or phrase that has been used so much that its original meaning is lost. In addition, clichés, such as **a ton of homework,** are boring.

Now it's time to make sure my word choice is interesting. I looked at my draft again, and I thought that some sections sounded dull and stale. I need to get rid of any clichés and make sure that all my language is appealing and fresh! Look at how I livened up this paragraph.

[DRAFT]

[added fresh language]

Sometimes she gives me ~~fresh, homemade~~ oven-warm cookies with melted

chocolate chips. Or she might give me a bowl of her volcano chili.

~~It's as hot as fire,~~ It's so hot it makes me want to dunk my whole face in the creek but I love it! Whatever she makes is special.

[replaced cliché]

Reflect

Did the changes make the language fresher and more lively? Are there other clichés in the descriptive article that should be replaced?

Apply

Read through your draft and replace any tired, old language with fresh, interesting words and phrases. Replace any clichés with fresh phrases as well.

Revise

Focus on Sentence Fluency

The Rubric Says   Repetitive sentence patterns are used to emphasize a point.

Writing Strategy   Repeat a sentence pattern to emphasize a point.

The rubric says to repeat a sentence pattern to emphasize a point. At first, I didn't understand how to do that because I've always tried to use a variety of sentences for flow. Then I understood that a repetitive pattern could help strengthen a point in the paragraph below. Does the repetition make you feel that time is passing as Grandma and I sit there quietly?

[DRAFT]

While I eat, Grandma sits with me and drinks a cup of coffee.

Sometimes we're quiet. We listen to whatever's bubbling on the stove. ^We hear^ The refrigerator hums, ~~and the old house creaks~~ ^its one-note song.^ It's a nice, comfortable quiet.

[repeated sentence pattern] ——→ We notice the creaks the old house makes as it settles.

Apply

Use a repetitive sentence pattern to emphasize one of your points.

Edit

The Rubric Says   Verb tenses are consistent throughout. The writing is easy to read and understand.

Writing Strategy   Recognize and correct inappropriate shifts in verb tense.

Writer's Term___

Verb Tense
Verb tenses tell whether an action is taking place in the past, present, or future. Most past- and present-tense verbs are formed by adding *-s, -ed, -en,* or *-ing*. Most future-tense verbs are formed by placing the helping verb *will* in front of the verb.

The rubric says to use the proper tense for verbs. If I make the verb tenses consistent, my reader will be able to understand when things happen. Sometimes I have a hard time keeping present, past, and future tenses straight. You can see some of my edits below.

[DRAFT]

[correct present-tense verb]

Usually
~~Usualy,~~ we talk. Grandma's voice is low and husky and I ~~liked~~ like to

listen to her tell stories about how she lived back in the day. When I'm

sympathetic
talking, Grandma makes ~~simpathetic~~ noises. I feel like she understands

care
me, and she'll always ~~cared~~ about me.   [correct future-tense verb]

Reflect

How can repeating a sentence pattern strengthen a point? How do Denise's edits help the reader better understand her article?

Apply   Conventions

Edit your draft for spelling, grammar, and punctuation. Be sure to fix any errors in verb tense.

For more practice with verb tenses, use the exercises on the next two pages.

Present, Past, and Future Tenses

Know the Rule

A **present-tense verb** is used to indicate that something happens regularly or is true now.

> Example: Our family **holds** a reunion every summer.

A **past-tense verb** tells about something that has already happened. Regular verbs form the past tense by adding *-ed*.

> Example: Mom and I **created** a scrapbook to take to this year's reunion.

Irregular verbs change their spelling in the past tense.

> Example: The scrapbook **took** hours and hours of work.

A **future-tense verb** tells what is going to happen. Add the helping verb *will* to the present-tense form of a verb to form the future tense.

> Example: Everyone **will enjoy** looking at the family scrapbook.

Practice the Rule

Copy the sentences onto a sheet of paper. Underline each past-tense verb, circle each present-tense verb, and draw a box around each future-tense verb.

1. We started the scrapbook six months before the reunion.
2. Mom and I take our time with projects.
3. First we looked through all our boxes of old photos.
4. An old family photo really brings back memories!
5. Someone labeled most of the photos, but we will never know all the people in the really old pictures.
6. From now on, we will label all our photos for future generations.
7. That way everyone will know the names of family members who came before them.
8. I look forward to this family reunion!
9. We will all look at the photos together.
10. Maybe Grandpa will know the names of some of the people in the older pictures.

Present-Perfect and Past-Perfect Tenses

Know the Rule

The **perfect tenses** are made with the helping verb *has*, *have*, or *had* and the past participle of a verb.

- The **present-perfect tense** shows action that started in the past and was recently completed or is still happening.
  Example: I **have helped** my grandmother cook since I was little.

- The **past-perfect tense** shows action that was definitely completed in the past.
  Example: I **had learned** about spices from Grandma before I cooked my first meal by myself.

Practice the Rule

Read the following sentences. Complete each sentence by writing the present-perfect or the past-perfect form of the verb in parentheses.

1. Every summer my sister and I (help) my dad plant his vegetable garden.
2. Before we started last summer, I (read) a new book about gardening.
3. I (learn) to use organic methods to produce the best vegetables.
4. This summer I (choose) to plant broccoli and carrots.
5. My sister (want) to plant corn before my dad told her our garden isn't big enough.
6. My dad (enjoy) planting small gardens since he was my age.
7. His family (own) a farm for two generations before my grandfather sold it.
8. My dad says that if he (like) farming, we would be living on a farm now.
9. I'm glad my dad (teach) us to appreciate planting and tending a vegetable garden each summer.
10. I (eat) our own tasty vegetables since I was a baby!

Publish

✚ Presentation

Publishing Strategy Publish your article in a family scrapbook.

Presentation Strategy Use the computer to prepare a neat and attractive article.

My descriptive article is finished, and I can't wait for my family to read it! I'm going to make a good copy and put it in our big family scrapbook. I'll type the article on the computer to make it neat and easy to read. To attract my reader's attention, I'll start with a decorative and readable font for the title. Afterwards, I'll check my article once more, using this checklist.

My Final Checklist

Did I—

✔ make sure all the verb tenses are consistent?

✔ use present perfect and past perfect tenses correctly?

✔ make sure the article is designed for visual appeal?

✔ check my spelling, punctuation, and grammar?

Apply

Make a checklist for a final check of your descriptive article. Then make a final copy to publish.

Cooking Up Love

by Denise

Nobody in our family goes to my grandmother's front door. That's for company! We all use the back door, the family entrance. It leads straight to her kitchen—and right into her heart!

I visit often since we live on the same street. Every time I step onto Grandma's back porch, I smell something wonderful. Sometimes, the home-baked scents of vanilla and cinnamon welcome me. At other times, mouth-watering chocolate promises a sweet surprise. If it's near suppertime, I'll smell roasting meat, zesty spices, or something else delicious!

Grandma greets me with a wide smile and twinkling eyes. Usually her strong hands are chopping or stirring something, so I give her a sideways hug. The kitchen has fresh, white cabinets and green walls that make the place cheery and bright. As soon as I sit down, she fixes me something to eat!

Sometimes she gives me oven-warm cookies with melted chocolate chips. Or she might give me a bowl of her volcano chili. It's so hot it makes me want to dunk my whole face in the creek, but I love it! Whatever she makes is special.

While I eat, Grandma sits with me and drinks a cup of coffee. Sometimes we're quiet. We listen to whatever's bubbling on the stove. We hear the refrigerator hum its one-note song. We notice the creaks the old house makes as it settles. It's a nice, comfortable quiet.

Usually, we talk. Grandma's voice is low and husky, and I like to listen to her tell stories about how she lived back in the day. When I'm talking, Grandma makes sympathetic noises. I feel like she understands me, and she'll always care about me.

When it's time to go, I wash my dishes in warm, soapy water and dry my hands on a crisp, cotton towel. Then Grandma wraps me tightly in her arms, soft and warm and strong. After she lets go, it feels like she's still holding me. I hurry home, full of good food and Grandma's love!

Reflect

Do you see all the traits of a good descriptive article in Denise's writing? Check it against the rubric. Don't forget to use the rubric to check your own descriptive article.

What's a Poem?

A poem is a piece of writing that expresses thoughts, feelings, and ideas. It's a creative way to describe any topic or emotion.

What's in a Poem?

Haiku
A haiku is a form of Japanese poetry that is often about nature. It contains three unrhymed lines with five, seven, and five syllables, respectively.

Line
The words of a poem are grouped in lines. A word, phrase, or complete sentence can form one line in a poem. Lines have a rhythmic flow to them, sometimes rhyming and sometimes not. The lines of a poem are grouped in stanzas.

Figurative Language
Figurative language, or figures of speech, help paint a picture in the reader's mind. Poets use figurative language—such as metaphor, simile, personification, and alliteration—to make their topic come alive for readers.

Why write a Poem?

There are many reasons to write a poem. I can think of three good ones. What other ideas can you think of?

Description
I can write a poem to describe any subject I choose. A creative description allows readers to see a topic more clearly or in a different light. In a poem, I can describe and share my feelings.

Personal Reflection
Writing a poem is a great way to reflect on what something means to me personally. How I feel about something, how I'm affected, or what I'm thinking can all be expressed in a poem.

Understanding
A poem can help readers gain a new understanding of the subject I'm describing. Not only can a poem help my readers gain new insights, but the process of writing poetry also helps me appreciate and understand the work of a poet.

Linking Descriptive Writing Traits to a Poem

In this chapter, you will write a three-line poem about something in nature or another topic of your choosing. This type of descriptive writing is a form of poem called a haiku. Denise will guide you through the stages of the writing process: Prewrite, Draft, Revise, Edit, and Publish. In each stage, Denise will show you important writing strategies that are linked to the Descriptive Writing Traits below.

Descriptive Writing Traits

Ideas
- a clear topic that is supported and enhanced by specific sensory details

Organization
- well-organized paragraphs that follow the order of the description, whether by time, location, or another order

Voice
- a voice and tone that are appropriate for the purpose and audience

Word Choice
- precise, descriptive words, possibly with figurative language, that create an accurate picture for the reader

Sentence Fluency
- sentences that vary in length and type to add flow to the writing

Conventions
- no or few errors in grammar, usage, mechanics, and spelling

Before you write, read Taylor Spinelli's poems (three haiku) on the next page. Then use the poem rubric on pages 442–443 to decide how well he did. (You might want to look back at What's in a Poem? on page 438, too!)

Haiku

By Taylor Spinelli

Sea Song

Crashing waves retreat

Salty mist upon my cheek

Bright ball ever burns

figurative language

haiku poem

Wonderland

Fluffiest white flakes

Powdering icy landscapes

Wildlife tracks revealed

figurative language

Marking Time

Tick, tock three o'clock

Mid-afternoon right angle

Turns obtuse at four

figurative language

lines

Rubric

Use this 6-point rubric to plan and score a poem.

	6	5	4
Ideas	The topic is presented in an original, creative way. Descriptive details are vivid.	The topic is presented in an original, creative way. Details are descriptive.	The topic is presented in a creative way. A couple of details are descriptive.
Organization	Lines and stanzas, if used, organize the ideas.	Lines and stanzas, if used, organize most of the ideas.	Lines and stanzas, if used, organize many of the ideas.
Voice	The poet's voice sets the tone and mood of the piece. It connects with the audience.	The poet's voice sets the tone and mood of the piece. It connects with the audience most of the time.	The poet's voice sets the tone and mood at first but then fades. The connection is inconsistent.
Word Choice	Precise vocabulary and figurative language are used purposefully and effectively.	Most words are used purposefully. One example of figurative language could be more effective.	Most of the words are used purposefully. Several examples of figurative language could be more effective.
Sentence Fluency	The lines and stanzas, if used, convey ideas at a good pace. The line breaks establish the rhythm and flow.	Most of the lines and stanzas, if used, flow well. One or two line breaks interrupt the rhythm.	Some of the lines and stanzas, if used, flow well. Several line breaks interrupt the rhythm.
Conventions	The writing has been carefully edited. Comparative and superlative forms of modifiers are used correctly.	Minor errors are present but do not interfere with meaning. Modifiers are used correctly.	A few errors cause confusion. One or two modifiers may be misspelled. (Ex. "joyful or joyfully")
✛ Presentation	Visuals and audio are integrated effectively.		

3	2	1	
The topic is presented. Most details are ordinary or dull.	The topic is incomplete. Details are vague or weak.	The topic is not clear. Details may be unrelated or inaccurate.	**Ideas**
Lines and stanzas, if used, organize some of the ideas.	Lines and stanzas do not organize the ideas well.	Ideas are listed but not organized as verse.	**Organization**
The poet's voice sets a tone that may not be appropriate. A connection is not maintained.	The voice is very weak. The connection is very weak.	The voice is absent. A connection is not established.	**Voice**
Some of the words are used purposefully. Figurative language may be unclear.	Many words are ordinary or overused. Figurative language is unclear or absent.	Words are very basic and limited. Several words may be used incorrectly.	**Word Choice**
Lines do not flow well. Line breaks impede the pace and rhythm.	Lines do not flow well. Line breaks do not establish a rhythm.	Poetic lines are not established.	**Sentence Fluency**
Many errors are repeated and cause confusion. Modifiers may be used incorrectly. (Ex. "more joyfuller")	Serious errors interfere with meaning. Modifiers may be used incorrectly.	The writing has not been edited.	**Conventions**

See Appendix B for 4-, 5-, and 6-point descriptive rubrics.

Using the Poem Rubric to Study the Model

Did you notice that the model on page 441 points out some key elements of a haiku poem? As he wrote "Sea Song," "Wonderland," and "Marking Time," Taylor Spinelli used these elements to help him describe the sea, snow, and angles. He also used the 6-point rubric on pages 442–443 to plan, draft, revise, and edit the writing. A rubric is a great tool to evaluate writing during the writing process.

Now let's use the same rubric to score the model. To do this, we'll focus on each trait separately, starting with Ideas. We'll use the top descriptor for each trait (column 6), along with examples from the model, to help us understand how the traits work together. How would you score Taylor on each trait?

- **The topic is presented in an original, creative way.**
- **Descriptive details are vivid.**

In "Marking Time," Taylor chose to discuss types of angles in a creative way. I never thought about a clock having so many angles! The details are vivid because I can hear the sound of the clock ticking, and I can picture the arms turning. Can you picture it?

[from the writing model]

Tick, tock three o'clock
Mid-afternoon right angle
Turns obtuse at four

Organization

- Lines and stanzas, if used, organize the ideas.

The three lines of "Marking Time" follow the 5-7-5 syllable format of a haiku, and each line addresses an aspect of angles. The ideas are organized clearly so that in the second line, I can picture the right angle, and in the next, the wider obtuse angle.

[from the writing model]

Tick, tock three o'clock
Mid-afternoon right angle
Turns obtuse at four

Voice

- **The poet's voice sets the tone and mood of the piece.**
- **It connects with the audience.**

In "Wonderland," Taylor has carefully chosen certain words to create a carefree tone. *Wonderland* is a light and carefree word. It makes me think of *winter* wonderland, and that reminds me of my home here in Minnesota, where I've seen a lot of beautiful, snow-covered landscapes. By using other light and carefree words such as *fluffiest* and *powdering*, Taylor creates a captivating mood.

[from the writing model]

Fluffiest white flakes
Powdering icy landscapes
Wildlife tracks revealed

Word Choice

- Precise vocabulary and figurative language are used purposefully and effectively.

I like how Taylor chooses words that paint a picture in my mind. In "Sea Song," the use of *crashing* shows the fierce action of the waves. Taylor could have said *moving waves*, but *crashing waves* shows a sharper contrast between how the waves come in and how they go out, or *retreat*, a softer action. The alliteration in line three—the repetition of the *b* sound in *Bright ball ever burns*—is a good example of figurative language. The repeated sound puts emphasis on the image of the sun (the "bright ball"), making the description stand out and come alive for the reader. Not only that, but line three uses a metaphor, as it compares the sun to a bright ball burning. That's a lot of rich language in one short poem!

[from the writing model]

Crashing waves retreat
Salty mist upon my cheek
Bright ball ever burns

Sentence Fluency

- The lines and stanzas, if used, convey ideas at a good pace.
- The line breaks establish the rhythm and flow.

I like how Taylor introduces ideas one at a time in "Sea Song." First we hear the rhythm of the waves, next we taste and feel the salty sensation, and last we see the burning sun. Each image flows nicely into the next. Taylor has also followed the appropriate syllable counts for each line. Five for the first, seven for the second, and five for the third. This creates the classic flow of a haiku.

[from the writing model]

Crashing waves retreat
Salty mist upon my cheek
Bright ball ever burns

Conventions

- **The writing has been carefully edited.**
- **Comparative and superlative forms of modifiers are used correctly.**

I didn't come across any mistakes, so I know Taylor did a careful job when he edited. Also the superlative adjective *fluffiest* is used correctly. It appropriately compares many snowflakes. If Taylor were comparing just two snowflakes, he would have used the word *fluffier*.

[from the writing model]

Fluffiest white flakes
Powdering icy landscapes
Wildlife tracks revealed

✛Presentation Visuals and audio are integrated effectively.

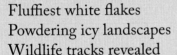

Now it's my turn to write a poem. I'll use the rubric and good writing strategies to help me. Follow along to see how I do it.

Prewrite

Focus on Ideas

The Rubric Says The topic is presented in an original, creative way. Descriptive details are vivid.

Writing Strategy Choose a topic. Make a list of descriptive details.

My assignment is to write a haiku. My teacher said we could write more than one. Since a traditional Japanese haiku is about something in nature, I'll jot down ideas and descriptions about some of my favorite outdoor spots. I'll write down ideas about other subjects that appeal to me, too. I'll also need to keep in mind that my final haiku will consist of three unrhymed lines. The first line will have five syllables, the next seven, and the last five.

Notes on topics for haiku

Notes about visiting my favorite pond

Water is still, calm, serene.
Water is high after a heavy rain and there's hardly any beach.
Surface of the water has a glare from the sun.

Notes about my garden

Tomatoes, peppers, cucumbers
Green and leafy, grow and grow
Need plenty of water and sunlight
Flowers form, fruits grow

Notes about my neighbor's baby

Always looking around with wide eyes
Loves to be cuddled
Learns to clap hands
Mother takes good care of him

Apply

Choose something in nature or another topic that interests you. Write down some notes about it.

Focus on Organization

The Rubric Says   Lines and stanzas, if used, organize the ideas.

Writing Strategy   Use a Web to plan the poem.

Writer's Term
Web
A **Web** is a way to organize ideas around a topic. The topic is in the center. Attached to each topic are related categories. Attached to each category are related details.

To organize my ideas I'll use a graphic organizer called a Web. I have a few ideas that I'd like to use as the topics for the haiku I'm going to write. A haiku does not have stanzas. However, the Web will help me organize my notes so I can figure out the ideas I want to include in each line.

Web

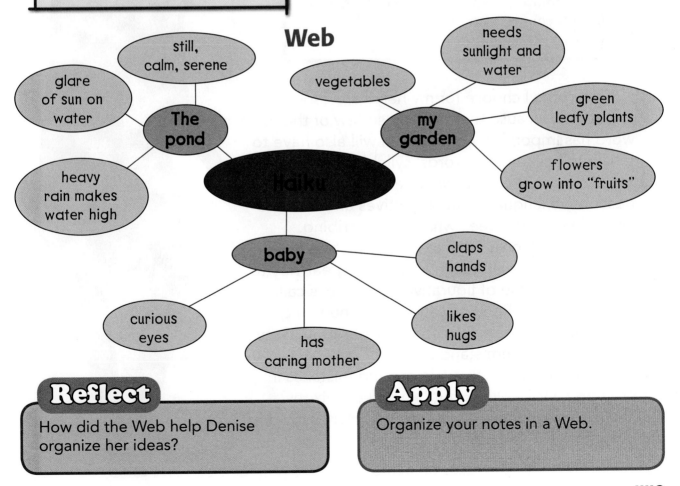

Reflect
How did the Web help Denise organize her ideas?

Apply
Organize your notes in a Web.

Draft

Focus on Word Choice

The Rubric Says	Precise vocabulary and figurative language are used purposefully and effectively.
Writing Strategy	Choose words and phrases for effect.

> **Writer's Term**
>
> **Personification and Alliteration**
> **Personification** makes writing come alive by giving human qualities to things or animals. **Alliteration** is repeating a consonant sound within a sentence or phrase. It can give a poem rhythm and emphasize an idea by drawing the reader's attention.

The words I choose for my haiku are especially important because there will be so few of them. Each word has important work to do! I will also have to take into account the words' syllables because the 5-7-5 count is essential to a haiku. Using descriptive language and adjectives and adverbs will help readers "see" what I'm describing.

I want the words I use to paint a picture in your mind. Figurative language is another great way to do this. One type of figurative language is called personification. Personification gives human qualities to things or animals. I'll also use alliteration in my poem titles to make them stand out.

As I write, I'll try to avoid making mistakes in grammar and spelling, but I know I can fix my mistakes later when I edit my work. Here's my draft.

[DRAFT]

Baby Boy

Boy claping his hands

Gazes up for approval

Wins Mama's tight squeeze

[alliteration]

Peaceful Place

The pond's high water

Sweeter than the fierce ocean

The Pond is calmer

[personification]

Harvest Home

Leaves take in the rays

Water quenches innate thirst

Pretty fruits emerge

Reflect

What words help you "see" what Denise describes? How does the figurative language make the poem come alive?

Apply

Use your Web to draft your own haiku. Choose your words carefully, because every word counts!

Revise

Focus on **Ideas**

The Rubric Says   Descriptive details are vivid.

Writing Strategy   Choose details that bring the topic to life.

I used my notes to write my draft, and now it's time to revise. The rubric says descriptive details are vivid. I had that in mind while I was drafting, but I found some places where I could make improvements. In my revision, do you see how *rosy fruits* is more vivid than *pretty fruits*? Using the adjective *rosy* helps paint a picture because you can "see" that color. I also changed *take* to *soak* because *soak* is a stronger, more vivid word than *take*. I can see and feel the hot sun *soaking* into the leaves! Can you?

[DRAFT]

[replaced weaker verb]

soak
Leaves ~~take~~ in the rays

Water quenches innate thirst

Rosy
~~Pretty~~ fruits emerge

[replaced dull description]

Apply

Look through your draft in search of descriptions needing improvement. Can you make details any stronger to make your poem more vivid?

| The Rubric Says | Lines and stanzas, if used, organize the ideas. |
| Writing Strategy | Make sure each line or stanza conveys one clear idea. |

As I revise, I need to look again at how I have organized my ideas. The way a poem is organized affects how the reader experiences the poem. I want my reader to "see" a short series of crystal-clear images in each haiku. That means each line should focus on one precisely described idea.

As I look at my writing, I notice that the second two lines of "Peaceful Place" blend images of the Pond and the ocean. I think my poem will convey my thoughts more clearly to the reader if I use a separate line to describe each body of water.

[DRAFT]

The pond's high water
Glistens most calmly and sweetly
~~Sweeter than the fierce ocean~~
Than the fierce, rushing ocean
~~The Pond is calmer~~

Reflect

How did Denise's revision help the organization and flow of ideas in the poem?

Apply

Check the lines of your poem to see that ideas are grouped logically.

Revise

Focus on Sentence Fluency

The Rubric Says	The lines and stanzas, if used, convey ideas at a good pace. The line breaks establish the rhythm and flow.
Writing Strategy	Place line breaks where they make sense.

As you can see, the flow of ideas in the lines of a poem is important. Equally important is the flow of the lines themselves. The lines are what give poetry its rhythm, and the syllable counts in each line of a haiku give it the form and feel of a haiku. The lines also determine which words will be read together or apart. A good trick I use to make sure the lines of my haiku sound okay and have the correct number of syllables is to read the lines aloud, counting out the syllables for 5-7-5.

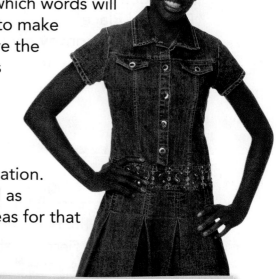

As I did this for my haiku, I noticed that a line that is supposed to have seven syllables has eight. See it in line two? I didn't catch it when I was revising that same line for organization. I thought up another word with the same feel as *glistens*, since *glistens* fits with the flow of ideas for that line. Have a look at what I did.

[DRAFT]   [adjusted syllable count]

Gleams
~~Glistens~~ most calmly and sweetly

Apply

Read your lines aloud to hear how they sound to you. Pay attention to rhythm and flow.

Focus on Conventions

The Rubric Says	The writing has been carefully edited. Comparative and superlative forms of modifiers are used correctly.
Writing Strategy	Check the use and form of comparative and superlative adjectives and adverbs.

Writer's Term

Comparative and Superlative Forms

The **comparative form** of an adjective or adverb compares two items. The **superlative form** is used to compare three or more items. For example, "This book is funnier than that book." (comparative) "This book is the funniest of all." (superlative)

Now I need to double-check my spelling, grammar, and punctuation. The rubric also says to use comparative and superlative forms correctly. I may have to use a dictionary for the tricky ones! Here are some corrections I made. I need to use the comparative form instead of the superlative since I'm comparing two things, the pond and the ocean.

[DRAFT]

more ←———————— [used correct comparative form]

Gleams ~~most~~ calmly and sweetly

Than the fierce, rushing ocean

Reflect

How do the edits Denise made affect her poem?

Apply   Conventions

Edit your draft for spelling, punctuation, and comparative and superlative forms.

For more practice with comparative and superlative forms of adjectives and adverbs, use the exercises on the next two pages.

Comparative and Superlative Adjectives

Know the Rule

The **comparative form** of an adjective compares two people, places, or things. Add -er to short adjectives to create the comparative form. Use the word *more* before long adjectives to create the comparative form.

The **superlative form** compares three or more people, places, or things. Add -est to create the superlative form. Use the word *most* before long adjectives to create the superlative form.

Practice the Rule

Number a sheet of paper 1–10. Write the correct form of the adjective in parentheses.

1. The second poem was (funny) than the first poem.
2. The first poem was (serious) than the second poem.
3. Of the three poems that Taylor wrote, I think "Sea Song" is the (descriptive).
4. Reading funny poems is (enjoyable) than reading serious ones.
5. Sometimes I have a (hard) time than my friends when I am thinking up vivid descriptions.
6. Choosing the right words to describe your ideas can be the (hard) work of all!
7. A poem may not use as many words as a story, so that means the poem's words are (important).
8. To create the (thoughtful) haiku, choose your words carefully and don't forget to count those syllables.
9. His poem was the (fine) one in the whole book.
10. His poem was also the (long) one in the whole book!

Comparative and Superlative Adverbs

Know the Rule

The **comparative form** of an adverb compares two actions. Add -er to short adverbs to create the comparative form. Use the word *more* before long adverbs to create the comparative form.

The **superlative form** compares three or more actions. Add -est to create the superlative form. Use the word *most* before long adverbs to create the superlative form. Most of the time, you will use *more* or *most*.

Practice the Rule

Number a sheet of paper 1–10. Write the correct form of the adverb in parentheses.

1. The first poem read (smoothly) than the second poem.
2. The second poem read (awkwardly) than the first poem.
3. Out of the whole class, Jake read his haiku the (seriously).
4. Emma revised her poem (fast) than I did because I needed more time to choose a better word for my description.
5. Out of the whole class, I worked the (slow).
6. My hard work paid off, though. My haiku described mountains (beautifully) than the teacher's poem!
7. I may have worked (slowly) than others, but it was worth it.
8. You might say I worked on my haiku the (hard)!
9. Jake read his poem aloud (clearly) than Emma did.
10. Kavitha was the last one to read aloud, so she had to wait the (long).

Publish

✚ Presentation

Publishing Strategy Present your poem in a multimedia presentation.

Presentation Strategy Choose video and audio that enhances the poem.

Our assignment is to showcase our poetry in a multimedia presentation. I'll need to choose images and sounds that work well together to enhance and support the ideas in my poems. I'm going to tape record my neighbor's baby playing and giggling to go along with the haiku about him clapping his hands. I'll play that for the class while I read the haiku. I will also use a computer to project the lines of my haiku on the board for the class to see, and I'll include a photograph of the baby, too. These sights and sounds will enhance my poem by making my readers feel like they are right there playing with the baby. I'll also choose appropriate images and sounds for my other two poems. But first, I'll use my final checklist to check over my poems.

My Final Checklist

Did I—

✔ check my spelling, grammar, and punctuation?

✔ make sure I used comparative and superlative forms of adjectives and adverbs correctly?

✔ choose visuals and sounds that will enhance the audience's experience of my poem?

Apply

Make a final checklist and use it to create the final copy of your poetry.

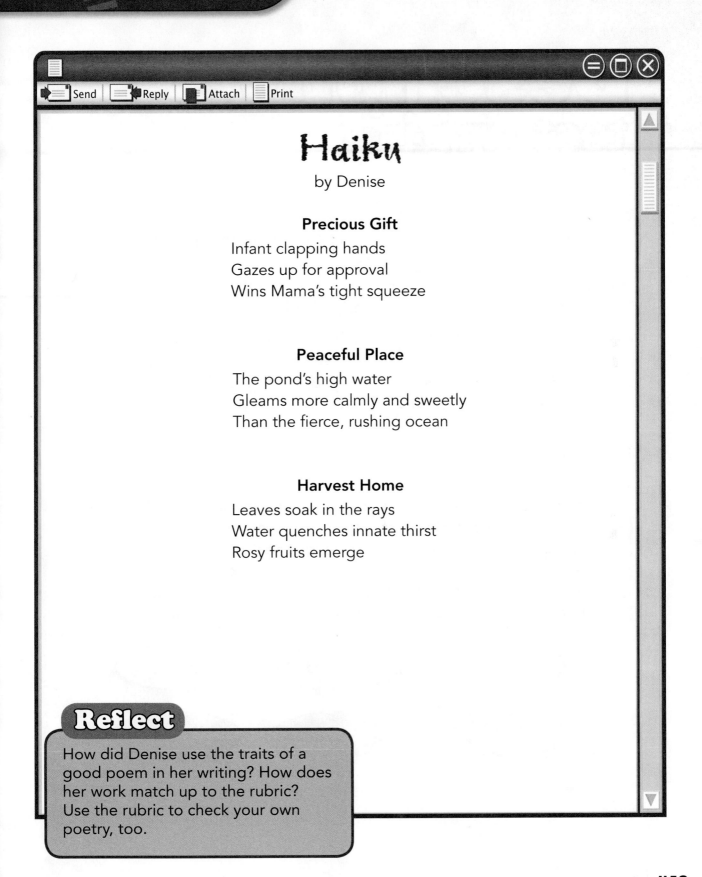

Haiku

by Denise

Precious Gift

Infant clapping hands
Gazes up for approval
Wins Mama's tight squeeze

Peaceful Place

The pond's high water
Gleams more calmly and sweetly
Than the fierce, rushing ocean

Harvest Home

Leaves soak in the rays
Water quenches innate thirst
Rosy fruits emerge

Reflect

How did Denise use the traits of a good poem in her writing? How does her work match up to the rubric? Use the rubric to check your own poetry, too.

Descriptive test writing

Read the Writing Prompt

When you take a writing test, you'll be given a writing prompt. Most writing prompts have three parts:

Setup This part of the writing prompt gives you the background information you need to get ready to write.

Task This part of the writing prompt tells you exactly what you are supposed to write: a descriptive essay.

Scoring Guide This section tells how your writing will be scored. To do well on the test, you should make sure your writing does everything on the list.

Remember the rubrics you used earlier in the unit? When you take a writing test, you don't always have all of the information that's on a rubric. However, the scoring guide is a lot like a rubric. It lists everything you need to think about to write a good paper. Like the rubrics you've used in this unit, many scoring guides are based upon the six important traits of writing:

 Ideas

 Organization

 Voice

 Word Choice

 Sentence Fluency

Conventions

Think about a place that's very special to you. Maybe it's your room or a favorite park you like to visit.

Write an essay describing this place in detail.

Be sure your writing

- includes relevant, sensory details that create a vivid picture for the reader.

- is organized so that all the related information is together.

- has a voice that matches the audience and purpose.

- creates a picture with descriptive words and figurative language.

- contains sentences that flow smoothly.

- contains correct grammar, punctuation, capitalization, and spelling.

Writing Traits
in the Scoring Guide

The scoring guide in the prompt on page 461 has been made into this chart. Does it remind you of the rubrics you've used? Not all prompts include all of the writing traits, but this one does. Use them to do your best writing. Remember to work neatly and put your name on each page.

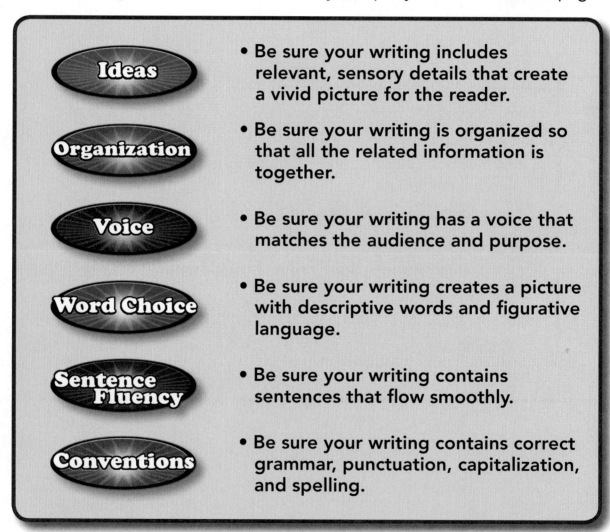

Ideas
- Be sure your writing includes relevant, sensory details that create a vivid picture for the reader.

Organization
- Be sure your writing is organized so that all the related information is together.

Voice
- Be sure your writing has a voice that matches the audience and purpose.

Word Choice
- Be sure your writing creates a picture with descriptive words and figurative language.

Sentence Fluency
- Be sure your writing contains sentences that flow smoothly.

Conventions
- Be sure your writing contains correct grammar, punctuation, capitalization, and spelling.

Look at Daniel Maloney's essay on the next page. Did he follow the scoring guide?

Sitting on the Dock

by Daniel Maloney

I really didn't want to spend my summer vacation with my family at Bass Lake—I wanted to stay home with my friends. But by the end of our vacation, my parents practically had to drag me away from what had quickly become my favorite place. You see, Bass Lake, with its calm, crystal-blue morning water and its choppy, loud, and fun-filled afternoons, is a truly magnificent place.

On our last day there, I got up early and walked the few steps from our rented log cabin to the dock on the lake for a final goodbye. At this hour, the lake was still. The water, a deep navy blue, had a glassy sheen to it that I hated to disturb. As I walked to the end of the dock, the wood planks creaked and gave slightly, causing small ripples in the water below.

Two small boats were tied to the dock—an old, messy rowboat and a speed boat ready to take its passengers for water-skiing adventures after dawn turned to day. On either side, not far from my dock, were other similar docks, quietly waiting for the day to begin. Homes old and new, large and small, lined the shore and rose up into the hills above it. In the distance, I heard a dog bark and thought it must be eager for its morning swim. Across the vast lake there were no homes, just pine trees bunched together thickly, leaving a dark impression of their outline in the water.

I took a deep breath, inhaling the strong scent of pine and the slightly fishy smell of the water. I also smelled the faint odor of fuel from the boat. Though the sun was quickly rising, the air was still crisp, and my toes caught a chill when I took off my shoes. I wanted to get one last feel of the lake's cool, clean water, a final reminder of my visit. I could see rocks below the surface of the lake as I carefully stuck my toe into its chilly bath. The rocks became blurry and faded from my view with the movement of the water, and I got up to leave for the last time.

Using the Scoring Guide to Study the Model

Now let's use the scoring guide to check Daniel's writing test, "Sitting on the Dock." Let's see how well his essay meets each of the six writing traits.

Ideas

- The writing includes relevant, sensory details that create a vivid picture for the reader.

Daniel does a good job providing details that are both relevant and sensory. For instance, he talks about how still the lake was. He even describes what it smelled like outside.

> At this hour, the lake was still. The water, a deep navy blue, had a glassy sheen to it that I hated to disturb.

> I took a deep breath, inhaling the strong scent of pine and the slightly fishy smell of the water. I also smelled the faint odor of fuel from the boat.

Organization

- The writing is organized so that all the related information is together.

Daniel takes care to describe stepping in the water in great detail. He puts information about the crisp air, cool water, and rocks under the surface—all related details—together in the same paragraph.

> Though the sun was quickly rising, the air was still crisp, and my toes caught a chill when I took off my shoes. I wanted to get one last feel of the lake's cool, clean water, a final reminder of my visit. I could see rocks below the surface of the lake as I carefully stuck my toe in to its chilly bath.

Voice

- **The writing has a voice that matches the audience and purpose.**

Daniel uses first-person point of view because his purpose is to share a personal experience. He connects with his audience right from the start by explaining why he loves Bass Lake.

But by the end of our vacation, my parents practically had to drag me away from what had quickly become my favorite place. You see, Bass Lake, with its calm, crystal-blue morning water and its choppy, loud, and fun-filled afternoons, is a truly magnificent place.

Word Choice

- **The writing creates a picture with descriptive words and figurative language.**

Daniel makes his writing more interesting by using colorful, descriptive words. I know, for instance, that docks can't wait for the day to begin, but it helps to give the reader a clearer picture when Daniel uses figurative language like this.

On either side, not far from my dock, were other similar docks, quietly waiting for the day to begin. Homes old and new, large and small, lined the shore and rose up into the hills above it. In the distance, I heard a dog bark and thought it must be eager for its morning swim. Across the vast lake there were no homes, just pine trees bunched together thickly, leaving a dark impression of their outline in the water.

Using the Scoring Guide to Study the Model

Sentence Fluency

- The writing contains sentences that flow smoothly.

Daniel's sentences flow smoothly because he's careful to vary their lengths and structures. I never got lost trying to follow a series of too-long sentences or confused by too many short, choppy sentences together. Look how well these sentences flow.

> On our last day there, I got up early and walked the few steps from our rented log cabin to the dock on the lake for a final goodbye. At this hour, the lake was still. The water, a deep navy blue, had a glassy sheen to it that I hated to disturb.

Conventions

- The writing contains correct grammar, punctuation, capitalization, and spelling.

I didn't notice any mistakes in Daniel's writing. When you take a test, it's important to check for mistakes in your work, including errors in grammar, punctuation, capitalization, and spelling. Be sure to go through and edit your work before you turn it in!

Planning My Time

Before giving us a writing test prompt, my teacher tells us how much time we'll have to complete the test. Since I'm already familiar with the writing process, I can think about how much total time I have and then divide it up into the different parts of the writing process. If the test takes an hour, here's how I can organize my time. Planning your time will help you, too!

Step 4:
Edit
5 minutes

Step 1:
Prewrite
25 minutes

Step 3:
Revise
15 minutes

Step 2:
Draft
15 minutes

Prewrite

Focus on **Ideas**

Writing Strategy   Study the writing prompt to find out what to do.

When I am handed a test, the first thing I do is study the writing prompt so I will know what to do. The writing prompt usually has three parts. The parts probably won't be labeled, so you'll have to identify them on your own, like I did with my writing prompt. Locate and label the setup, task, and scoring guide on your writing prompt. Circle key words in the setup and the tasks that tell what kind of writing you need to do and who your audience will be. Here, I circled the setup in blue and the task in orange. I'm going to write my test for my teacher, since the writing prompt doesn't identify who the reader is.

My Writing Test Prompt

Setup — Think about an (event that you attended or witnessed) that really stands out in your mind.

Task — Write an (essay describing the event in detail.)

Scoring Guide — Be sure your writing

- includes relevant, sensory details that create a vivid picture for the reader.
- is organized so that all the related information is together.
- has a voice that matches the audience and purpose.
- creates a picture with descriptive words and figurative language.
- contains sentences that flow smoothly.

Let's think about how the scoring guide for my descriptive writing test relates to the writing traits you've studied in the rubrics. All of the traits might not be included in every scoring guide, but you need to remember them all to write a good essay.

Ideas

- Be sure your writing includes relevant, sensory details that create a vivid picture for the reader.

My descriptions should include sensory details that are relevant and create a clear mental image.

Organization

- Be sure your writing is organized so that all the related information is together.

I'll put information that goes together in the same paragraph so my reader won't be confused.

Voice

- Be sure your writing has a voice that matches the audience and purpose.

I'll use first-person point of view and a personal tone to share my thoughts and impressions.

Word Choice

- Be sure your writing creates a picture with descriptive words and figurative language.

My writing will be more interesting if I use colorful words and figurative language that give the reader a clear picture of my descriptions.

Sentence Fluency

- Be sure your writing contains sentences that flow smoothly.

I'll check that my sentences flow easily and do not repeat the same structure or length too many times.

Conventions

- Be sure your writing contains correct grammar, punctuation, capitalization, and spelling.

Editing my work for grammar and spelling mistakes is really important!

Prewrite

Focus on **Ideas**

Writing Strategy   Respond to the task.

I know that good writers prepare to write even before they put their pens to paper. Before I begin writing my essay, I'll gather information and take notes. The writing prompt provides me with a lot of information, so I'll start by looking at that. First, look at the task to find out what you are supposed to write. Then think about how you'll respond to the task before you start writing. Since you don't get much time when you write for a test, these steps are helpful.

The task that I identified from my writing prompt is to write a descriptive essay about an event that stands out in my mind. The thing that comes to my mind is my brother's first football game at his high school—it was really exciting. I'll quickly jot down some notes to get started.

Task —— [Write an essay describing the event in detail.

Notes

✔ Wow, it was loud!

✔ The stands were full of people of all ages.

✔ The team ran through the banner to get on the field.

Apply

Think about how you are going to respond to the task before you start writing. Then you can write notes to help you gather information.

Prewrite

Writing Strategy   Choose a graphic organizer.

Now I need to start organizing my ideas with the help of a graphic organizer. A graphic organizer will help me gather ideas and organize them at the same time. That will help, since my time is limited! A Spider Map will help me remember and organize all the details and ideas I want to include.

TOPIC: first football game of year

Where I was
- My brother's first football game was at the high school.
- My grandmother, my mom, and I were all excited!
- The stadium is next to the school.

What I saw
- Lights were on, so it looked like daylight on the field.
- The team came running out, tearing through a banner held by cheerleaders.
- The stands were filled with people of all ages and the band in their uniforms.
- People were wearing green and yellow to support the Eagles, our team.
- I spotted my brother, Number 67.

What I smelled
- Popcorn and hot dogs were being sold at the stadium.

What I heard
- Everyone stood up and yelled and shouted as the team ran through the banner to the field.
- The band was playing team fight songs.
- It was loud as the team took to the field to play.

What I felt
- Even though it was cold, all the excitement kept me warm.
- From my seat, I could feel the rumble of the crowd, stomping feet, and yelling.

Reflect

Does the Spider Map list enough details for a complete essay?

Apply

Choose a graphic organizer that will help you organize the details you want to include in your essay.

Prewrite

Focus on **Organization**

Writing Strategy Check my graphic organizer against the scoring guide.

Prewriting is important since you won't have much time to revise when you take a test. So before I begin writing, I'll take another look at my Spider Map and check it against the scoring guide.

Where I was
- My brother's first football game was at the high school.
- My grandmother, my mom, and I were all excited!
- The stadium is next to the school.

What I saw
- Lights were on, so it looked like daylight on the field.
- The team came running out, tearing through a banner held by cheerleaders.
- The stands were filled with people of all ages and the band in their uniforms.
- People were wearing green and yellow to support the Eagles, our team.
- I spotted my brother, Number 67.

TOPIC: first football game of year

What I smelled
- Popcorn and hot dogs were being sold at the stadium.

What I heard
- Everyone stood up and yelled and shouted as the team ran through the banner to the field.
- The band was playing team fight songs.
- It was loud as the team took to the field to play.

What I felt
- Even though it was cold, all the excitement kept me warm.
- From my seat, I could feel the rumble of the crowd, stomping feet, and yelling.

Ideas

- Be sure your writing includes relevant, sensory details that create a vivid picture for the reader.

I included lots of sensory details in my Spider Map to choose from. Using them will help my reader "see" what I am describing.

Organization

- Be sure your writing is organized so that all the related information is together.

My Spider Map helped me get my ideas organized so information that goes together will be in the same paragraph in my essay.

Voice

- Be sure your writing has a voice that matches the audience and purpose.

I want to give my readers a feel for all the excitement of the big game. Using first-person point of view will really help me connect.

Word Choice

- Be sure your writing creates a picture with descriptive words and figurative language.

I'll try to use colorful words and figurative language to describe things as I write.

Sentence Fluency

- Be sure your writing contains sentences that flow smoothly.

Using my Spider Map as a guide, I'll write a variety of sentence structures that flow smoothly.

Conventions

- Be sure your writing contains correct grammar, punctuation, capitalization, and spelling.

After I complete my draft, I will be sure to thoroughly edit it so that I don't have any mistakes.

Reflect

How will Denise's Spider Map help her write a descriptive and well-organized essay?

Apply

Reviewing your graphic organizer against the scoring guide will help you determine what you're going to write even before you start writing.

Draft

Focus on **Ideas**

Writing Strategy   Include relevant sensory details.

The scoring guide says to use details that are both sensory and relevant. I want my reader to picture everything in my essay, so I'll choose details that will make it easy for them to imagine they are right there at the game with me. I'll be sure all my details relate to the topic so I don't confuse the reader.

[DRAFT]

Go, Eagles!
by Denise

The crowd roars. The cheerleaders kick and yell cheers. The band plays team songs to get us in the spirit. Eagle stadium is about to hold its first game of the season, and the crowd is going wild!

Along with my mother and my grandmother. I have come to watch the Eagles, the team that which my brother plays defense, compete. As we enter the stadium just before the game begins, I can feel the energy of the crowd! Even though it's a cold fall night, the excitement inside the stadium makes it seem warm.

We make our way to seats in the stands that surround the stadium. The smell of popcorn and hot dogs comes drafting through the stands as we walk up the steps. It even smells like a football game! Popcorn is one of my very favorite foods. As I look around, I see a green and yellow blur, with fans of all ages—students, parents, grandparents, and members of the community sporting the Eagles green and yellow colors and waving handheld pompons to show their spirit. The band in their ornate uniforms and hats were seen sitting on the bleachers near the field. They were heard playing a team song as the cheerleaders on the field in their green and yellow skirts and sweaters could be seen opening up a huge paper banner that reads, "Go, eagles!"

Although it's after dark, the huge lights illuminate the field so that it looks like daytime. Across the field I sea the stands filled with blue and black and more people. Their there to support the opposing team, the Panthers.

I know it must be time for the team to come on the field. The stands start to vibrate with all the stomping, and then almost all at once, the Eagles fans rise to their feet.

Our team comes running through the Banner the cheerleaders are holding, ripping it as they cross, and the sound of the crowd is almost defening. I finally spot Number 67, my brother, runs onto the field and over to the sidelines. My mom and grandma and I yell even louder. The game is about to begin!

Reflect

How does the essay capture the excitement for the reader?

Apply

It's important to think about and write for your audience whenever you write for a test.

Revise

Focus on **Organization**

Writing Strategy Organize the information into paragraphs.

I know that all the sentences in a paragraph need to be about the same topic. Any details that aren't relevant to the topic of the paragraph must be removed, because they might confuse my reader. I'll go through my story again looking for any sentences that are off topic. I see one I can delete!

[DRAFT]

[deleted off-topic sentence]

We make our way to seats in the stands that surround the stadium. The smell of popcorn and hot dogs comes drafting through the stands as we walk up the steps. It even smells like a football game! ~~Popcorn is one of my very favorite foods~~. As I look around, I see a green and yellow blur, with fans of all ages—students, parents, grandparents, and members of the community sporting the Eagles green and yellow colors and waving handheld pompons to show their spirit.

Apply

Read your story to see if any sentences do not relate to the topic of the paragraph.

Focus on **Voice**

Writing Strategy Use a casual tone.

My story will be judged on how well I connect to my reader as I describe the event. When I talk about a personal event that I have attended myself, I need to use an appropriate casual tone, like I am talking in a friendly way to my reader. See these changes I made to add a more casual tone.

[DRAFT]

On the bleachers near the field sits the band in their ornate uniforms and hats. They're playing a team song as the cheerleaders on the field in their green and yellow skirts and sweaters open

~~The band in their ornate uniforms and hats were seen sitting on the~~
~~bleachers near the field. They were heard playing a team song as the~~
~~cheerleaders on the field in their green and yellow skirts and sweaters~~
~~could be seen opening~~ up a huge paper banner that reads, "Go, eagles!"

Apply

A casual tone is appropriate to describe a personal event. Look for places where you can use more friendly language. Imagine you're talking to your reader.

Revise

Focus on **Word Choice**

Writing Strategy   Use lively and interesting language.

The scoring guide says that I should use writing that's lively and interesting. I'm going to read through my essay again to see if any of my descriptions are boring. I notice a few areas where the words I use don't really convey what I am trying to explain. I can jazz it up with more personal language.

[DRAFT]

[added colorful and interesting language]

Along with my mother and grandmother. I have come to watch the ~~show their might against the Panthers~~

Eagles, the team ~~that~~ on which my brother plays defense, ~~compete~~. As we

enter the stadium just before the game begins, I can feel the energy of , and it feels electrifying

the crowd! Even though it's a cold fall night, the excitement inside the feel like a warm summer day

stadium makes it ~~seem warm~~.

Reflect

Do the added words make the story read better?

Apply

Boring words and phrases will make your essay seem uninteresting. You can make your descriptions stand out by using words that are lively and exciting.

Focus on Conventions

Writing Strategy Check the grammar, punctuation, capitalization, and spelling.

Now I need to do a final edit on my test. I don't want to have any mistakes!

Go, Eagles!
by Denise

The roar of the crowd! The cheerleaders kicking and yelling cheers! The band playing team songs to get us in the spirit!
~~The crowd roars. The cheerleaders kick and yell cheers. The band plays team songs to get us in the spirit.~~ Eagle stadium is about to hold its first game of the season, and the crowd is going wild!

Along with my mother and my grandmother, I have come to watch the
                                                    show their might against the Panthers
Eagles, the team ~~that~~ which my brother plays defense, ~~compete.~~ As we

enter the stadium just before the game begins, I can feel the energy of
, and it feels electrifying
the crowd! Even though it's a cold fall night, the excitement inside the
           feel like a warm summer day
stadium makes it ~~seem warm.~~

We make our way to seats in the stands that surround the stadium.
                                      drifting
The smell of popcorn and hot dogs comes ~~drafting~~ through the stands

Apply

It's important to check your grammar, punctuation, capitalization, and spelling every time you write for a test.

Descriptive Test Writing 479

[FINAL DRAFT]

On the bleachers near the field sits the band in their ornate uniforms and hats. They're playing a team song as the cheerleaders on the field in their green and yellow skirts and sweaters open as we walk up the steps. It even smells like a football game! ~~Popcorn is one of my very favorite foods.~~ As I look around, I see a green and yellow blur, with fans of all ages—students, parents, grandparents, and members of the community, sporting the Eagles green and yellow colors and waving handheld pompons to show their spirit. ~~The band in their ornate uniforms and hats were seen sitting on the bleachers near the field. They were heard playing a team song as the cheerleaders on the field in their green and yellow skirts and sweaters could be seen opening~~ up a huge paper banner that reads, "Go, Eagles!"

Although it's after dark, the huge lights illuminate the field so that it looks like daytime. Across the field I see ~~see~~ the stands filled with blue and black and more people. They're ~~Their~~ there to support the opposing team, the Panthers. ; I can literally feel it as the crowd starts I know it must be time for the team to come on the field. stamping and yelling so loudly that my grandma can't even hear my mom asking her a question. The stands start to vibrate with all the stomping, and then almost all at once, the Eagles fans rise to their feet as the announcer comes over the speaker saying, "Please welcome last year's state champions, the Eagles!" Our team comes running through the banner the cheerleaders are holding, ripping it as they cross, and the sound of the crowd is almost deafening ~~defening~~. I finally spot Number 67, my brother, as he runs onto the field and over to the sidelines. My mom and grandma and I yell even louder. The game is about to begin!

Reflect

This is your last chance! Take one more look at the scoring guide to be sure you didn't miss anything.

That's it! We've finished the test. Pretty easy, don't you think? Here are some helpful tips to remember when you write for a test.

TEST TIPS

1. **Study the writing prompt before you start to write.** Most writing prompts have three parts: the setup, the task, and the scoring guide. The parts probably won't be labeled. You'll have to figure them out for yourself!

2. **Make sure you understand the task before you start to write.**
   - Read all three parts of the writing prompt carefully.
   - Circle key words in the task part of the writing prompt that tell what kind of writing you need to do. The task might also identify your audience.
   - Make sure you know how you'll be graded.
   - Say the assignment in your own words to yourself.

3. **Keep an eye on the clock.** Decide how much time you will spend on each part of the writing process and try to stick to your schedule. Don't spend so much time prewriting that you don't have enough time left to write.

4. **Reread your writing. Compare it to the scoring guide at least twice.** Remember the rubrics you have used all year? A scoring guide on a writing test is like a rubric. It can help you keep what's important in mind.

5. **Plan, plan, plan!** You don't get much time to revise during a test, so planning is more important than ever.

6. **Write neatly.** Remember: If the people who score your test can't read your writing, it doesn't matter how good your essay is!

Appendix A
Grammar Practice

Simple Sentences

Know the Rule

A **simple sentence** expresses a complete thought. It has a simple subject and a simple predicate. Helping verbs may or may not be part of the simple predicate.

Examples:

Tomás's **watch needed** repairs. (The simple subject is *watch*. The simple predicate is the verb *needed*.)

He will take his watch to a jewelry store tomorrow. (The simple subject is *He*. The simple predicate is *will take*.)

Practice the Rule

Number a sheet of paper 1–10. Copy the sentences. Underline the simple subject of each sentence once. Underline the simple predicate twice.

1. Tomás took his watch to a jewelry store.
2. The owner of the store examined Tomás's watch.
3. She suggested a new battery for the watch.
4. Two girls had entered the store before Tomás.
5. They were looking at bracelets and earrings.
6. An assistant removed the bracelets from the showcase.
7. Tomás's repairs to his watch cost five dollars.
8. He paid the owner with a ten-dollar bill.
9. His mother had given Tomás the money for the repair.
10. Tomás will give the change to his mother.

Predicate Nouns

Know the Rule

A **predicate noun** follows a linking verb and renames the subject of the sentence. A linking verb does not show action. Rather, it "links" a subject with another noun in the sentence. The forms of the verb *be* (*is, are, was, were*) are commonly used as linking verbs. Other verbs that may be linking verbs include *become, seem, feel, taste, look,* and *appear*. In the sentence below, the predicate noun *goalie* follows the linking verb *is* and renames the simple subject *Janice*.

> **Example:**
> **Janice** is the **goalie** on the soccer team.

Practice the Rule

Number a sheet of paper 1–10. Find the subject and the predicate noun in each sentence. Then write them in this form: **Janice=goalie**.

1. Devon's favorite sport is soccer.
2. His sister is the captain of our school soccer team.
3. Her goal in yesterday's game was a controversial event.
4. It was the fatal blow to the opposing team's hope for victory.
5. Devon was certainly the most enthusiastic spectator at the game.
6. By contrast, golf seems a really dull sport.
7. My uncle, however, is an excellent golfer.
8. He was the winner of this year's county championship.
9. The championship has become an annual competition.
10. Generally, though, my friends are not fans of golf.

Predicate Adjectives

Know the Rule

A **predicate adjective** follows a linking verb and describes the subject. In the sentence below, the predicate adjective *dull* follows the linking verb *seems* and describes the simple subject *book*.

> **Example:**
> This **book** about the environment seems **dull**.

Practice the Rule

Number a sheet of paper 1–10. Find the subject and the predicate adjective in each sentence. Then write them in this form: **book=dull**.

1. The first chapter about oil spills in the ocean seemed interesting.
2. One company was responsible for an oil spill in the Gulf of Mexico.
3. The first attempts at stopping the oil leak were unsuccessful.
4. Plumes of oil in the water appeared endless.
5. Many residents along the Gulf of Mexico coast became angry about the company's failures.
6. The effects of the spilled oil on coastal wildlife seemed devastating.
7. The damage from the oil was similar to a large spill back in 1989.
8. After that spill, the future of fishing in part of Alaska looked bleak.
9. After an oil spill, many people become more aware of their energy use.
10. We should always be careful about how much energy we use.

Clauses

Know the Rule

An **independent clause** makes sense by itself and can be written as a sentence. A **dependent clause** has a subject and a verb, but it does not make complete sense by itself. It needs to be used with an independent clause. A **complex sentence** is made up of a dependent clause and an independent clause. Dependent clauses usually begin with a subordinating conjunction, such as *although, because, if, as, when,* or *unless.* At the beginning of a sentence, a dependent clause is followed by a comma.

Examples:

Abraham Lincoln was elected President of the United States in 1860. (independent clause written as a simple sentence)

Because Lincoln was against slavery, his election enraged many people in the South. (complex sentence beginning with a dependent clause followed by an independent clause)

Practice the Rule

Number a sheet of paper 1–8. Copy each sentence. Underline each dependent clause twice. Circle the subordinating conjunction. Underline each independent clause once.

1. Although I have read about the American Civil War, I am not sure about its causes.

2. Because southern plantation owners depended upon the continued practice of slavery, they opposed all attempts by the U.S. government to end it.

3. Many southern states threatened to form a separate country unless they were allowed to continue the practice of slavery.

4. People from the South and North were sharply divided over the issue of slavery as the war began.

5. When the Civil War finally ended, slaves in all the states of the union had gained their freedom.

6. Although enslaved people had gained their freedom, many were not truly free.

7. The war was hard on the whole country because more than 600,000 people had died in the war.

8. If I ever have to write a report about the Civil War, I will already know a lot of the facts.

Compound Sentences

Know the Rule

A **compound sentence** is made of two closely related independent clauses. The two clauses can be joined by a comma and a conjunction (*and, but, or*) or by a semicolon (;).

Examples:
Service dogs help people in many ways, **but** not everyone knows very much about them.
Uncle Nate uses a service dog; he is very fond of the dog.

Practice the Rule

Number a sheet of paper 1–8. Read each sentence pair. Combine the sentences in 1–3 with a semicolon. Combine the rest of the sentences with a comma and a conjunction.

1. Dogs that help individuals with disabilities are called service dogs. Dogs that help farmers and law enforcement officials are called working dogs.
2. One kind of service dog is a guide dog that helps blind people. Another valuable service dog is a signal dog that helps deaf people.
3. A signal dog can help deaf people know when the telephone rings. It can also alert the person when a smoke alarm goes off.
4. Service dogs often help people with physical disabilities. They can also help people with psychological disabilities, such as autism.
5. A person does not need a special certificate or license for a service dog. The person who uses a service dog may require some special training.
6. Golden retrievers and Labrador retrievers make the best service dogs. There are exceptions.
7. People who enjoy working with animals train service dogs. Not all people who love animals are capable of training them.
8. Training a dog for service takes a long time. A person has to be willing to work many hours.

Dangling and Misplaced Modifiers

Know the Rule

Modifying phrases must always refer to a noun or a pronoun in the main part of a sentence. **Dangling modifiers** are phrases that do not refer to any particular word in the sentence.

> **Examples:**
> **While eating supper,** the phone rang. (incorrect)
> **While eating supper, I** heard the phone ring. (correct)

Misplaced modifiers are words or phrases that seem to describe the wrong part of the sentence.

> **Examples:**
> It took only me five minutes to change my clothes. (not clear)
> It took me only five minutes to change my clothes. (clear)

Practice the Rule

Number a sheet of paper 1–10. Identify the sentences that are correct (have no dangling modifier) by writing **Correct**.

1. Hoisting the main sail, the boat was prepared for sailing.
2. The passengers boarded the boat wearing life jackets.
3. Sitting at the tiller, the captain guided the boat among the other boats.
4. The captain almost looked out to see the whole bay.
5. While heading away from the shore, the stars began to twinkle in the sky.
6. Silently gliding over the water, the boat moved swiftly across the bay.
7. Leaping from the boat onto the dock, the boat was secured with a rope by a crew member.
8. The only passengers were on the boat for an hour, but they had a great time.
9. Standing on the dock, several passengers watched the boat glide away.
10. The passengers told each other goodbye while holding their souvenirs.

Direct Objects

Know the Rule

The **direct object** is the noun or pronoun that receives the action of the verb. Only action verbs can take a direct object. To find the direct object, say the verb and then ask "What?" or "Whom?"

Examples:

Our neighbor keeps her **books** in a separate room. (Ask: The neighbor keeps "what"? Answer: The neighbor keeps books. The direct object is *books*.)

Once in a while, her friends ask **her** for an interesting book. (Ask: Her friends ask "whom"? Her friends ask her. The direct object is *her*.)

Practice the Rule

Number a sheet of paper 1–10. Write the action verb in each sentence. Then write the direct object.

1. My cousin Raphael collects stamps.
2. He cuts them from mailed letters and postcards.
3. Raphael owns several books about stamp collecting.
4. He really loves his hobby.
5. Aunt Janelle owned a valuable collection of coins.
6. My family often visited her on weekends.
7. She once gave an old coin to me as a present.
8. I keep her gift in a small box under my bed.
9. My grandfather collected electric toy trains.
10. He built an elaborate track for his trains.

Concrete and Abstract Nouns

Know the Rule

A **concrete noun** (*teacher, library, clarinet*) names a person, a place, or a thing that can be touched or recognized through the senses. An **abstract noun** (*joy, dream, trust*) names a feeling, an idea, or a quality.

Practice the Rule

Number a sheet of paper 1–10. Copy each sentence. Underline the concrete nouns. Circle the abstract nouns.

1. My friends and I had fun at the picnic.
2. We played soccer before lunch.
3. The excitement of the game exhausted us.
4. Our teachers barbecued hamburgers on a grill.
5. Later in the afternoon, we hiked along paths through the park.
6. The girl walking beside me stubbed her toe on the root of a tree.
7. We saw turtles along the banks of a pond.
8. Their shells glistened in the bright sunlight.
9. The day provided me with many great memories.
10. I will always remember the beauty of the sunset that night.

Singular and Plural Nouns

Know the Rule

A **singular noun** names one person, place, thing, or idea. A **plural noun** names more than one. Most nouns add *-s* or *-es* to form the plural. The spelling of some nouns changes when *-es* is added to form the plural (*puppy/puppies; life/lives*). Some nouns do not add *-s* or *-es* to form the plural; instead, they change spelling (*cactus/cacti*). Other nouns have the same form in the singular and plural (*fish*).

Examples:
Many of the **children** in the fourth grade class have **pets**.
Two **girls** own pet **mice**.
Birds can make the **lives** of their **owners** more musical.
Geese would probably not make good **pets**.

Practice the Rule

Number your paper 1–12. Copy the following chart. Give the missing singular or plural form of each noun.

Singular Nouns	Plural Nouns
1. country	
2.	classmates
3. child	
4. sheep	
5.	cities
6. tooth	
7.	men
8. body	
9.	echoes
10. deer	
11.	parties
12. dance	

Possessive Nouns

Know the Rule

A **possessive noun** shows ownership. To form the possessive of a singular noun, add an apostrophe and *-s* (*girl/girl's*). To form the possessive of most plural nouns that end with *-s*, add an apostrophe after the *-s* (*raccoons/raccoons'*). To form the possessive of plurals that don't end in *-s* (*children, mice*) add an apostrophe and *-s* (*children's, mice's*).

Examples:
the **man's** car
the **students'** test results
the **women's** shoes

Practice the Rule

Number a sheet of paper 1–5. Rewrite each phrase to use a possessive noun.

1. the attitude of the boy
2. the experiences of other children
3. the parents of her friends
4. the jokes of his brothers
5. the instructions of his mother

Number your paper 6–10. Write each sentence using the correct possessive form of the singular or plural noun in parentheses.

6. Samantha picked up the (kittens) toys and put them in a box.
7. Next she helped with her (brother) school project.
8. After that, she helped to straighten her (mother) office.
9. She wondered if other (women) offices had as many piles of paper.
10. That night, her (parents) praise made Samantha feel good about having finished her chores.

Personal Pronouns

Know the Rule

A pronoun can take the place of a noun. Use the **personal pronouns** *I*, *me*, *we*, and *us* and the **compound personal pronouns** *myself* and *ourselves* to speak or write about yourself. Use the personal pronouns *she, her, it, he, him, you, they,* and *them* and the compound personal pronouns *herself, himself, itself, yourself, yourselves,* and *themselves* to refer to other people and things.

Example:
The **coach** asked **herself** what **she** needed to do to inspire the team. (The compound personal pronoun *herself* and the personal pronouns *she* refers to the noun *coach*.)

Practice the Rule

Number a sheet of paper 1–10. Write the personal pronouns you find in each sentence.

1. Joel asked himself how he could best help his team win the relay race.
2. He wondered if he should run before Dina or after her.
3. Joel was not sure how fast she could run.
4. Joel and Dina had never tested themselves against one another.
5. Mr. Strand asked the two runners, "Have you two ever timed yourselves in a fifty-yard dash?"
6. Joel said, "My sister timed me last week."
7. Dina said, "I timed myself during practice yesterday."
8. Mr. Strand told Joel and Dina to prepare themselves for a short race.
9. Dina's friends urged her on as she shot from the starting line.
10. The race itself proved nothing because the two runners crossed the finish line at the same time.

Possessive Pronouns

Know the Rule

The **possessive pronouns** *my, your, her, his, its, our,* and *their* show possession. They can replace possessive nouns.

Examples:

Tyrell will play a trumpet as part of <u>Tyrell's</u> report on music.
Tyrell will play a trumpet as part of **his** report on music.

Tyrell and Mona carry <u>Tyrell's and Mona's</u> instruments in leather cases.
Tyrell and Mona carry **their** instruments in leather cases.

Practice the Rule

Number a sheet of paper 1–10. Write the possessive pronoun from the box that best completes each sentence.

my	your	her	his	its	our	their

1. Kyle and Caitlyn are working on _____ project about classical music.
2. Kyle created a timeline as part of _____ contribution to the project.
3. The timeline showed the births and deaths of famous composers as well as the dates of _____ important compositions.
4. Caitlyn drew a portrait of the composers Mozart and Beethoven as part of _____ contribution to the project.
5. You might choose to write about twentieth-century classical music for _____ report.
6. In the public library, we found a book about the Spanish composer Joaquín Rodrigo as well as CDs of _____ music.
7. Everyone in _____ class was excited about hearing a real classical music concert.
8. Before the concert, the conductor asked us to name _____ favorite instruments.
9. I told him that the clarinet was _____ favorite.
10. I don't know why I chose the clarinet; I guess that I just like _____ sound.

Relative and Interrogative Pronouns

Know the Rule

When the pronouns *who, whom, whose, which,* and *that* are used to introduce an adjective clause, they are called **relative pronouns**. A relative pronoun always follows the noun that the adjective clause is describing. When the pronouns *who, whom, whose, which,* and *what* are used to begin a question, they are called **interrogative pronouns**.

Examples:
Our homeroom teacher, **who** made us feel comfortable on our first day, is Mr. Streep.
What kinds of new things do sixth graders encounter as they begin middle school?

Practice the Rule

Number a sheet of paper 1–5. Write the relative pronoun or interrogative pronoun in each sentence. Then write **relative** or **interrogative** to identify the kind of pronoun each is.

1. What do you think are the issues facing American students today?
2. The practice of bullying is one problem that I think must be solved.
3. Which concern does Kasha think is most important to today's students?
4. The problem that Kasha has is how to score well on standardized tests.
5. Anyone who takes standardized tests knows how hard they can be.

Number your paper 6–10. Write the relative pronoun or interrogative pronoun that completes each sentence.

6. _____ is that boy waving his hand in the air at the back of the class?
7. His name is Todd, a boy _____ always has something to say about everything.
8. _____ makes him so interested in all sorts of different topics?
9. He reads only books _____ give information.
10. _____ magazines do you read for information or for fun?

The Perfect Tenses

Know the Rule

The **present-perfect tense** shows action that started in the past and was completed at some time or may still be occurring. To form the present-perfect tense, use the helping verb *has* or *have* with the past participle of a verb (*have known*). The **past-perfect tense** shows action that was definitely completed in the past. To form the past-perfect tense, add the helping verb *had* to the past participle of a verb (*had believed*).

Example:
Have you ever **heard** of the English explorer Henry Hudson? I **had known** just a little bit about him before I read his biography.

Practice the Rule

Number a sheet of paper 1–10. Write the sentences, using the helping verb in parentheses to form the present-perfect tense or the past-perfect tense that correctly completes each sentence.

1. Henry Hudson (has/had) made several voyages to the northeastern coasts of North America before he sailed farther south.
2. He didn't know it at the time, but he (have/had) sailed into what would become New York harbor.
3. He and his crew (has/had) landed on the coast of what would become New York City.
4. His name (has/have) survived as the name of the Hudson River in New York State.
5. Many books and Hollywood movies (has/have) recounted Hudson's brave explorations.
6. An explorer who also (has/had) made several voyages to North America in the early 1600s was Samuel de Champlain.
7. Champlain's name (has/have) survived as the name of a large lake between Vermont, New York, and Canada.
8. Champlain (has/had) named it after himself after he first saw it in 1609.
9. Only one president (has/have) had a state named after him.
10. (Has/Have) you ever wondered how your state got its name?

Transitive and Intransitive Verbs

Know the Rule

Action verbs may or may not take an object to complete the action of the verb. An action verb that has an object is called a **transitive verb**. A verb that expresses action without an object is called an **intransitive verb**. Many verbs can be either transitive or intransitive, depending on how they are used in the sentence.

Examples:
The pitcher **threw** a wild **pitch**. (transitive verb with the direct object *pitch*)
The batter **ducked**. (intransitive verb, no object needed)
Luckily, the ball **missed** the **batter**. (transitive verb with the direct object *batter*)
The fans **yelled**. (intransitive verb, no object needed)
They **yelled** threats at the pitcher. (transitive verb with the object *threats*)

Practice the Rule

Number a sheet of paper 1–10. Write the action verb in each sentence. Label it **transitive** or **intransitive**. If the verb is a transitive verb, write the object that goes with it.

1. The umpire raised his hands, signaling time out.
2. He explained the rules to the managers of both teams.
3. They listened carefully.
4. Both managers shrugged their shoulders.
5. After the brief dispute, the game resumed.
6. The next batter swung the bat hard.
7. The ball rolled out of play.
8. Then the rain began.
9. The ground crew covered the field with a tarp.
10. At the end of the game, the fans cheered.

Articles

Know the Rule

Adjectives describe nouns. The words *a*, *an*, and *the* are adjectives called **articles**. Use *a* or *an* to refer to a general noun. Use *a* before a singular word that begins with a consonant sound and *an* before a singular word that begins with a vowel sound. Use *the* when you refer to a specific noun, whether singular or plural.

Examples:
Mom needs **a** new computer.
Her computer is **an** old model.
The computer we have at home is broken.
Unfortunately, **the** computers we've seen in stores are expensive.

Practice the Rule

Number a sheet of paper 1–10. Write each sentence, using the correct article or articles in parentheses. Then underline the word it modifies.

1. (A/An) computer is (a/an) machine that receives and stores information.
2. The first electronic computers were about the size of (a/an) room.
3. Today people can carry (a/an) computer easily.
4. Adults and children use computers for (a/an) number of purposes.
5. (A/An) child might use (a/an) computer to play (a/an) game or to write (a/an) essay for school.
6. Almost everyone has used some sort of electronic device to write (a/an) e-mail or another kind of message.
7. The world of today almost requires that (a/an) individual own (a/an) cell phone and (a/an) computer.
8. The scientists who created computers probably did not foresee (a/an) world like ours.
9. If you could create (a/an) invention, what would it be?
10. Remember, the person who first thought of computers started out as (a/an) kid just like everyone else.

Interjections

Know the Rule

An **interjection** expresses emotion and is not related grammatically to any of the other words in a sentence. Words like *hurray*, *oh*, *ah*, *wow*, and *hush* are interjections because they exclaim, protest, or command. An interjection usually appears at the beginning of a sentence. An exclamation mark or a comma may follow it. When you write, choose the punctuation for the effect that you want to convey.

Examples:
Hey! Why are we going to the museum's dinosaur room?
Hush, just listen to me and you'll find out.

Practice the Rule

Number a sheet of paper 1–10. Write the interjection in each sentence. Then add the appropriate punctuation after the interjection.

1. Wow _____ Look at this great dinosaur skeleton!
2. Ah _____ that's all you ever want to see when we visit the museum.
3. Oh _____ I don't think that's true at all.
4. Hey _____ Check out this dinosaur footprint preserved in tar.
5. Good grief _____ There must be more interesting things in the museum!
6. Well _____ let's try to find the animal habitat displays.
7. Okay _____ Now you're talking about something that interests me!
8. Whew _____ I thought I'd never find anything that you liked.
9. Oh, no _____ The guard says that the animal habitats are closed for repairs.
10. Hurray _____ It's back to the dinosaurs we go!

Subordinating Conjunctions

Know the Rule

Subordinating conjunctions, such as *although, because, before, if, since,* and *so that,* show how one clause is related to another. Subordinating conjunctions are used at the beginning of adverb clauses. Notice that a comma is used at the end of the adverb clause when it comes first in a sentence.

Examples:

If Chante had not been assigned the report, she would not have learned about wind power.

She and her group members went to the library **so that** they could research the topic.

Practice the Rule

Number a sheet of paper 1–10. Choose a subordinating conjunction from above to complete each sentence.

1. Chanté was looking for articles on wind power _____ she was working on a group project on that topic for class.

2. She did not know how wind turbines worked, _____ she had seen some turning in a field.

3. _____ wind power became popular among environmentalists, solar power had been promoted as the best renewable energy.

4. _____ wind power has become popular, a lot of controversy has surrounded it.

5. Some people don't want wind turbines near them _____ they are noisy.

6. Other people wonder what will happen _____ we don't use more renewable energy sources.

7. Chanté tried to find out as much as she could _____ she gave her report.

8. You can look on a website about wind power _____ you want to know more about it.

9. _____ she began her report, Chanté had never thought about wind power.

10. Chanté has become a believer in wind power _____ she did her report.

Compound Personal Pronouns

Know the Rule

The **compound personal pronouns** are these: *myself, yourself, himself, herself, itself, ourselves, yourselves,* and *themselves*. Depending on how they are used in a sentence, they are also known as **reflexive** or **intensive pronouns**.

- A reflexive pronoun reflects back on the subject.
  Example:
  Grandpa and Grandma built their house **themselves**.

- An intensive pronoun emphasizes the subject. It often appears right after the subject.
  Example:
  Grandma **herself** put on all the shingles.

Practice the Rule

Number a sheet of paper 1–10. Write each sentence with the correct compound personal pronoun. Underline the antecedent (the word or words to which the pronoun refers) for each sentence.

1. I _____ had a tough time finding a quiet place to do my homework last night.
2. My older sister was doing homework _____, too.
3. She and one of her friends closed _____ in her room.
4. Suddenly, the bedroom door seemed to open all by _____.
5. The noise from my sister's TV was so loud that I couldn't hear _____ think.
6. My sister should know better than to distract _____ with noise while doing homework.
7. She _____ always tells me to keep quiet when she's studying.
8. I asked my father for help, but he said we should settle the problem _____.
9. My father _____ prefers to have some quiet time in the evening.
10. Finally, everyone had settled _____ down for the rest of the evening.

Using the Right Word

Know the Rule

Some words are often misused in writing. Some words, such as *new* and *knew*, sound the same but have different meanings. Other words, such as *fewer* and *less*, have similar meanings but different uses. It is important to know how to use the right word so your readers will not be confused.

Examples:

I cannot **accept** the invitation to the party.

I'm free every night **except** the night of the party.

Practice the Rule

Number a sheet of paper 1–10. Write each sentence, using the correct word in parentheses. Check the meanings of the words in a dictionary if necessary.

1. Please (bring/take) these color markers back to your desk.

2. Would you please (bring/take) your report up to my desk?

3. We have (fewer/less) minutes between classes this year than we had last year.

4. This means that we have (fewer/less) time to talk with friends in the hallways.

5. I had to build something from wood for my art (coarse/course).

6. I used a (coarse/course) piece of sandpaper to work on my birdfeeder.

7. Hearing about natural disasters, such as floods, usually (affects/effects) people in different ways.

8. The newspaper article described the damaging (affects/effects) of the tornado.

9. Each student was (allowed/aloud) just five minutes to present his or her oral report.

10. As part of her report, Janelle read (allowed/aloud) some poems she had written.

Irregular Verbs

Know the Rule

Many commonly used verbs are **irregular;** the past tense of these verbs is not formed by adding -*ed*. The chart lists some irregular verbs.

Present	Past	With *has, have, or had*
begin	began	begun
become	became	become
draw	drew	drawn
keep	kept	kept

Practice the Rule

Number a sheet of paper 1–10. Write each sentence, using the correct form of the irregular verb in parentheses.

1. A professional artist (speak) to our class yesterday.
2. She (tell) us about an artist named Pablo Picasso.
3. I had (hear) of Picasso before from my older brother.
4. Picasso (begin) painting when he was seven years old.
5. By the age of twenty-five, Picasso had (become) a famous artist.
6. Last year Jon always (draw) the best pictures.
7. The school (keep) most of his drawings on display.
8. Jon (become) interested in drawing when he visited the art museum.
9. After his visit, he (begin) to draw pencil sketches.
10. Eventually he (become) interested in working with charcoal.

Avoiding Double Negatives

Know the Rule

A **negative** is a word that means "no" or "not." The words *no, not, nothing, none, never, nowhere,* and *nobody* are negatives. The *n't* in a contraction (*don't, can't*) is also a negative. Use only one negative word in a sentence. You can use positive words in place of a negative word to write a correct sentence. Positive words include *any, anybody, anything, either,* and *ever.*

Examples:
I have**n't** done **nothing** all morning. (incorrect)
I have done **nothing** all morning. (correct)
I have**n't** done **anything** all morning. (correct)

Practice the Rule

Number a sheet of paper 1–10. Write the word or words in parentheses that complete each sentence.

1. I don't know (nothing/anything) I like more than soccer.
2. Nobody could (ever/never) convince me that basketball was more exciting.
3. As for excitement, baseball doesn't come close to soccer, (neither/either).
4. I can't stand watching (any/no) other sport on television.
5. Nothing (no one/anyone) says could ever change my mind.
6. There is (nothing/anything) better than watching an exciting soccer game.
7. If I can't (either/neither) play or watch soccer, then I read about it.
8. I don't (ever/never) read books just about soccer.
9. When I can't find (no/any) soccer books, I read about world history.
10. Still, I couldn't (ever/never) imagine a world without soccer.

Subject-Verb Agreement

Know the Rule

The **subject** and its **verb** must **agree** in number. That is, a singular subject takes a singular verb. A plural subject takes a plural verb. There are special rules for certain kinds of subjects. A **collective noun,** such as *family, country, team,* or *herd,* names more than one person or object acting together as one group. These nouns are almost always considered singular. (*The country is changing its form of money.*) Most indefinite pronouns, including *everyone, nobody, nothing,* and *anything,* are considered singular. (*Not everyone is happy about the change.*) A few **indefinite pronouns,** such as *many* and *several,* are considered plural. (*Many plan to protest.*)

Practice the Rule

Number a sheet of paper 1–10. Write each sentence, using the verb in parentheses that agrees in number with the subject. Then underline the simple subject in the sentence.

1. Many people (use/uses) spices when cooking meals.
2. Spices (add/adds) flavor to food.
3. Also, several (appear/appears) in certain perfumes and cosmetic products.
4. One of the more common spices (are/is) pepper.
5. Everyone (sprinkle/sprinkles) a little pepper on scrambled eggs.
6. Cinnamon trees (grow/grows) in Southeast Asia, Africa, and South America.
7. The spice (come/comes) from the bark of the cinnamon tree.
8. Nothing (taste/tastes) better than cinnamon in applesauce!
9. The production of spices (is/are) a huge business around the world.
10. Many (lose/loses) their fragrance and taste after a year on a kitchen shelf.

Writing Sentences Correctly

Know the Rule

Begin every sentence with a capital letter. A **declarative sentence** makes a statement and ends with a period. An **interrogative sentence** asks a question and ends with a question mark. An **imperative sentence** gives a command and ends with a period or an exclamation point. An **exclamatory sentence** shows excitement and ends with an exclamation point. When you write, choose the punctuation that is right for the effect you want to convey.

Examples:
Have you ever watched a silent movie**?** (interrogative sentence)
We don't know what a silent movie is**.** (declarative sentence)
Wow! I can't believe you've never heard of silent movies**!** (exclamatory sentence)
Tell me what they are**.** (imperative sentence)

Practice the Rule

Number a sheet of paper 1–10. Write each sentence correctly. Use capital letters and appropriate punctuation marks.

1. before the 1920s, most movies did not have sound
2. how could you tell what was going on in the movie
3. captions that the audience had to read were inserted in the movie
4. good grief! watching a movie back then must have been really boring
5. come with me to the library
6. does the library have any silent movies that we could check out
7. you bet! the library probably has a hundred silent movies
8. tell me the titles of a few famous silent movies
9. was D. W. Griffith a famous silent movie director
10. we want to learn more about silent movies

Capitalization

Know the Rule

Begin the following with a capital letter: proper noun (*India*), proper adjective (*Boston baked beans*), title of respect (*Doctor Johnson*), initial (*J. S. Bach*), first word in a sentence, month (*April*), and day of the week (*Saturday*).

Practice the Rule

Number a sheet of paper 1–5. Write each phrase using capital letters correctly.

1. the first monday in october
2. my dentist doctor Sanchez
3. the asian country of vietnam
4. our neighbor pastor kim
5. my birthday in june

Number your paper 6–10. Write each sentence, using capital letters correctly.

6. robert louis stevenson is a famous scottish author.
7. he was born in november 1850 in the city of edinburgh.
8. edinburgh is the capital of scotland.
9. the author who created the character peter pan, j. m. barrie, admired stevenson's work.
10. this friday, I am going to get some of r. l. stevenson's books from the public library.

Initials and Abbreviations
Know the Rule

An **abbreviation** is a shortened form of a word. **Titles of respect** are often abbreviated (*Dr., Rev.*). So are words in **addresses,** such as Street (*St.*), Road (*Rd.*), and Apartment (*Apt.*). **Days** (*Fri.*), some **months** (*Nov.*), and parts of **business names** (*Co. for Company*) are often abbreviated in informal notes. Abbreviations usually begin with a capital letter and end with a period. An **initial** can replace the name of a person or place. An initial is written as a capital letter followed by a period (*W. S. Merwin for William Stanley Merwin*).

Practice the Rule

Number a sheet of paper 1–5. Write the word that each abbreviation stands for.

1. Mr.
2. Oct.
3. Ave.
4. Thurs.
5. Gov.

Number your paper 6–10. Write each item using initials and abbreviations where possible.

6. the waiting room of Doctor Kelly's office
7. a magazine article about General Patton
8. the poet Thomas Stearns Eliot
9. the last Sunday in August
10. 280 75th Street, Apartment 2

Titles

Know the Rule

When writing, underline the **titles** of longer works, such as **books, magazines, newspapers,** and **movies**. In printed texts, such as papers that you prepare on the computer, these titles appear in italics. Use quotation marks around the titles of shorter works, such as **songs, stories,** and **poems**. Capitalize the first word and the last word in titles. Capitalize all other words except articles, short prepositions, and coordinating conjunctions. Also, capitalize short verbs, such as *is* and *are*.

Practice the Rule

Number a sheet of paper 1–5. Rewrite each sentence, punctuating and capitalizing each title correctly.

1. I have never seen the movie batman returns.
2. You could probably find a review of it at the website for a major newspaper, such as the washington post.
3. You could also check the websites for the magazines time and newsweek.
4. I found the Robert Frost poem stopping by woods on a snowy evening online.
5. The lyrics of the star-spangled banner (our national anthem) can also be found online.

Number your paper 6–10. Write each title correctly.

6. america the beautiful (song)
7. the emperor of ice cream (poem)
8. the dallas morning news (newspaper)
9. maniac magee (novel)
10. the legend of sleepy hollow (short story)

Commas

Know the Rule

A series is a list of three or more words or phrases. **Commas** are used to separate items in a series. Each item in a series might consist of one word or a longer phrase. The last comma in a series goes before the conjunction (*and, or*).

Examples:

My **friend,** my friend's **parents,** and **I** went to a baseball game last week.

Did you have a **pizza,** a **hot dog,** or just a **soda** for a snack?

Practice the Rule

Number a sheet of paper 1–10. Rewrite each sentence, adding commas where appropriate. Underline the conjunction used in each series.

1. My favorite player hit a single a double and a home run.
2. My friends Dina Miguel and Felix also attended the game.
3. The batter the catcher and the umpire got into a heated argument.
4. Is your favorite sport baseball football basketball or soccer?
5. Should we play baseball at the park on Thursday Friday or Saturday?
6. My friends and I will play summer league baseball in June July and August.
7. Florida Texas and Ohio each have two Major League baseball teams.
8. The teams in Toronto Phoenix and Tampa play indoors.
9. Five California cities have baseball teams: San Francisco Oakland Anaheim Los Angeles and San Diego.
10. Dina Miguel Felix and I think it would be fun to see baseball games in different cities.

More Commas

Know the Rule

A **comma** is used to separate an **introductory word** from the rest of the sentence (*Hey, wait for me! Bob, tell me where you were born.*). Commas are also used to set off information that is useful but not necessary to a sentence (*Next year, when I am 13, I will probably get braces.*). Nonessential information is called *nonrestrictive*. A comma is also used between the name of a city or town and state (*My aunt lives in Asheville, North Carolina.*).

Practice the Rule

Number a sheet of paper 1–10. Write each sentence, adding commas where appropriate.

1. Mom can you tell me what time of the day I was born?
2. Well I think you were born around midnight.
3. Have we always lived in Fort Worth Texas?
4. Yes but your father and I were not born here.
5. He and I grew up in Lexington Kentucky.
6. Oh is that where the Kentucky Derby is run?
7. No that race is run in Louisville Kentucky.
8. In 1999 a year before you were born we moved to Texas.
9. Eliot who happens to be my best friend was born in Tucson Arizona.
10. Last year just as he was about to start middle school Eliot moved here.

Semicolons and Colons

Know the Rule

A **semicolon** can be used instead of a comma and a conjunction to separate independent clauses in a compound sentence. A **colon** can be used to separate two independent clauses when the second clause states something that is a direct result of the first.

Examples:

Almost everyone does some traveling at some point; knowing a few basic things about packing can make the trip more enjoyable. I once forgot to pack a toothbrush: I had to buy one at a store in the airport.

Practice the Rule

Number a sheet of paper 1–10. Combine each pair of sentences, using a semicolon or a colon as appropriate.

1. Pack only essential items when you go to camp or on a long trip. Light packing makes traveling a lot easier.

2. No one likes to carry a lot of luggage on a trip. The bags are heavy and clumsy when you have to move through a crowd of people.

3. Most camps provide you with a list of items. This list usually includes the suggested number of each item.

4. Parents often drive their children to camp. Doing so cuts down a bit on the lugging of suitcases.

5. Sometimes the campers all travel together on a bus. This is a great way to get to know the kids you'll be camping with.

6. Find out where the bus stops. The bus does not go to every town or city.

7. Children come from all over. Last year children came from ten different states.

8. Camp can be hard at first. It's worth adjusting because it can be a great experience.

9. My sister went to camp last summer. She hasn't stopped talking about it.

10. Be sure to register early. Many camps fill up quickly.

Brackets and Dashes

Know the Rule

Brackets are used within quoted material to set off text added by someone other than the person who wrote or spoke the quotation. There are two types of **dashes.** They differ in length. An **em dash,** which is the longer dash, is used to set off text from the rest of the sentence. *(The Pony Express lasted only nineteen months—a very short time, considering how well known it is.)* An **en dash,** which is about half the length of the em dash, is used to show a range *(pages 4–10, Monday–Thursday).*

Example:

"Ladies and gentlemen," said the school board president, "I am extremely honored by this [her election as board president], and I hope to serve our community honorably."

Practice the Rule

Number a sheet of paper 1–8. Write the sentences. Where necessary, add an em dash or an en dash. After the sentence, identify the dash you used by writing **em** or **en**. Add brackets where needed.

1. I found the article about the opening of the new zoo on pages 4 _____ 5 in yesterday's newspaper.

2. The zoo director said, "We all hope that it the new zoo will be visited by people of all ages."

3. The zoo was several years in the planning _____ a process that was often interrupted by disagreement.

4. The zoo is scheduled to be open every week, Tuesday _____ Sunday.

5. The director hopes the zoo will be fun and educational _____ educational in the sense that the display will be accompanied by interactive programs for young children.

6. The program director stated, "They interactive programs are an important part of the zoo."

7. Activities will be available for children ages 2 _____ 12.

8. The zoo should appeal to everyone _____ unless, of course, something goes wrong.

More Practice

Simple Sentences

Copy the sentences. Underline the simple subject of each sentence. Then circle the simple predicate.

1. Lions live on the plains of Africa and Asia.
2. A male can weigh over five hundred pounds.
3. The females usually survive longer than the males.
4. A mane of long hair around its neck distinguishes the male lion.
5. Lions travel in large groups called prides.

Predicate Nouns

Write the subject in each sentence. Then write the predicate noun that renames it.

1. Florida is a state in the southeastern United States.
2. The capital of the state is Tallahassee.
3. Florida's northern neighbor is Georgia.
4. Tourism is the largest industry in the state.
5. The Atlantic is the ocean that borders the eastern coast of Florida.

Predicate Adjectives

Copy the sentences. Underline the simple subject of each sentence. Then circle the predicate adjective that describes the subject.

1. Last summer my sister became interested in collecting butterflies.
2. Her collection is now pretty extensive.
3. The wings of butterflies are usually very beautiful.
4. Catching butterflies is very difficult.
5. Butterflies are very delicate.

More Practice

Clauses

Copy the sentences. Underline each independent clause once. Underline each dependent clause twice. Circle the subordinating conjunction that begins each dependent clause.

1. Whenever I have some free time, I like to play electronic games.
2. I play the games until my mother tells me to quit.
3. My older sister sometimes tells me to turn off the computer because the noise annoys her.
4. When I grow up, I will still like electronic games.
5. Unless I get a better idea, my career will be designing electronic games.

Compound Sentences

Combine each pair of sentences with a comma and a conjunction to make a compound sentence.

1. Should we do our own research on rivers of the world? Should we ask our teacher or the librarian for help locating resources?
2. The Mississippi River begins in Minnesota. Many other smaller rivers feed into it as it flows toward the Gulf of Mexico.
3. I always thought that the Amazon River was the longest river in the world. I recently learned that the Nile River in Africa is longer.
4. Rivers have many important uses. This is one reason why many of the important cities on Earth are located near major rivers.
5. Rivers can provide many fun activities. They can also be extremely dangerous.

Conventions Grammar, Usage & Mechanics

More Practice

Dangling and Misplaced Modifiers

Select the sentence in each pair that is written correctly (has no dangling or misplaced modifiers).

1a. Supporting unpopular issues, many people disliked the candidate for mayor.
 b. As a candidate supporting unpopular issues, he was disliked by many people.
2a. Having been in office for a year, those same people liked him.
 b. Having been in office for a year, he was liked by some people.
3a. People carrying signs of protest stood outside the mayor's office.
 b. Carrying signs of protest, the mayor's office had people standing outside.
4a. Having learned about politics in class, I now know how important voting is.
 b. Having learned about politics in class, voting is very important.
5a. My only sister is 18 years old, so she can vote in the next election.
 b. My sister is only 18 years old, so she can vote in the next election.

Direct Objects

Write each sentence. Underline the direct object and draw an arrow from it to the transitive verb.

1. At the concert, the band played their most popular songs.
2. The audience loved the performance.
3. I framed my ticket as a souvenir.
4. My brother downloaded the band's most recent release.
5. I played the song on repeat for hours.

Concrete and Abstract Nouns

Copy the sentences. Underline the concrete nouns. Circle the abstract nouns.

1. The article I read about the human brain was a pure joy.
2. Our brain controls our breathing and contains our memories.
3. At night, our brains generate our dreams.
4. I have an illustration of the human body on the wall of my bedroom.
5. Of all the parts of the human body, I find the brain most interesting.

More Practice

Singular and Plural Nouns

Copy the following chart. Give the missing singular or plural form of each noun.

Singular Nouns	Plural Nouns
1. knife	
2.	women
3. goose	
4.	sheep
5. wolf	

Possessive Nouns

Write the possessive form of the noun in parentheses that correctly completes each sentence.

1. The (children) theater will present a play this Saturday.
2. Have you picked up your (parents) tickets yet?
3. My (brother) seat is in the front row.
4. I helped design the (actors) costumes for the play.
5. My (grandparents) video camera will capture the entire play.

Personal and Compound Personal Pronouns

Write the pronoun in parentheses that correctly completes each sentence.

1. Mary and (me/I) have set a personal goal for (ourself/ourselves).
2. (Us/We) both intend to read two books every month.
3. Some friends of ours think (us/we) have a good idea.
4. They are going to try reading a book every week (ourselves/themselves).
5. If (we/us) meet our goal, (we/us) are going to celebrate!

Possessive Pronouns

Write the possessive pronoun that could replace each possessive noun.

1. Roberto's notebook
2. Ms. Greene's desk
3. the car's tires
4. the players' celebration
5. the bird's nest

More Practice

Relative and Interrogative Pronouns

Identify each underlined pronoun as a **relative** or an **interrogative**.

1. <u>Who</u> from your class is on the Student Council?
2. Tell me about some of the issues <u>that</u> the Student Council is working on.
3. One issue, <u>which</u> I think is very important, concerns the elimination of free periods.
4. <u>Which</u> solution to this problem do you favor?
5. <u>Which</u> points of the argument do you find most convincing?

The Perfect Tenses

Write each sentence using the correct helping verb to form the present-perfect tense or past-perfect tense of the verb.

1. Pakistan (has/had) experienced severe flooding.
2. (Have/Had) you known anything about Pakistan before we began studying it in class?
3. Countries around the world (has/have) offered emergency assistance.
4. The Pakistani government (has/had) stated that the country will take years to recover.
5. (Has/Have) your school done anything to help out people in need in times of emergency?

Transitive and Intransitive Verbs

Write the action verb in each sentence. Label it **transitive** or **intransitive**. If the verb is a transitive verb, write the object that goes with it.

1. My father quit smoking last week.
2. He threw his cigarettes in the garbage can.
3. Since quitting, he runs two miles every day.
4. Have your parents quit yet?
5. Some people develop health problems from secondhand smoke.

More Practice

Articles

Write each sentence, using the correct article in parentheses. Underline the article *the* each time it appears and the word to which it refers.

1. Last summer I worked part-time in (a/an) orchard.
2. I swept the store area with (a/an) long broom.
3. The job involved working only (a/an) few hours each week.
4. As (a/an) perk of the job, I could eat (a/an) apple whenever I wanted one.
5. One day, I ate so many apples I got (a/an) stomachache!

Interjections

Use the interjections *Wow, Hey, Ah, Ick,* and *Well* to complete the sentences. Use each interjection only once. Use the appropriate punctuation after the interjection.

1. _____ would you like to go swimming today?
2. _____ I have a little homework to do before I can go.
3. _____ You do homework on Saturdays?
4. _____ the water feels so refreshing.
5. _____ There's a bug in the water.

Subordinating Conjunctions

Write the subordinating conjunction in parentheses that correctly completes each sentence.

1. (Although/If) the war was unpopular with the people, the president and his staff thought that it was necessary.
2. (Before/If) people disagree with an elected official's actions, they can choose not to vote for him or her in the next election.
3. Voters should learn as much as they can about candidates (although/before) they vote for one or another.
4. My parents read newspapers and watch TV news shows (because/if) they want to be well informed about issues.
5. Some voters develop strong opinions about the candidates (before/if) they vote.

More Practice

Using the Right Word

Write each sentence, using the correct word in parentheses.

1. (Among/Between) you and me, we have a lot of baseball cards.
2. I have most of the cards I want (accept/except) for Derek Jeter's rookie card.
3. Who is standing (beside/besides) the manager on that team card?
4. My uncle knows a (hole/whole) lot about baseball players.
5. He even (knew/new) Babe Ruth's real first name.

Irregular Verbs

Write each sentence, using the correct form of the irregular verb in parentheses.

1. Our class has (begin) a unit on the Holocaust.
2. We learned about a girl who (keep) a diary while hiding from the Nazis.
3. Her book later (become) very famous.
4. I had never (hear) of Anne Frank before.
5. Since learning about the Holocaust in class, I have (read) several books on the topic.

Avoiding Double Negatives

Write each sentence, using the correct word in parentheses to avoid a double negative.

1. Haven't you (ever/never) learned to swim?
2. People who can't swim don't have (no/any) business wading in a river.
3. They shouldn't wander into the deep end of a pool (neither/either).
4. I can't think of (anything/nothing) more important than learning to swim.
5. I don't know if there's (anything/nothing) better than swimming on a hot summer day.

More Practice

Subject-Verb Agreement

Write the verb in parentheses that agrees with the subject of the sentence. Then identify the verb as a singular verb or plural verb.

1. Our country (has/have) many people from other countries living in it.
2. Not everyone (agree/agrees) that this is a good policy.
3. Many strongly (oppose/opposes) America's immigration laws.
4. Others (believe/believes) in the fairness of the laws.
5. Many senators (has/have) tried to pass new laws.

Writing Sentences Correctly

Write **declarative, interrogative, imperative,** or **exclamatory** to identify the type of each sentence.

1. What are the three branches of the United States government?
2. The legislative, judicial, and executive branches make up our government.
3. Tell me who the head of the executive branch is.
4. Everyone knows that the president heads the executive branch!
5. What is the main function of the executive branch?

Capitalization

Write each phrase, using capitalization where needed.

1. the end of december
2. the british author j. k. rowling
3. the capital of puerto rico
4. vice president biden
5. dr. matthew perez of houston medical center

More Practice

Initials and Abbreviations

Write the abbreviation of each word.

1. Monday
2. February
3. Doctor
4. Street
5. California

Titles

Write each sentence. Use correct punctuation and capitalization for titles.

1. Have you ever heard the Beatles' song something?
2. What about the song here comes the sun?
3. No, but I've seen the movie yellow submarine, which is based on the group's music.
4. I saw Paul McCartney's picture in a magazine called newsweek.
5. You can read about pop stars in the entertainment section of the houston chronicle.

Commas

Write the sentences, using commas where needed.

1. My family feeds finches chickadees and cardinals in the winter.
2. We don't put out birdseed in the spring summer or fall.
3. Chipmunks will eat unsalted peanuts dried corn and other kinds of seeds.
4. My friends Debbie Shauna and Cory like to watch the animals with me.
5. We eat snacks like popcorn cereal and fruit as we watch the animals nibble on birdseed.

More Practice

More Commas

Write each sentence, using commas where needed.

1. Pedro can you tell me where the ballpark for the Texas Rangers is located?

2. The Rangers ballpark is in Arlington Texas.

3. Arlington which is located between Fort Worth and Dallas is also the home of a theme park.

4. Two rivers one of which is the Trinity River flow through the city.

5. Mary can you tell me any of facts about the city of Arlington Texas?

Semicolons and Colons

Use a semicolon or a colon to combine each pair of sentences.

1. Forests are valuable resources in nature. People should protect forests when they can.

2. Forests provide habitats for many animals and insects. Thousands of different plants also live in forests.

3. Logging and urban sprawl are two ways humans affect forests. Disease and weather are two natural conditions that affect forests.

4. Too often campers are careless about their use of fire. Resulting fires have destroyed millions of acres of forests.

5. Campers must take precautions when using fire. Making sure coals are completely dead before going to sleep is one way to prevent forest fires.

Brackets and Dashes

Write each sentence, using brackets and em dashes or en dashes where needed. Identify the dashes you used by writing **em** or **en**.

1. My homeroom period is 7:24 A.M. _____ 7:58 A.M. each morning.

2. During her morning address, our principal Ms. Weinstein said, "There will be a change in this policy _____ roaming freely through the hallways after lunch _____ starting tomorrow."

3. Then the class read pages 36 _____ 42 in our history textbook.

4. The upcoming spring break _____ and a very welcome break it is _____ falls in April.

5. I will be going to the Bahamas with my family April 4 _____ 10 for vacation.

Transitions

Certain words and phrases can help make the meaning of your writing clearer. Below are lists of words and phrases that you can use to help readers understand more completely what you are trying to say.

Time Order

about	first	today	later
after	second	tomorrow	finally
at	to begin	until	then
before	yesterday	next	as soon as
during	meanwhile	soon	in the end

Cause and Effect

and so	as a result	because	besides
consequently	once	since	so
therefore			

Compare and Contrast

Compare:	also	as	both
	in the same way	like	likewise
	one way	similarly	
Contrast:	although	but	even though
	however	still	on the other hand
	otherwise	yet	

Words and phrases that can show location:

above	across	around	behind
below	beneath	beside	between
down	in back of	in front of	inside
near	next to	on top of	outside
over	under		

Words and phrases that can conclude or summarize:

finally	in conclusion	in the end	lastly
therefore	to conclude		

Appendix B
Rubrics

Narrative Writing Rubric

	4	3	2	1
Ideas	An engaging topic, experience, or series of events is supported by relevant details. Memorable descriptions develop the narrative. Carefully selected ideas completely satisfy the reader.	Most of the details are relevant and supportive. Descriptions are adequate. The ideas selected by Descriptions are inadequate. The the author frequently meet the needs of the reader.	The narrative is not supported by enough relevant details. Descriptions are inadequate. The ideas selected by the author sometimes meet the needs of the reader.	The topic is not clear. Details are unrelated to the topic.
Organization	The narrative has an engaging beginning and an ending that leaves the reader thinking or feeling. Events are logically and creatively sequenced. A variety of effective transition words, phrases, and clauses signifies shifts in the setting and plot.	The beginning and the conclusion are functional, but one may be stronger than the other. The sequence of events is logical, but may have a flaw or two. More or better transitions may be needed to guide the reader.	The beginning does not get the reader's attention, or the ending does not satisfy. Some events are out of order. Transitions are needed.	The writing is not organized into a beginning, middle, and ending.
Voice	The voice, mood, and tone are perfect for the purpose and audience. Dialogue, if used, is realistic and fits all the characters.	The voice, mood, and tone are appropriate in places, but inconsistent. Dialogue, if used, usually fits the characters.	The voice sounds disinterested. Mood and tone are weak. Dialogue, if used, is unrealistic or does not fit the characters.	Voice, mood, and tone are not established.
Word Choice	Clear and precise nouns and verbs consistently capture the imagery and action of the story. Descriptive language clearly conveys the experiences and events. Modifiers are strong.	Some nouns and verbs are strong, but others are weak. Descriptive language conveys most of the imagery, experiences, and events. Modifiers are satisfactory.	Many nouns and verbs do not capture the imagery or action of the story. The descriptive language is overly dependent on modifiers, and many of these are weak.	Words are overused, very weak, or incorrect. Descriptive language is not used.
Sentence Fluency	A variety of sentence structures and sentence beginnings makes the narrative flow smoothly. To read this paper aloud with inflection and feeling is effortless.	A few sentences share the same structures, lengths, or beginnings. The writing flows reasonably well. It is possible to read this writing aloud with inflection and feeling.	Many sentences have the same structures, lengths, or beginnings. The flow is robotic or rambling. It is difficult to read this writing aloud with inflection and feeling.	Sentences are incorrectly written or incomplete. The writing is difficult to follow.
Conventions	The narrative has been carefully edited. Grammar, usage, and mechanics are correct.	The narrative contains some minor errors that may distract the reader, but meaning remains clear.	The narrative contains many errors. Line-by-line editing in specific places is needed.	The writing has not been edited. Serious errors affect or alter the meaning.

Informative/Explanatory Writing Rubric

	4	3	2	1
Ideas	The topic is introduced clearly. It is developed and supported with relevant facts and concrete details. If included, quotations are relevant, accurate, and insightful. Carefully selected ideas completely answer the reader's main questions.	The topic is introduced adequately. Some facts, details, and quotations (if included) support the topic adequately. The reader's main questions are frequently answered.	The topic is introduced. Facts, details, and quotations (if included) do not develop and support the topic effectively. A few of the reader's questions are answered.	The topic is not clear. The topic is not supported by facts and details. The author did not think about what questions the reader might have.
Organization	The ideas, concepts, and information are organized into a strong introduction, body, and conclusion. Varied, appropriate, and unique transitions connect and clarify relationships among ideas.	The ideas, concepts, and information are organized into an introduction, body, and conclusion. More or better transitions may be needed.	An introduction, body, and conclusion are present. Some transitions may be inappropriate or incorrect.	The text is not organized into an introduction, body, and conclusion. It is hard or impossible to follow the ideas.
Voice	The writer's voice is appropriate for the purpose and audience. The tone is informative, respectful, and consistent.	The writer's voice is mostly appropriate for the purpose and audience. The tone is mostly informative and respectful, but may be too informal in some places.	The writer's voice is not very appropriate for the purpose or audience. The tone is inconsistent.	The writer's voice is very weak or absent. The tone is not established.
Word Choice	The language is exact and concise. Domain-specific vocabulary is used correctly and explained, as needed. Nouns and verbs are clear and precise, supported by a few carefully selected modifiers.	Some of the language is exact, but some is too general or vague. Some domain-specific vocabulary is used but not explained. Some nouns and verbs are weak, requiring too much help from modifiers. Modifiers are satisfactory.	Some language is confusing. Domain-specific vocabulary may be used incorrectly. Nouns and verbs lack clarity and precision. Too many or too few modifiers are used, and many of these are weak.	Many words are repeated or used incorrectly. Domain-specific vocabulary is not used.
Sentence Fluency	The sentences vary greatly in length and structure, adding style and interest. Almost all sentences begin differently. The text flows smoothly and is effortlessly read aloud with inflection.	Sentence length and structure vary somewhat, with some sentences adding style or interest. Some sentence beginnings are repeated. Parts of the text flow smoothly. The paper can be read aloud with inflection.	In many places, the writing does not flow smoothly because sentences are the same length or begin the same way. The paper is difficult to read aloud with inflection.	Sentences are incomplete or incorrect. The text does not flow smoothly.
Conventions	The text has been carefully edited. Grammar, usage, and mechanics are correct.	The text contains some minor errors that may distract the reader, but meaning remains clear.	Many errors are repeated. Line-by-line editing in specific places is needed. The errors interfere with meaning in some places.	The text has not been edited. Serious errors affect or alter the meaning.

Argument Writing Rubric

	4	3	2	1
Ideas	The writer's claim is stated clearly. Counterclaims are anticipated and addressed very well. Accurate reasons and evidence from reliable sources support the claim.	The writer's claim is stated adequately. The author may fail to anticipate or address one or more common counterclaims. One or two reasons or pieces of evidence may not be from reliable sources.	A claim is stated. Counterclaims are not anticipated or are not addressed well. There is little accurate support for the writer's claim.	The writer does not state a claim. Reasons and evidence are not provided.
Organization	The argument is organized logically, including a strong introduction. A compelling conclusion restates the thesis and includes a call to action. Clear and unique transitions clarify the relationships between the claim, reasons, supporting evidence, and counterclaims.	The argument is organized logically, including an introduction. The conclusion may not restate the thesis or may not include a call to action. More or better transitions may be needed to clarify the relationships between the claim, reasons, supporting evidence, and counterclaims.	The argument is not organized logically. The introduction or conclusion is missing (or problematic). Transitions are not appropriate or effective. Counterclaims are not addressed effectively.	The writing is not organized as an argument. The introduction and conclusion are missing. Transitions are not used. Counterclaims are not addressed.
Voice	The voice strongly supports the writer's purpose and consistently connects with the audience. A respectful, confident tone is maintained.	The voice mostly supports the writer's purpose. The tone is mostly respectful and confident, but may be too informal in some places.	The voice is fairly weak or passive throughout the piece and fails to connect with the audience. The tone is inconsistent.	The voice is flat or absent.
Word Choice	Compelling language conveys the writer's ideas and engages the reader. Nouns and verbs are clear and precise, supported by a few carefully selected modifiers.	Some of the language is compelling, but some is vague or ineffective. Some nouns and verbs are strong, but others are weak, requiring too much help from modifiers. Modifiers are satisfactory.	Much of the language is vague or ineffective. Nouns and verbs lack clarity or precision. Too many or too few modifiers are used, and many of these are weak.	The language is not compelling. Words are weak, negative, or used incorrectly.
Sentence Fluency	The sentences vary greatly in length and structure, adding style and interest. Almost all sentences begin differently. The text flows smoothly and is effortlessly read aloud with inflection.	Sentence length and structure vary somewhat, with some sentences adding style or interest. Some sentence beginnings are repeated. Parts of the text flow smoothly. The paper can be read aloud with inflection.	In many places, the writing does not flow smoothly because sentences are the same length or begin the same way. The paper is difficult to read aloud with inflection.	Sentences are incomplete or incorrect. Sentence beginnings are repeated over and over again. The text does not flow smoothly.
Conventions	The writing has been carefully edited. Grammar, usage, and mechanics are correct.	The writing contains some minor errors that may distract the reader, but meaning remains clear.	Many errors are repeated. Line-by-line editing in specific places is needed. The errors interfere with meaning in some places.	The writing has not been edited. Serious errors affect or alter the meaning.

Descriptive Writing Rubric

	4	3	2	1
Ideas	The topic is focused and exactly the right size. Sensory details clearly develop, describe, and reveal the subject. Carefully chosen ideas help the reader to completely experience what is being described.	The topic may need to be more carefully focused. Some sensory details reveal the subject. The author's ideas sometimes help the reader experience what is being described.	The topic is not well focused. Too few sensory details reveal the subject. The ideas fail to consistently help the reader experience what is being described.	The topic is unfocused or unclear. Details are random or missing. The ideas do not support the reader's experience of the topic.
Organization	The description is organized logically and creatively, including an engaging introduction and a thoughtfully crafted conclusion. Varied and appropriate transitions clarify relationships between ideas.	The description is organized logically, including a functional introduction and conclusion. More or better transitions may be needed to clarify relationships between ideas.	The description is not well organized. The introduction or the conclusion is weak or missing. Transitions are weak or confusing. Some of the ideas are hard to follow.	The writing is not organized. The introduction and the conclusion are missing. Transitions are not used.
Voice	An authentic, clear voice conveys the writer's purpose and connects with the reader. The mood is perfect, and the tone conveys respect for the subject and the audience.	The voice connects with the reader in some places. The tone is appropriate but inconsistent. An appropriate mood is somewhat established.	The voice may convey purpose but does not connect with the reader. The mood and tone may not be appropriate.	The voice is weak or absent. Mood and tone are not established.
Word Choice	Precise, descriptive words (including nouns, verbs, and modifiers) bring the subject to life. Figurative language and comparisons create a clear, coherent picture.	Some words are precise and descriptive, but others are not. Some nouns and verbs may rely too heavily on modifiers for clarity. Figurative language and/or comparisons sometimes create a clear picture.	Nouns and verbs lack precision and clarity. Too many or too few modifiers are used, and many of these are weak. Figurative language and/or comparisons do not create a clear picture.	Words are basic and very limited. Figurative language and comparisons are not used.
Sentence Fluency	A variety of sentences and/or lines adds interest and energy to the description. The writing flows very smoothly. Reading this aloud with inflection and feeling is effortless.	Some sentences and/or lines are varied and interesting. The writing flows smoothly some of the time. It can be read aloud with inflection and feeling.	Many sentences and/or lines are not varied or interesting. Most of the writing does not flow smoothly. It is difficult to read aloud with inflection or feeling.	Sentences and/or lines are incomplete or incorrect. The writing does not flow.
Conventions	The description has been carefully edited. Grammar, usage, and mechanics are correct.	The description contains some minor errors that may distract the reader, but meaning remains clear.	Many errors are repeated. Line-by-line editing in specific places is needed. Errors interfere with meaning in places.	The writing has not been edited. Serious errors affect or alter the meaning.

Narrative Writing Rubric

	5	4	3	2	1
Ideas	An engaging topic, experience, or series of events is supported by relevant details. Memorable descriptions develop the narrative. Carefully selected ideas completely satisfy the reader.	Most of the details are relevant and supportive. Most descriptions are memorable. Carefully selected ideas satisfy most of the reader's needs.	Some of the details may be unrelated or marginally supportive, but descriptions are adequate. The ideas selected by the author frequently meet the needs of the reader.	The narrative is not supported by enough relevant details. Descriptions are inadequate. The ideas selected by the author sometimes meet the needs of the reader.	The topic is not clear. Details are unrelated to the topic.
Organization	The narrative has an engaging beginning and an ending that leaves the reader thinking or feeling. Events are logically and creatively sequenced. A variety of effective transition words, phrases, and clauses signifies shifts in the setting and plot.	The narrative has an interesting beginning and satisfying ending. Events are logically sequenced. Most transitions are effective, especially as they signify shifts in the setting and plot.	The beginning and the conclusion are functional, but one may be stronger than the other. The sequence of events is logical, but may have a flaw or two. More or better transitions may be needed to guide the reader.	The beginning does not get the reader's attention, or the ending does not satisfy. Some events are out of order. Transitions are needed.	The writing is not organized into a beginning, middle, and ending.
Voice	The voice, mood, and tone are perfect for the purpose and audience. Dialogue, if used, is realistic and fits all the characters.	The voice, mood, and tone are appropriate. Dialogue, if used, is realistic and usually fits the characters well.	The voice, mood, and tone are appropriate in places, but inconsistent. Dialogue, if used, sometimes fits the characters.	The voice sounds disinterested. Mood and tone are weak. Dialogue, if used, is unrealistic or does not fit the characters.	Voice, mood, and tone are not established.
Word Choice	Clear and precise nouns and verbs consistently capture the imagery and action of the story. Descriptive language clearly conveys the experiences and events. Modifiers are strong.	Most of the nouns and verbs are clear, capturing the imagery and action of the story. Descriptive language conveys the experiences and events well. The majority of the modifiers are strong.	Some nouns and verbs are strong, but others are weak. Descriptive language conveys most of the imagery, experiences, and events. Modifiers are satisfactory.	Many nouns and verbs do not capture the imagery or action of the story. The descriptive language is overly dependent on modifiers, and many of these are weak.	Words are overused, very weak, or incorrect. Descriptive language is not used.
Sentence Fluency	A variety of sentence structures and sentence beginnings makes the narrative flow smoothly. To read this paper aloud with inflection and feeling is effortless.	Most sentence structures and sentence beginnings are varied and flow well. Most of the sentences are well crafted. It is easy to read this writing aloud with inflection and feeling.	A few sentences share the same structures, lengths, or beginnings. The writing flows reasonably well. It is possible to read this writing aloud with inflection and feeling.	Many sentences have the same structures, lengths, or beginnings. The flow is robotic or rambling. It is difficult to read this writing aloud with inflection and feeling.	Sentences are incorrectly written or incomplete. The writing is difficult to follow.
Conventions	The narrative has been carefully edited. Grammar, usage, and mechanics are correct.	The narrative contains one or two minor errors that are easily corrected.	The narrative contains some minor errors that may distract the reader, but meaning remains clear.	The narrative contains many errors. Line-by-line editing in specific places is needed.	The writing has not been edited. Serious errors affect or alter the meaning.

Informative/Explanatory Writing Rubric

	5	4	3	2	1
Ideas	The topic is introduced clearly. It is developed and supported with relevant facts and concrete details. If included, quotations are relevant, accurate, and insightful. Carefully selected ideas completely answer the reader's main questions.	The topic is introduced well. Almost all the facts and details support the topic well. If included, quotations are relevant and accurate. Almost all of the reader's main questions are answered.	The topic is introduced adequately. Some facts, details, and quotations (if included) support the topic adequately. The reader's main questions are frequently answered.	The topic is introduced. Facts, details, and quotations (if included) do not develop and support the topic effectively. A few of the reader's questions are answered.	The topic is not clear. The topic is not supported by facts and details. The author did not think about what questions the reader might have.
Organization	The ideas, concepts, and information are organized into a strong introduction, body, and conclusion. Varied, appropriate, and unique transitions connect and clarify relationships among ideas.	The ideas, concepts, and information are organized into an introduction, body, and conclusion. Most transitions are appropriate and helpful.	The ideas, concepts, and information are organized into an introduction, body, and conclusion. More or better transitions may be needed.	An introduction, body, and conclusion are present. Some transitions may be inappropriate or incorrect.	The text is not organized into an introduction, body, and conclusion. It is hard or impossible to follow the ideas.
Voice	The writer's voice is appropriate for the purpose and audience. The tone is informative, respectful, and consistent.	The writer's voice is appropriate for the purpose and audience. The tone is almost always informative and respectful.	The writer's voice is mostly appropriate for the purpose and audience. The tone is mostly informative and respectful, but may be too informal in some places.	The writer's voice is not very appropriate for the purpose or audience. The tone is inconsistent.	The writer's voice is very weak or absent. The tone is not established.
Word Choice	The language is exact and concise. Domain-specific vocabulary is used correctly and explained, as needed. Nouns and verbs are clear and precise, supported by a few carefully selected modifiers.	Most of the language is exact and concise. Domain-specific vocabulary is used correctly and usually explained, as needed. Most nouns and verbs are clear and precise. Most modifiers are carefully selected.	Some of the language is exact, but some is too general or vague. Some domain-specific vocabulary is used but not explained. Some nouns and verbs are weak, requiring too much help from modifiers. Modifiers are satisfactory.	Some language is confusing. Domain-specific vocabulary may be used incorrectly. Nouns and verbs lack clarity and precision. Too many or too few modifiers are used, and many of these are weak.	Many words are repeated or used incorrectly. Domain-specific vocabulary is not used.
Sentence Fluency	The sentences vary greatly in length and structure, adding style and interest. Almost all sentences begin differently. The text flows smoothly and is effortlessly read aloud with inflection.	Most of the sentences vary in their beginnings, lengths, and structures. Several add style or interest. Most of the text flows smoothly and is easy to read aloud with inflection.	Sentence length and structure vary somewhat, with some sentences adding style or interest. Some sentence beginnings are repeated. Parts of the text flow smoothly. The paper can be read aloud with inflection.	In many places, the writing does not flow smoothly because sentences are the same length or begin the same way. The paper is difficult to read aloud with inflection.	Sentences are incomplete or incorrect. The text does not flow smoothly.
Conventions	The text has been carefully edited. Grammar, usage, and mechanics are correct.	The text contains one or two minor errors, but the meaning remains clear.	The text contains some minor errors that may distract the reader, but meaning remains clear.	Many errors are repeated. Line-by-line editing in specific places is needed. The errors interfere with meaning in some places.	The text has not been edited. Serious errors affect or alter the meaning.

Argument Writing Rubric

	5	4	3	2	1
Ideas	The writer's claim is stated clearly. Counterclaims are anticipated and addressed very well. Accurate reasons and evidence from reliable sources support the claim.	The writer's claim is stated clearly. Counterclaims are anticipated and addressed well. Most of the reasons and evidence are accurate and from reliable sources.	The writer's claim is stated adequately. The author may fail to anticipate or address one or more common counterclaims. One or two reasons or pieces of evidence may not be from the writer's claim.	A claim is stated. Counterclaims are not anticipated or are not addressed well. There is little accurate support for the writer's claim.	The writer does not state a claim. Reasons and evidence are not provided.
Organization	The argument is organized logically, including a strong introduction. A compelling conclusion restates the thesis and includes a call to action. Clear and unique transitions clarify the relationships between the claim, reasons, supporting evidence, and counterclaims.	The argument is organized logically, including a good introduction. The conclusion restates the thesis and may include a call to action. Most transitions clarify the relationships between the claim, reasons, supporting evidence, and counterclaims.	The argument is organized logically, including an introduction. The conclusion may not restate the thesis or may not include a call to action. More or better transitions may be needed to clarify the relationships between the claim, reasons, supporting evidence, and counterclaims.	The argument is not organized logically as an argument. The introduction or conclusion is missing (or problematic). Transitions are not appropriate or effective. Counterclaims are not addressed effectively.	The writing is not organized logically. There is no introduction and conclusion are missing. Transitions are not used. Counterclaims are not addressed.
Voice	The voice strongly supports the writer's purpose and consistently connects with the audience. A respectful, confident tone is maintained.	The voice supports the writer's purpose and almost always connects with the audience. A respectful, confident tone is maintained.	The voice mostly supports the writer's purpose. The tone is mostly respectful and confident, but may be too informal in some places.	The voice is fairly weak or passive throughout the piece and fails to connect with the audience. The tone is inconsistent.	The voice is flat or absent.
Word Choice	Compelling language conveys the writer's ideas and engages the reader. Nouns and verbs are clear and precise, supported by a few carefully selected modifiers.	Most of the language is compelling. Nouns and verbs are mostly clear and precise. Most modifiers are carefully selected.	Some of the language is compelling, but some is vague or ineffective. Some nouns and verbs are strong, but others are weak, requiring too much help from modifiers. Modifiers are satisfactory.	Much of the language is vague or ineffective. Nouns and verbs lack clarity or precision. Too many or too few modifiers are used, and many of these are weak.	The language is not compelling. Words are weak, negative, or used incorrectly.
Sentence Fluency	The sentences vary greatly in length and structure, adding style and interest. Almost all sentences begin differently. The text flows smoothly and is effortlessly read aloud with inflection.	Most of the sentences vary in their beginnings, lengths, and structures. Several add style or interest. Most of the text flows smoothly and is easy to read aloud with inflection.	Sentence length and structure vary somewhat, with some sentences adding style or interest. Some sentence beginnings are repeated. Parts of the text flow smoothly. The paper can be read aloud with inflection.	In many places, the writing does not flow smoothly because sentences are the same length or begin the same way. The paper is difficult to read aloud with inflection.	Sentences are incomplete or incorrect. Sentence beginnings are repeated over and over again. The text does not flow smoothly.
Conventions	The writing has been carefully edited. Grammar, usage, and mechanics are correct.	The writing contains one or two minor errors, but the meaning remains clear.	The writing contains some minor errors that may distract the reader, but meaning remains clear.	Many errors are repeated. Line-by-line editing is needed. The errors interfere with meaning in some places.	Many errors are repeated. The writing has not been edited. Serious errors affect or alter the meaning.

Descriptive Writing Rubric

	5	4	3	2	1
Ideas	The topic is focused and exactly the right size. Sensory details clearly develop, describe, and reveal the subject. Carefully chosen ideas help the reader to completely experience what is being described.	The topic is focused and the right size. Many sensory details develop, describe, and reveal the subject. The ideas selected usually enable the reader to experience what is being described.	The topic may need to be more carefully focused. Some sensory details reveal the subject. The author's ideas sometimes help the reader experience what is being described.	The topic is not well focused. Too few sensory details reveal the subject. The ideas fail to consistently help the reader experience what is being described.	The topic is unfocused or unclear. Details are random or missing. The ideas do not support the reader's experience of the topic.
Organization	The description is organized logically and creatively, including an engaging introduction and a thoughtfully crafted conclusion. Varied and appropriate transitions clarify relationships between ideas.	The description is organized logically, including a strong introduction and a strong conclusion. Most of the transitions clarify relationships between ideas.	The description is organized logically, including a functional introduction and conclusion. More or better transitions may be needed to clarify relationships between ideas.	The description is not well organized. The introduction or the conclusion is weak or missing. Transitions are weak or confusing. Some of the ideas are hard to follow.	The writing is not organized. The introduction and the conclusion are missing. Transitions are not used.
Voice	An authentic, clear voice conveys the writer's purpose and connects with the reader. The mood is perfect, and the tone conveys respect for the subject and the audience.	The voice is clear and connects with the reader most of the time. The mood is appropriate, and the tone conveys respect for the subject and audience most of the time.	The voice connects with the reader in some places. The tone is appropriate but inconsistent. An appropriate mood is somewhat established.	The voice may convey purpose but does not connect with the reader. The mood and tone may not be appropriate.	The voice is weak or absent. Mood and tone are not established.
Word Choice	Precise, descriptive words (including nouns, verbs, and modifiers) bring the subject to life. Figurative language and comparisons create a clear, coherent picture.	Most words (including nouns, verbs, and modifiers) are precise and descriptive. Figurative language and comparisons create a clear, coherent picture most of the time.	Some words are precise and descriptive, but others are not. Some nouns and verbs may rely too heavily on modifiers for clarity. Figurative language and/or comparisons sometimes create a clear picture.	Nouns and verbs lack precision and clarity. Too many or too few modifiers are used, and many of these are weak. Figurative language and/or comparisons do not create a clear picture.	Words are basic and very limited. Figurative language and comparisons are not used.
Sentence Fluency	A variety of sentences and/or lines adds interest and energy to the description. The writing flows very smoothly. Reading this aloud with inflection and feeling is effortless.	Most sentences and/or lines are varied and interesting. The writing flows smoothly most of the time. It is easy to read aloud with inflection and feeling.	Some sentences and/or lines are varied and interesting. The writing flows smoothly some of the time. It can be read aloud with inflection and feeling.	Many sentences and/or lines are not varied or interesting. Most of the writing does not flow smoothly. It is difficult to read aloud with inflection or feeling.	Sentences and/or lines are incomplete or incorrect. The writing does not flow.
Conventions	The description has been carefully edited. Grammar, usage, and mechanics are correct.	The description contains one or two minor errors that are easily corrected. Meaning is clear.	The description contains some minor errors that may distract the reader, but meaning remains clear.	Many errors are repeated. Line-by-line editing in specific places is needed. Errors interfere with meaning in places.	The writing has not been edited. Serious errors affect or alter the meaning.

	6	5	4	3	2	1
Ideas	An engaging topic, experience, or series of events is supported by relevant details. Memorable descriptions develop the narrative. Carefully selected ideas completely satisfy the reader.	Most of the details are relevant and supportive. Most descriptions are memorable. Carefully selected ideas satisfy most of the reader's needs.	Some of the details may be unrelated or marginally supportive, but descriptions are adequate. The ideas selected by the author frequently meet the needs of the reader.	The narrative is not supported by enough relevant details. Descriptions are inadequate. The ideas selected by the author sometimes meet the needs of the reader.	The topic may not be clear. Many details are unrelated. The author did not consider the needs of the reader.	The topic is not clear. Details are unrelated to the topic.
Organization	The narrative has an engaging beginning and an ending that leaves the reader thinking or feeling. Events are logically and creatively sequenced. A variety of effective transition words, phrases, and clauses signifies shifts in the setting and plot.	The narrative has an interesting beginning and satisfying ending. Events are logically sequenced. Most transitions are effective, especially as they signify shifts in the setting and plot.	The beginning and the conclusion are functional, but one may be stronger than the other. The sequence of events is logical, but may have a flaw or two. More or better transitions may be needed to guide the reader.	The beginning does not get the reader's attention, or the ending does not satisfy. Some events are out of order. Transitions are needed.	The beginning and ending are weak. The sequence of events is seriously flawed. Transitions are not used.	The writing is not organized into a beginning, middle, and ending.
Voice	The voice, mood, and tone are perfect for the purpose and audience. Dialogue, if used, is realistic and fits all the characters.	The voice, mood, and tone are appropriate. Dialogue, if used, is realistic and usually fits the characters well.	The voice, mood, and tone are appropriate in places, but inconsistent. Dialogue, if used, sometimes fits the characters.	The voice sounds disinterested. Mood and tone are weak. Dialogue, if used, is unrealistic or does not fit the characters.	The voice, mood, and tone are inappropriate for the audience. Dialogue, if used, is unrealistic.	Voice, mood, and tone are not established.
Word Choice	Clear and precise nouns and verbs are perfect for the purpose and audience. Descriptive language clearly conveys the experiences and events. Modifiers are strong.	Most of the nouns and verbs are clear, capturing the imagery and action of the story. Descriptive language conveys the experiences and events well. The majority of the modifiers are strong.	Some nouns and verbs are strong, but others are weak. Descriptive language conveys most of the imagery, experiences, and events. Modifiers are satisfactory.	Many nouns and verbs do not capture the imagery or action of story. The descriptive language is overly dependent on modifiers, and many of these are weak.	Words are not powerful or precise. Descriptive language is not used.	Words are overused, very weak, or incorrect.
Sentence Fluency	A variety of sentence structures and sentence beginnings makes the narrative flow smoothly. To read this paper with inflection and feeling is effortless.	Most sentence structures and sentence beginnings are varied and flow well. Most of the sentences are well crafted. It is easy to read this writing aloud with inflection and feeling.	A few sentences share the same structures, lengths, or beginnings. The writing flows reasonably well. It is possible to read this writing aloud with inflection and feeling.	Many sentences have the same structures, lengths, or beginnings. The flow is robotic or rambling. It is difficult to read this writing aloud with inflection and feeling.	Sentences have little variation. The narrative does not flow well.	Sentences are incorrectly written or incomplete. The writing is difficult to follow.
Conventions	The narrative has been carefully edited. Grammar, usage, and mechanics are correct.	The narrative contains one or two minor errors that are easily corrected.	The narrative contains some minor errors that may distract the reader, but meaning remains clear.	The narrative contains many errors. Line-by-line editing in specific places is needed.	Serious errors affect or alter the meaning.	The writing has not been edited.

Informative/Explanatory Writing Rubric

	6	5	4	3	2	1
Ideas	The topic is introduced clearly. It is developed and supported with relevant facts and concrete details. If included, quotations are relevant, accurate, and insightful. Carefully selected ideas completely answer the reader's main questions.	The topic is introduced well. Almost all the facts and details support the topic well. If included, quotations are relevant and accurate. Almost all of the reader's main questions are answered.	The topic is introduced adequately. Some facts, details, and quotations (if included) support the topic adequately. The reader's main questions are frequently answered.	The topic is introduced. Facts, details, and quotations (if included) do not develop and support the topic effectively. A few of the reader's questions are answered.	The topic is not introduced, or more than one topic is introduced. Details are not relevant. Facts are not included. The author did not think about what questions the reader might have.	The topic is not clear. The topic is not supported by facts and details.
Organization	The ideas, concepts, and information are organized into a strong introduction, body, and conclusion. Varied and unique transitions connect and clarify relationships among ideas.	The ideas, concepts, and information are organized into an introduction, body, and conclusion. Most transitions are appropriate and helpful.	The ideas, concepts, and information are organized into an introduction, body, and conclusion. More or better transitions may be needed.	An introduction, body, and conclusion are present. Some transitions may be inappropriate or incorrect.	The text is not well organized. The introduction and conclusion are weak or missing. Transitions are not used.	The text is not organized into an introduction, body, and conclusion. It is difficult to follow the ideas.
Voice	The writer's voice is appropriate for the purpose and audience. The tone is informative, respectful, and consistent.	The writer's voice is appropriate for the purpose and audience. The tone is almost always informative and respectful.	The writer's voice is mostly appropriate for the purpose and audience. The tone is mostly informative and respectful, but may be too informal in some places.	The writer's voice is not very appropriate for the purpose or audience. The tone is inconsistent.	The writer's voice is not appropriate. The tone is too informal.	The writer's voice is very weak or absent. The tone is not established.
Word Choice	The language is exact and concise. Domain-specific vocabulary is used correctly and explained, as needed. Nouns and verbs are clear and precise, supported by a few carefully selected modifiers.	Most of the language is exact and concise. Domain-specific vocabulary is used correctly and usually explained, as needed. Most nouns and verbs are clear and precise. Most modifiers are carefully selected.	Some of the language is too general or vague. Some domain-specific vocabulary is used but not explained. Some nouns and verbs are weak, requiring too much help from modifiers. Modifiers are satisfactory.	Some language is confusing. Domain-specific vocabulary may be used incorrectly. Nouns and verbs lack clarity and precision. Too many or too few modifiers are used, and many of these are weak.	The language is very basic and limited. Domain-specific vocabulary is used incorrectly. Nouns and verbs are vague, unclear, or confusing. Modifiers may be missing.	Many words are repeated or used incorrectly. Domain-specific vocabulary is not used.
Sentence Fluency	The sentences vary greatly in length and structure, adding style and interest. Almost all sentences begin differently. The text flows smoothly and is effortlessly read aloud with inflection.	Most of the sentences vary in their beginnings, lengths, and structures. Several add style or interest. Most of the text flows smoothly and is easy to read aloud with inflection.	Sentence length and structure vary somewhat, with some sentences adding style or interest. Some sentence beginnings are repeated. Parts of the text flow smoothly. The paper can be read aloud with inflection.	In many places, the writing does not flow smoothly because sentences are the same length or begin the same way. The paper is difficult to read aloud with inflection.	Most sentences are the same length and structure. Sentence beginnings are repeated over and over again. The flow is too robotic or rambling.	Sentences are incomplete or incorrect. The text does not flow smoothly.
Conventions	The text has been carefully edited. Grammar, usage, and mechanics are correct.	The text contains one or two minor errors, but the meaning remains clear.	The text contains some minor errors that may distract the reader, but meaning remains clear.	Many errors are repeated. Line-by-line editing in specific places is needed. The errors interfere with meaning in some places.	Serious errors affect or alter the meaning.	The text has not been edited.

Argument Writing Rubric

	6	5	4	3	2	1
Ideas	The writer's claim is stated clearly. Counterclaims are anticipated and addressed very well. Accurate reasons and evidence from reliable sources support the claim.	The writer's claim is stated clearly. Counterclaims are anticipated and addressed. Most of the reasons and evidence are accurate and from reliable sources.	The writer's claim is stated adequately. The author may fail to anticipate or address one or more common counterclaims. One or two reasons or pieces of evidence may not be from reliable sources.	A claim is stated. Counterclaims are not stated clearly. Counterclaims are not addressed well. There is little accurate support for and evidence from the writer's claim.	The writer's claim is inaccurate. Counterclaims are not addressed. Reasons and evidence are unrelated or not accurate.	The writer does not state a claim. Reasons and evidence are not provided.
Organization	The argument is organized logically, including a strong introduction. A compelling conclusion restates the thesis and includes a call to action. Clear and unique transitions clarify the relationships between the claim, reasons, supporting evidence, and counterclaims.	The argument is organized logically, including a good introduction. The conclusion restates the thesis and may include a call to action. Most transitions clarify the relationships between the claim, reasons, supporting evidence, and counterclaims.	The argument is organized logically, including an introduction. The conclusion may not restate the thesis or may not include a call to action. More or better transitions may be needed to clarify the relationships between the claim, reasons, supporting evidence, and counterclaims.	The argument is not organized logically. The introduction or conclusion is missing (or problematic). Transitions are not appropriate or effective. Counterclaims are not addressed.	The argument is not organized logically. The introduction and conclusion are missing. Transitions are not used. Counterclaims are not addressed.	The writing is not organized as an argument.
Voice	The voice strongly supports the writer's purpose and consistently connects with the audience. A respectful, confident tone is maintained.	The voice supports the writer's purpose and almost always connects with the audience. A respectful, confident tone is maintained.	The voice mostly supports the writer's purpose. The tone is mostly respectful and confident, but may be too informal in some places.	The voice is fairly weak or passive throughout the piece and fails to connect with the audience. The tone is inconsistent.	The voice is weak or inappropriate for the purpose and audience. A respectful, confident tone is not established.	The voice is flat or absent.
Word Choice	Compelling language conveys the writer's ideas and engages the reader. Nouns and verbs are clear and precise, supported by a few carefully selected modifiers.	Most of the language is compelling. Nouns and verbs are mostly clear and precise. Most modifiers are carefully selected.	Some of the language is compelling, but some is vague or ineffective. Some nouns and verbs are strong, but others are weak, requiring too much help from modifiers. Modifiers are satisfactory.	Much of the language is vague or ineffective. Nouns and verbs lack clarity or precision. Too many or too few modifiers are used, and many of these are weak.	The language is not compelling. Many words are very basic. Nouns and verbs are vague, unclear, or confusing. Modifiers may be missing.	Words are weak, negative, or used incorrectly.
Sentence Fluency	The sentences vary greatly in length and structure, adding style and interest. Almost all sentences begin differently. The text flows smoothly and is effortlessly read aloud with inflection.	Most of the sentences vary in their beginnings, lengths, and structures. Several add style or interest. Most of the text flows smoothly and is easy to read aloud with inflection.	Sentence length and structure vary somewhat, with some sentences adding style or interest. Some sentence beginnings are repeated. Parts of the text flow smoothly. The paper can be read aloud with inflection.	In many places, the writing does not flow smoothly because sentences are the same length or begin the same way. The paper is difficult to read aloud with inflection.	Most sentences are the same length and structure. Sentence beginnings are repeated over and over again. The flow is too robotic or rambling.	Sentences are incomplete or incorrect. The text does not flow smoothly.
Conventions	The writing has been carefully edited. Grammar, usage, and mechanics are correct.	The writing contains one or two minor errors, but the meaning remains clear.	The writing contains one or two minor errors that may distract the reader, but meaning remains clear.	The writing contains some minor errors that may distract the reader, but meaning remains clear.	Many errors are repeated. Line-by-line editing is needed. The errors interfere with meaning in some places.	Serious errors affect or alter the meaning. The writing has not been edited.

Descriptive Writing Rubric

	6	5	4	3	2	1
Ideas	The topic is focused and exactly the right size. Sensory details clearly develop, describe, and reveal the subject. Carefully chosen ideas help the reader to completely experience what is being described.	The topic is focused and the right size. Many sensory details develop, describe, and reveal the subject. The ideas selected usually enable the reader to experience what is being described.	The topic may need to be more carefully focused. Some sensory details reveal the subject. The author's ideas sometimes help the reader experience what is being described.	The topic is not well focused. Too few sensory details reveal the subject. The ideas fail to consistently help the reader experience what is being described.	The topic is not focused. Details are scarce, or may relate to more than one subject. The ideas do not support the reader's experience of the topic.	The topic is unfocused or unclear. Details are random or missing.
Organization	The description is organized logically and creatively, including an engaging introduction and a thoughtfully crafted conclusion. Varied and appropriate transitions clarify relationships between ideas.	The description is organized logically, including a strong introduction and a strong conclusion. Most of the transitions clarify relationships between ideas.	The description is organized logically, including a functional introduction and conclusion. More or better transitions may be needed to clarify relationships between ideas.	The description is not well organized. The introduction or the conclusion is weak or missing. Transitions are weak or confusing. Some of the ideas are hard to follow.	The description is not organized. The introduction and the conclusion are missing. Transitions are incorrect or missing. The ideas are hard to follow.	The writing is not organized. Transitions are not used.
Voice	An authentic, clear voice conveys the writer's purpose and connects with the reader. The mood is perfect, and the tone conveys respect for the subject and the audience.	The voice is clear and connects with the reader most of the time. The mood is appropriate, and the tone conveys respect for the subject and audience most of the time.	The voice connects with the reader in some places. The tone is appropriate but inconsistent. An appropriate mood is somewhat established.	The voice may convey purpose but does not connect with the reader. The mood and tone may not be appropriate.	The voice does not convey purpose or connect with the reader. The mood and tone are inappropriate.	The voice is weak or absent. Mood and tone are not established.
Word Choice	Precise, descriptive words (including nouns, verbs, and modifiers) bring the subject to life. Figurative language and comparisons create a clear, coherent picture.	Most words (including nouns, verbs, and modifiers) are precise and descriptive. Figurative language and comparisons create a clear, coherent picture most of the time.	Some words are precise and descriptive, but others are not. Some nouns and verbs may rely too heavily on modifiers for clarity. Figurative language and/ or comparisons sometimes create a clear picture.	Nouns and verbs lack precision and clarity. Too many or too few modifiers are used, and many of these are weak. Figurative language and/ or comparisons do not create a clear picture.	Words are vague or confusing. Figurative language or comparisons are incomplete or missing.	Words are basic and very limited. Figurative language and comparisons are not used.
Sentence Fluency	A variety of sentences and/ or lines adds interest and energy to the description. The writing flows very smoothly. Reading this aloud with inflection and feeling is effortless.	Most sentences and/or lines are varied and interesting. The writing flows smoothly most of the time. It is easy to read aloud with inflection and feeling.	Some sentences and/or lines are varied and interesting. The writing flows smoothly some of the time. It can be read aloud with inflection and feeling.	Many sentences and/or lines are not varied or interesting. Most of the writing does not flow smoothly. It is difficult to read aloud with inflection or feeling.	Sentences and/or lines are very basic, limited, or repetitive. The writing is predictable and dull.	Sentences and/or lines are incomplete or incorrect. The writing does not flow.
Conventions	The description has been carefully edited. Grammar, usage, and mechanics are correct.	The description contains one or two minor errors that are easily corrected. Meaning is clear.	The description contains some minor errors that may distract the reader, but meaning remains clear.	Many errors are repeated. Line-by-line editing in specific places is needed. Errors interfere with meaning in places.	Serious errors affect or alter the meaning.	The writing has not been edited.

Index